ONLY
BELIEVE

OTHER TITLES BY PAUL L. KING

Finding Your Niche: 12 Keys to Opening God's Doors for Your Life
Universal biblical principles from more than 35 years of ministry experience for unlocking the gateways to your assignment from God and encountering new vistas of God's purposes for your life and calling. Discussion and study questions included.
ISBN 10: 0-9785352-8-6 [paperback]
ISBN 13: 978-0-9785352-8-5

Moving Mountains: Lessons in Bold Faith from Great Evangelical Leaders
Amazing stories and teachings of bold, wise faith from George Müller, Hudson Taylor, Charles Spurgeon, Andrew Murray, A.B. Simpson, Hannah Whitall Smith, Oswald Chambers, E.M. Bounds, Amy Carmichael, A.W. Tozer, and more! Study guide included. *"Feast on wind and fire!"—Calvin Miller*
ISBN 0-8007-9375-7 Paperback

A Believer with Authority: The Life and Message of John A. MacMillan
The ground-breaking biography and teachings of the Christian and Missionary Alliance missionary and professor who was a trailblazing pioneer in spiritual warfare and the seminal writer on the authority of the believer. *Endorsed by Jack Hayford and Neil Anderson.*
ISBN 0-87509-917-3 Paperback

Genuine Gold: The Cautiously Charismatic Story of the Early Christian and Missionary Alliance
The rediscovered and fully-documented history of the supernatural in the C&MA, featuring first-hand testimonies of early Alliance charismatic experiences (even before Azusa Street), relationships between the C&MA and the early Pentecostal movement, and evidences of historical drift and recovery. *"[A] valuable book. . . . King's research is impressive."—Pneuma: The Journal of the Society for Pentecostal Studies*
ISBN 0-9785352-0-0 Paperback

Binding and Loosing: Exercising Authority over the Dark Powers (co-authored with K. Neill Foster)
Understanding properly the biblical and theological concept and sound practice of combating the powers that war against Christ and His Church through binding and loosing according to Matthew 16:19—when it is appropriate, when it works and when it does not. Illustrated from real life experiences. Study guide included.
ISBN 0-87509-852-5 Paperback

To order copies see www.higherlifeministries.com or e-mail plking1@juno.com.

ONLY BELIEVE

Examining *the* Origin
and Development
of Classic *and*
Contemporary
Word *of* Faith
Theologies

Paul L. King, D.Min., Th.D.

WORD & SPIRIT PRESS

Published in Tulsa, Oklahoma, by Word & Spirit Press
WordSP@gmail.com • http://WandSP.com

Book design and composition by Bob Bubnis / Booksetters, Bowling Green, Kentucky

ISBN 10: 0-9785352-6-X ISBN 13: 978-0-9785352-6-1 — paperback
ISBN 13: 978-0-9819526-0-4 — hardcover

The paper used in this publication meets the minimum requirements of the American National Standard for Information Sciences—Permanence of Paper for Printed Library Materials, ANSI Z39.48-1992.

Dedicated to the Memory of

Charles ("Chuck") Farah, Jr., Ph.D.

Pastor, scholar, theologian,
mentor and friend

Acknowledgements

Special thanks to my wife Kathy and my children Sarah and Christopher for their patience and support during my Doctor of Theology program. Professors Jacques Theron of the University of South Africa and Henry Lederle of Sterling College and formerly Oral Roberts University have given me much great insight and constructive criticism to strengthen the doctoral thesis from which this book is adapted. The late Dr. Charles Farah, formerly a professor from Oral Roberts University and personal mentor, has challenged me theologically and intellectually, and encouraged me to pursue a doctorate, research this book, and write for publication. He passed away before seeing the completed work, but we dialogued together over many of the issues covered in this book. Jim Garrett and Bill Sullivan, friends and pastors, have also challenged me intellectually and spiritually.

Dr. Dale Simmons, Rev. Troy Edwards, Rev. Joe McIntyre, Rev. Geir Lie, Rev. Derek Vreeland, all members of an e-mail group discussing many of the faith issues presented in this book, have contributed thoughtful insights and research information. Dr. Mark Roberts, my colleague and literary agent, also has encouraged me in this research and writing and given many helpful suggestions in preparing this book for publication.

Table of Contents

Abbreviations Used

ANF	*Ante-Nicene Fathers*
AW	*The Alliance Weekly*
C&MA	*The Christian and Missionary Alliance*
CITB	*Christ in the Bible Commentary*
CMAW	*The Christian and Missionary Alliance Weekly*
DPCM	*Dictionary of Pentecostal and Charismatic Movements*
KJV	*King James Version Bible*
NIV	*New International Version Bible*
NPNF	*Nicene and Post-Nicene Fathers*

Introduction

*"Only believe, only believe,
all things are possible, only believe."*
—Paul Rader

This hymn was written in 1921 by Paul Rader, president of The Christian and Missionary Alliance (C&MA) and pastor of Moody Church in Chicago. It has been sung for nearly a century in holiness and Pentecostal churches. Oral Roberts used the song in his healing crusades. It has been a theme song of Robert Schuller's possibility thinking ministry. The song epitomizes the sentiment of the movements of faith in late 19th and early 20th centuries as well as the contemporary word of faith movement.

One of the most popular and most controversial movements in today's Christian world is sometimes known as the "Word Movement," "Word of Faith," "Health, Wealth, and Prosperity Gospel," or more pejoratively, "Name It and Claim It." Although some consider it to be the same as the charismatic movement, it is really one branch of many streams in the charismatic movement. Not all charismatics subscribe to word of faith tenets, although the vast majority of contemporary word of faith advocates are charismatic or Pentecostal. Some believe such word of faith teaching is fresh revelation from God; others believe it is cultic or heretical. This is where the controversy lies.

On one hand, we are encouraged by Scripture to "walk by faith, not by sight" (2 Corinthians 5:7), because "without faith it is impossible to please God" (Hebrews 11:6). On the other hand, although A.W. Tozer emphasizes this Scripture, he also cautions, "Not all faith pleases God."[1] Accordingly, the Apostle Paul exhorts, "Teach what is in accord with sound doctrine. Teach the older men to be . . . sound in faith" (Titus 2:1-2, NIV). A "healthy" faith, therefore, is a faith that is both sound and strong—a faith that is both sound doctrinally and also strong in practice. So how are we to discern what is truth and what is error in contemporary-day teaching about walking by faith? Adapted from my Doctor of Theology thesis from the University of South Africa, *A Practical-theological Investigation of Nineteenth and Twentieth "Faith Theologies,"*[2] this study is designed to guide and encourage believers to exercise faith with discernment and confidence, avoiding the pitfalls and excesses of some contemporary teaching on faith, yet gleaning sound, practical insights on faith by rediscovering classic faith teaching and practice.

For the purposes of this study the term "contemporary faith" will be used to describe the movement, leaders, and teachings of what has been referred to above as the "Word Movement," "Word of Faith," "Health, Wealth, and Prosperity Gospel," or "Name It and Claim It." The teachings of evangelical leaders of the late nineteenth and early twentieth century holiness and healing movements emphasize many principles of faith similar to the "contemporary faith" movement, and therefore can also be called a "word of faith" movement, though there are significant differences as well. Thus for the purpose of this study, in order to distinguish the two, these nineteenth and early twentieth century movements, leaders, and teachings will be designated by the term "classic faith" (though I recognize that "classic" is commonly used of older writings and that it could be argued that in a broad sense the contemporary faith movement began in the nineteenth century). By "healthy faith" I mean a faith that is sound both theologically and hermeneutically and also demonstrates strong exercise of faith practically.

THE PRACTICAL-THEOLOGICAL PROBLEM

Sincere and earnest Christians in the contemporary faith movement have laid down principles for the strong exercise of faith in everyday life issues such as finances, sickness, anxiety, depression, demonic harassment and attack. Their purpose has been to promote greater health, prosperity, well-being, and victory over difficulties of life. On the other hand, critics have pointed out, sometimes with scathing condemnation, what appear to be serious errors in teaching that border on the heretical and cultic, as well as questionable practices of faith that in some cases have resulted in financial loss or irresponsibility, broken relationships, questionable morality, physical harm and even death.

The practical-theological problem of this investigation is thus three-fold: 1) The concern that aberrant doctrine and praxis in contemporary faith movement has often resulted in unsound faith practice, sometimes with harmful consequences. 2) On the other hand, many of the contemporary faith teachings and practices are quite similar in nature to, and often derived from, those of the classic faith movement, advocated by respected and solidly evangelical leaders. 3) Thirdly, the critics of contemporary faith movement have been so condemning that one is left wondering how a person can really walk by faith. The critics have not supplied an adequate alternative model of faith praxis.

SORTING OUT TRUTH FROM ERROR—BALANCING EXTREMES

This study seeks to sort out truth from error, balance from imbalance, wheat from chaff, in order to develop a theory of faith practice that is healthy, in other words, that is sound, balanced, and encourages a strong exercise of faith. Whereas the contemporary faith movement has presented a distinct theory of faith practice, which proponents often consider as revelation from God, its antagonists have labeled it as "hyper-faith" and have presented, often in polemic and diatribe fashion, an opposing theory. This has resulted in two seemingly irreconcilable ends of a continuum.

In contradistinction to both poles, I believe that there is a balanced viewpoint between the two extremes, based substantially on classic faith teachings and practice, in which some of the contemporary faith teachings and practices are recognized as valid, while some of the anti-faith camp's concerns are also recognized as valid. This may appear to follow the Hegelian dialectic of thesis → antithesis → synthesis. While this may be true to a degree, I prefer to view it as recovering the original evangelical teachings and practices on faith without the contemporary divergences and modifications which have resulted in extremes and excesses on one hand, and, on the other hand, without the evangelical skepticism and criticism which has lumped all contemporary faith teaching as heretical and unorthodox.

The major criticisms of the contemporary faith movement, oftentimes scathing, have been voiced by Hank Hanegraaff in *Christianity in Crisis* (1993), Dave Hunt in *Seduction of Christianity* (1985) and *Beyond Seduction* (1987), Dan R. McConnell in *A Different Gospel* (1988), and John MacArthur in *Charismatic Chaos* (1992).[3] More moderate critiques include Bruce Barron in *The Health and Wealth Gospel* (1987), Gordon Fee in *The Disease of the Health and Wealth Gospel* (1979), Jimmy Swaggart in *The Balanced Faith Life* (1981), Charles Farah in *From the Pinnacle of the Temple: Faith or Presumption* (c. 1980), Robert M. Bowman in *The Word-Faith Controversy: Understanding the Health and Wealth Gospel* (2001), and Andrew Perriman, in *Faith, Health and Prosperity* (2003), as well as others.[4] A more recent article in the *Journal of the American Academy of Religion* (2007), "The Word-Faith Movement: A Theological Conflation of the Nation of Islam and Mormonism" by Kirk R. MacGregor, proposes to link some teachings of Mormonism and the Nation of Islam to some of the more recent teaching of contemporary faith leaders such as Frederick Price and Kenneth Copeland, claiming that "the two major historical roots of the contemporary Faith infrastructure lie in the Nation of Islam and Mormonism."[5]

While *some* of the criticisms of some anti-faith writers have a legitimate base, one finishes reading many of the more derisive denunciations wondering if there is such a thing as a "walk of faith." With so much emphasis on the negative, there is little room left for positive principles to guide a person to exercising faith soundly and confidently. Further, upon investigating classic faith teachings, we will find both areas of agreement with and opposition to the contemporary faith movement. Although books such as *A Different Gospel* by McConnell and *Christianity in Crisis* by Hanegraaff have declared the contemporary faith teaching cultic and heretical, some of those very teachings are remarkably similar to orthodox Christianity and the teaching of classic evangelical faith writers. In fact, the contemporary faith movement makes wide use of the writings of three leaders affiliated with The Christian and Missionary Alliance, a twentieth-century denomination which grew out of the nineteenth century Higher Life holiness movement, namely: *Bodily Healing in the Atonement* by T.J. McCrossan, *Christ the Healer* by Fred F. Bosworth, and *The Authority of the Believer* by J.A. MacMillan.[6]

While certain elements of contemporary faith teaching may appear cultic and heretical to critics of the movement, those same critics also attack teachings on faith that have been taught by other respected evangelical leaders of the early healing and holiness movements. Some have thus not only rejected contemporary faith teaching, but also valid principles of faith that sound similar to the excesses of contemporary faith teaching, and may sometimes, in fact, be precursory of contemporary faith teaching.

It is my belief that not all principles taught by contemporary faith teachers are invalid. The Latin phrase *abusus non tollit usus* applies here: "The abuse does not bear away the use," or in other words, the abuse should not obscure or invalidate legitimate use. One of the prominent classic faith teachers, A.B. Simpson, put it this way, "The best remedy for the abuse of anything is its wise and proper use."[7] Similarly, a more recent advocate of the classic faith movement, A.W. Tozer rephrased it as: "Never allow the abuse of a doctrine to cancel out its use."[8]

"TRUTH HAS TWO WINGS"—THE ELLIPTICAL NATURE OF TRUTH

The nature of truth is elliptical, that is, truth tends to revolve around distinct polarities (e.g., God's sovereignty vs. man's free will). Neither pole possesses the totality of truth. Rather, a divinely-designed dynamic tension exists between the two focal points.[9] Tozer explains it in the motto, "Truth has two wings."[10] Both wings are needed to make truth fly properly. Contemporary faith teaching and its critics, therefore, represent contra-polarities. Each holds elements of truth, but also elements of error, and thus has broken the dynamic tension between the focal points of truth.[11] Conversely, classic faith teaching, we shall see, to a great degree preserved a balance between the poles.

On one hand, many of the headaches of the contemporary faith controversies could have been avoided if their leaders had been more careful conveyors of their own evangelical/classic faith forebears. Perhaps they were blinded by prejudice against mainline traditionalism. On the other hand, their critics have been ignorant of the evangelical heritage of faith teaching and practice (especially from the last two centuries) out of which contemporary faith theory and praxis has sprung. This book entails a more discerning understanding of the evangelical faith heritage common to both polarities.

In this analysis, I want to point out the areas of legitimate use in practical principles of faith especially taught by classic evangelical holiness/healing leaders such as Andrew Murray, E.M. Bounds, A.J. Gordon, S.D. Gordon, A.B. Simpson, Reuben A. Torrey, Charles Spurgeon, George Müller, and many more. These classic teachings that are generally considered sound in faith will be compared and contrasted with contemporary faith teaching. It is the thesis of this study that classic evangelical leaders, particularly of the nineteenth and early twentieth centuries, by and large taught an orthodox, balanced walk of faith that can be trusted and emulated by believers today.

Other critiques of the contemporary faith movement have focused primarily on perceived theological aberrations, sometimes even considered as heretical or cultic. This study focuses more on the practical implications of a theological viewpoint of faith in the interest of developing a sound model of faith praxis.

AN ALTERNATIVE FOR HEALTHY FAITH PRACTICE

Maddox writes that "a truly practical theology should be inherently transformative, i.e., it should seek not only to understand but also to correct Christian life."[12] Therefore, this study will seek to correct the excesses in belief and practice in the contemporary faith movement and also to correct the excesses of its critics. It so doing, it will be transformational, providing a viable alternative of faith practice that will enable believers to become both strong and sound in their faith-walk.

While I will make references to historical faith foundations from earlier times such as church fathers, reformers, and mystics, I am necessarily limiting this study to a sampling of contemporary faith and classic faith teaching. In particular, the healing and holiness movements of the nineteenth century have been recognized by scholars as forerunners to the Pentecostal and contemporary faith movements.[13] Chappell, for example, maintains, "The Holiness movement provided the theological environment for faith healing in America."[14]

This holiness movement was manifested in three different streams representing three disparate, yet similar, theological beliefs about sanctification, encompassing a broad variety of denominational backgrounds: Wesleyan (eradication), Higher Life (habitation/transformation), and Keswick (suppression). The Higher Life and Keswick movements represent more Reformed views of sanctification as opposed to the Wesleyan-Arminian position, and though close cousins, are often confused as being the same movement. It is this broad body of teaching and practice that is studied here in relationship to teaching and practice in regard to faith. These three related holiness streams represent a wide variety of denominational backgrounds and theological viewpoints. They would not all agree theologically, but they share common teachings and practices of faith. These classic faith teachers have been chosen because they are known to be both orthodox evangelical leaders (that is, sound in their theology of faith) and also people known for their strong exercise of faith. Most of these leaders have been touted through the years as great evangelical leaders, leaders whose lives have exemplified integrity, holiness, power, and orthodoxy—people who are models of faith.

Not all facets of faith theology and practice can be studied here, so the issues chosen for study are issues of relevance and importance. The matters discussed here are not comprehensive of all relevant faith issues, but deal with the major questions of faith praxis. They have been focal points of controversy, which have been defended or condemned vociferously by opposing camps. We want to get beyond the rhetoric and name-calling and discover the legitimacy or unsoundness of these teachings and practices through examining the teachings of the classic orthodox leaders of faith. Misunderstanding of these issues and misinterpretation of Scripture have caused much confusion and heartache in the church. Resolution of these issues is vital for a sound practical theology of faith. Those who would like a non-academic approach with stories of classic faith leaders can refer to my book, *Moving Mountains: Lessons in Bold Faith from Great Evangelical Leaders*.[15]

STRUCTURE OF THIS STUDY

The general structure of this investigation of the issues of faith will be four-fold: 1) identify the teaching or practice of the contemporary faith movement regarding a particular issue, 2) state the criticism against the contemporary faith tenet, 3) identify classic faith teaching and practice on the issue, 4) critically reflect upon the issue, pointing out areas of agreement and disagreement between classic and contemporary faith teaching and the contemporary faith critics, and developing conclusions for a sound practical theology on the issue.

There may be some from the anti-faith camp who would consider such teaching from earlier evangelicals as the aberration of a few. In order to demonstrate that this is not true, I will cite several classic faith writers, illustrating their widespread acceptance in the evangelical community. Likewise, I will include multiple citations from several classic faith writers expressing disagreement with a certain viewpoint of the contemporary faith camp, in order to show the widespread classic evangelical disagreement with certain contemporary faith teachings. To some this might seem to be needless redundancy, repetitiously piling one quote upon another. On the contrary, I am making a conscious and intentional effort to build the case block-by-block that these teachings were not uniquely limited to only one or two people, but were characteristic teachings of many leaders of evangelicalism, thus confirming the acceptability and soundness of the teachings. Further, this material is intended to provide a resource for quotations from classic faith leaders on these issues.

---

1. A.W. Tozer, *Of God and Men* (Harrisburg, Penn.: Christian Publications, 1960), 54.

2. Paul L. King, *A Practical-Theological Investigation of Nineteenth and Twentieth-Century "Faith Theologies."* Doctor of Theology thesis. Pretoria, South Africa: University of South Africa, November 2001.

3. Hank Hanegraaff, *Christianity in Crisis* (Eugene, Ore.: Harvest House, 1993); Dave Hunt and T.A. McMahon, *Seduction of Christianity* (Eugene, Ore.: Harvest House, 1985); Dave Hunt, *Beyond Seduction* (Eugene, Ore.: Harvest House, 1987), Dan R. McConnell, *A Different Gospel* (Peabody, Mass.: Hendrickson, 1988); John F. MacArthur, *Charismatic Chaos* (Grand Rapids: Zondervan, 1992).

4. Bruce Barron, *The Health and Wealth Gospel* (Downers Grove, Ill.: IVP, 1987); Gordon Fee, *The Disease of the Health and Wealth Gospel* (Cosa Mesa, Calif.: Word for Today, 1979); Jimmy Swaggart in *The Balanced Faith Life* (Baton Rouge, La.: Jimmy Swaggart Evangelistic Assn., 1981); Charles Farah, Jr., *From the Pinnacle of the Temple: Faith or Presumption* (Plainfield, N.J.: Logos, n.d.); Charles Farah, Jr., "A Critical Analysis: The 'Roots and Fruits' of Faith Formula Theology," paper presented at the Annual Meeting of the Society

for Pentecostal Studies (Tulsa, Okla.: Oral Roberts University, 1980); Robert M. Bowman, *The Word-Faith Controversy: Understanding the Health and Wealth Gospel* (Grand Rapids: Baker, 2001); Andrew Perriman, ed., *Faith, Health and Prosperity* (Carlisle, Cumbria, U.K.; Waynesboro, Ga.: Paternoster Press, 2003).

5. Kirk R. MacGregor, "The Word-Faith Movement: A Theological Conflation of the Nation of Islam and Mormonism?," *Journal of the American Academy of Religion*, Vol. 75, No. 1, (Mar. 2007), 89.

6. T.J. McCrossan, *Bodily Healing in the Atonement*, reedited by Roy Hicks and Kenneth E. Hagin (Tulsa, Okla.: Kenneth Hagin Ministries, [1930] 1982); F.F. Bosworth, *Christ the Healer* (Grand Rapids: Fleming H. Revell, 1973); John A. MacMillan, *The Authority of the Believer* (Harrisburg, Penn.: Christian Publications, 1980).

7. A.B. Simpson, *Christian and Missionary Alliance Weekly (CMAW)*, Mar. 27, 1891, 195.

8. A.W. Tozer, cited in "Minutes of General Council 1995 and Annual Report 1994," The Christian and Missionary Alliance, 142.

9. See Abraham Joshua Heschel, *God in Search of Man: A Philosophy of Judaism* (New York: The Noonday Press/Farrar, Straus and Giroux, 1955), 12-15, 336-347, for a discussion of elliptical thinking and polarities in biblical theology and philosophy, especially in Judaism.

10. A.W. Tozer, *That Incredible Christian* (Harrisburg, Penn.: Christian Publications, 1964), 59.

11. Henry H. Knight III, "God's Faithfulness and God's Freedom: Comparison of Contemporary Theologies of Healing," *Journal of Pentecostal Theology* (1993), 2:65-89, discusses the polarities of God's freedom and God's faithfulness in relationship to faith theologies of healing.

12. Randy L. Maddox, "The Recovery of Theology as a Practical Discipline," *Theological Studies* 51 (1990), 6:667.

13. Cf. Donald W. Dayton, *Theological Roots of Pentecostalism* (Peabody, Mass.: Hendrickson, 1987), 15-33, 87-141; P.G. Chappell, "Healing Movements," *Dictionary of Pentecostal and Charismatic Movements (DPCM)*, Stanley M. Burgess and Gary B. McGee, eds. (Grand Rapids: Zondervan, 1988), 353-374; Vinson Synan, *The Holiness-Pentecostal Tradition: Charismatic Movements in the Twentieth Century* (Grand Rapids: Eerdmans, 1991, 1997), 14-83, 143-145; Henry I. Lederle, *Treasures Old and New: Interpretations of "Spirit-Baptism" in the Charismatic Renewal Movement* (Peabody, Mass.: Hendrickson, 1988), 1-36.

14. Chappell, 357.

15. Paul L. King, *Moving Mountains: Lessons in Bold Faith from Great Evangelical Leaders* (Grand Rapids: Chosen Books, 2004).

PART 1

**HISTORY AND SOURCES OF WORD OF FAITH
TEACHING AND PRACTICE**

CHAPTER 1

Faith of Our Fathers: Word of Faith Roots in the Early Church Fathers, Mystics, Reformers, Puritan, Pietist, and Wesleyan Movements

INTRODUCTION

"Stand at the crossroads and look: ask for the ancient paths, ask where the good way is, and walk in it" (Jer. 6:16, NIV).

Some people have the impression that faith teaching is new twentieth and twenty-first-century revelation from the Holy Spirit. However, in reality, teaching on the truths of faith is indeed very ancient. Many people, especially from the charismatic and word of faith camps, emphasize the Scriptures that say that God is doing a new thing (Isa. 42:9; 43:19). However, they often ignore Jeremiah's exhortation to ask for the ancient paths.

God *is* doing new things, but He has not changed truth. As E.M. Bounds wrote toward the end of the nineteenth-century, "It is not new truth that the world needs, so much as the constant iteration of old truths, yet ever new truths of the Bible."[1] Again Bounds counseled shortly before his death in 1913, "Hold to the old truths—double distilled [refined]."[2] A.B. Simpson, commenting on Jeremiah 6:16 in the first decade of the twentieth-century, declared in a similar vein, "We are not originators of truth. We are not sent to formulate a new gospel or a new theology. Rather, we are to 'stand . . .

in the ways, and ask for the old paths, where is the good way, and walk therein.'"[3] Simpson also held that God causes old truths to become "present truths."[4] The walk of faith is one of those ancient truths that has become a present truth.

Webster's Dictionary defines a classic as "a work of enduring excellence," "serving as a standard of excellence," "of recognized value," "authoritative," "historically memorable."[5] The writings of many evangelical Christians of earlier times cited in this book are considered to have become classics, particularly in American evangelical circles, because their insights have abided through the generations. What has often gone unnoticed is that these classic leaders were men and women of great faith.

As we study church history, we can see that seeds of faith were planted which germinated and grew into greater movements of faith. What began with a few individuals continued to snowball in the nineteenth and early twentieth centuries into a revival of faith. The nineteenth-century "Higher Life" holiness movement was sometimes called "the life of faith."[6] This classic faith movement was interdenominational in scope and included people of a wide variety of theological persuasions—Presbyterian (A.B. Simpson, W.E. Boardman, A.T. Pierson), Lutheran (August Francke, Johannes Blumhardt, Otto Stockmayer), Baptist (A.J. Gordon, C.H. Spurgeon, F.B. Meyer, Oswald Chambers), Methodist (Phoebe Palmer, E.M. Bounds, R.K. Carter, George D. Watson, J. Hudson Taylor), Quaker (Hannah Whitall Smith), Congregational (Thomas Upham, Charles Finney, R.A.Torrey, Horace Bushnell), Plymouth Brethren (George Müller, Watchman Nee), Dutch Reformed (Andrew Murray), Episcopalian/Anglican (Charles Cullis, Amy Carmichael), Salvation Army (Carrie Judd Montgomery). The classic faith movement was also international, beginning in mainland Europe (emerging out of German and Swiss Pietism—Blumhardt, Stockmayer, Trudel) and spreading to England (Müller, Spurgeon, Taylor, Meyer, Penn-Lewis, Chambers), South Africa (Murray), Asia (Taylor, Carmichael, Nee) and America (Moody, Gordon, Simpson, Torrey).

The rudiments of classic and contemporary faith teaching and practice can be found in the Early Church Fathers, the Reformers, Lutheran and Dutch Reformed Pietism, and the evangelical mystics of the church. Therefore, before we get acquainted with the nineteenth and early twentieth century faith leaders, in this chapter we want to acknowledge some of those earlier pioneers who influenced their faith.

EARLY CHURCH FATHERS

Faith and the First Principles. One of the earliest Church Fathers who stressed the importance of a life of faith was Theophilus, a second century Bishop of Syrian Antioch. He laid down the axiom, "Faith is the leading principle in all matters."[7] Clement of Alexandria expanded upon this thought further, commenting on the nature of faith: "The knowledge of God can be attained only through faith. . . . Faith is the way. . . . Faith is discovered to be the beginning of action, being the foundation of rational choice, . . . the first principle of understanding. . . . Faith the foundation of all knowledge. . . . rest in the infallible criterion of faith, . . . since . . . we believe God through His voice. . . . the first cause of the universe can be apprehended by faith alone."[8] Clement (and probably Theophilus as well) drew upon the philosophical language of Aristotle with his use of the terminology "first principles." For Aristotle "first principles" are the essences or self-evident truths.[9] To the Early Church Fathers, faith was a first principle or essence, a self-evident truth.

This Aristotelian phrase applied to faith would be paraphrased centuries later by Baptist holiness leader F.B. Meyer: "Faith . . . is the root-principle of character."[10] Again, he wrote, "Faith is preeminently the receptive faculty. . . . Faith is the one law of the Divine household."[11] Higher Life leader A.B. Simpson echoed, asserting that faith is "the foundation principle of spiritual life."[12] Likewise, Methodist pastor E.M. Bounds declared, "Faith is not a subordinate principle, but supreme."[13] From the early church fathers to the nineteenth and twentieth centuries, faith is thus regarded as the primary principle of the Christian life.

Revelation and Sense Knowledge. Some contemporary faith critics assert that the concepts of revelation knowledge and sense knowledge are a new form of the Gnostic heresy.[14] However, Clement of Alexandria, arguing specifically against Gnosticism in the late second century, taught a distinction between knowledge by the senses and knowledge by faith, which is superior, "advancing over the pathways of the objects of sense, leav[ing] Opinion behind."[15] Although he does not use the specific language "revelation knowledge," for Clement, such "faith of knowledge" is "God-taught wisdom."[16] Clement's concept of "intelligent faith," H.B. Timothy explains, involves "a comprehensive grasp of essentials, acquaintance with heavenly things," and "rests on Christ, the Logos and the revelation of the universal reason and of reality itself."[17] Variations and expansions upon his ideas would later be alluded to by later writers, especially the mystics, and in the early twentieth century by Oswald Chambers, E.W. Kenyon and others. Chapter 13 on "Revelation and Sense Knowledge" will discuss these concepts. Clement also viewed faith as "a power of God," a harbinger of contemporary faith teaching that faith is a force from God.[18]

Cyril of Jerusalem wrote of faith as spiritual sense, describing faith as "an eye that enlightens every conscience. . . . For, when enlightened by faith, the soul hath visions of God."[19] He also distinguished between "two distinct senses" of faith, which commentator Edwin Gifford notes "seems to be derived from Clement of Alexandria."[20]

Further, the contemporary faith teaching that emphasizes ignoring one's senses is not a new concept, but rather is prefigured in early Roman Catholic teaching, especially regarding the doctrine of transubstantiation. Cyril of Jerusalem exhorted regarding the elements of the Eucharist, "So do not think of them as bread and wine. As the Lord himself has declared, they are body and blood. And if your senses suggest otherwise, then let faith reassure you. Do not decide the question on the basis of taste, but on the basis of faith."[21] Likewise, centuries later Thomas Aquinas used a similar argument for transubstantiation, saying that "it is obvious to our senses" that the bread and wine remain after consecration, but they are "appearances" on the basis of faith.[22] While there is not a direct connection between contemporary faith teaching and these beliefs regarding faith and sense as applied to eucharistic doctrine, it does show that the concept of operating by faith rather than trusting senses is an ancient one.

Faith Confessions. Augustine (354-430) also emphasized the role of faith: "Faith is to believe what we do not see, and the reward of this faith is to see what we believe."[23] He advocated making confessions of praise which can be "effected by God" to have supernatural results.[24] So also, the roots of the positive confession teaching and practice can be traced back to the Church Fathers such as Augustine. Chapter 17 will investigative the classic and contemporary faith thinking regarding positive confession.

Hilary of Poitiers (c. 315-368) taught that the Church is built on the rock of confession of faith: "This faith it is which is the foundation of the Church; through this faith the gates of hell cannot prevail against her. This is the faith which has the keys of the kingdom of heaven. Whatsoever this faith shall have loosed or bound on earth shall be loosed or bound in heaven. This faith is the Father's gift by revelation."[25] He also connected faith confession and the exercise of the spiritual authority of the believer. In addition, he drew on Clement of Alexandria's concept of "faith knowledge" with his idea that faith is a gift through revelation from God.

Patrick Henry Reardon notes that the early monks made verbal confessions of the Scriptures: "In order to become alive, God's word had to take the living form of sound. In the patristic and middle ages, therefore, it was common and normal to read the Scriptures out loud, at least loud enough to be heard by the reader, even in private reading. 'Faith,' after all, 'comes by hearing, and hearing by the word of God' (Rom. 10:17)."[26]

MEDIEVAL PERIOD

The Middle Ages brought a time of decline in understanding what it meant to walk by faith, although faith teaching was not absent. By the time of Leo the Great (fifth century) and Gregory the Great (sixth century), Peter was viewed as the Rock and the spiritual authority of binding and loosing was conveyed through the Apostolic office of Peter.[27] Nevertheless, like Hilary, Leo recognized that the exercise of the authority of binding and loosing is a faith that "conquers the devil, and breaks the bonds of his prisoners. It uproots us from this earth and plants us in heaven, and the gates of Hades cannot prevail against it."[28] Theologian and philosopher Anselm (1033-1109) began to reawaken the principles of faith with his conception of "faith seeking understanding." Combining intellectual study with pursuit of faith, Anselm declared, "I do not seek to understand so that I may believe; but I believe that I may understand. For I believe this also, that 'unless I believe, I shall not understand.'"[29] This idea of faith preceding and informing reason is basic to eighteenth through twentieth-century faith teaching.

THE CHRISTIAN MYSTICS

The latter part of the medieval period, in particular, brought an awakening of what is considered by many as "evangelical" mysticism. This not to say that all mystics would be considered evangelical, nor that everything "evangelical" mystics taught would be accepted as evangelical truth. Those considered as "evangelical mystics" were men and women of great faith who had a deep and close walk with God. They believed in a deep personal communion with God through faith. When reading the writings of nineteenth and early twentieth century holiness and deeper life leaders who taught on faith, one can find many references to these mystics in conceptualizing and practicing faith. The rise of mysticism in the church is thus pivotal in the development of classic and contemporary faith theology and practice.

There are some contemporary Christian leaders like MacArthur and Hunt who are flatly opposed to mysticism of any sort, mistakenly thinking that mysticism is only a feature of Eastern religions, and failing to understand the distinctness of Christian mysticism.[30]   Certainly, such Eastern forms found in Buddhism, Hinduism, and the contemporary New Age movement need to be avoided, and not all Catholic mysticism would be accepted by evangelical Protestants.   However, many evangelicals have a mystical frame of mind without embracing the questionable beliefs of Eastern mysticism.   Oswald Chambers and A.W. Tozer, for instance, are considered as twentieth-century evangelical mystics. Chambers defined mysticism as "direct and immediate communion with God."[31] Tozer says of mysticism:

> As short a time as, say, forty years ago, the words 'mystic' and 'mystical' were altogether unacceptable in evangelical circles. Among the gospel churches the words suggested someone who was emotionally unstable, visionary, and worst of all, unsound theologically. . . . The word 'mystic'. . . refers to that personal spiritual experience common to saints of Bible times and well-known to multitudes in the post-Biblical era. I refer to the evangelical mystic who has been brought by the gospel into intimate fellowship with the Godhead. . . . He differs from the ordinary orthodox Christian only because he experiences his faith down in the depths of his sentient being while the other does not. . . . He is quietly, deeply, and sometimes almost ecstatically aware of the Presence of God in his own nature and in the world around him.[32]

Martyn Lloyd-Jones also advocates a true Christian mysticism.[33] A.T. Pierson asserted that the mystics were a prominent influence on the holiness movement of the late nineteenth century: "Every great movement in the direction of holier life is inseparable from this great current of thought that is associated with such as Jacob Böhme, St. Theresa, Catherine of Siena, Madame Guyon, Fenelon, Tauler, and William Law."[34] Many others could be mentioned such as Bernard of Clairvaux, Julian of Norwich, Meister Eckhart, John of the Cross, Thomas a Kempis, the anonymous author of *The Cloud of Unknowing* and later mystics, along with Guyon, Fenelon, and

Law, such as Jean-Nicolas Grou, Brother Lawrence, Henry Scougal and Michael Molinos. The classic faith leaders would not accept all that was taught by the mystics, but gleaned much wheat from the chaff.

A Sampling of Faith Influences from the Medieval Mystics

The limits of this book permit only a sampling of the faith influences from the mystics, but even just a sampling demonstrates their impact. Bernard of Clairvaux (1090-1153), often considered the greatest of all mystics, is known for his classic hymns "Jesus, Thou Joy of Loving Hearts" and "Jesus, the Very Thought of Thee." In opposition to Peter of Abelard, he stressed faith over reason, and was a forerunner of both classic and contemporary faith theology.[35] Bernard also emphasized the importance of confession in maintaining close communion with Christ, saying, "If we wish to have Christ for a guest often, we must keep our hearts fortified by the testimony of our faith."[36] His friend and biographer, William of St. Thierry, referred to the "powers of faith, hope and charity," in some way representing a precursor to classic and contemporary faith teaching on faith as a force.[37] Catherine of Siena (1347-1380) counseled a walk of faith that Baptist Keswick holiness leader F.B. Meyer explained as "reckoning on God's faithfulness."[38] Julian of Norwich's (1343-1413) popular work *Revelations of Divine Love* is considered a classic on prayer and intimacy with God. She emphasized praying in the will of God with implicit trust, a popular theme among the classic faith leaders like Tozer and Carmichael.[39]

Meister Eckhart (c. 1260-c. 1327), though less evangelical due to his leanings toward Neoplatonism and pantheism, nonetheless, had great influence on more evangelical mystics, as well as classic faith leaders. Tozer, for instance, frequently quoted Eckhart and other mystics, even though he made clear that he did not unconditionally approve all their teachings.[40] Eckhart joined together scholarship (sometimes speculative) and mysticism. He posited three modes of knowledge: 1) sensory knowledge, 2) rational knowledge on a higher level, and 3) pure divine knowledge, or "unknowing knowledge," which transcends the "human knower," coming to the place of knowing God through God.[41] Eckhart's categories of sensory and rational knowledge correspond to the contemporary faith concept of sense knowledge, and his divine knowledge is similar to what contemporary faith leaders call revelation knowledge. He also presented faith in an active, rather than passive sense: "God's gifts are meted out according to the taker, not according to the giver."[42]

This would prefigure classic and contemporary faith teaching by Murray and others on "faith that takes."

John Tauler (1300-1361), though mentored by Eckhart, was more evangelical. His teaching and the related writing of the *Theologia Germanica* had a great impact on the life and thought of Martin Luther.[43] The classic faith view of prosperity as exemplified by Simpson is derived from Tauler, who avowed, "I have never been unprosperous."[44] The *Theologia Germanica* (c. 1350), a document formulated by a reforming revivalist group known as the "Friends of God," stressed moving "our knowledge and experience of God from the 'outer person' to the 'inner person.'"[45] The *Theologia* cited Dionysius the Areopagite (c. 500 A.D.) about forsaking sense "and all that the senses can apprehend, and that reason of her own powers can bring forth."[46] These are harbingers of the contemporary faith emphases on revelation and sense knowledge. Luther declared that "next to the Bible and St. Augustine, he had never read anything as helpful as the *Theologia*."[47]

The fourteenth-century anonymous writing *The Cloud of Unknowing*, recommended by Tozer, distinguished between spiritual knowledge and sense knowledge in much the same way as Clement of Alexandria, thus foreshadowing the twentieth century teaching on revelation knowledge and sense knowledge.[48] The author also alluded to Augustine, Tauler, St. John of the Cross, and others.[49] Thomas a Kempis' (1380-1471) book *Of the Imitation of Christ* is considered a spiritual classic and has had a major impact on the faith of great Christians through the centuries. For Thomas, all of life is centered around the Cross: "How few are the lovers of the Cross of Jesus. . . . Many reverence His miracles, few follow the ignominy of His Cross. . . . The higher a person hath advanced in the Spirit, so much the heavier crosses he oftentimes findeth."[50] Presaging contemporary faith teaching, he counseled trusting faith over sense and reason: "Submit thyself to God, and humble thy sense to faith, and the light of knowledge shall be given thee, in such degree as shall be profitable and necessary for thee. . . . Human reason is feeble and may be deceived, but true Faith cannot be deceived. All reason and natural search ought to follow faith, and not to go before it, nor to break in upon it."[51]

THE REFORMERS

Martin Luther (1483-1546). Building on the personal faith of later medieval mystics, the Reformation further reversed the medieval decline in faith understanding. Martin Luther, more than any other, reawakened the role of faith by insisting on salvation by grace alone (*sola gratia*) through faith alone (*sola fide*). "Deeply influenced by the *Theologia Germanica*," Underhill comments, "The Lutheran 'faith,' which is the foundation-stone of [Luther's] theology, has far more the character of mystical adherence to God than of mere belief."[52] Luther originated a maxim, *Glaube und Gott gehören zuhaufe* ("faith and God belong together"), meaning that God is to be approached "solely through God rather than reason."[53] This is a common theme in contemporary faith teaching. In fact, Lederle concludes that Luther is saying, "faith is what makes God God."[54]

Prefiguring contemporary faith teaching on the creative nature of faith, Luther posited a unique and controversial concept that faith is "the creator of divinity—*fides creatrix divinitatis*."[55] He explained it as: "That to which you put your heart in pawn and on which you rely, that is truly your God."[56] So Luther was, in effect, also warning against a false faith that creates an idol: "The trust and faith of the heart alone make both God and an idol. If your faith and trust are right, then your God is the true God. On the other hand, if your trust is false and wrong, then you have not the true God. For these two belong together, faith and God. That to which your heart clings and entrusts itself, I say is really your God."[57] Unlike the implications of some contemporary faith teaching that seem to make man sovereign, Lederle, however, cautions that "it would be absurd to interpret Luther's formulation . . . as if this meant that man is the creator and God the creature."[58]

Additionally, Luther reclaimed the idea taught in classic and contemporary faith circles that "faith makes us heirs," stressing "faith which clings to the Word of the promising God."[59] Luther's emphasis on the priesthood of the believer supplied a basis for faith principles regarding the state and privileges of the believer. This, in turn, awakened the understanding that believers are not just priests, but a *royal* priesthood, or "kings and priests" (from 1 Pet. 2:9-10 and Rev. 1:6), as later taught by Dorothy Trudel, Andrew Bonar, Andrew Murray, A.B. Simpson, and others. It also provides the basis for the concept of the authority of the believer, taught in classic and contemporary faith circles. Precursor to contemporary faith "little gods" teaching (though he would not take its meaning as far), Luther taught a similar concept based on Psalm 82:6: "This is what I have often said, that faith makes of us lords, and love makes of us servants. Indeed, by faith we become gods and partakers of the divine nature and name. . . . Of this we have spoken often enough, namely, that we also must by faith be born God's sons and gods, lords and kings, even as Christ is born true God of the Father in eternity.[60] If one did not know this quote was from Luther, it might sound like it came from the lips of a contemporary faith teacher.

In Luther we also find recovery of the practice of anointing with oil and praying for healing by faith. Considering the Roman Catholic sacrament of Extreme Unction as a rite for the dying a departure from the sacrament's original intent of praying for healing, he writes, "But in Extreme Unction as practiced in our day, there is no prayer of faith. No one prays in faith over the sick, confidently expecting their restoration. Yet James describes that kind of faith in this passage [James 5:15]. . . . There is no doubt at all that if, at the present day, this kind of prayer were offered over the sick, i.e., by the older and graver men, men saintlike and full of faith, as many as we desired would be healed. Nothing is impossible for faith."[61] Luther's remarks prefigure the classic and contemporary faith emphasis on expectancy for God to heal by faith.

John Calvin (1509-1564). Calvin built upon Luther's emphasis on *sola fide*, but avoided Luther's controversial formulations. He stressed that faith is a gift from God and the work of the Holy Spirit, not man's effort, though man exercises the faith that God implants in him.[62] He was heavily influenced by Bernard of Clairvaux, whom he quotes more frequently than any other person except Augustine in his *Institutes of Christian Religion.* Calvin did hold an unusual view regarding the "spiritual" death of Christ, which some have considered similar to the teachings of contemporary faith founder Kenyon and subsequent contemporary faith leaders regarding a spiritual death of Christ in hell.[63] McConnell and Hanegraaff consider such views in the contemporary faith movement as heretical.[64] However, Calvin's teaching does not appear to be substantially related to contemporary faith teaching, for he was merely seeking an explanation for the "descent into hell" by spiritualizing it to include the suffering of Christ's soul in addition to the physical torment.

COVENANT THEOLOGY

Another significant paradigm shift in faith understanding emerged from Covenant theology, developed by other Reformation leaders such as Zwingli and Bullinger. It was adopted by one strain of the Calvinist Reformed tradition and especially found its consummation in the Dutch Puritan theology of Cocceius. Covenant theology, which teaches that the Church is spiritual Israel in covenant relationship with God, provided a foundation for nineteenth and twentieth-century faith teaching on inheriting the promises of the Covenant. These doctrinal foundations of the Reformation period were further developed by the Puritans and Pietists, and adopted into nineteenth-century Reformed holiness beliefs as taught by Andrew Murray, A.B. Simpson, A.T. Pierson and others in the Higher Life/Keswick Reformed holiness movement, as well as by Spurgeon, who is sometimes called the last of the Puritans.

A SAMPLING OF FAITH INFLUENCES FROM POST-REFORMATION MYSTICS

Guyon and Fenelon. Francois Fenelon (1651-1715) and Madame Jeanne Guyon (1648-1717), his spiritual mentor, were later mystics who greatly influenced the eighteenth to twentieth century holiness leaders, especially John Wesley, Andrew Murray, J. Hudson Taylor, Jessie Penn-Lewis, Watchman Nee, Hannah Whitall Smith, and a host of others.[65] Guyon emphasized the importance of maintaining a positive mental attitude: "I entreat you, give no place to despondency. This is a dangerous temptation—a refined, not a gross temptation of the adversary. Melancholy contracts and withers the heart, and renders it unfit to receive the impressions of grace. It magnifies and gives a false coloring to objects, and thus renders your burdens too heavy to bear. God's designs regarding you, and His methods of bringing about these designs, are infinitely wise."[66] Likewise, Fenelon advised, "The strivings of the human mind not only impair the health of your body, but also bring dryness to the soul. You can actually consume yourself by too much inner striving. And to no purpose at all! Your peace and inner sweetness can be destroyed by a restless mind."[67] Guyon also practiced the concept of "praying the Scripture," which was adopted by George Whitefield, George Müller, and others as a practice of faith.[68]

Guyon emphasized what might be called the "passive side of faith": "Many people want to direct God, instead of resigning themselves to be directed by Him; to show Him a way, instead of passively following where He leads."[69] Faith and stillness go hand in hand for Guyon.[70] Further, Guyon advises, "Great faith produces great abandonment."[71]

Fenelon and Guyon both taught the importance of the cross in the life of faith: "Faith and the cross are inseparable: the cross is the shrine of faith, and faith is the light of the cross."[72] Fenelon declared that we should both "live by faith and live by the cross. . . . Trial and strength are portioned out in equal measures. Living by this kind of faith demands the deepest kind of death to self."[73] For Fenelon, "Pure faith sees God alone," both in blessings and in trials.[74] The concepts of abandoning self and the crucified life as vital to the life of faith, were taught by holiness leaders from Andrew Murray, A.B. Simpson, Amy Carmichael, to Oswald Chambers, and echo the teachings of St. John of the Cross, Guyon, Fenelon, and others.

Scougal and Grou. Other later mystics impacting classic faith leaders include Henry Scougal and Jean-Nicolas Grou. Scougal (1650-1678) had an intensely close relationship to God, and though he died at the age of 28, wrote the classic *The Life of God in the Soul of Man.* His book was a strong influence on the Wesleys, the early Methodist movement, George Whitefield, nineteenth-century Higher Life leaders like William Boardman, and twentieth century mystics like Tozer. Similar to the Church Fathers, he emphasized, "The root of the divine life is faith."[75] In his little book he mentions various faith teachings commonly taught today, such as spiritual laws and forces, the relationship between faith and sense, all centered in the divine life, which is a life of faith in Jesus Christ. Grou (1730-1803) was a classic French scholar-mystic writer on prayer whose writings had influence among classic faith leaders, especially upon Simpson and Tozer. He is best known for his work *How to Pray.* He was possibly one of the earliest writers to speak of prayer as a force, having an impact on nineteenth century holiness teaching on spiritual force.[76]

COCCEIUS, EDWARDS, AND THE PURITAN MOVEMENT

As mentioned earlier, Johannes Cocceius (1603-1669) most fully developed Reformational Covenant theology. One scholar avows that "Cocceius unlocked the treasure of the Bible by means of the control idea of the covenantal God."[77] Moreover, McCoy asserts, "Along with others, Cocceius influenced the development of pietism both in the Reformed and Lutheran churches," noting his impact on Spener, Francke, Bengel and the school of Halle. He pioneered several concepts that provided seeds for classic and contemporary faith teaching. Similar to faith teaching, he taught that "God binds Himself to the whole man" in the Covenant.[78] He maintained the sovereignty of God, but also stressed a divine/human interaction, in which God's will for governing the world is carried out through human activity in the covenant relationship.[79] Further, McCoy notes that he taught, "Within the covenant will of God, there is a succession of activities determined upon to be put into effect when certain events come to pass. This succession is described by Cocceius as the system of covenants."[80] This presents in an embryonic form the cause and effect concept of spiritual laws, later taught by classic and contemporary faith leaders.

The Puritan ethic that righteousness and diligence result in blessing and prosperity is a forerunner of contemporary faith teaching (and some classic faith teaching) on prosperity. Seventeenth-century Puritan leader Thomas Brooks made reference to the blessings of Deuteronomy 28:13, commonly cited in contemporary faith teaching, saying, "There will come a time, even in this life, in this world, when the reproach and contempt that is now cast on the ways of God, by reason of poverty and paucity of those that walk in those ways, shall be quite taken away, by his making them the head that have days without number been the tail, and by his raising them up to much outward riches, prosperity, and glory, who have been as the outcast because of their poverty and paucity."[81] If one did not know that this statement came from Puritanism, one might reasonably think that it came from the pen of one of the contemporary faith leaders. It is obvious that Puritans believed that this Scripture meant that prosperity can be claimed through this Scripture.

Deeply influenced by Puritanism, Jonathan Edwards (1703-1758) wedded together mystical experience and intellectual endeavor. While he valued the use of reason and was even considered by some the epitome of a rationalist, he exalted revelation as a type of knowledge above reason, providing foundation for later teaching on revelation knowledge.[82] Surprisingly, though a staunch Calvinist emphasizing the sovereignty of God, he also believed that believers play a significant role in accomplishing God's heavenly purposes on earth, to the point that "the heavenly church depends upon the earthly one."[83] Edward's understanding of the dynamic tension between God's providence and man's response set the stage for classic faith teaching on the active role of faith.

PIETISM—SPENER, BENGEL, AND FRANCKE

Donald Dayton, in *Theological Roots of Pentecostalism*, states, "Pietism may have been one of the most important forces in the rise of the doctrine of divine healing. . . . Pietism's biblical realism and pastoral orientation combined with a belief in the continuation of miracles produced a doctrine of healing through prayer and faith."[84] Thus much of what we are here calling the "classic faith movement" really found its germination in the German Pietist movement.

Significant leaders included founder Philip Jacob Spener (1635-1705), and scholars Johann Albrecht Bengel (1687-1752), who believed in the supernatural power of God to work by faith, and August Hermann Francke (1663-1727) who received remarkable answers to prayer by faith and taught those principles to students at the Universities of Tubingen and Halle. Sattler notes, "For Francke faith was a verb, a way of being which was the necessary authority of intellectual and emotional assent to the claim that Jesus is Savior. . . . Faith is in fact a living relationship with Jesus Christ and means illumination and responsibility for the believer."[85] Dorsett summarizes the significance of the pietistic tradition in evangelical spirituality: "Pietists advocate a personal, spiritual new birth manifested in a heartfelt personal relationship with Jesus Christ. This personal relationship must be experienced individually, not just as a part of the community of the faithful. This experiential faith, to be valid, should bring an assurance of salvation, a new life of piety or holy living, and a zeal for evangelism and missions."[86] This pietistic faith also has practical implications for Christian living: "Furthermore, the Pietist movement has always been marked by a profound social consciousness that has usually been applied through outreach and care for the poor, especially widows, orphans, prisoners, and those locked in the chains of prostitution and alcohol or drug addiction."[87]

Dorsett concludes that "the seeds of Pietism have taken hold in fertile ground for 300 years. The plants have continued to blossom, bear fruit, and reproduce through sermons and mentoring processes but most importantly through the publication and dissemination of devotional literature. . . . In the late nineteenth and early twentieth centuries a number of women and men wrote books on various devotional topics that have continued to be extremely useful in spiritual formation. These books have become classics in the fields of devotional and disciple-making literature."[88] Among these Dorsett includes many of the classic faith leaders to which I will be referring here: George Müller, Andrew Murray, E.M. Bounds, A.B. Simpson, Amy Carmichael, Oswald Chambers, Jonathan Goforth, A.J. Gordon, F.B. Meyer, Jessie Penn-Lewis, Watchman Nee, and A.W. Tozer.[89]

The Pietist movement thus had an impact on the development of the nineteenth century holiness and healing movements that branched in four directions: the Wesleyan holiness movement, the development of faith ministries and missions through George Müller, the influence of Pietism on scholarship, and the European healing/holiness movement emerging out of the ministries of Johannes Blumhardt and Dorothea Trudel.

ZINZENDORF AND THE MORAVIANS

Count Nicholaus von Zinzendorf (1700-1760) and the Moravians practiced the Pietist principles of faith and power and experienced a mighty outpouring of the Holy Spirit. Zinzendorf and the Moravians, in turn, had an impact on the Wesleys and nineteenth century leaders. The teaching of Francke influenced the mother of John Wesley, and the Moravians themselves had a lasting impression on Wesley. It was Moravian missionary Peter Bohler who counseled John Wesley, "Preach faith until you have it; and when you have it, preach faith." This is a form of faith confession akin to classic and contemporary faith teaching on positive confession.

THE WESLEYS AND WESLEYAN THEOLOGIANS

John Wesley (1703-1791) influenced belief and practice of faith both at the grass roots level with common people and was also an able scholar who taught principles of faith. He emphasized holiness, which he called "the fullness of faith."[90] Following Wesley, a theological foundation for faith in the supernatural working of God was laid by eighteenth-century Methodist leaders such as John Fletcher, Hester Ann Rogers, and William Corvosso and theologians such as commentators Joseph Bensen and Adam Clarke, and later by nineteenth-century Boston University professor Daniel Steele.[91]

SUMMATION

These are just a sampling the roots of faith principles in the Early Church Fathers, Mystics, Reformers, and the Pietist, Puritan, and Wesleyan movements. This brief overview is not intended to be a thorough study of faith principles in the earlier Christian writing since the focus of this study is on the nineteenth and twentieth century faith leaders. The purpose has been to show that contemporary principles of faith are not new, but find their roots in ancient Christian faith teaching and practice. This overview has noted some of the significant developments and paradigm shifts in faith thinking that lay a foundation for classic and contemporary faith theology and practice.

---

1.   Lyle Wesley Dorsett, *E.M. Bounds: Man of Prayer* (Grand Rapids: Zondervan, 1991), 72.

2.   Ibid., 60.

3.   A.B. Simpson, cited in MacMillan "Our Alliance Message," *The Alliance Weekly (AW)*, Dec. 27, 1941, 826.

4.   A.B. Simpson, *Present Truths or the Supernatural* (Harrisburg, Penn.: Christian Publications, 1967), 9-10.

5.   *Merriam-Webster's Collegiate Dictionary*, Tenth Edition (Springfield, Mass.: Merriam-Webster, Inc., 1993), 211.

6.   Hannah Whitall Smith, *The Christian's Secret of a Happy Life* (Old Tappan, N.J.: Fleming H. Revell, 1942), 20, 25, 32, 47, 96, 101, 104, 121, 132, 134, 140.

7.   Theophilus, *To Autolycus*, 8, *The Ante-Nicene Fathers* (*ANF*), Alexander Roberts and James Donaldson, eds. (Grand Rapids: Eerdmans, 1979), 2:91.

8.   Clement of Alexandria, *The Stromata, or Miscellanies*, Book 2, Chapters 2, 4, *ANF*, 2:348-350. David Hazard gives this paraphrase of Clement: "But far above this way of knowing are the first principles of our knowledge—the knowledge of God, given to us by revelation. For the principles of our faith were revealed to us by God, from above, by the Spirit. . . ." Clement of Alexandria, "First Principles of Faith," cited in *You Give Me New Life*, ed. David Hazard (Minneapolis: Bethany House, 1995), 37.

9.   Peter Kreeft and Ronald Tacelli, *Handbook of Christian Apologetics* (Downers Grove, Ill.: IVP, 1994), 369. See also H.B. Timothy, *The Early Christian Apologists and Greek Philosophy* (Assen, Netherlands: Van Gorcum & Co., 1972), 73.

10.   F.B. Meyer, *Abraham or the Obedience of Faith* (Ft. Washington, Penn.: Christian Literature Crusade, 1983), 118.

11.   F.B. Meyer, *The Secret of Guidance* (Chicago: Moody, n.d.), 53, 122.

12.   A.B. Simpson, *AW*, Feb. 10, 1917, 290.

13.   Dorsett, *E.M. Bounds*, 152.

14.   McConnell, 103-115.

15.   Clement, *Stromata*, 2:4, *ANF*, 2:350.

16.   Clement, *Stromata*, 2:11, *ANF*, 2:358.

17.   Timothy, 72.

18.   Clement, *Stromata*, 2:11, *ANF*, 2:358.

19.   Cyril of Jerusalem, *Catechetical Lectures*, Lecture V, 4, 11; *The Nicene and Post-Nicene Fathers* (*NPNF*), Philip Schaff, ed. (Grand Rapids: Eerdmans, 1979), 2:7:29, 32.

20.   Cyril of Jerusalem, *Catechetical Lectures*, Lecture V, 10, 11, *NPNF*, 2:7:31n5.

21.   Allister E. McGrath, *The Christian Theology Reader* (Cambridge, Mass.: Blackwell Publishers, 1995), 292-293.

22.   Ibid., 301.

23.   Augustine, cited in Mrs. Charles Cowman, *Streams in the Desert* (Grand Rapids: Zondervan, [1925] 1972), 1:219.

24.   Augustine, *Sermons on St. John*, Tractate 49, *NPNF*, 1:7:277; see also Augustine, *Sermons on NT Lessons*, 17:24, *NPNF*, 1:6:310-313.

25.   Hilary of Portier, *On the Trinity*, vii. 37, *NPNF*, 2:9:112.

26.   Patrick Henry Reardon, "Scripture Saturation," *Christian History*, Issue 80, Vol. XXII, No. 4, 32.

27.   *NPNF*, 2:12:117, 228-229.

28.   Leo, *Sermons,* 3:3, *NPNF*, 2:12:117.

29.   Justo L. Gonzalez, *A History of Christian Thought* (Nashville: Abingdon Press, 1971), 2:158.

30.   See MacArthur, *Charismatic Chaos*, 35-53; Hunt and McMahon, *Seduction of Christianity*, 107-109, 118, 119.

31. Oswald Chambers, *Biblical Psychology* (Grand Rapids: Discovery House, [1962] 1995), 157.

32. A.W. Tozer, *The Christian Book of Mystical Verse* (Camp Hill, Penn.: Christian Publications, 1963), v-vi. For a treatise on Tozer's mystic spirituality, see E. Lynn Harris, *The Mystic Spirituality of A.W. Tozer, A Twentieth-Century American Protestant* (San Francisco: Mellen Research University Press, 1992).

33. D. Martyn Lloyd-Jones, *The Christian Warfare* (Grand Rapids: Zondervan, 1976), 122.

34. A.T. Pierson, *The New Acts of the Apostles* (New York: Baker and Taylor, 1894), 1, 2.

35. Gonzalez, *A History of Christian Thought*, 2:167, 171-172.

36. Bernard of Clairvaux, *The Works of Bernard of Clairvaux: Treatises II* (Washington, D.C.: Cistercian Publications, 1974), 101.

37. William of St. Thierry, *The Mirror of Faith* (Kalamazoo, Mich.: Cistercian Publications, 1979), 8-9.

38. F.B. Meyer, *Five Musts of the Christian Life* (Chicago: Moody, 1927), 99; see also F.B. Meyer, *The Secret of Guidance* (Chicago: Moody, n.d.), 36.

39. Richard J. Foster and James Bryan Smith, eds., *Devotional Classics* (San Francisco: HarperSanFrancisco, 1993), 69; A.W. Tozer, *Man: The Dwelling Place of God* (Camp Hill, Penn.: Christian Publications, 1966), 98, 100, 129; A.W. Tozer, *Jesus Is Victor* (Camp Hill, Penn.: Christian Publications, 1989), 45, 72; Elizabeth Elliott, *A Chance To Die: The Life and Legacy of Amy Carmichael* (Old Tappan, N.J.: Fleming H. Revell, 1987), 91; Amy Carmichael, *Thou Givest . . . They Gather* (Ft. Washington, Penn.: Christian Literature Crusade, 1958), 18.

40. See Tozer, *That Incredible Christian*, 66, 77; A.W. Tozer, *The Divine Conquest* (Old Tappan, N.J.: Fleming H. Revell, 1950), 13; A.W. Tozer, *The Next Chapter After the Last* (Camp Hill, Penn.: Christian Publications, 1987), 96, 102-105; A.W. Tozer, *The Size of the Soul* (Camp Hill, Penn.: Christian Publications, 1992), 47; James L. Snyder, *In Pursuit of God: The Life of A.W. Tozer* (Camp Hill, Penn.: Christian Publications, 1991), 231.

41. C.F. Kelley, *Meister Eckhart on Divine Knowledge* (New Haven, Conn., and London: Yale University Press, 1977), 196, 204, 211, 214.

42. Eckhart, cited in Tozer, *That Incredible Christian*, 77.

43. See also Mrs. Charles Cowman, *Streams in the Desert* (Grand Rapids: Zondervan, [1925] 1972), 1:152.

44. A.B. Simpson, *In the School of Faith* (New York: Christian Alliance Publishing Co., [1894]), 90.

45. Foster and Smith, *Devotional Classics*, 147. See Thomas S. Kepler, ed., *Theologia Germanica* (Cleveland, Ohio: The World Publishing Co., 1952), Chapters 7, 39, 40.

46. Kepler, ed., *Theologia Germanica*, Chapter 8, 51-52. See also Chapter 9, 54.

47. Foster and Smith, *Devotional Classics*, 147.

48. *The Cloud of Unknowing, The Book of Privy Counseling*, ed. William Johnson (Garden City, N.Y.: Image Books, 1973), 138, 139, 160; see A.W. Tozer, *The Pursuit of God* (Camp Hill, Penn.: Christian Publications, [1948, 1982] 199), 18.

49. *The Cloud of Unknowing*, 30-31.

50. Thomas a Kempis, *Of the Imitation of Christ* (Grand Rapids: Baker, 1973), 69, 73.

51. Ibid., 225-226.

52. Evelyn Underhill, *The Mystics of the Church* (Cambridge: James Clarke and Co., Ltd., [1925] 1975), 212.

53. Henry I. Lederle, *Systematic Theology: Honors B.Th. STH403: Guide 2* (Pretoria, South Africa: University of South Africa, 1980), 4, 6.

54. Ibid., 4.

55. Ibid.

56. Ibid.

57. Ibid., 4-5.

58. Ibid., 6.

59. McGrath, *The Christian Theology Reader*, 304.

60. Martin Luther, "Sermon for the 3rd Sunday of Epiphany, Matthew 8:1-13," *The Sermons of Martin Luther* (Grand Rapids: Baker, 2000), 2:73-74

61. John Dillenberger, *Martin Luther: Selections from His Writings* (New York: Doubleday, 1961), 354.

62. John Calvin, *A Compendium of the Institutes of the Christian Religion by John Calvin*, Hugh T. Kerr, ed. (Philadelphia: Westminster Press, [1939] 1964), 91-94; Geoffrey W. Bromiley, *Historical Theology: An Introduction* (Grand Rapids: Eerdmans, 1978), 236.

63. Cf. John Calvin, *The Institutes of the Christian Religion* (Grand Rapids: Eerdmans, 1949), 1:564, as cited in Joe McIntyre, *E.W. Kenyon and His Message of Faith: The True Story* (Lake Mary, Fla.: Creation House, 1997), 186-187; see also Derek E. Vreeland, "Reconstructing Word of Faith Theology: A Defense, Analysis and Refinement of the Theology of the Word of Faith Movement." Paper presented at the 30th Annual Meeting of the Society for Pentecostal Studies, Oral Roberts University, Tulsa, Okla., Mar. 2001, 5.

64. McConnell, 129; Hanegraaff, 162.

65. Madame Guyon, *Experiencing God through Prayer* (Springdale, Penn.: Whitaker, 1984), 5; Foster and Smith, 320.

66. Cowman, *Streams in the Desert*, 1:165.

67. Francois Fenelon, *Let Go* (Springdale, Penn.: Whitaker, 1973), 9.

68. Foster and Smith, *Devotional Classics*, 320.

69. Cowman, *Streams in the Desert*, 1:348.

70. Guyon, 23-24.

71. Ibid., 27.

72. Pere La Combe, "Spiritual Maxims," Francois Fenelon and Madame Guyon, *Spiritual Progress*, http://ccel.org/f/fenelon/progress/spirit06.htm, accessed 2000.

73. Fenelon, 24.

74. Ibid., 27-28.

75. Henry Scougal, *The Life of God in the Soul of Man* (Minneapolis: Bethany Fellowship, 1946), 37-38.

76. See Foster and Smith, 138-141.

77. Charles Sherwood McCoy, *The Covenant Theology of Johannes Cocceius*. Ph.D. Thesis, Yale University, 1956, 148.

78. Ibid., 170.

79. Ibid., 274.

80. Ibid., 249-250.

81. Thomas Brooks, *Precious Remedies Against Satan's Devices* (London: Banner of Truth Trust. [1652, 1866] 1968), 131.

82. Alfred Owen Aldridge, *Jonathan Edwards* (New York: Washington Square Press, 1964), 150-162.

83. Ibid., 161.

84. Dayton, 119.

85. Gary R. Sattler, *God's Glory, Neighbor's Good: A Brief Introduction to the Life and Writings of Aug. Herman Francke* (Chicago: Covenant Press, 1982), 105.

86. Lyle Wesley Dorsett, "The Pietist Tradition in Evangelical Spirituality: A Bibliographic Essay," *The Christian Educator's Handbook on Spiritual Formation*, Kenneth L. Gangel and James C. Willhoit, eds. (Grand Rapids: Baker, 1994), 296.

87. Ibid.

88. Ibid., 298

89. Ibid., 298-304.

90. J. Steven Harper, "Renewal—The Wesley Way," *The Asbury Herald*, Spring 1996, 10.

91. Harold E. Raser, *Phoebe Palmer: Her Life and Thought* (Lewiston, N.Y.: E. Mellon Press, 1987), 249-250.

CHAPTER 2

Classic Word of Faith Movements:
Nineteenth/Early
Twentieth-Century Men
and Women of Faith

In our brief survey of the role of faith teaching in church history, we have seen that seeds of faith were planted which germinated and grew into greater movements of faith. What began with a few individuals continued to snowball in the nineteenth and early twentieth centuries in a revival of faith. These revivals of faith took place through the Wesleyan holiness movement, scholarly influences, faith ministries and missions, the faith home movement, the Keswick/Higher Life holiness movements, The C&MA movement, the early Young Men's Christian Association/Young Women's Christian Association (YMCA/YWCA), and Pentecostalism. The people and movements listed below, though not comprehensive, are among the most influential teachers and practitioners of faith.[1]

WESLEYAN HOLINESS MOVEMENT[2]

Phoebe Palmer (1807-1874). Phoebe Palmer was a Methodist holiness leader who wrote extensively on faith in a collection of writings first published in 1848 entitled *Faith and Its Effects.* Her teachings on faith were developed from eighteenth century Methodist leaders John Fletcher, Adam Clarke, Hester Ann Rogers, and William Corvosso.[3] She is especially known for propagating the idea of actively confessing one's faith, what she termed "professing the blessing," picked up and adapted by Hannah Whitall Smith, A.B. Simpson, Oswald Chambers, and others. Palmer's teaching lies at the roots of contemporary faith teaching on positive confession, although she would not have applied the concept in the manner and to the extent of contemporary faith teaching.

Edward McKendree Bounds (1835-1913). E.M. Bounds, a leading Methodist pastor known for his deep prayer life and strong faith, wrote several classic books on prayer that contain principles of faith, including *Power Through Prayer, Purpose in Prayer,* and *Prayer and Praying Men.* Bounds was also influenced by Pietist pastor Johannes Blumhardt's teaching on faith, prayer, and spiritual authority, as well as Methodist theologians and Wesley himself. Having been a Civil War military chaplain, his writings show military applications in his thoughts on prayer. He taught on "commanding faith" and believing prayer as a force, foreshadowing contemporary faith teaching on these ideas.

SCHOLARLY INFLUENCES

Thomas Upham (1799-1872). Upham was a Congregational professor of philosophy and psychology (then called "mental philosophy") who became a Methodist holiness leader after contact with Phoebe Palmer. He studied Fenelon and Guyon, writing a biography of the latter entitled *Life, Religious Opinions and Experience of Madame Guyon.* His 300+ page book *The Life of Faith* along with Palmer's *Faith and Its Effects* were the most comprehensive on the subject in the early nineteenth century and undoubtedly influenced much of nineteenth and early twentieth century thinking on faith, including A.B. Simpson and A.W. Tozer, leaders of C&MA. He taught on the law and energy of faith, foundational to classic and contemporary faith teaching on faith as a law and as a force.

Other Scholars—Christlieb, Bushnell and Drummond. The writings of Professor Theodore Christlieb of the University of Bonn, *Contemporary Doubt and Christian Belief,* Horace Bushnell (1802-1876), *Nature and the Supernatural* and Henry Drummond (1851-1897), *Natural Law and the Spiritual World,* were all written to counteract the "de-supernaturalizing" of faith due to the philosophy of the Age of Reason, reinforcing the idea that God was and still is a miracle-working God. Thus faith in the continuing operation of the supernatural had a solid theological evangelical basis in the seventeenth and eighteenth centuries. Drummond became a close friend of American evangelist D.L. Moody, who popularized many classic faith ideas.

FAITH MINISTRIES AND MISSIONS

George Müller (1805-1898). Known as "The Apostle of Faith," George
Müller was probably the greatest catalyst of faith of the nineteenth century. A Prussian by birth, Müller went to England to engage in evange-
lizing Jews. He became involved with the Plymouth Brethren and was
led by the Lord to establish an orphanage based on the faith principles
of Prussian Pietist professor Francke.[4] His *Autobiography* chronicles
his walk of faith. Many of the contemporary faith principles regarding
Mark 11:24, praying in faith for healing, claiming the promises of God
for provision of needs and answers to prayer all came from the practical
exercise of his faith. He thus became an apostle of faith by his example
even more than his teaching. For instance, Müller did not publicize his
financial and material needs, so as to prove God faithful. While he did
preach on various aspects of faith, he never formulated a comprehensive
theology of faith. Contemporary faith leader Kenneth Hagin cites Müller's faith walk as an example.[5]

James Hudson Taylor (1832-1905). J. Hudson Taylor, pioneer missionary to
China and founder of the China Inland Mission, was considered the "Father of Faith Missions." As a friend of Müller, he put into practice Müller's
faith principles in his missions ventures, especially in not telling others of
his needs.[6] He was known for his deep life of prayer and close fellowship
with God. Many remarkable and supernatural answers to prayer occurred
as a result of his bold faith. His best-known published work is *Union and
Communion with Christ*, an allegorical study of the Song of Solomon related
to fellowship with Christ. Taylor also influenced many holiness leaders
such as Murray, Carmichael, and Simpson.[7] As with Müller, his walk of
faith became a model for classic and contemporary faith praxis.

Charles Haddon Spurgeon (1834-1892). Spurgeon, renowned British
Baptist expositor and pastor of the Metropolitan Tabernacle in London,
was considered the "Prince of Preachers." A close friend of both Müller and Taylor, he practiced the same principles of faith. He had one of
the earliest and largest ministries of healing in England, even before the
ministries of William Boardman and Elizabeth Baxter, and preached a
faith message similar to his contemporaries such as Simpson, Murray,
and A.J. Gordon. His devotional book *Faith's Checkbook* was based on
the premise that the promises of God are appropriated by an act of faith
like endorsing and cashing a check, a common teaching in classic and

contemporary faith movements. A series of his sermons on faith have been compiled into a book entitled *The Triumph of Faith in a Believer's Life*. Though he is not usually identified with the Higher Life and Keswick holiness movements, he nonetheless maintained close friendships with leaders of those movements such as Taylor, Murray, Pierson, and Meyer, and his teachings reflected many of the same themes and beliefs. Contemporary faith leader Kenneth Hagin is reported to have read and absorbed many of his writings.

C.T. Studd (1860-1931). A famous cricket player who gave away all his fortune and launched into faith missions, Studd became founder of World Evangelization Crusade. He also followed the faith principles of Müller with amazing results, including miraculous financial provisions and health and healing without medicine or doctors. Hudson Taylor and Hannah Whitall Smith also influenced Studd's way of life and thinking.[8] His brother later became actively involved in the early Pentecostal movement, and their walk of faith has been a model in both evangelical and charismatic/contemporary faith circles.

Amy Carmichael (1867-1951). An Irish Anglican missionary to the Far East, Carmichael founded Dohnavur Fellowship in India, ministering especially to young girls sold into prostitution. A friend of Hudson Taylor's daughter-in-law, her ministry was influenced heavily by his faith principles, trusting God for provision of needs. Many extraordinary answers to prayer, including miraculous provision, conversions, deliverance from demons, and healings came through her life of faith. She was also involved with the Keswick holiness movement, and contributed articles to its magazine, *The Life of Faith*, edited by Jessie Penn-Lewis. She especially taught about receiving a fresh word from the Lord in due season, akin to contemporary faith teaching on the concept of *logos* and *rhema* (see Chapter 12), but differed from contemporary faith teaching in such issues as prosperity and suffering.

THE EUROPEAN FAITH HOME MOVEMENT[9]

Johannes Christoph Blumhardt (1805-1880). Blumhardt, a German Lutheran pastor who has been called "a latter day Pietist," began a healing ministry in 1843 when a dying girl was dramatically healed and delivered from demonic attack through prayer and the laying on of hands.[10] He thus also became a pioneer in the ministry of spiritual warfare and exorcism. In 1852 he established a "faith home" for the purpose of instructing the sick in "the biblical message of healing within a faith-building atmosphere to enable them to obtain spiritual power over their sickness."[11] Within thirty-five years more than thirty similar healing centers were established in America, including those of Charles Cullis, Carrie Judd Montgomery, and A.B. Simpson.[12] His ministry of healing and deliverance laid a foundation for classic and contemporary faith praxis.

Dorothea Trudel (1813-1862). Trudel was a Swiss woman who learned faith practically from her experiences of life. A.J. Gordon commented, "She looked to Him for food for her family when they must otherwise have starved; for deliverance when they must otherwise have perished; for healing when they must otherwise have died."[13] In 1851 several of her coworkers became sick and grew worse in spite of medical treatment. She anointed them with oil according to the promise of James 5:14-15, and they were healed instantly. She began several faith homes to handle the masses of people who came to her for healing. Samuel Zeller became her assistant and continued her work when she died, also with a strongly anointed ministry of healing. She taught one of the basic classic and contemporary faith tenets, claiming the promises of God as the believer's privilege.

Otto Stockmayer (1838-1917). Swiss pastor Otto Stockmayer (or Stockmaier) was healed through the ministry of Zeller on Easter 1867, and subsequently began a faith home. Laying a doctrinal foundation for healing and faith practice, he became known as the "theologian of the doctrine of healing by faith,"[14] and was a speaker at Keswick and Simpson's Old Orchard Conventions. His influence was multiplied especially when rising Dutch Reformed South African leader Andrew Murray was healed through his ministry at Bethshan home in England in 1882.

Mrs. Michael (Elizabeth) Baxter (1837-1926). In 1882 Mrs. Baxter, with the help of William Boardman and Charlotte C. Murray, established a faith healing home in London called Bethshan where her husband was editor of magazines that published teaching on holiness, faith, and healing. She became a popular speaker at Cullis' faith conventions and frequent writer in Carrie Judd Montgomery's magazine *Triumphs of Faith* and A.B. Simpson's *C&MA Weekly*. As mentioned above, Murray received miraculous healing after spending three weeks at Bethshan under the ministry of Otto Stockmayer.

CLASSIC WORD OF FAITH MOVEMENTS

EARLY AMERICAN FAITH HEALING PIONEERS

Charles Cullis (1833-1892). Episcopalian medical doctor Charles Cullis received the sanctifying baptism in the Spirit through the ministry of Phoebe Palmer in 1862 and was also influenced by the book *Life of Dorothea Trudel* in 1869. "Following a four month trip to Europe in 1873, where he visited the faith works of Blumhardt, Trudel, and George Müller, he began conducting annual faith conventions at Framingham, Massachusetts, and later at Old Orchard Beach, Maine."[15] Simpson, who was dramatically healed at one of those conventions, would later establish similar conventions at Old Orchard. Cullis also established a school of faith and a healing home. His ministry resulted in the mushrooming of what was sometimes called the "faith-cure" movement, especially through Simpson, Carrie Judd Montgomery and A.J. Gordon.

Ethan O. Allen (1813-1902). Descendent of the renowned Colonial leader of furniture fame, Allen was healed of tuberculosis through a Methodist class meeting in 1846. He began a healing and deliverance ministry which spanned more than 50 years. He became a speaker at many conferences, including A.B. Simpson's Old Orchard Convention, and had a significant impact on the teaching and practice of the early C&MA regarding faith, healing, spiritual warfare, and deliverance ministry.[16] Claiming Mark 16:17-18, he frequently repeated the phrase, "I'm believin' and receiving.'"[17] He was also an early teacher and practitioner of the authority of the believer according to Luke 10:19 and binding the strongman (Matt. 12:29).[18] He founded a faith home in Springfield, Massachusetts, and was considered by A.B. Simpson as the "Father of Divine Healing."[19] Ironically, his supernatural ministry contradicted his famed grandfather's deistic belief, published in his 1784 pamphlet *Reason the Only Oracle of Man*: "In those parts of the world where learning and science have prevailed, miracles have ceased; but in those parts of it as are barbarous and ignorant, miracles are still in vogue."[20]

Mrs. Edward Mix (1832-1884). Mrs. Mix appears to be the first black evangelist to have a healing ministry. Healed of tuberculosis through the ministry of Allen in 1877, she sometimes ministered with Allen and became renowned as a "faith cure physician."[21] It was through her healing ministry that Carrie Judd (Montgomery) was healed about 1880, who then edited a magazine on faith and wrote on *The Prayer of Faith*. Significantly, Allen called himself Judd's "grandfather" because of the healing anointing passed to her through Mrs. Mix.[22] There seemed to be a domino effect as Allen's ministry impacted Mix's ministry, which impacted Judd's ministry, which in turn stimulated much more faith teaching and practice.

CHARLES G. FINNEY (1792-1875)—OBERLIN THEOLOGY[23]

While Müller was preaching and exercising faith in the 1830s in England, a popular American contemporary, Charles Finney, was preaching similar principles on prayer and faith. It seems the Holy Spirit was revealing the same truths at the same time in locations thousands of miles apart. While he had a collection of sermons *Principles of Faith*, most of that teaching on faith was on the relationship of faith and salvation. However, in his lectures on *Revivals of Religion* in 1835, he taught principles relating to the exercise of faith in the Christian life such as the prayer of faith in prevailing prayer and the will of God. Arising out of Finney's modified Reformed Oberlin theology (similar to Keswick with some Wesleyan-Arminian influence) were holiness leaders such as Asa Mahan.[24]

Finney's teaching became pivotal for both classic and contemporary faith teaching. In fact, Farah maintains that the roots of contemporary faith theology are found in Finney, whom he claimed baptized Jeremy Bentham's utilitarian philosophy with moral principles and theology.[25] In particular, Finney's teaching that prevailing prayer must "pray for a definite object," "pray in faith," and "expect to obtain the blessing,"[26] provided a foundation for classic and contemporary faith praxis. His emphasis that "faith always receives its object" is similar to the cause and effect teaching of contemporary faith leaders. In fact, he was accused by some, as contemporary faith leaders have been, of trying to manipulate God.[27] Farah attributes to Finney an indirect influence, rather than direct, but believes that it "seriously weakened the sovereignty of God and opened the flood gate to humanist influences."[28]

THE KESWICK/HIGHER LIFE HOLINESS MOVEMENTS[29]

William E. Boardman (1810-1886). Boardman, a Presbyterian advocate of the Keswick holiness and healing movements in England, wrote *The Higher Christian Life* in 1858, which contained fresh teaching on faith. Along with Pearsall and Hannah Whitall Smith and others, Boardman helped to found the Keswick movement in 1875, which advocated the "rest of faith," claiming the promises of God, and appropriating the power of Christ.[30] He also wrote one of the earliest nineteenth-century books on divine healing, *The Lord That Healeth Thee*, which had significant impact on many classic faith leaders, especially Simpson.[31]

Andrew Murray (1828-1917). Murray, a highly respected South African Dutch Reformed leader, was also influenced by Boardman and Stockmayer. His voice became so strained that he could not speak for two years, and he was miraculously healed at Elizabeth Baxter's Bethshan healing home in 1882. Two years later he wrote *Divine Healing* on principles of healing by faith. Other books containing classic faith principles include *With Christ in the School of Prayer*, *Two Covenants*, and *The Prayer Life*. He was also instrumental in establishing the Keswick movement in South Africa. Murray spoke at one of Simpson's Old Orchard Conventions, as well as at Moody and Torrey's Northfield Conventions.[32] On the basis of covenant theology, he taught that believers can claim the promises, inheritance and authority of the Covenant, providing the basis for similar contemporary faith theology.

Hannah Whitall Smith (1832-1911). Another healing/holiness leader associated with Boardman and the Keswick movement, Quaker Hannah Smith, in the 1870s published *The Christian's Secret of a Happy Life* on the "Higher Christian Life," which she also called the "life of faith." This book has been considered a classic by people from people of many different denominational and theological backgrounds. Other books she wrote which contain faith principles were *The God of All Comfort* and *The Unselfishness of God*. She was influenced by Fenelon, Guyon, the Plymouth Brethren movement with which Müller was associated, and the Methodist understanding of sanctification.[33] Smith was influenced by Guyon to exercise positive attitude and confession, as well as trusting the Lord passively, saying, "Thy will be done." She testified, "I was much helped, too, by a saying of Madame Guyon's, that she had learned to be thankful for every snub and mortification, because she had found that they helped to advance her in the spiritual life; and in time I learned something of the same lesson."[34] Smith also refers to a collection of Guyon's and Fenelon's writings called *Spiritual Progress*, saying, "This book was very dear to me."[35] She advocated many of the same themes as other classic, as well as contemporary, faith leaders, including faith as a law and a force, positive confession, and the believer's inheritance.

Arthur T. Pierson (1837-1911). A.T. Pierson, a Presbyterian holiness leader and respected scholar, became one of the chief leaders of the

Keswick movement. As a strong faith advocate, he wrote the first full-length authorized biography of Müller, entitled *George Müller of Bristol*, which further popularized Müller's example of faith. It is not surprising that Pierson, though Presbyterian and not Baptist, followed Spurgeon as interim pastor of Metropolitan Tabernacle in London. He was also a friend and associate of A.B. Simpson and a frequent speaker at meetings of the C&MA, and his book *The Acts of the Holy Spirit* is published by the C&MA. He also wrote a commentary on the autobiography of renowned Baptist leader A.J. Gordon, who founded what is known today as Gordon College and Gordon-Conwell Seminary.[36] Pierson expounded from a scholarly standpoint on such principles as commanding faith and faith as a law and a force.

Frederick Brotherton Meyer (1847-1929). A friend of Spurgeon and Taylor, F.B. Meyer was a Baptist minister who served as a key spokesman for the Keswick movement, and also a speaker at Moody's Northfield conferences and Simpson's deeper life conferences.[37] He was a strong proponent of classic faith principles, echoing the belief of Church Father Theophilus, saying, "All God's dealings with men are on the same principle, by faith."[38] Some of his books containing classic faith principles include *Five Musts of the Christian Life*, *The Secret of Guidance*, and *Abraham: The Obedience of Faith*. He taught faith principles such as the inheritance and authority of the believer and exercising the faith of God.

Jessie Penn-Lewis (1861-1927). Penn-Lewis was a leader in the Keswick holiness movement in Great Britain and associate of Evan Roberts in the Welsh Revival. She published a weekly journal entitled *The Life of Faith*, the official periodical of the Keswick movement and taught on principles of prayer, revival, and the authority of the believer in spiritual warfare in such books as *The Warfare with Satan*, *War on the Saints*, *The Conquest of Canaan* and *Prayer and Evangelism*. Later she parted with the Keswick movement, moving into what was known as the Overcomer movement. Her teachings especially had significant impact on John MacMillan, the seminal writer on the authority of the believer and whose material was used extensively by contemporary faith leader Kenneth Hagin.[39]

Dwight L. Moody (1837-1899). Although D.L. Moody concentrated on evangelism, he accepted the classic faith, healing, and holiness movements, and people experienced healing in his meetings. A close friend of professor Henry Drummond, he maintained close friendships with

Higher Life and Keswick leaders such as Murray, Simpson, A.J. Gordon, Spurgeon, Meyer, and many others who taught classic faith principles. His Northfield conventions touted many of these leaders and speakers.[40] It was in one of Moody's meetings that Gordon witnessed an instantaneous healing and transformed his theology of healing. Paul Rader's ministry as pastor of Moody Church also furthered the classic faith teaching in early Moody circles. Moody Bible Institute was a center that taught healing, holiness, and the baptism in the Spirit in the early twentieth century.

Reuben A. Torrey (1856-1928). R.A. Torrey, an associate of Moody who did evangelistic work in America and Europe, also touted classic faith themes. He served as the chief executive officer of Moody Bible Institute and Dean of the Bible Institute of Los Angeles (later named Biola). He was a speaker at the Old Orchard Conventions led by Simpson. In 1924 he wrote the classic *The Power of Prayer*, which contained many classic faith principles, including those of Müller. In the same year he also published the booklet *Divine Healing*, in which he described healing as a provision of the atonement.

The YMCA/YWCA Movement. In contrast to the social movement that it is today, the early YMCA/YWCA movement acted as a strong advocate of healing, holiness, and faith principles. Keswick leader Jessie Penn-Lewis was actively involved in the YWCA. S.D. Gordon (1859-1936), one of the early leaders of the YMCA, was well-known for his "Quiet Talks" series of publications. He too was a speaker for Simpson at C&MA conventions. He taught on prayer, faith, healing, and spiritual warfare and published *Quiet Talks on Prayer* in 1911 and *Quiet Talks on the Healing Christ* in 1924.

Oswald Chambers (1874-1917). Chambers, a Baptist leader who was superintendent of the YMCA work in Egypt in World War I, also taught classic principles of faith, some of which are recorded in his famous devotional *My Utmost for His Highest*. He was saved under the ministry of Spurgeon and his father was ordained to the ministry by Spurgeon. He was also active in the Keswick movement. More than any other classic faith leader, Chambers taught a form of what is known today as revelation knowledge and sense knowledge, remarkably similar to the terminology of E.W. Kenyon.

THE CHRISTIAN AND MISSIONARY ALLIANCE MOVEMENT[41]

Perhaps the most prolific propagation of classic faith teaching and practice came through A.B. Simpson and those associated with the organization he founded, The Christian and Missionary Alliance. Simpson established the C&MA in 1887 as an interdenominational Higher Life movement promoting worldwide missions and a Fourfold Gospel of Jesus Christ as Savior, Sanctifier, Healer, and Coming King. While the C&MA eventually became a denomination, in its early stages it emerged as the largest interdenominational movement combining the classic principles of faith, healing, and holiness. Many evangelical leaders, such as Presbyterians A.T. Pierson and Jonathan Goforth, Baptist A.J. Gordon, Episcopalian Kenneth MacKenzie, later Assemblies of God leaders George and Carrie Judd Montgomery, and Methodists Charles and Lettie Cowman remained a part of their denominations while also being associated with the C&MA. By 1889 the C&MA (then known as the "Christian Alliance") was considered "the faith healing school of America."[42]

Albert Benjamin Simpson (1843-1919). In 1881 Presbyterian minister A.B. Simpson received a miraculous healing from a life-threatening heart condition at one of the conferences of Charles Cullis. Simpson's experience of healing and resulting publication of works on healing paralleled Andrew Murray's very closely and Murray spoke at one of Simpson's Old Orchard Conventions.[43] While a wide variety of classic writers taught various principles of faith, apart from Upham's 300+ pages *Life of Faith*, written in 1845 and Palmer's *Faith and Its Effects* in 1848, there appears to be no more extensive and comprehensive teaching addressing the practical issues of faith taught in the contemporary word of faith movement than that of Simpson.

His chief book on faith, now entitled *Seeing the Invisible* (originally *In the School of Faith*) was based primarily upon exposition of the characters of Hebrews 11. *The Gospel of Healing* and *Lord for the Body* lay down many principles of faith with regard to healing. *The Life of Prayer* contains many classic faith principles. The *Land of Promise* gives faith teaching on the believer's inheritance and authority. *Present Truths or the Supernatural* lays the groundwork for supernatural faith. *A Larger Christian Life* challenges believers to larger faith possibilities. Simpson was not by any means the first faith teacher, but he was the leading faith teacher of his time. He was influenced by several other people of faith (Francke, Müller, Spurgeon, Hannah Whitall Smith, Boardman, Trudel, Stockmayer,

Cullis, Palmer, Murray, Montgomery), and also had great impact on the faith teaching of other leaders who followed him, including Watchman Nee and contemporary faith leader Kenneth Hagin.

Boardman's book *The Higher Christian Life* had a major impact on Simpson's experience of the baptism in the Holy Spirit as a crisis experience of sanctification and also shaped some of his ideas on faith. It was at one of Cullis' conventions at Old Orchard in 1881 that Simpson received a miraculous healing by faith. Simpson himself eventually began similar conventions at Old Orchard. Chappell writes, "No single individual in the movement who was influenced by Charles Cullis touched so many lives with the message of healing as Simpson or persuaded so many individuals to enter full-time ministry with faith healing as a vital aspect of that ministry."[44]

Simpson and the C&MA have also been influenced by Thomas Upham. Upham's hymn "The Great Healer" is found in the C&MA hymnal *Hymns of the Christian Life*. His influence in the C&MA is also found in the publishing of several excerpts of his writings on faith and the Holy Spirit in several issues of *The Alliance Weekly* while A.W. Tozer was editor. Nienkirchen comments, "Upham (like Simpson) married Quietist mysticism to his holiness theology without surrendering the essentials of his own Protestant theological tradition."[45] While some consider Simpson to be radical, C.I. Scofield proclaimed of him, "He was the greatest man of his age."[46] Moody commented of Simpson's preaching, "No man gets to my heart like A.B. Simpson."[47]

Carrie Judd Montgomery (1859-1946). Carrie Judd (who married George Montgomery in 1890) was healed through the ministry of Mrs. Edward Mix, the first black healing evangelist, and was also influenced by fellow Episcopalian Charles Cullis. As a popular journalist, she strongly propagated faith teaching through her monthly magazine *Triumphs of Faith*, subtitled *A Monthly Journal Devoted to Faith Healing and the Promotion of Christian Holiness*. Articles by such faith leaders as Cullis, Elizabeth Baxter, Otto Stockmayer, Simpson, Mrs. Cornelia Nuzum, F.F. Bosworth, Murray, S.D. Gordon, A.J. Gordon, Aimee Semple McPherson, Charles Price, Müller, Spurgeon, and even contemporary faith founder E.W. Kenyon, appeared in her journal over several decades. In its early years, the journal promoted the work and message of the C&MA. She opened a faith home in Buffalo, New York, called "Faith Rest Cottage." Chappell observes the similarity of her teaching on healing to that of Phoebe

Palmer.[48] Simpson himself was influenced by Carrie Judd's 1880 book *The Prayer of Faith*, and frequently exhorted people to "act" their faith, a term that seems to have originated with Judd's book. Judd was one of the earliest members of the Board of Managers of the C&MA. She later married George Montgomery, who was appointed as an honorary Vice President of the C&MA until his death in 1930. They later became active in the Salvation Army and the Pentecostal movement, holding dual associations with the C&MA and the Assemblies of God. Aside from Simpson, her *Triumphs of Faith* most widely advanced classic faith teaching and practice.

Russell Kelso Carter (1849-1928). Captain R. Kelso Carter is considered by Chappell as "one of the leading apologists" for the faith healing movement.[49] He was a military academy teacher and captain and ordained Methodist minister who became an associate of Simpson and author of the hymn of faith "Standing on the Promises." In 1884 he wrote *The Atonement for Sin and Sickness*, giving a defense for belief in healing in the atonement. This work is particularly notable, because at that time his views of faith were very similar to those of some in the contemporary faith movement. In 1897 he wrote *Faith Healing Reviewed after Twenty Years*, in which he answered questions, clarified misunderstandings, retracted some of his more radical beliefs, and presented modifications and corrections of his beliefs regarding faith and healing. His change in viewpoints is especially of interest as an example of one who became less radical and controversial in his faith beliefs and practice. It is noteworthy that he later trained to be a physician, since in his earlier days he discouraged use of medicine and doctors.

Adoniram Judson Gordon (1836-1895). A.J. Gordon, another associate of Cullis and Simpson, was a popular Baptist pastor and founder of Gordon College who embraced the message of healing. He was a frequent speaker at C&MA, Keswick and Higher Life gatherings, and was a lecturer at Simpson's Missionary Training Institute, which opened in 1883. Writer of the music for the hymn "My Jesus, I Love Thee," Gordon also authored the book *The Ministry of Healing* in 1882, which gives a history of healing through the centuries and a basic theological defense for the reality of present-day healing and miracles. He came to believe in the reality of healing when he observed people instantaneously healed at one of Moody's meetings. His book on healing along with those of

Murray and Simpson are currently published together in one volume by the publishing house of the C&MA.

George D. Watson (1845-1924). Watson, a popular Methodist holiness leader, wrote on the higher Christian life in such books as *Throne Life* and *Bridehood Saints.* Watson was close friend with the C&MA and spoke in many C&MA meetings. Even his funeral was conducted in a C&MA church. He had significant impact on the life of C&MA leader John Mac-Millan, the seminal writer on the authority of the believer. MacMillan later wrote on Watson's idea of "throne power" and other holiness themes similar to those of Watson in relationship to the believer's authority. Watson's teachings, though for the most part not in print today, are found in many of the classic faith/higher life/Keswick writings, as well as in the more recent writing of Paul Billheimer (see Chapter 7).

Charles (1864-1924) and Lettie Cowman (1870-1960). The Cowmans were Methodist missionaries who founded the Oriental Missionary Society. Their lives were transformed through Simpson's ministry when he preached at one of Moody's meetings.[50] Lettie is best known as the editor and devotional writer of *Streams in the Desert* and *Springs in the Valley,* which have become popular devotional books. Her devotionals contain many quotes and teachings on faith and holiness from Simpson, Hudson Taylor, Spurgeon, A.J. Gordon, Meyer, Montgomery, Müller, Torrey, Stockmayer, Murray, Hannah Whitall Smith, S.D. Gordon, Chambers, Pierson and other Higher Life leaders. Her devotional compilations have probably promulgated the classic faith message more than any other source other than Simpson and Montgomery.

Jonathan Goforth (1859-1936). Goforth, pioneer Canadian Presbyterian missionary to China, associated closely with the C&MA and fellow Canadian A.B. Simpson. He and his wife Rosalind had a strong ministry of faith, healing, and exercise of spiritual authority. His daughter was a student of the C&MA Missionary Training Institute at Nyack and served under the C&MA on the mission field. He was also a friend and colleague of fellow Toronto native John MacMillan. His book *By My Spirit* recounts the moving of the Holy Spirit in the Far East. He was used by God as a catalyst of the early twentieth-century Chinese revival. The book *Goforth of China* by his wife Rosalind recounts his ministry of faith and power.

Charles A. Blanchard (1848-1925). Blanchard, President of Wheaton College (1882-1925) and an honorary Vice President of the C&MA, wrote a book on faith and prayer entitled *Getting Things from God.*[51] He writes that he was influenced by Müller, Murray, Bounds, and Torrey. His indebtedness to Simpson's thought is also shown through his reference to the Fourfold Gospel of Jesus Christ as Savior, Sanctifier, Healer, and Coming King.[52] C&MA scholar Keith Bailey notes that Wheaton College and Moody Bible Institute were centers that taught healing, holiness, and the baptism in the Spirit in the early twentieth century.[53]

Fred Francis Bosworth (1877-1958). F.F. Bosworth, who had been associated with John Alexander Dowie[54] in his earlier days, moved away from Dowie's extreme position on healing, launching an interdenominational church in Dallas in 1910 loosely affiliated with the C&MA. In 1914 he became involved with the founding of the Assemblies of God. However, disavowing the doctrine of tongues as the initial evidence of the baptism in the Spirit, he left the Assemblies of God in 1918 and rejoined the C&MA. As a C&MA evangelist, he published a series of sermons entitled *Christ the Healer* in 1924, and added additional chapters in later editions. In one of his later messages on positive confession in the 1948 edition he acknowledges the influence of E.W. Kenyon on his thought. At one time, his book was required reading for ordination in the C&MA. He has been frequently cited by contemporary faith leaders and his book is used as a textbook at Kenneth Hagin's Rhema Bible Training School. While some of his beliefs reflect those of Kenyon, most of his teaching is rooted in the teachings of Simpson, Murray, and other leaders of the classic faith/Higher Life movement.

Thomas J. McCrossan (1868-1960). T.J. McCrossan was a prominent Presbyterian pastor and professor of Greek and classical languages at the University of Manitoba. Falling under the power of the Spirit at one of Charles Price's meetings in 1921, he was baptized in the Spirit and had a dramatic vision, but never spoke in tongues. He began pastoring with the C&MA in 1923, and was a friend of F.F. Bosworth and independent Pentecostal evangelist Charles Price, frequently traveling and ministering with Price. He taught at Simpson Bible Institute and served as interim president for a year. His book *Speaking in Tongues: Sign or Gift—Which?* was published by the C&MA in 1927, teaching a similar position to Bosworth and Simpson on tongues. His book *Bodily Healing and the Atonement*, published in 1930, gives an exegetical defense for the doctrine of healing in the atonement. It has been reprinted by contemporary faith teachers Kenneth Hagin and Roy Hicks, and is used at Rhema Bible Training School.

John A. MacMillan (1873-1956). MacMillan, a Presbyterian lay elder who became a C&MA missionary to the Far East and an editor of *The Alliance Weekly*, wrote a series of articles on *The Authority of the Believer* in 1932, eventually published in book form. MacMillan was the seminal writer on the concept of the authority of the believer, popularized by contemporary faith leader Kenneth Hagin, who used much of his material.[55] Specializing in spiritual warfare, MacMillan also later published *Encounter with Darkness* (formerly published as *Contemporary Demon Possession*) and taught courses at Nyack College. Chapter 7 will discuss his teachings on the authority of the believer.

Paul Rader (1879-1938). Paul Rader, who served as evangelist, radio preacher, pastor of Moody Church, and president of the C&MA following Simpson, propagated widely the classic themes of faith, healing, and holiness. He was also associated with Aimee Semple McPherson and preached at Angelus Temple during her absence for three months. He is author of hymns on faith and the power of the Spirit such as "Only Believe" (used as a hymn of benediction on Robert Schuller's TV programs) and "Old Time Power" and wrote a book entitled *Harnessing God* on the power of faith and the Holy Spirit. One of his descendents has recently served as President of the Salvation Army and President of Asbury College.

Aiden Wilson Tozer (1897-1963). A.W. Tozer, a vice president of the C&MA and editor of *The Alliance Witness* following MacMillan, is a more recent advocate of classic faith theology. He is considered a twentieth century prophet and mystic whose insights speak clearly to our times. He authored more than forty books, including books on faith entitled *Faith Beyond Reason* and *Jesus, The Author of Our Faith*. He is best known for his books *The Pursuit of God* and *Knowledge of the Holy*, both considered classics. He frequently quoted mystics such as Fenelon, Guyon, Bernard, Thomas a Kempis, and many others. His influence in the evangelical community is the greatest of any in the C&MA movement, even more so than its founder A.B. Simpson.

1. For more biographical information on some of these classic faith leaders, as well as several others not mentioned here, see Nancy A. Hardesty, *Faith Cure: Divine Healing in the Holiness and Pentecostal Movements* (Peabody, Mass.: Hendrickson, 2003).

2. For more on the Wesleyan holiness roots of the healing, faith, and Pentecostal movements, see Synan, *The Holiness-Pentecostal Tradition*, 1-43; and Dayton, 35-84.

3. Raser, 249-250.

4. Kenneth Scott Latourette, *A History of Christianity* (New York: Harper and Row, [1953] 1975), 2:1185.

5. Kenneth Hagin, *Mountain Moving Faith* (Tulsa, Okla.: Kenneth Hagin Ministries, 1993), 39-41.

6. Arthur T. Pierson, *The Acts of the Holy Spirit* (Harrisburg, Penn.: Christian Publications, 1980), 92.

7. Andrew Murray, *Key to the Missionary Problem*, contemporized by Leona Choy (Ft. Washington, Penn.: Christian Literature Crusade, 1979), 88. On Carmichael, see Elliot, 58-60; and on Simpson, see Robert L. Niklaus, John S. Sawin, and Samuel J. Stoesz, *All for Jesus* (Camp Hill, Penn.: Christian Publications, 1986), 7.

8. Norman P. Grubb, *C.T. Studd: Cricketer and Pioneer* (Ft. Washington, Penn.: Christian Literature Crusade, 1933), 37, 41, 61.

9. For more on healing homes, see Hardesty, 56-71.

10. Dayton, 120.

11. Chappell, 355.

12. Russell Kelso Carter, *Faith Healing Reviewed After Twenty Years* (Boston, Chicago: Christian Witness Co., 1897), 35.

13. A.J. Gordon, *The Ministry of Healing* (Harrisburg, Penn.: Christian Publications, n.d.), 147. For a current edited and updated version of Gordon's original book, see A.J. Gordon, *The Ministry of Healing*, in *Healing: The Three Great Classics on Divine Healing*, comp and ed. Jonathan L. Graf (Camp Hill, Penn.: Christian Publications, 1992).

14. Chappell, 356.

15. Chappell, 358.

16. William T. MacArthur, *Ethan O. Allen* (Philadelphia: The Parlor Evangelist, n.d.).

17. Ibid., 4.

18. Ibid., 4-6, 12, 14.

19. Ibid., 14.

20. Ethan Allen, *Reason the Only Oracle of Man*, accessed online at http://atheism.about.com/library/quotes/bl_q_EAllen.htm.

21. Hardesty, 10-11.

22. MacArthur, *Ethan O. Allen*, 17.

23. For more on Finney and Oberlin theology, see Dayton, 66-72, 100-101; Synan, *The Holiness-Pentecostal Tradition*, 14-15; Richard Gilbertson, *The Baptism of the Holy Spirit* (Camp Hill, Penn.: Christian Publications, 1993), 13-15, 151-157.

24. Dayton, 64, 66-67; Gilbertson, 13-14, 156.

25. Farah, "A Critical Analysis," 3.

26. Dayton, 122.

27. Ibid.

28. Farah, "A Critical Analysis," 4.

29. For more on the Keswick and Higher Life movements, see Dayton, 104-108; Synan, *The Holiness-Pentecostal Tradition*, 33, 144-145; Gilbertson, 176-185.

30. Pierson, *The New Acts of the Apostles*, 38.

31. Lindsay Reynolds, *Footprints* (Beaverlodge, Alberta: Buena Book Services, 1981), 62.

32. Chappell, 361-362.

33. Smith, *The Unselfishness of God and How I Discovered It*, 174, 175, 184.

34. Hannah Whitall Smith, *The Unselfishness of God and How I Discovered It* (New York: Garland Publishers, [1903] 1985), 164.

35. Hannah Whitall Smith, *The God of All Comfort* (New Kensington, Penn.: Whitaker, 1984), 174.

36. See A.T. Pierson, "The Life Story, and the Dream as Interpreting the Man." in A.J. Gordon, *How Christ Came to Church: A Spiritual Autobiography* (Philadelphia: American Baptist Publishing Co., 1895), 95-149.

37. Gilbertson, 183.

38. Ibid.

39. Paul L. King, *A Case Study of a Believer with Authority: The Impact of the Life and Ministry of John A. MacMillan*. Doctor of Ministry dissertation. Tulsa, Okla.: Oral Roberts University, 2000, 281-283, 299.

40. Gilbertson, 157.

41. See Niklaus, et al, *All for Jesus*, for a history of the C&MA.

42. Reynolds, *Footprints*, 96.

43. Chappell, 361-362.

44. Ibid., 364.

45. Charles W. Nienkirchen, *A.B. Simpson and the Pentecostal Movement* (Peabody, Mass.: Hendrickson, 1992), 10.

46. Eunice Perkins, *Fred Francis Bosworth, The Joybringer: His Life Story* (River Forest, Ill.: F.F. Bosworth, 1927), 109.

47. A.B. Simpson, *A Larger Christian Life* (Camp Hill, Penn.: Christian Publications, 1988), 2.

48. Chappell, 364.

49. Chappell, 359.

50. David F. Hartzfeld and Charles Nienkirchen, eds., *The Birth of a Vision* (Camp Hill, Penn.: Christian Publications, 1986), ix.

51. Later Wheaton College President V. Raymond Edman was also a C&MA minister and former missionary.

52. Charles A. Blanchard, *Getting Things from God: A Study of the Prayer Life* (Chicago: Bible Institute Colportage Assn., 1915), 218.

53. Keith Bailey, audiotape of message delivered Jan. 1996.

54. Dowie was a more radical faith healing leader who was opposed to doctors and medicine, and thus criticized Simpson's more moderate position.

55. See King, *A Case Study of a Believer with Authority*, 281-283.

CHAPTER 3

Twentieth-Century Classic
and Contemporary Word of Faith
Movements

THE PENTECOSTAL MOVEMENT

Smith Wigglesworth (1859-1946). Known as "The Apostle of Faith" among Pentecostals, Wigglesworth wrote *The Ever-Increasing Faith* and *Faith That Prevails*. He had a powerful ministry of faith and healing. He has been frequently cited by many in the contemporary faith movement, especially Kenneth Hagin. As will be seen later, however, some of his teaching is actually opposed to some contemporary faith teaching.[1]

Aimee Semple McPherson (1890-1944). Founder of the Foursquare Church, McPherson was one of the most popular, though sometimes controversial, leaders of faith and healing in the Pentecostal movement. Her "Foursquare Gospel" of Jesus as Savior, Baptizer, Healer, and Coming King, was adapted and modeled after Simpson's Fourfold Gospel. Charles Price received the baptism in the Spirit under her ministry, and Paul Rader and other C&MA leaders preached for her in her church. Her ministry also acted as a forerunner of the healing ministry of Kathryn Kuhlman.

Cornelia Nuzum. Known usually as "Mrs. C. Nuzum," she was an Assemblies of God missionary to Mexico. A friend of Carrie Judd Montgomery, she frequently contributed articles on faith in Montgomery's *Triumphs of Faith*, and wrote the book *The Life of Faith*. Her writings also appeared in the evangelical periodical *Herald of His Coming* and the Pentecostal magazine *Herald of Faith*. She taught classic faith principles, but some of her teaching showed variations from classic leaders and similarity to some contemporary faith teaching.

John G. Lake (1870-1935). Lake and his wife experienced healing through the ministry of John Alexander Dowie and became an elder in his church. He later left Dowie's ministry and became involved in the Pentecostal movement, doing missionary work in Africa, becoming a healing evangelist, and establishing healing clinics and healing rooms in various places. He is considered to be the source of the contemporary faith teaching on "little gods."[2]

Later Pentecostal Leaders in the Classic Faith Tradition

T.L. Osborn. Missionary and evangelist T.L. Osborn was mentored by Bosworth, and was influenced by the writings of Kenyon, Wigglesworth, and others. While he taught some of the positive confession teachings of Bosworth and Kenyon, his ministry was characterized primarily by evangelism, missions, and healing in the classic Pentecostal and holiness traditions.

Gordon Lindsay. Editor of *Voices of Healing* and founder of Christ for the Nations Institute, Lindsay followed in the classic Pentecostal teaching on healing and faith. He was a major leader in the healing revivals of the 1940s and following.

Kathryn Kuhlman. Kuhlman's popular ministry of healing beginning in the 1940s arose out of McPherson's healing ministry. She attended the C&MA's Simpson Bible Institute and McPherson's L.I.F.E. College in the 1920s and became close friends with a daughter of T.J. McCrossan.

Oral Roberts. Although Oral Roberts is labeled by some as a contemporary faith leader,[3] his ministry and teachings came out of the more classical Pentecostal Holiness Church and show influence from the Wesleyan and Higher Life holiness backgrounds. Nonetheless, he has maintained close relationships with those in the contemporary faith camp. His most popular concepts of "seed-faith" and "point of contact" for prayer and healing find their roots in the teachings of Spurgeon, Murray and Simpson.

EVANGELICAL/PENTECOSTAL BRIDGE-BUILDERS

Maria Woodworth-Etter (1844-1924). Woodworth-Etter, a holiness and healing evangelist of the late 1800s and a long-time friend of Montgomery, embraced the Pentecostal movement, but also continued to circulate in non-Pentecostal holiness circles. Her view of doctors and medicine, however, tended to be more negative than most of the classic leaders and closer to those of Dowie and some contemporary faith advocates. However, she was also critical of some Pentecostal practices and their lack of discernment regarding counterfeit manifestations. In 1912 she carried on a series of revival meetings in connection with Bosworth's church.

Charles S. Price (1887-1947). Price, a Congregational minister, received the baptism in the Spirit at one of Aimee Semple McPherson's meetings, and became an independent pastor and evangelist, holding evangelistic and healing meetings throughout the world. He described McCrossan as "one of my closest friends."[4] He was strongly influenced by Simpson, calling him "revered" and a man of "spiritual revelation."[5] McCrossan, Bosworth, and Price were friends and spoke highly of each other. McCrossan dedicated his book *Christ's Paralyzed Church X-Rayed* to Price and called Price and Bosworth "real men of God."[6] He wrote several books on faith and healing in the 1940s, including *The Real Faith, The Creative Word,* and *Spiritual and Physical Health,* including some teachings that would be contrary to contemporary faith teaching. Similar to Montgomery, Bosworth, Rader, and McCrossan, he endeavored to act as a bridge and a balance between evangelicals and Pentecostals in an attempt to bring moderation to some of the more extreme faith teachings and practices in the Pentecostal and healing movements, as well as to encourage evangelicals to become open to the moving of the Spirit and the walk of faith.

Watchman Nee (1903-1972). Nee was a Chinese spiritual leader in the first half of the twentieth-century and was influenced by the lives of Müller and Taylor, and followed their examples and faith principles. He was also strongly shaped by the teachings of Guyon, Penn-Lewis, Simpson, Murray, and Keswick teaching. His wife was the daughter of a Chinese C&MA pastor, and his views on sickness and healing show dependency on Simpson. He wrote on the authority of the believer and the deeper Christian life. His writings have been popular in both evangelical and charismatic circles.

Paul Billheimer (1899-1984). A more recent advocate of classic faith teaching is Paul Billheimer, a radio preacher and Bible College president in the Wesleyan holiness tradition. His ministry began in the 1930s and blossomed in the 1950s. He is best known for his books on prayer and spiritual authority entitled *Destined for the Throne* and *Destined to Overcome.* His teachings on "throne life" and the authority of the believer are an expansion of the teachings of C&MA leaders John MacMillan and George D. Watson, as well as other leaders in the holiness tradition.[7] Due to his appearances on TBN, a Christian TV network that propagates the contemporary faith message, and a questionable theological statement by Billheimer similar to some contemporary faith teaching, Hanegraaff mistakenly categorizes Billheimer in the contemporary faith camp, apparently not being aware of the classic faith movement.[8]

Observations on the Classic Faith Movement

Carrie Judd Montgomery, F.F. Bosworth, T.J. McCrossan, and Paul Rader, all mentioned earlier, were also active in Pentecostal circles as well as non-Pentecostal and circulated the common classic faith teachings. They maintained a middle ground as a bridge and buffer between the two movements, believing in the supernatural gifts and manifestations of the Spirit, but avoiding Pentecostal excesses. Montgomery's *Triumphs of Faith* journal was probably the largest contributor of faith teaching to the early Pentecostal movement.

The people listed above make up most of the prominent leaders in the classic faith movement. Still others could be listed. Further distinction could be made between classic Pentecostal leaders (those who believed tongues was the evidence of the baptism in the Spirit) and classic non-Pentecostal or semi-Pentecostal faith leaders (those who believed in the reality of supernatural gifts and powers, but not in the "tongues as evidence" doctrine), such as Simpson, Bosworth, McCrossan, Price, and William Seymour, catalyst of the 1906 Azusa Street Pentecostal revival. These latter were not anti-*charismata*, just anti-initial evidence doctrine.

There appear to be cycles of emphasis on faith and healing in late nineteenth and early twentieth evangelical movements. For instance, Simpson's *Gospel of Healing*, Murray's *Divine Healing*, Carter's *The Atonement for Sin and Sickness*, Carrie Judd (Montgomery)'s *The Prayer of Faith*, Cullis' *Faith Cures*, and Boardman's *The Lord That Healeth Thee*, all were published about 1880-1884. Similarly, Bosworth's *Christ the Healer*, S.D. Gordon's *Quiet Talks on the Healing Christ*, and Torrey's *Divine Healing* and *The Power of Prayer* were all published in 1924. The evangelistic and healing ministries of Oral Roberts, Kathryn Kuhlman, Gordon Lindsay, and several others blossomed in the 1940s.[9]

The writings of all of these classic leaders are too extensive to cite substantially in this book. The most prominent or significant of these leaders of faith will be cited the most frequently. These include George Müller, Charles Spurgeon, J. Hudson Taylor, Hannah Whitall Smith, Phoebe Palmer, Andrew Murray, E.M. Bounds, Amy Carmichael, Oswald Chambers, R.A. Torrey, A.B. Simpson, Carrie Judd Montgomery, Charles Price, and A.W. Tozer. Of these, Müller, Spurgeon, Murray, Bounds, Chambers, Simpson, and Tozer have written the most extensively or comprehensively on issues of faith.

THE CONTEMPORARY WORD OF FAITH MOVEMENT

Contrary to claims otherwise, the contemporary faith movement, for the most part, arose out of the classic Higher Life, Keswick, and Pentecostal movements, but also expanded in new directions, doctrines and practices. The contemporary faith movement is distinguished by its emphasis on certain concepts and practices of faith, healing, and prosperity, which, as will be seen in the ensuing study, vary from classic faith teaching. Some earlier Pentecostal leaders such as John G. Lake, who originally taught the "little gods" concept; Alexander Dowie, who held more radical views on healing; and Smith Wigglesworth have also influenced the contemporary faith movement. The main teachers of the contemporary faith movement are mentioned here.

E.W. Kenyon (1867-1948). While roots of the contemporary faith movement can be found in the nineteenth and early-twentieth century Keswick/Higher Life/Wesleyan holiness movements, Kenyon is generally recognized as the chief originator of the contemporary faith movement. Simmons, in his doctoral dissertation on Kenyon, avows, "Kenyon is the *primary* source of the health and wealth gospel of the independent Charismatic movement."[10] Bowman prefers to consider him the grandfather of the word of faith movement.[11]

Although some writers such as McConnell and Hanegraaff have considered Kenyon a product of the cultic and heretical New Thought movement,[12] the more recent and more thorough scholarship of Dale Simmons, Joe McIntyre, Robert Bowman, Geir Lie, and others, has debunked much of their thesis, demonstrating the prime influences upon Kenyon to be leaders of the Higher Life and Keswick movements, such as A.J. Gordon, A.B. Simpson, A.T. Pierson, S.D. Gordon, and others.[13]

Simmons' doctoral thesis written on Kenyon concludes that Kenyon most appropriately categorized as part of the Keswick/Higher Life movement. Yet, Simmons also notes, "This is not to say that there are not aspects of Kenyon's teaching—specifically those centering on one's confession—that he stresses to a point that is only comparable to that of New Thought. . . . It would be going too far to conclude that New Thought was *the* major contributing factor in the initial development of Kenyon's thought."[14] In other words, *most* of Kenyon's thought remained in the realm of orthodox evangelical teaching represented by the Higher Life movement, although he developed some ideas that would be considered aberrational, stretching the bounds of orthodoxy. In his later ministry, he became more of a maverick in his teachings. Simmons comments, "In thrashing out his own teachings, Kenyon displayed an independent streak and an overwhelming need to come up with teachings that no one else had ever discovered."[15]

Through statistical analysis comparing 23 New Thought concepts with Christian Science and Kenyon's teachings, Bowman has demonstrated that "Kenyon's system appears to have little resemblance to overall to New Thought. . . . Kenyon's doctrine is actually more unlike New Thought than like it," and was "far closer to orthodoxy than is Christian Science."[16]

McConnell's error was in not recognizing the parallels and similarities between New Thought (which was unorthodox and more secular in theology) and Keswick/Higher Life teaching (which maintained evangelical orthodoxy). In a personal conversation with McConnell he admitted to me he was not aware of Kenyon's Keswick/Higher Life connections. Hyatt, a church historian, comments further, "These critics, however, display a lack of knowledge concerning the historical development of the twentieth century Pentecostal movement from its nineteenth century antecedents and its influence of the contemporary movement. It is in the religious mileau [sic] out of the Holiness and Healing movements of the nineteenth century that the contemporary "Faith Movement" finds its primary emphasis."[17]

Kenneth E. Hagin (1917-2003). Hagin has been the most extensive propagator of contemporary faith teaching. In 1967 he instituted The Faith Chapel of the Air and founded Rhema Bible Training Center. He also published *Word of Faith*, a monthly magazine. The majority of his teaching appears to be derived from Kenyon. His teaching on the authority of the believer comes most directly from C&MA leader John MacMillan. He also acknowledges the influence of evangelical and Higher Life leaders

Müller, Spurgeon, Simpson, McCrossan, and Bosworth, and Pentecostal leaders John G. Lake and Smith Wigglesworth. Bosworth's book *Christ the Healer* and McCrossan's book *Bodily Healing and the Atonement* are used in classes at Rhema Bible Training Center. He also claimed that many of his teachings came through revelation knowledge from God. He has been a prolific writer of more than two hundred booklets on various aspects of faith (many of which are transcribed sermons). Among them are *The Believer's Authority, Have Faith in Your Faith,* and *Writing Your Own Ticket with God.* Among the faith principles he taught are faith as a law and a force, positive confession, revelation and sense knowledge, believers as "little gods," among others.

Frederick K.C. Price (b. 1932). Price served as a minister in the African Methodist Episcopal Church and the C&MA before building his large independent Crenshaw Christian Center.[18] His teachings are a mixture of the teachings of A.B. Simpson, Hagin, and other faith teachers, along with his own concepts. Among his writings are *Is Healing for All?, Faith, Foolishness or Presumption?,* and *How to Obtain Strong Faith.*[19] He especially emphasizes prosperity and healing, and the chief leader to introduce the contemporary faith teaching to the African-American community. His most controversial teachings are the claim that faith heals, not God (see Chapter 10), and that God has abdicated control to man, and is no longer in control (see Chapter 7). A recent study by Kirk MacGregor claims that Price has borrowed and modified concepts from the Nation of Islam,[20] but if so, they are later adaptations and not direct sources of Price's earlier teaching.

Charles Capps (b. 1934). Capps was a farmer and lay minister who came in contact with Kenneth Hagin's teaching in 1969. After establishing his own ministry in 1973, he was ordained by Kenneth Copeland in 1980.[21] He especially emphasizes positive confession and faith as a force in his booklets *The Tongue, a Creative Force* and *God's Creative Power.*

Kenneth Copeland (b. 1937). Copeland studied for one year at Oral Roberts University in 1967 and served as Roberts' co-pilot, then after hearing Hagin's teachings and absorbing his tapes began his own evangelistic ministry. In 1973 he began publishing *The Believer's Voice of Victory.* "Heavily influenced by E.W. Kenyon, Copeland emphasizes that for those who do not love their own lives but submit themselves totally to God's purposes, there is great prosperity: a flourishing of spirit, soul, and body."[22] He has also written a proliferation of booklets and tapes, among which are *The*

Force of Faith, The Laws of Prosperity, and *Freedom from Fear.* MacGregor's recent study alleges that Copeland is borrowing concepts and terminology from Mormonism, citing circumstantial evidence and claims from Mormon scholars themselves. [23]

Robert Tilton (b. 1946). Tilton was founder and pastor of Word of Faith Outreach Center, a mega-church in Dallas. Eventually, through alleged scandals and TV exposes, his ministry was virtually destroyed. Tilton taught "that Christians are 'the righteousness of Christ' and that they can be all God intends. He insists that Christ has redeemed us from the curse of the law, which includes sickness, poverty, and death. Some have accused Tilton of preaching a 'gospel of success' that leaves out aspects of the gospel dealing with suffering."[24]

Former Contemporary Faith Teachers. Jimmy Swaggart and Jim Bakker are two Pentecostal leaders who at one time embraced the prosperity message, but later disclaimed the teachings. Swaggart wrote a series of articles in his magazine and a book entitled *The Balanced Faith Life,* which detailed his change in beliefs. Bakker, following the PTL scandal and his release from imprisonment, wrote about recanting his advocacy of prosperity teaching in his book *I Was Wrong.* Benny Hinn, who has more recently emerged with an international healing ministry and claimed to be in the legacy of Kathryn Kuhlman, also taught the prosperity message for a time, but has recanted some of its teachings.

SUMMATION

These are the chief early leaders of the contemporary faith movement. Many others could be listed who have followed in the footsteps of these main leaders. Also there are some who have been classed by some with contemporary faith teachers who really fit more into the classic faith tradition, including Oral Roberts and Paul Billheimer. It should also be noted, however, that not all contemporary faith teachers believe the same things. The contemporary word of faith movement far from monolithic, though Hanegraaff and others have presented it in that fashion. This brief overview has demonstrated that contemporary faith teaching, contrary to McConnell's and Hanegraaff's claims, finds its heritage primarily in the classic faith teachers, though sometimes deviating from classic faith teaching and practice. Further chapters will discuss the classic faith roots of the contemporary faith movement, pointing out both similarities and differences.

ONLY BELIEVE

1. For in-depth doctoral study on the teachings and ministry of Smith Wigglesworth, see Johanes Lilik Susanto, "A Practical Theological Evaluation of the Divine Healing Ministries of Smith Wigglesworth and John G. Lake: A Continuationist Reformed Perspective," Doctor of Theology Thesis, University of South Africa, Pretoria, South Africa, June 2007, accessed at: http://etd.unisa.ac.za/ETD-db/theses/available/etd-06262008-113048/unrestricted/thesis.pdf

2. Bowman, *The Word-Faith Controversy*, 71. See John G. Lake, *Spiritual Hunger and Other Sermons*, ed., Gordon Lindsay (Dallas: Christ for the Nations, 1994), 20, 86, 90. For in-depth doctoral study on the teachings and ministry of John G. Lake, see Susanto, "A Practical Theological Evaluation of the Divine Healing Ministries of Smith Wigglesworth and John G. Lake," referenced above.

3. See Hanegraaff, 31, 187, 195-198, 201-205; Hunt, *Beyond Seduction*, 72-73; MacArthur, *Charismatic Chaos*, 241-243, 348.

4. Charles S. Price, *The Story of My Life* (Pasadena, Calif.: Charles S. Price Publishing Co., 1935), 50.

5. Charles S. Price, *The Creative Word* (Pasadena, Calif.: Charles S. Price Publishing Co., 1941), 66, Charles S. Price, *Two Worlds* (Pasadena, Calif.: Charles S. Price Publishing Co., 1946), 19.

6. T.J. McCrossan, *Christ's Paralyzed Church X-Rayed* (Youngstown, Ohio: Rev. C.E. Humbard, 1937), 267.

7. King, *A Case Study of a Believer with Authority*, 271-276, 320-321.

8. Hanegraaff, 164-165, 363.

9. See David Edwin Harrell, Jr., *All Things Are Possible: The Healing and Charismatic Revivals in Contemporary America* (Bloomington, Ind.: Indiana University Press, 1975).

10. Dale H. Simmons, *E.W. Kenyon and the Postbellum Pursuit of Peace, Power, and Plenty* (Lanham, MD and London: Scarecrow Press, 1997), x.

11. Bowman, *The Word-Faith Controversy*, 36, 38. Bowman considers Oral Roberts, William Branham and the Latter Rain movement, and Kenneth Hagin as the fathers of the movement (pp. 85-94), but I would disagree.

12. McConnell, *A Different Gospel*; Hanegraaff, *Christianity in Crisis*.

13. Simmons, *E.W. Kenyon*; Joe McIntyre, *E.W. Kenyon and His Message of Faith: The True Story* (Lake Mary, Fla.: Creation House, 1997); William DeArteaga, *Quenching the Spirit* (Lake Mary, Fla.: Creation House, 1996); Geir Lie, "E.W. Kenyon: Cult Founder or Evangelical Minister? An Historical Analysis of Kenyon's Theology with Particular Emphasis on Roots and Influences," masters thesis, Norwegian Lutheran School of Theology, 1994; see also Vreeland, "Reconstructing Word of Faith Theology; Bowman, *The Word-Faith Controversy*.

14. Simmons, *E.W. Kenyon*, 304.

15. Simmons, *E.W. Kenyon*, xii.

16. Bowman, *The Word-Faith Controversy*, 46-47.

17. Eddie Hyatt, "The Nineteenth Century Roots of the Modern Faith Movement," unpublished paper, Tulsa, Okla.: Oral Roberts University, Apr. 25, 1991, 1, 2.

18. I personally met Price in 1972 when he spoke at the C&MA church in Pennsylvania where I was serving as youth pastor and for a period of time fully embraced his teachings.

19. G.W. Gohr, "Price, Frederick K.C.," *DPCM*, 727.

20. MacGregor, 93-102.

21. H. Vinson Synan, "Capps, Charles Emmitt," *DPCM*, 107.

22. R.M. Riss, "Copeland, Kenneth," *DPCM*, 226.

23. MacGregor, 102-109.

24. S. Strang, "Tilton, Robert," in *DPCM*, 845.

PART 2

FOUNDATIONS OF WORD OF FAITH TEACHING AND PRACTICE

C H A P T E R   4

———————•◦•———————

Faith and the Supernatural Today

Most teachers of faith, both classic and contemporary, believe in the reality of supernatural power from God available to believers today—in miracles, healing, supernatural gifts such as prophecy and tongues. Practically speaking, they would argue that it is difficult to be both a cessationist and to operate in the realm of great faith. However, even some of those who believe some of the supernatural gifts like tongues have ceased, nonetheless, believe in God's power to heal today by faith. Müller, for example, believed in healing in answer to prayer of faith, but there is no evidence that he believed the gift of tongues was continuing.

OPPOSITION TO CLASSIC AND CONTEMPORARY FAITH SUPERNATURALISM—RATIONALISM AND CESSATIONISM

Opposition to the belief that God works supernaturally in contemporary times comes from two mutually exclusive philosophical and theological bases: rationalism and cessationism. Rationalists believe that the universe is a closed system in which God does not intervene supernaturally. Such supernatural phenomena as miracles, healing, demonic spirits, etc., cannot occur according to this belief. The Bible must be "demythologized," stripped of its supposed supernatural mythology. The events that purport to be supernatural in the Scriptures either are exaggerated legends designed to authenticate divine presence and power or are real events that can be explained naturally. Cessationists, on the other hand, believe in the veracity of supernatural events in biblical times. Yet they insist that God no longer needs to work supernaturally today because we have Christ and the Bible to believe in, and do not need the supernatural today to authenticate God's working. The supernatural gifts of the Spirit such as tongues, healing, miracles and prophecy were intended to be temporary—lasting only for the initial establishing of the church in the Apostolic age.[1] Both of these viewpoints are opposed to the contemporary faith belief in the supernatural, as well as classic faith belief. Contemporary and classic faith teaching find these explanations to be false. Contemporary faith supernaturalism finds its roots in classic faith supernaturalism. We will thus look next at the foundations of classic faith belief in the supernatural today as a basis for contemporary faith teaching.

THE CLASSIC FAITH RESPONSE TO RATIONALISM—FAITH IN A SUPERNATURAL GOD AND A SUPERNATURAL BOOK

Answering to rationalism, classic and contemporary faith leaders believed in a supernatural God and the Bible as a supernatural book. They believed in a God who is all-powerful, all knowing, and everywhere present. Belief in the supernatural nature and power of God was central to nineteenth and twentieth century evangelical theology and practice of faith: "The secret of Abraham's faith was his realization of the supernatural God."[2] Hudson Taylor, pioneer faith missionary to China, proclaimed, "We are a supernatural people born again by a supernatural birth, kept by a supernatural power, sustained on supernatural food, taught by a supernatural Teacher from a supernatural Book. We are led by a supernatural Captain in right paths to assured victories."[3] Murray quoted Taylor in agreement with his statement.

In a time when the divine inspiration and infallibility of the Bible was being challenged, Simpson, typical of the classic faith leaders, believed that there was nothing more important than the inspiration and supreme authority of the Word of God. The malignity of Satan and the pride of human culture are striving as never before to eliminate the supernatural from the Holy Scriptures and change the Book of God into a mere collection of ancient writings, saved out of the wreck of the world's literature. . . . Like a chain which depends upon its weakest link, if God's Word is not absolutely and completely true, it is too weak a cable to fix our anchorage and guarantee our eternal peace. Thank God, we have reason to accept it as the supernatural revelation of the supernatural God, the word not of man, but the Word of God that liveth and abideth forever.[4]

THE CLASSIC FAITH RESPONSE TO CESSATIONISM—FAITH IN GOD'S CONTINUING SUPERNATURAL WORKING

Classic faith teaching would agree with cessationists that God by nature is supernatural and that the Scriptures are supernatural in origin.

However, in contrast to cessationists, they believed that because God is omnipotent, omniscient and omnipresent, logically speaking, He continues to manifest His power, wisdom, and presence at all times, not just in biblical days, thus He continues to work supernaturally today. The church is now a supernatural people of God, with supernatural experiences, gifts and manifestations. They thus not only opposed the anti-supernaturalism of rationalism, but also the truncated supernaturalism of cessationism. They argue that the supernatural was not meant just for the apostolic age, but for all times. Their reasoning was both theological and practical.

Theological Basis for Continuing Supernaturalism—The Great "I Am." Such classic faith leaders as George Müller, A.J. Gordon, Simpson, and Murray all touted the Scripture, "Jesus Christ is the same yesterday and today and forever" (Heb. 13:8, NIV). The understood implication was that all of God's power, gifts, and promises are therefore applicable for all times. As Jonathan Goforth, Presbyterian missionary to China, put it, "All the resources of the Godhead are at our disposal!"[5] Simpson explained, "Our Lord's ministry began . . . in the manifestation of His healing power, and He is still the 'same yesterday, today, and forever.'"[6] This view was also held by A.J. Gordon and Spurgeon.[7] They believed He is the Great I AM, not "the great I was." Simpson emphasized the real life manifestation of the supernatural presence of God according to this Scripture, "I am courage in your difficulties . . ."[8] He believed, "All difficulties and dangers must give way before the omnipotence of faith. . . . Faith is . . . one of the attributes of God Himself. . . . There is no doubt that while the soul is exercising, through the power of God, the faith that commands what God commands, a mighty force is operating that moment upon the obstacle. God has put into our hands one of His own implements of omnipotence and permitted us to use it in the name of Jesus, according to His will and for the establishment of His Kingdom."[9]

Secondly, classic faith leaders often noted that Paul writes in Ephesians that we are seated together in Christ in the heavenly places, so that the heavenly supernatural life begins in the here and now, not just in the sweet by-and-by. Typical of this understanding, Simpson wrote, "We anticipate in the present life to a certain extent the power of our future resurrection, and that we have a foretaste of this part of our salvation here even as we have a foretaste of heaven."[10] Ladd would later describe it as a partially realized eschatology—the "already here now, but not yet (fully)" status of the kingdom of God.[11]

Practical Basis for Continuing Supernaturalism

1. *Evidence of the Supernatural throughout Church History.* The classic faith leaders also had a practical-theological basis for believing in continuing supernaturalism in the church age. First, they would cite evidence of the supernatural throughout church history. Typical of classic faith belief, A.J. Gordon declared, "Whenever we find a revival of primitive faith and Apostolic simplicity, there we find the Evangelical miracles which surely characterize the Apostolic age."[12] According to Gordon, the supernatural is the birthright of the Church.[13] In his book *The Ministry of Healing*, Gordon demonstrated that John Wesley, Methodist commentator Joseph Benson, reformed pastor Richard Baxter, Count Nicholas Zinzendorf and the Moravians, and Horace Bushnell, all believed that the supernatural gifts of the Spirit are to abide in the Church.[14] Gordon himself witnessed the supernatural healing power of God in one of Moody's meetings, confirming his faith in the miraculous.

2. *All Gifts Are for All Times.* Classic faith leaders like Murray taught that "all the spiritual graces" are promised to believers today and that the signs of Mark 16 are "applicable to all times."[15] Taylor believed in the supernatural power of God to provide miraculous protection, calm storms, send rain in drought, bring healing to the dying, and speak through words of prophecy.[16] As noted above, Murray was in accord with Taylor, quoting his statement on the supernatural in a missionary conference at the beginning of the twentieth century.[17] Keswick missionary to India Amy Carmichael likewise came to believe in the power of God according to Mark 16:17, and operated in gifts of healing, casting out demons, receiving prophetic words from the Lord, prophetic dreams and visions, miraculous provision and protection, extraordinary answers to prayer, and other supernatural encounters.[18]

3. *What Jesus Did, He Continues through the Church.* The classic faith leaders would assert that what Jesus did, He continues to do through the Church. For example, Simpson declared according to Acts 1:1 that what Jesus began to do and teach during His life on earth, "He continued to do and teach after His ascension" through the Church.[19] In other words, the Church as the Body of Christ is the extension of Jesus' life to carry on His supernatural ministry. Simpson viewed this as a fulfillment of Jesus' words: "Truly, truly, I say to you, he who believes in Me, the works that I do shall he do also; and greater works than these shall he do; because I go to the Father" (John 14:12).

4. The Supernatural Is a Neglected Truth. Related to this, the classic faith leaders would affirm the reality of the supernatural as a neglected truth. They believed that God was restoring in their day long-forgotten or neglected truths. In *Present Truths or the Supernatural* (more recently reprinted under the title *The Supernatural*) Simpson elaborated on some of these "present truths": "While all inspired truth is necessary and important yet there are certain truths which God emphasizes at certain times. He is ever speaking to the age and generation, and He never speaks at random but always to the point and to the times. . . . From age to age God speaks the special message most needed, so that there is always some portion of divine truth which might properly be called *present* truth, God's message to the times."[20] Simpson considered the supernatural as the "pre-eminently present truth" of his day.[21] His book includes chapter titles that could be an elaboration of Taylor's themes: The Supernatural God, The Supernatural Book, The Supernatural Life, The Supernatural Church, The Supernatural Body, The Supernatural Hope, The Supernatural Work. In 1899 in an article entitled "Aggressive Christianity," an apparent allusion to Catherine Booth's earlier book of the same title, Simpson declared that the C&MA "stands for an absolute faith in supernatural things and a supernatural God."[22]

5. The Need for Supernatural Power Today. Fifth, the classic faith leaders emphasized the *need* of the church for supernatural power today, as well as in the New Testament church. Spurgeon anticipated the on-going operation of the supernatural power of the Spirit: "If at the commencement of the gospel we see the Holy Spirit work great signs and wonders, may we not expect a continuance—if anything, an increased display—of His power as the ages roll on?"[23] In fact, Spurgeon not only believed that the supernatural power of God is available today, but also that it is necessary, even crucial: "If there is not a miraculous spiritual power in the church of God today, the church is an imposter. . . . Only let men come back to the real gospel and preach it ardently, not with fancy words and polished speech but as a burning heart compels them and as the Spirit of God teaches them to speak it; then will great signs and wonders be seen. We must have signs following; we cannot otherwise answer the world."[24] He leaned toward believing that the gift of tongues was temporary, but he did not rule out the possibility as long as the emphasis was not on the gift: "Even if you could obtain miraculous gifts, you ought not to be satisfied to speak with tongues or to work miracles, but you should press on to know the Spirit within—indwelling, communing, quickening you."[25]

Spurgeon not only believed in the supernatural gifts, but also personally experienced and knew of supernatural dreams and visions, words of knowledge, prophecy, and healing.[26] His biographer declared the year after his death, "No man probably, in England or America, in this century, has healed so many people as Mr. Spurgeon."[27] He devoted an entire chapter on a few examples of the thousands of healings that occurred in Spurgeon's ministry. Though he himself said he was unworthy of possessing the gift of healing,[28] he would be considered in the ranks of a Kathryn Kuhlman or an Oral Roberts today (though he did not use their methods). Spurgeon's interim successor, A.T. Pierson, also affirmed the reality and importance of supernatural power: "A supernatural gospel is meant to accomplish supernatural results, and needs a supernatural power behind it and its messengers."[29]

E.M. Bounds believed in the reality of healing, saying, "Sickness dies before prayer. Health comes in answer to prayer." [30] Commenting on James 5:15, "The prayer of faith shall save the sick," Bounds declared, "Prayer in its highest form of faith is that prayer which carries the whole man as a sacrificial offering. . . . Such an attitude of self-devotement to God mightily helps praying."[31] More than half a century before Oral Roberts taught the "whole man" concept of health and healing, Bounds mentioned the concept in embryonic form, implying that a whole man wholly devoted to God can exercise great power in prayer to bring wholeness or healing to the whole person: "Prayer takes in man in his *whole* being, mind, soul, and body. It takes the *whole* man to pray and prayer effects the *entire* man in its gracious results. . . . Holiness is *wholeness*."[32]

While Moody Bible Institute and Moody Press have a reputation today for cessationist dispensationalism, both Moody and his associate R.A. Torrey believed in the reality of the supernatural power of God operating in a believer today. Though critical of the excesses of the Pentecostal movement, Torrey considered the Christian faith "a supernatural religion from start to finish," writing that "we should live our lives in supernatural power" and "should perform our service with supernatural power."[33] He believed that the Holy Spirit gives supernatural gifts for each believer's individual calling.[34] As mentioned earlier, C&MA scholar Keith Bailey has shown that Moody Bible Institute and Wheaton College were centers for proclaiming the healing message in the early twentieth century. Many people would be surprised to discover that Moody Memorial Church once had a pastor who believed in the reality of speaking in tongues continuing today, Paul Rader, who became successor to Simpson as president of the C&MA. Rader also was involved in a ministry of exorcism and preached for Pentecostal leader and Foursquare Church founder Aimee Semple McPherson.

6. *The Need for the Supernatural to Combat Evil Forces.* Classic faith leaders stressed the need for the supernatural to combat supernatural powers of darkness. A.J. Gordon quoted German professor Christlieb: "In the last epoch of the consummation of the Church she will again require for the final decisive struggle with the powers of darkness the miraculous interference of her risen Lord; and hence the scriptures lead us to expect miracles once more for this period."[35] As the church approaches the end of this present age, he reasoned, so the church will need the supernatural powers of God to combat the supernatural powers of darkness.

7. *Reasons for Lack of the Supernatural.* The classic faith writers provided the following reasons for the lack of supernatural phenomena:

- *Loss of New Testament Church Life and Power.* Amy Carmichael commented in the 1890s, "I don't wonder apostolic miracles have died. Apostolic living certainly has."[36]
- *Ignorance about Life in the New Covenant.* Murray declared, "Until we learn to form our expectation of a life in the New Covenant, according to the inconceivable worth and power of the blood of God's Son, we never can have even an insight into the entirely supernatural and heavenly life that a child of God may live."[37]
- *Compromise.* Simpson asserted, "There is no truth that has more need of emphasis in these days of compromise than the supernatural character and destiny of the church of the Lord Jesus."[38]
- *Unbelief.* Simpson argued, "What right have we to go to the unbelieving world and demand their acceptance of our message without these signs following? . . . Nay, Christ did give them, and they did follow as long as Christians continued to 'believe' and expect them. . . . The signs shall correspond to the extent of their faith."[39] Simpson pointed out the inconsistency of believing healing is for the Church today, but not the other gifts.

8. *Need for a Larger Faith.* The chief reason for lack of supernatural signs and power according to Simpson, Murray, Gordon and other evangelical

leaders is unbelief. Simpson averred, "The signs of healing do not follow all believers, but they follow those who believe for the signs."[40] Murray similarly explained, "If divine healing is seen but rarely in our day, we can attribute it to no other cause than that the Spirit does not act with power. The unbelief of worldlings and the want of zeal among believers stop His working."[41] A.J. Gordon set this maxim: "Faith for healing cannot rise above the general level of the Church's faith."[42] A century earlier Bible commentator Bengel had written in response to those who believed that the church only needed to be launched by supernatural faith: "The reason why many miracles are not now wrought is not so much because faith is established, as that unbelief reigns."[43] Theologian Theodore Christlieb, professor of Bonn University, echoed the same truth: "It is the want of faith in our age which is the greatest hindrance to the stronger and more marked appearance of that miraculous power which is working here and there in quiet concealment. Unbelief is the final and most important reason for the retrogression of miracles."[44]

Other evangelical leaders also bewailed the lack of faith for the supernatural within the church. Meyer, writing before the advent of the Pentecostal movement, acknowledged that he believed the gifts of the Spirit belonged to the Apostolic age, and were withdrawn, but he had doubts that this was God's intention, adding, "though it is a serious question whether they might not have been continued if only the Church had been more faithful to her sacred trust."[45] In a later book he seems to admit the possible reality of tongues, but advised avoiding the Pentecostal movement because of its excesses.[46] Cowman, in her popular devotional book, wrote, "The supernatural always slumbers when faith lies sleeping, or dead."[47] Many more could be cited, but these give evidence of the extensive belief in the continuance of the supernatural. Simpson sums up the tenor of all these leaders, proclaiming, "We need a larger faith. . . . We need a faith that will personally appropriate all that we understand, a faith so large that it will reach the *fullness* of God's great promises. A faith so large that it will rise to the level of each emergency that comes into our lives."[48]

CAUTIONS ABOUT THE SUPERNATURAL

It should be pointed out, however, classic faith leaders would not approve of all of the practices and purported supernatural manifestations in the charismatic and contemporary faith movements. Classic faith teachers believed in the supernatural, but also cautioned about indiscriminate and undiscerning acceptance of seemingly supernatural phenomena.

Pre-nineteenth Century Cautions. John Wesley, who argued for the continuance of supernatural gifts such as speaking in tongues, nevertheless counseled, "Do not hastily ascribe things to God. Do not easily suppose dreams, voices, impressions, visions, or revelations to be from God. They may be from Him. They may be from Nature. They may be from the devil. Therefore believe not every spirit, but 'try the spirits whether they be from God.'"[49] Jonathan Edwards concluded concerning physical manifestations accompanying God's supernatural work of revival during the Great Awakening of the 1700s:

> A work is not to be judged of by any effects on the bodies of men; such as tears, trembling, groans, loud outcries, agonies of body, or the failing of bodily strength. The influence persons are under is not to be judged of one way or other by such effects on the body; and the reason is because Scripture nowhere gives us any such rule. We cannot conclude that persons are under the influence of the true Spirit because we see such effects on their bodies, because this is not given as a mark of the true Spirit; nor on the other hand, have we any reason to conclude, from any such outward appearances, that persons are not under the influence of the Spirit of God, because there is no rule of Scripture given us to judge of spirits by, that does neither expressly or indirectly exclude such effects on the body, nor does reason exclude them.[50]

Classic Faith Cautions. On the basis of her experiences in the aftermath of the Welsh and Pentecostal revivals, Jessie Penn-Lewis counseled that "a sign or a wonder coming to pass is no proof that it is of God." Rather, she advised that the believer needs to discern the effect in one's own spiritual life: "Does it lead you nearer to God, and nearer to His children? Does it tend to unite or disunite the people of God? Does it make you more loyal to God or lead to the worship of "other gods"—even in the sense of placing your "experience" as of greater value than the bare word of God?"[51]

Simpson, who in pre-Pentecostal days encouraged restoration of the supernatural gifts probably more than any other of his time, cautioned to be wary about counterfeits of the work of the Holy Spirit, especially as the second coming of Christ draws nearer. He advised that any experience that becomes an end in itself and does not clearly lead to glorifying Jesus Christ as Lord may be suspect, because the Holy Spirit testifies of Christ (John 15:26-27) and does not exalt man or the Spirit's own work.

Fanaticism and excess in supernatural manifestations do not glorify Christ, but rather sabotage the believer's witness.[52]

Hannah Whitall Smith regarded much of speaking in tongues as fanaticism, particularly the belief that "the Lord takes hold of your vocal organs."[53] Taking her cue from Fenelon, she believed that anything not controlled in the will is of the flesh and emotion, so that according to 1 Corinthians 14, true tongue-speaking is under the control of the speaker.[54] She does not make mention of the occurrences of *glossolalia* in her Quaker roots. Perhaps she was not aware, or found the excessive emotionalism of many tongues-speakers foreign to the quieter, calmer expressions of tongues in the Quaker tradition. She also considered going off to a foreign land expecting to be given the native tongue supernaturally an expression of fanaticism.

However, Smith was not totally opposed to the supernatural. She believed in supernatural divine guidance, but recognized the possibility of deception: "Every peculiarly precious spiritual gift is always necessarily linked with some peculiar danger. When the spiritual world is opened to the soul, both the good and the evil there will meet it. But we must not be discouraged by this. Who would not rather take manhood with all its risks and dangers than remain forever in the ignorance and innocence of childhood; and who would not rather grow up into the stature of Christ, even if it shall involve new and more subtle forms of temptation? Therefore we must not be deterred from embracing the blessed privilege of Divine guidance by a dread of the dangers that environ it."[55] She also considered some forms of faith healing as fanatical.[56] But she nonetheless believed in the reality of divine healing, and many people were healed through her prayers. Others claimed she had the gift of healing, but she denied it, saying that she sensed no power or anointing or special faith, and was just being obedient to the Lord by praying for others.[57]

Similarly, Chambers believed in the supernatural power of the Spirit, though he was cautious about getting wrapped up in it: "Our Lord did not say that signs and wonders would not follow, but that the one set purpose for us is that we do God's will in His way, not our way."[58] He was not opposed to the supernatural, just the misuse and overemphasis on them. He was concerned that the emphasis on the spectacular often successfully tempts the Church to go into "show business."[59] Chambers especially cautioned about passively accepting impressions without discernment, resulting in yielding to any influence.[60] (This will be discussed further in Chapter 19). Meyers and Bounds likewise believed in the supernatural, but warned about excesses and misuse of supernatural power. Meyers shared a story about a man who experienced no pain while conscious without anesthetic on an operating table, and had a vision of the pierced feet of Jesus.[61] Yet he was negative about the "tongues movement" as a whole, because, in his judgment, it "has led to such excesses that it is wisest to avoid it altogether. Too seldom do its promoters observe the . . . principles laid down in 1 Corinthians 14:27-29."[62] His opposition to the Pentecostal movement was thus not on the basis of cessationism or doctrinal orthodoxy, but on the basis of perceived excesses or errors of practice. Bounds also believed in the reality of the supernatural, but warned of its misuse: "Satan perverts the things which are truly works of God and misemploys miracles to obscure God's glory."[63]

Pentecostal Cautions. Some early Pentecostals also had cautions about accepting all supernatural manifestations as genuinely from God. Charles Parham, considered by some to be the originator of the Pentecostal movement due to occurrences of *glossolalia* in Topeka, Kansas, in 1901, startlingly wrote ten years later:

> Hear this: three-fourths of the so-called Pentecosts in the world are counterfeits, the devil's imitation to deceive the poor earnest souls. . . . Many hundreds, in seeking Pentecost, were taught to yield to any force, as God would not permit them to be misled; under those conditions they were ripe for hypnotic influence. . . . Two-thirds of the people professing Pentecost are either hypnotized or spook-driven, being seized in the first place with a false spirit or coming under the control of one afterward. We cannot be too careful to try or test the spirits and any person unwilling to have their experience tested by going to God for themselves or with the brethren, reveal the fact that they are demon-controlled. . . . They plead the blood, and claim to be Jesus, giving messages, and imitate every gift of the Holy Spirit and Pentecostal tongues.[64]

If one did not know the source of this quote, it might well be assumed that it was written by an anti-Pentecostal! While his estimated percentages of false manifestations are skewed by his racial prejudice and his belief that genuine tongues could only be *xenolalia* (also called *xenoglossa*), tongues that are actual languages, nevertheless, he does cite a number of examples of discernible demonic and psychic manifestations.[65] William Seymour, catalyst of the Azusa Street revival who was mentored by Parham, also admonished, "Wherever the doctrine of the baptism in the Holy Spirit will only be known as the evidence of speaking in tongues, that work will be an open door for witches and spiritualists, and free loveism. . . . When we leave the word of God and begin to go by signs and voices we will wind up in Spiritualism."[66]

Maria Woodworth-Etter, active in both the holiness and the Pentecostal movements, also warned of the dangers of counterfeit manifestations, citing several instances:

> Don't take up with every vision that comes along. . . . In the midst of a vision, a woman heard a voice say to her, "You are going to die." But it was of the devil. . . . In one of our meetings there was a woman who had a wonderful experience spiritually; that is the kind the devil gets after. One day she commenced to go about on her knees, twisting about like a serpent. God does not tell anyone to do that. She spoke in tongues; then she said, "I don't want to do it. I don't want to do it." Everyone knew it was not of God; and I said to her, "that is not of God; the enemy has got hold of you. . . . Some people when they pray for anyone and lay on hands, throw their slime off. That is spiritualism. . . . Be careful who lays hands on you, for the devil is counterfeiting God's work.[67]

OBSERVATIONS

The classic faith leaders affirmed the reality of the supernatural, not just in the Bible and the early New Testament church, but for the entire church age. The Pentecostal, charismatic and contemporary faith movements embraced this classic faith position, but sometimes went beyond classic faith teaching and practice regarding the supernatural. Classic faith teaching often provides a balance, a moderation, in the practice of faith in relationship to the supernatural that is sometimes lacking today. Some classic faith leaders backed away from Pentecostalism and supernatural manifestations, over-reacting to excesses in the movement, whereas some Pentecostals acknowledged and warned of the problems of excesses and counterfeits, yet maintained the genuineness of the movement as a whole.

Practically speaking, I would conclude that if those in the Pentecostal, charismatic, and contemporary faith movements would exercise more discernment and be more self-critical as did some early Pentecostal leaders, they would be criticized less. While some like MacArthur criticize from a cessationist point of view, Hunt and Hanegraaff are purported not to be cessationists. McConnell comes from a solidly Pentecostal camp, as does Fee. So it should be noted that one can exercise faith in the supernatural realm and believe that God works supernaturally today without embracing all of the teachings, practices, and phenomena often associated with charismatic, Pentecostal, and contemporary faith practice.

---

1. MacArthur, *Charismatic Chaos*, 127-154, 237-299.

2. Simpson, *Present Truths or the Supernatural*, 15.

3. Murray, *Key to the Missionary Problem*, 88.

4. Simpson, *Present Truths or the Supernatural*, 22, 24.

5. J. Hudson Taylor, cited in *World Shapers: A Treasury of Quotes from Great Missionaries* (Wheaton, Ill.: Harold Shaw Publishers, 1991), 107.

6. A.B. Simpson, *Christ in the Bible* (Camp Hill, Penn.: Christian Publications, 1992), 1:123.

7. A.J. Gordon, *The Ministry of Healing*, 51; on Spurgeon, see Lewis Drummond, *Spurgeon: Prince of Preachers* (Grand Rapids: Kregel, 1992), 291.

8. Simpson, *Present Truths or the Supernatural*, 15.

9. Simpson, *A Larger Christian Life*, 6, 11.

10. Simpson, *Present Truths or the Supernatural*, 53.

11. See George Eldon Ladd, *A Theology of the New Testament* (Grand Rapids: Eerdmans, 1974), 70-80.

12. A.J. Gordon, cited in Bosworth, *Christ the Healer*, 29-30.

13. A.J. Gordon, *The Ministry of Healing*, 140.

14. *Graf*, 136, 152, 159-162, 169, 189; see also Horace Bushnell, *Nature and the Supernatural* (New York: Charles Scribner's Sons, 1885).

15. Andrew Murray, *Divine Healing* (London: Victory Press, 1934), 12.

16. Howard Taylor, *Hudson Taylor's Spiritual Secret* (Chicago: Moody Press, 1932), 117, 118; Dr. and Mrs. Howard Taylor, *Hudson Taylor in the Early Years* (London: China Inland Mission, [1911] 1930), 478-479, 488.

17. Murray, *Key to the Missionary Problem*, 88.

18. Elliot, 89-90, 99, 168, 181, 193, 210, 221, 222, 235, 253, 276, 292-293.

19. A.B. Simpson, *Christ in the Bible: Gospel of John and the Acts of the Apostles* (Christian Alliance Publishing Co., 1891), Vol. X, 256.

20. Simpson, *Present Truths or the Supernatural*, 9-10.

21. Ibid., 10.

22. Hartzfeld and Nienkirchen, 200.

23. Charles H. Spurgeon, *What the Holy Spirit Does in a Believer's Life* (Lynnwood, Wash.: Emerald Books, 1993), 14.

24. Ibid., 51-52.

25. Ibid., 128; see also 97, 104.

26. Lewis Drummond, 81, 167, 173, 181, 184, 221, 235-236, 271, 281, 285.

27. Russell Conwell, *Life of Charles Haddon Spurgeon: The World's Great Preacher* (Philadelphia: Edgewood Publishing Co., 1892), 173.

28. Ibid., 186.

29. Pierson, *The Acts of the Holy Spirit*, 92.

30. E.M. Bounds, *Prayer and Praying Men* (Grand Rapids: Baker, 1977), 62.

31. Ibid., 17.

32. E.M. Bounds, *Book 2: The Essentials of Prayer*, from *The Complete Works of E.M. Bounds* (Grand Rapids: Baker, 1996), Book 2, 81, italics mine.

33. R.A. Torrey, *The Power of Prayer and the Prayer of Power* (Grand Rapids: Zondervan, 1924), 21.

34. Ibid.

35. A.J. Gordon, *The Ministry of Healing*, 140.

36. Elliot, 85.

37. Andrew Murray, *The Two Covenants* (Ft. Washington, Penn.: Christian Literature Crusade, 1974), 78.

38. Simpson, *Present Truths or the Supernatural*, 45.

39. Simpson, *The Gospel of Healing*, 19-20, see also p. 8.

40. Simpson, *Present Truths or the Supernatural*, 4:338.

41. Murray, *Divine Healing*, 18.

42. A.J. Gordon, *The Ministry of Healing*, 210.

43. Ibid., 24.

44. Ibid., 25.

45. F.B. Meyer, "The Fulness of the Spirit," cited in *Twenty Centuries of Great Preaching*, Clyde E. Fant, Jr. and William M. Pinson, Jr., eds. (Waco, Tex.: Word, 1971), 6:380.

46. Meyer, *Five Musts of the Christian Life*, 73-74.

47. Mrs. Charles Cowman, *Springs in the Valley* (Minneapolis: World Wide Publications, [1939] 1968), 167.

48. Simpson, *A Larger Christian Life*, 53-54.

49. John Wesley, cited in Martin Wells Knapp, *Impressions* (Cincinnati: Revivalist Publishing House, 1892), 34.

50. Jonathan Edwards, "The Distinguishing Marks of the Work of the Spirit of God," *Jonathan Edwards on Revival* (Edinburgh: The Banner of Truth Trust, 1984), 91.

51. Jessie Penn-Lewis, *The Conquest of Canaan* (Ft. Washington, Penn.: Christian Literature Crusade, 1989), 70.

52. A.B. Simpson, *The Holy Spirit* (Harrisburg, Penn.: Christian Publications, 1896), 2:546.

53. Hannah Whitall Smith, cited in Ray Strachey, *Religious Fanaticism: Extracts from the Papers of Hannah Whitall Smith* (London: Faber & Gwyer, Ltd., 1928), 260.

54. Ibid., 270.

55. H.W. Smith, *The Christian's Secret*, 71.

56. Strachey, 262-267.

57. Ibid., 253-256.

58. Oswald Chambers, *The Psychology of Redemption* (London: Marshall, Morgan and Scott, ([1930] 1963), 68.

59. Ibid., 66-67.

60. Oswald Chambers, *Biblical Psychology*, 144-145.

61. Meyers, *Five Musts of the Christian Life*, 122.

62. Ibid., 73.

63. Dorsett, *E.M. Bounds: Man of Prayer*, 238.

64. Charles Parham, *The Everlasting Gospel* (Baxter Springs, Kan.: n.p., 1911), 55, 72, 120-121.

65. Ibid., 71-73, 118-119; King, *A Case Study of a Believer with Authority*, 429-430.

66. William Seymour, *The Doctrines and Disciplines of the Azusa St. Apostolic Faith Mission* (Los Angeles: Apostolic Faith Mission, 1915), 3.

67. Maria Woodworth-Etter, *Marvels and Miracles* (Indianapolis: M.B.W. Etter, 1922), 503, 506-508.

CHAPTER 5

Faith and the Believer's Inheritance:
Claiming God's Promises Today

The concept of an inheritance that can be claimed by believers through faith is based on such Scriptures as:

> *The Spirit Himself bears witness with our spirit that we are children of God, and if children, heirs also, heirs of God and fellow-heirs with Christ* (Rom. 8:16-17a).

> *Therefore you are no longer a slave, but a son, and if a son, then an heir through God* (Gal. 4:7).

With his emphasis on *sola Scriptura* and *sola fide*, Martin Luther thus taught on the basis of these Scriptures that "faith makes us heirs," describing it as "faith which clings to the Word of the promising God."[1] This set the stage for further understanding the inheritance of believers. Moreover, Reformed covenant theology, which views the church as spiritual Israel, provided the foundation for believing that Christians inherit the promises of Israel. Both the contemporary faith and classic faith movements believe on the basis of these theological roots and Scriptures that believers can claim the promises of their inheritance today.

CONTEMPORARY FAITH TEACHING ON THE BELIEVER'S INHERITANCE

Contemporary faith leaders typically teach many of the same principles of the believer's inheritance as classic faith leaders, as we will see shortly. In addition, they attach other implications to the concept of the believer's inheritance. For instance, they take the blessings and curses of the covenant in Deuteronomy 28 in a literal, physical sense as applied to believers today, citing Galatians 3:13 as the New Testament justification for this belief.[2] E.W. Kenyon and some of those who follow him emphasize that believers are "the righteousness of God in Christ," interpreting that to mean that the believer has been imparted righteousness at conversion.[3] Some in the contemporary faith movement interpret "partakers of divine nature" (2 Peter 1:4) and "ye are gods" (Psalm 82:6) to mean that believers are "little gods."[4] Kenyon described victorious believers as "supermen."[5] Another implication of the believer's inheritance, according to contemporary faith teachers, is that God wants to prosper believers. Some even say that God wants believers to be wealthy, and to be poor is a sin.[6]

CRITICISM OF CONTEMPORARY FAITH TEACHING

Critics of the contemporary faith movement do not usually dispute the concept of inheriting the promises of God. However, they criticize what contemporary faith teaching means by claiming the inheritance of the believer and the practical implications of that interpretation. For instance, MacArthur especially decries the beliefs and practices of some contemporary faith leaders that because of the believer's position, they "have what they say."[7] Another criticism of contemporary faith teaching is that some give the impression that a Christian can receive *all* of his inheritance now. McConnell cites a problem of over-realized eschatology in contemporary faith teaching.[8] MacArthur and Hanegraaff assert that the "little gods" teaching appears to deify man while demoting God.[9] Many of the contemporary faith leaders such as Kenyon and others emphasize the New Covenant. However, they tend to view the Covenant as a legal contract rather than a relationship.[10] Hanegraaff argues against the contemporary faith belief regarding the blessings and cursings of Deuteronomy 28, charging, "Another example of text abuse is found in their correlation of Galatians 3:13 with Deuteronomy 28."[11]

CLASSIC FAITH TEACHING ON THE BELIEVER'S INHERITANCE

Classic faith teaching on the believer's inheritance, exemplified especially by Charles Spurgeon, Andrew Murray, and A.B. Simpson, begins with the believer knowing his identity in Christ. Practically speaking, a person cannot exercise faith adequately unless he knows that he has the right, authority, and ability to exercise such faith because of his position in Christ. Once the believer knows his identity, he can discover the nature of his inheritance, the rights and provisions of that inheritance, and the extent and limits to which he can receive that inheritance.

Knowing the Believer's Position in Christ. Exercising faith involves understanding who we are in Christ, our exalted position as a child of God. Simpson regarded knowledge of the believer's identity as a child of the King as vital: "How rich our inheritance as children of the King! How infinite our resources! How glorious our prospects! How we should dwell on high, above all low and groveling things, and bear the dignity of princes of heaven. . . . How unworthy to be living a life of discontent, strife and misery. 'All things are yours' (1 Cor. 3:21)."[12] In contrast to some contemporary faith teachers who would claim that the "all things" means material riches, Simpson stressed that the chief riches are contentment, peace, and joy.

Because of Christ's work of redemption in identification, classic leaders say, believers take on the identity of the righteous Christ. Referring to 2 Corinthians 5:21, Murray claimed that believers are the righteousness of God in Christ, exhorting, "Believer, abide in Christ as your righteousness. . . . Take time to realize that the King's own robe has indeed been put on, and that in it you need not fear entering into His presence. It is the token that you are the man whom the King delights to honour. . . . Live your daily life in the full consciousness of being righteous in God's sight, an object of delight and pleasure in Christ."[13] In a similar vein, Simpson asserted:

> "Do we dare to believe that we are absolutely, utterly, eternally accepted in Jesus Christ, in the same sense as He is accepted, and righteous even as He is righteous? Can we believe that our very name before God is: 'The Lord Our Righteousness;' His own name of ineffable holiness (Jer. 23:6) given to us (Jer. 33:16), even as the bride bears the husband's name? Now, this all comes by a simple act of believing God's testimony. God declares it of us simply because we have accepted Christ's atonement and we believe the declaration; and take the new place assigned us."[14]

In contrast to Kenyon and other contemporary faith leaders, classic faith leaders understood this righteousness to be *imputed* righteousness, reckoned to the believer and worn as a garment, not *imparted* righteousness within the believer, which is related to sanctification.

Classic leaders also emphasized that believers are partakers of the divine nature (2 Peter 1:4). Referring to this Scripture, Murray encouraged, "You may learn how it is possible, if you are a believer, that the Spirit of God is in you as a seed of God. . . . Begin to esteem that seed of the divine nature."[15] We can see in these words the roots of the concept of seed faith. Simpson wrote further that because we are partakers of the divine nature, "there are tens of thousands of these 'very great and precious promises' (2 Peter 1:4). But they must be appropriated, applied and inherited or they become dead letters and drafts that have gone by default."[16] Simpson also viewed faith as creating a partnership with Christ, and thus has all of Christ's resources at his command.[17]

According to classic faith leaders, believers are partakers of the New Covenant as well. Drawing on covenant theology in the Reformed tradition, Murray taught that every believer is a partaker of the New Covenant, and thus heir to all its promises.[18] Spurgeon espoused the same covenant theology, saying that the young believer has as much right to the benefits of the covenant "as the most advanced believers, for your right to covenant mercies lies not in your growth but in the covenant itself."[19] Also based on Reformed covenant theology is the idea that the church is spiritual Israel. Simpson was characteristic of this viewpoint, finding parallels between Israel and the Christian life such as the leadership of Joshua, conquest of the Promised Land, and obtaining their inheritance.[20]

Citing Isaiah 61:6, "Ye shall be named priests of the Lord," Spurgeon noted, "This literal promise to Israel belongs spiritually to the seed after the Spirit, namely, to all believers."[21] A.J. Gordon affirmed the believer's inheritance as the privilege of the believer as a royal priesthood, quoting Dorothy Trudel: "In the New Testament we are called kings and priests. Power accompanied the anointing of the kings, and if we really belong to the kingly priesthood shall not strength to heal the sick by prayer come on us also through the anointing of the Spirit?"[22] Murray made the same point, declaring, "He has made us kings and priests. . . . Jesus fills us with a kingly nature. He enables us to rule over sin, over the world, over men."[23] Again Murray exhorted, "Let each disciple of Jesus seek to avail himself of the rights of the royal priesthood."[24] Commenting on Romans 5:17, Hannah Whitall Smith expanded upon the theme: "What do we know of that *much more* reigning in life by Christ Jesus? . . . Do we reign over things much more than they once reigned over us? . . . We have been reigned over by thousands of things—by the fear of man, by our peculiar temperaments, by our outward circumstances, by our irritable tempers, even by

ONLY BELIEVE

bad weather. We have been slaves where we ought to have been kings. We have found our reign to be *much less* rather than *much more*. . . . We have been called to be kings, and we were created to have dominion over the earth (see Gen. 1:28)."[25]

One implication of that exalted position claimed by both contemporary and classic faith teaching is that, based on Deuteronomy 28:13, believers are "the head and not the tail, above and not beneath." As cited in Chapter 1, this concept finds its roots before the nineteenth-century classic faith movement in Puritanism, in seventeenth-century Puritan leader Thomas Brooks, who claimed this Scripture, asserting that believers would one day in this life receive "outward riches, prosperity, and glory." This belief carried over into nineteenth-century evangelical teaching, as Spurgeon, known as "the last of the Puritans," also claimed this Scripture: "Though this be a promise of the law, yet it stands good to the people of God; for Jesus has removed the curse, but He has established the blessing. It is for saints to lead the way among men by holy influence; they are not to be the tail, to be dragged hither and thither by others. . . . Are we not in Christ made kings to reign upon the earth?"[26]

The Nature of the Believer's Inheritance. On the basis of the believer's identity with Christ and in Christ, the concept of the inheritance of the believer is built. The nature of the inheritance is two-fold: (a) believers are co-heirs with Christ, (b) inheritance can be claimed in this life. Regarding both of these, Spurgeon declared, "What innumerable gifts faith has already bought us. It is though a key has been given to God's storeroom and we are allowed to feast upon all that the Lord has prepared for them that love Him. To know the privilege of heirship with Christ, does not this bind you fast to your Elder Brother?"[27] Again he wrote, "But we have not yet brought out the real meaning of this life of faith till we dwell upon another word. 'As ye have received.' Received what? . . . we have received Christ Himself. . . . Not merely the blessings of the covenant, but Himself."[28] Simpson and Murray also taught that as His Body the Church is co-heir to the throne of Christ according to Ephesians 1:21-23.[29] This concept is related to the authority of the believer, which is discussed in Chapter 7.

Like Spurgeon, Simpson believed very strongly that believers can claim their inheritance in Christ now: "We anticipate in the present life to a certain extent the power of our future resurrection, and that we have a foretaste of this part of our salvation here even as we have a foretaste of heaven."[30] In his book *The Land of Promise*, he puts forth his principles of claiming the believer's inheritance.[31] Likewise, Moody, a friend of both Spurgeon and Simpson, taught that believers should not just pray and believe for the promises of God, but claim them authoritatively: "Prayer is pleading the promises. Faith is claiming them."[32]

The Believer's Inheritance Rights. The practical-theological element of the concept of the believer's inheritance lies in the content of what can be claimed as rights of inheritance. For the classic faith teachers, the content of those rights is primarily spiritual, although they can be expressed physically and materially as well, as asserted by Simpson: "So our inheritance is all the fullness of God's exceedingly great and precious promises: all the unclaimed wealth of these forty thousand checks in the Bank Book of the Bible—promises for the soul, promises for the body, promises for ourselves, promises for others, promises for our work, promises for our trials, promises for time, and promises for eternity."[33] According to classic faith leaders, the believer's spiritual inheritance includes:

- *Godly character*—truth, holiness, faith, love, and unity.[34]
- *Supernatural power and the baptism in Holy Spirit.* For instance, Torrey declared, "It is the privilege of every child of God to have the power of God in his service."[35] Almost all leaders in the classic faith movements believe in a baptism or filling with the Spirit subsequent to conversion.[36] Contemporary faith leaders do as well. The major difference is that most of the classic faith leaders do not believe that tongues is the evidence of the baptism in the Spirit, as do contemporary faith leaders. (This will be discussed in Chapter 15).
- *Sonship*—intimacy with and access to God the Father.[37]
- *Restoration to divine image.*[38]
- *Triumph over Satan.*[39]
- *Supernatural help in crisis.*[40]
- *Divine guidance and Divine providence.*[41]
- *Divine protection.* Spurgeon prayed Isaiah 54:17, "We will stand on Your promise, 'No weapon that is formed against thee shall prosper.'"[42] This Scripture is also popularly claimed in the contemporary faith movement. Simpson gave specific examples of such divine protection: "He promises safety amid all danger. . . . The man or woman who is in the Master's will cannot perish until His work is accomplished. How often God has carried His chosen ones through battles and oceans, tempests and wild beasts."[43]

- *Redeemed from the curse of the law.* Classic faith leaders cite Galatians 3:13 in reference to the blessings and cursings of Deuteronomy 28. As cited earlier, Spurgeon related these two Scriptures together.[44] Penn-Lewis likewise quoted Murray in connecting redemption from the curse in Galatians 3:13 with the curses of Deuteronomy: "The cross and the curse are inseparable."[45]
- *Rest and fellowship in communion with God* –"above the scenes of earthly strife and sin."[46]
- *Victorious faith.*[47]
- *Spiritual freedom.*[48]
- *Illumination of the Word by the Spirit.*[49]
- *"Faith may claim healing, complete life, blessing without lack, finished service for God."*[50]

For classic faith leaders, the believer's inheritance does not include only spiritual blessings, but also material and physical blessings. As Simpson indicated above, there are "promises for the body." Those may include financial provision, strength and healing for the body, and provision for ministry needs.

- *Financial prosperity.* As mentioned above, this concept is rooted in seventeenth-century Puritanism, where Thomas Brooks believed that God would raise Christians out of poverty "to much outward riches, prosperity, and glory."[51] The Puritan belief was based on the belief that God would exalt the righteous.
- *Healing as a privilege of believers through the Atonement.* This is the belief that Isaiah 53:4-5 can be claimed as a redemption right. Typical of classic faith teaching, Murray wrote, "Healing and health form part of Christ's salvation."[52] Again, "The body also shares in the redemption effected by Christ."[53] Similarly, Simpson taught, "He reveals Himself throughout the ages as a Living Presence, who can sustain our entire being from His own life, and who Himself 'took up our infirmities . . . and carried our diseases' (Matthew 8:17) as well as our sins. . . . Why should the unbelief of the Church put away these ancient promises, and neutralize so large a part of our redemption?"[54] Although Spurgeon does not appear to have embraced the teaching of healing in the atonement fully, he nonetheless connected healing with the atonement when he made reference to Isaiah 53:5, commenting, "The Church on earth is full of souls healed by our beloved

Physician."[55] This question of healing in the atonement will be discussed in Chapter 14.

- *Provision for ministry needs.* Simpson asserted, "There is no Christian who cannot claim and exercise the very power of God . . . for everything connected with His cause, and our ministry shall touch every part of His work. Faith is the true channel of effectiveness, simply because faith is merely the hand by which the forces of Omnipotence are brought to bear upon the work. The removing of obstacles, the influencing of human hearts and minds, the bringing together of workers, the obtaining of helpers, the supply of financial needs; all these are proper subjects for believing prayer and proper lines for demonstrating the all-sufficiency of God."[56]

It should be noted that among the classic faith leaders, the emphasis on financial provision was not so much on personal wealth, as the provision for needs to enable believers to serve others. The practical issues of prosperity will be discussed in Chapter 23.

REFLECTIONS AND CONCLUSIONS ON CLAIMING THE PROMISES OF GOD

The Extent and Limits of the Believer's Inheritance. Of prime practical-theological concern is the extent to which a believer can obtain inheritance in this life. As mentioned above, one of the criticisms of contemporary faith teaching is that some give the impression that a Christian can receive *all* of his inheritance now. However, Simpson recognized that believers receive a "sample of the inheritance of glory which Christ has purchased for us and is in due time to convey in all its fullness."[57] He also indicated that God puts limits on His blessings: "He exercises a loving oversight in His blessings; and while He freely gives to all who ask and trust Him, and the only limitation in the measure of our blessings is our own faith and obedience, yet even when He gives most largely it is in the line which His wisdom and love see most consistent with our highest good and His supreme glory."[58]

Murray viewed reception of inheritance as dependent upon maturity: "The death of the testator gives the heir immediate right to the inheritance. And yet the heir, if he be a minor, does not enter into the possession. A term of years ends the stage of minority on earth, and he is no longer under guardians. In the spiritual life the state of pupilage ends, not with the expiry of years, but the moment the minor proves his fitness for being made free from the law, by accepting the liberty there is in Christ Jesus."[59] In similar fashion, A.J. Gordon aptly put it: "The promises of God are certain, but they do not all mature in ninety days."[60]

Spurgeon gave fuller explanation, counseling that a believer can rightly claim a promise of inheritance when it is "in due season":

> Often you cannot get at a difficulty so as to deal with it aright and find your way to a happy result. You pray, but have not the liberty in prayer which you desire. A definite promise is what you want. You try one and another of the inspired words, but they do not fit. You try again, and in due season a promise presents itself which seems to have been made for the occasion; it fits exactly as a well-made key fits the lock for which it was prepared. Having found the identical word of the living God you hasten to plead it at the throne of grace, saying, 'Oh Lord, Thou hast promised this good thing unto Thy servant; be pleased to grant it!' The matter is ended; sorrow is turned to joy; prayer is heard."[61]

Some might recognize the validity of spiritual inheritance but question material and physical inheritance. While classic faith leaders believed that financial prosperity could be included in the believer's inheritance, Simpson exemplified their attitude regarding material promises, avowing that Christ Himself is the believer's supreme inheritance.[62] He illustrated the point from the Old Testament incident of Abraham and Lot, perceiving that it is a matter of motivation and inner attitude: "He [Abraham] allowed Lot to have his choice of the land, and when he, full of his strong self-life, claimed the best, Abraham let him have it. When we believe God, we can let people have many things which really belong to us. If God has them for us, no one can possibly take them from us. So Lot took the rich plain of the Jordan. God had given it all to Abraham, and he knew he could not lose it."[63]

Although some take the blessings and curses of the covenant in Deuteronomy 28 in a literal, physical sense as applied to believers, Simpson stressed that they primarily apply to the church as spiritual Israel spiritually, not materially.[64] Further, they belong to the Mosaic covenant, and are only types of the New Covenant. Some contemporary faith teaching confuses what belongs to the Mosaic covenant and what belongs to the Abrahamic covenant, thus mistakenly identifying the material blessings in this Scripture with the Abrahamic covenant.[65]

Other Reflections on Criticisms Regarding Claiming the Promises of God

Imputed vs. Imparted Righteousness. While both contemporary and classic faith teaching emphasize that believers are "the righteousness of God in Christ," contemporary faith teachers such as Kenyon fail to distinguish between *imputed* righteousness and *imparted* righteousness.[66] Murray makes clear that believers are clothed with the robe of *imputed* righteousness.[67] The view that righteousness is imparted at conversion results in a two-fold practical-theological problem: (1) lack of seeing the need for believers to seek growth in sanctification and also (2) the lack of realizing the on-going problem with sin in the believer's life.

Over-Realized Eschatology. As Simmons argued, there is a problem of over-realized eschatology in contemporary faith teaching.[68] The problem lies not in the teaching that a believer can claim an inheritance, but in the extent of claims being made. For some, there is a failure to recognize the "already, but not yet" nature of the kingdom of God as explained by Ladd.[69] As mentioned in the last chapter, classic faith leaders make it clear that the believer's inheritance is a part of the kingdom "already, but not yet" status. Some contemporary faith teaching fails to understand that believers only receive the "firstfruits," a sampling of the inheritance, in this life.

Believers as Little Gods. There are similarities to the Eastern Orthodox theology of "theosis," or deification of believers, and the contemporary faith concept of believers as "little gods." Church father Athanasius declared, "He was God, and then became man, and that to deify us."[70] Some translate it, "God became man that man might become God" or "The divine became human that humans might become divine." He further asserted that God "made Moses God of Pharaoh."[71] As mentioned in Chapter 1, Luther taught, "by faith we become gods and partakers of the divine nature and name."[72] These statements seem to support contemporary faith teaching.

However, neither Athanasius or Luther would take the concept as far. For instance, Athanasius writes further, that these human sons of God or gods "were adopted and deified through the Word, and the Son Himself is the Word," and that "He Himself only is very Son, and He alone is very God from the very God, not receiving these prerogatives as a reward for His virtue, nor being another beside them, but being all these by nature and according to essence."[73] Thus, human believers cannot be "Gods" in the same way or to the same extent at Jesus Christ. Luther, as well, emphasized that believers are servants as well as gods, an emphasis often missing in contemporary "little gods" teaching.

Further, although the classic faith leaders' emphasis and terminology on believers partaking of the divine nature could engender controversy or misunderstanding, they would balk at the contemporary faith "little gods" interpretation. Simpson taught that "every true Christian is a reincarnation of Christ," which may sound like the "little gods" concept, but by that he meant that the believer is the representation of Christ to model the love and ministry of Christ.[74]

Likewise, Chambers referred to his spiritual mentor as "a re-incarnation of Jesus Christ by His Spirit."[75] Interpreting Paul's image of believers in 2 Corinthians 3:2, he commented, "an 'epistle of Christ' means a reincarnation of Jesus."[76] Yet Chambers also cautioned about "an amateur providence attitude" in which a believer becomes, "as it were, god almighty," thinking, "I am not likely to go wrong, but you are."[77] He especially warned, "The disposition of sin is not immorality or wrongdoing, but the disposition of self-realization—I am my own god."[78]

In contrast to Kenyon who described victorious believers as "supermen," Chambers decried the belief, saying, "We are not all excellent supermen."[79] Murray stated that believers have "an incipient Godlikeness," which he identified as their nature of "bearing God's image in having dominion, in being lord of all." This, he explained is the "root" of man's "inner likeness" to God.[80] Billheimer, a more contemporary representative of classic faith teaching, states it in this manner: "They are to be exact copies of Him, true genotypes, as utterly like Him as it is possible for the finite to be like the Infinite."[81]

Classic faith leaders thus used language similar to contemporary faith teaching to express the divine nature of the believers, but most would not go so far as to claim that believers are "little gods." Chambers made a clear distinction, "We are never in the relationship to God that the Son of God is in; but we are brought by the Son into the relation of sonship."[82] He warns, "The disposition of sin is not immorality and wrong-doing, but the disposition of self-realization—I am my own god. . . . It has the one basis, my claim to my right to myself."[83] Spurgeon also clarified:

> To be a partaker of the divine nature is not, of course, to become God. That cannot be. The essence of Deity is not to be

participated in by the creature. Between the creature and the Creator there must be a gulf fixed in respect of essence. But as the first man Adam was made in the image of God, so we, by the renewal of the Holy Spirit, are in a diviner sense made in the image of the Most High and are partakers of the divine nature. We are, by grace, made like God.[84]

Tozer gave this explanation, applying the "little god" concept to life in heaven: "Heaven is going to be a place where men released from tensions and inhibitions, released from prohibitions from the outside, released from sin, and made in the image of God can go to work like the young gods they are. For He said, 'Ye are gods'—He didn't mean you are God, but 'You are little images of Mine, born to do the kind of work that I do, creative work.'"[85] Without these clarifications, these classic faith leaders could well have been criticized for "little gods" teaching. While there is a qualified sense in which believers could be called "gods," as taught by classic faith leaders, because the terminology is prone to mis-understanding today, it should be avoided. It should be noted that some contemporary faith teachers such as Frederick Price and Casey Treat have abandoned the "little gods" concept and terminology.[86]

The Believer's Inheritance and Materialism. The classic faith leaders address the problem of materialistic attitudes in the contemporary faith movement. It should be noted that the classic faith leaders believe that while material blessing can be a part of the inheritance of the believer, the main focus is on the spiritual inheritance. As mentioned above, although some in the contemporary faith movement would claim "All things are yours" (1 Cor. 3:21) means that the believer is meant to be wealthy, classic faith leaders like Simpson interpret the phrase "all things are yours" as a life of con-tentment, peace and joy, not necessarily material prosperity, although that could be included in a secondary way.[87] Hannah Whitall Smith similarly claimed this verse for believers, including provision for material needs,[88] but also warned against materialistic abuse of this verse: "I knew one earnest Christian who had the text 'All things are yours' so strongly im-pressed upon her mind in reference to some money belonging to a friend, that she felt it was a direct command to her to steal that money, and after a great struggle she obeyed this apparent guidance, with of course most grievous after-results."[89] The counsels of the classic faith leaders need to be accepted by contemporary faith teaching. Additional implications of prosperity teaching will be discussed further in Chapter 23.

Contrary to Hanegraaff's charge that correlating Galatians 3:13 with Deuteronomy 28 is text abuse, as cited earlier, Spurgeon and Murray related these two Scriptures together. By so cavalierly dismissing the interpretative connection between Deuteronomy 28 and Galatians 3:13 understood by other older evangelical commentators, Hanegraaff finds himself in the dubious position of calling it text abuse. Hanegraaff fails to understand that the problem with contemporary faith teaching is not in textual abuse of the verses, but in misapplication, by over-emphasizing the "already" to the neglect of the "not yet." The interpretative connection between the verses is validated by the classic faith leaders. As Tozer has discerningly declared, "Truth has two wings."[90] The problem is found in the lack of balance in contemporary faith interpretation, trying to fly with one wing, once again breaking the dynamic tension of truth. Some contemporary faith leaders fail to see that redemption from the curse, though initiated and partially experienced through Christ today, is not yet fully consummated.

A problem also exists among some contemporary faith teaching of legalistic or materialistic application of the Covenant. Though Kenyon views the Covenant as a contract, he is in agreement with classic faith teachers when he declares, "Faith grows out of continual fellowship with the Father."[91] However, Capps, another contemporary faith teacher, misses Kenyon's caveat by claiming, "God does not answer prayer because of friendship. He answers prayer because of a legal document and the result is governed by the rules of this document. *That document is God's Word.*"[92] Contrary to both Kenyon and classic faith leaders, Capps reduces prayer to legalism—God must obey his contract. Murray, representing classic faith teaching, opposes such a view: "We must look for the fulfillment of the New Covenant *within*, the Covenant—not of laws—but of life."[93] Capps and Copeland also fail to understand that the biblical concept of covenant is not based on a contract between equals, but rather the ancient Mid-eastern suzerainty treaty between a superior and an inferior power.

Some over-emphasize the materialistic aspects of the covenant relationship.[94] For Simpson, however, claiming covenant rights is not a matter of claiming material blessings for oneself, but rather claiming inheritance that Satan would try to hold back or steal from the Christian.[95] Further, Simpson wrote, "Faith is contending for its inheritance when the enemy disputes it. . . . When Satan disputes our standing, and puts his foot upon our inheritance, we will arise in the name of he Lord against the most tremendous odds, and claim the victory through Jesus

Christ, by that aggressive and authoritative faith which treads on scorpions and serpents, and triumphs over all the power of the enemy; saying even to the mountain, 'Go, throw yourself into the sea' (Matthew 21:21), and withering the fig tree of evil in His name."[96]

Final Reflections on Claiming the Promises of God. From this research we can see that how believers views their position in Christ will affect in a practical way the manner in which they views themselves, which in turn affects their faith praxis. When believers see themselves as heirs of Christ, they can have confidence to claim the blessings of their inheritance. The classic faith leaders strike a balance between those who claim too little for the believer's inheritance today and those who try to claim too much in claiming their inheritance, maintaining the dynamic tension of truth. Spurgeon, Simpson, and Murray all represent respected evangelicalism, and their views are widely regarded as sound and led of the Spirit. Criticisms of some of the contemporary faith interpretations and applications of the believer's inheritance not withstanding, these classic faith leaders demonstrate wholesome faith praxis.

1. McGrath, 304.

2. See Kenneth Copeland, *Our Covenant with God* (Ft. Worth, Tex.: Kenneth Copeland Publications, 1976).

3. E.W. Kenyon, *The Two Kinds of Faith* (Seattle: Kenyon's Gospel Publishing Co., 1942), 26, 30, 41; E.W. Kenyon, *Two Kinds of Righteousness* (Seattle: Kenyon's Gospel Publishing Co., 1965), 20, 27; E.W. Kenyon, *In His Presence* (Seattle: Kenyon's Gospel Publishing Co., 1969), 52.

4. Hanegraaff, 379.

5. Kenyon, *The Two Kinds of Faith*, 87.

6. Hanegraaff, 186-189.

7. MacArthur, *Charismatic Chaos*, 325.

8. McConnell, 160.

9. MacArthur, *Charismatic Chaos*, 331-336; Hanegraaff, 105-143.

10. Kenyon, *In His Presence*, 28, 71; Hanegraaff, 212-213, 399-400.

11. Hanegraaff, 251.

12. Simpson, *Christ in the Bible (CITB)* (1992), 2:319.

13. Andrew Murray, *Abiding in Christ* (Springdale, Penn.: Whitaker, 1979), 59.

14. Simpson, *In the School of Faith*, 25-26.

15. Andrew Murray, *The Blood of the Cross* (Springdale, Penn.: Whitaker, 1981), 74.

16. Simpson, *CITB* (1992), 6:125-126.

17. Ibid., 6:125.

18. Murray, *The Two Covenants*, 73.

19. Charles H. Spurgeon, *Morning by Morning* (Old Tappan, N.J.: Fleming H. Revell, 1984), 295.

20. Simpson, *CITB* (1992), 2:139-140.

21. Spurgeon, *Faith's Checkbook*, 28.

22. A.J. Gordon, *The Ministry of Healing*, 149.

23. Murray, *The Blood of the Cross*, 132, 134.

24. Andrew Murray, *With Christ in the School of Prayer* (New York: Anson D.F. Randolph and Co., [1886]), 192. For an updated and revised version of Murray's book, see Andrew Murray, *With Christ in the School of Prayer* (Springdale, Penn.: Whitaker, 1981).

25. Hannah Whitall Smith, *Living Confidently in God's Love* (Springdale, Penn.: Whitaker, 1984), 145-146.

26. Spurgeon, *Faith's Checkbook*, 4.

27. Charles H. Spurgeon, "Faith Working by Love," Sermon #1553, Aug. 15, 1880, *Metropolitan Tabernacle Pulpit* (Pasadena, Tex.: Pilgrim Publications, 1977), Vol. 26 (1880), 460.

28. Charles H. Spurgeon, "Life and Walk of Faith," Sermon #483, Dec. 7, 1862, *Metropolitan Tabernacle Pulpit*, Vol. VIII (1862), 676-677.

29. Simpson, *CITB* (1992), 5:408; Murray, *Abiding in Christ*, 70, 143.

30. Simpson, *Present Truths or the Supernatural*, 53.

31. A.B. Simpson, *The Land of Promise* (Harrisburg, Penn.: Christian Publications, 1969), 85.

32. D.L. Moody, cited in Cowman, *Streams in the Desert*, Aug. 15.

33. Simpson, *The Land of Promise*, 85.

34. Simpson, *CITB* (1992), 2:143.

35. Torrey, *The Power of Prayer*, 21.

36. See Simpson, *CITB* (1992), 2:143; V. Raymond Edman, *They Found the Secret* (Grand Rapids: Zondervan, 1960); James Gilchrist Lawson, *Deeper Experiences of Famous Christians* (Anderson, Ind.: Warner Press, [1911] 1970).

37. Simpson, *Present Truths or the Supernatural*, 38.

38. A.B. Simpson, *Danger Lines in the Deeper Life* (Camp Hill, Penn.: Christian Publications, 1991), 100.

39. Simpson, *CITB* (1992), 4:238.

40. Simpson, *Danger Lines in the Deeper Life*, 80.

41. Simpson, *Present Truths or the Supernatural*, 40-42.

42. Spurgeon, *Morning by Morning*, 312.

43. Simpson, *CITB* (1992), 4:237; see also *CITB*, 3:420, 436, 484.

44. Spurgeon, *Faith's Checkbook*, 4.

45. Penn-Lewis, *The Conquest of Canaan*, 105, see also pp. 109, 114-115; Carter, *Faith Healing Reviewed After Twenty Years*, 62-63; Montgomery, *The Secrets of Victory*, 11.

46. Simpson, *In the School of Faith*, 121.

47. Simpson, *CITB* (1992), 4:236.

48. Murray, *The Two Covenants*, 79.

49. Ibid., 34.

50. Simpson, *A Larger Christian Life*, 8, 11.

51. Brooks, 131.

52. Murray, *Divine Healing*, 17.

53. William M. Douglas, *Andrew Murray and His Message* (Grand Rapids: Baker, 1984), 330.

54. Simpson, *CITB* (1992), 1:123.

55. Spurgeon, *Morning by Morning*, 130.

56. A.B. Simpson, *The Gentle Love of the Holy Spirit* (Camp Hill, Penn.: Christian Publications, 1983), 118-119.

57. A.B. Simpson, *The Highest Christian Life* (Harrisburg, Penn.: Christian Publications, 1966), 31.

58. Simpson, *The Land of Promise*, 86.

59. Murray, *The Two Covenants*, 74.

60. A.J. Gordon, cited in Cowman, *Streams in the Desert*, Jan. 3.

61. Spurgeon, cited in Cowman, *Streams in the Desert*, Jan. 13.

62. Simpson, *The Land of Promise*, 128.

63. Ibid., 34-35.

64. Simpson, *CITB* (1992), 1:358.

65. See Copeland, *Our Covenant with God*, 20-21.

66. Kenyon, *Two Kinds of Righteousness*, 20, 27; Kenyon, *In His Presence*, 52.

67. Murray, *Abiding in Christ*, 59.

68. Dale H. Simmons, "Mimicking MacMillan." Unpublished paper, Oral Roberts University Graduate School of Theology (Tulsa, Okla.: Oral Roberts University, 1984), 12.

69. Ladd, 68-69.

70. Athanasius, *Discourses Against the Arians*, Discourse I, 11:39, *NPNF*, 2:4:329.

71. Ibid.

72. Luther, "Sermon for the 3rd Sunday of Epiphany, Matthew 8:1-13," *The Sermons of Martin Luther*, 2:73-74.

73. Athanasius, 39.

74. Simpson, cited in Hartzfeld, and Nienkirchen, 201.

75. David McCasland, *Oswald Chambers: Abandoned to God* (Grand Rapids: Discovery House, 1993), 67.

76. Oswald Chambers, *The Place of Help* (Grand Rapids: Discover House, [1935] 1989), 181.

77. Ibid., 94.

78. Oswald Chambers, *My Utmost for His Highest* (New York: Dodd, Mead, and Co., [1935] 1963), 279, see also p. 99.

79. Chambers, *The Place of Help*, 174.

80. Murray, *With Christ in the School of Prayer*, 140.

81. Paul E. Billheimer, *Destined for the Throne* (Ft. Washington, Penn.: Christian Literature Crusade, 1975), 37.

82. Chambers, *My Utmost for His Highest*, 99.

83. Ibid., 279.

84. Spurgeon, *Morning by Morning*, 262.

85. A.W. Tozer, *Who Put Jesus on the Cross?* (Camp Hill, Penn.: Christian Publications, [1975] 1996), 227. This is quite similar to John G. Lake's interpretation of "ye are gods" as man's divine potential that will be fulfilled "when earth becomes a part of heaven": "He discovers the exalted purpose that Christ had in mind for every man, for the holy day when by the grace of God the sons of God will put the crown of glory on the head of Jesus Christ and the world will proclaim him King of kings and Lord of lords." Lake, 90-92. This is not to say that Tozer would agree with all that Lake taught about being gods.

86. Robert M. Bowman, Jr., "'Ye Are Gods?' Orthodox and Heretical Views on the Deification of Man," *Christian Research Journal* (Winter-Spring 1987), 18ff.; Bob and Gretchen Passantino, *Witch Hunt* (Nashville: Thomas Nelson, 1990), 145-156.

87. Simpson, *CITB* (1992), 2:319.

88. H.W. Smith, *Living Confidently*, 281-282.

89. H.W. Smith, *The Christian's Secret*, 67.

90. Tozer, *That Incredible Christian*, 59.

91. Kenyon, *The Two Kinds of Faith*, 101.

92. Charles Capps, *Releasing the Ability of God* (Tulsa, Okla.: Harrison House, 1978), 65.

93. Andrew Murray, *The Spirit of Christ* (Springdale, Penn.: Whitaker, 1984), 11.

94. Hanegraaff, 213-215.

95. A.B. Simpson, *Life More Abundantly* (New York: Christian Alliance Publishing Co., 1912; Harrisburg, Penn.: Christian Publications, 1965), 116; see also Simpson, *CITB* (1992), 1:361; Spurgeon, *Faith's Checkbook*, 36, 44, 55, 73.

96. Simpson, *CITB* (1992), 1:81.

CHAPTER 6

———◆·◆———

The Nature of Faith:
Active or Passive?

Controversy brews over the nature of faith, whether it is active or passive. Contemporary faith teaching emphasizes faith as active, while
its critics stress that it is passive. As with many other faith concepts,
classic faith teaching demonstrates that it is not a case of "either/or,"
but "both/and." We will see that faith has a passive side (trust, waiting,
looking, resting and yielding or surrender) and an active side (action,
claiming, stepping out, pressing forward, persevering, standing firm,
persisting, pressing forward, and confession). Quietism stressed passive
faith, as did some mystics and also some in the Keswick holiness movement who were influenced by these earlier movements. John Wesley,
while influenced in some respects by mystics and Quietists, nonetheless,
stressed a more active expression of faith. Throughout church history,
the pendulum has swung in both directions. However, classic faith leaders usually maintained a balance of both, viewing the active/passive nature of faith as two sides of the same coin.

CONTEMPORARY FAITH TEACHING

Contemporary faith teaching emphasizes acting by faith. Hagin explains, "The word 'believe' is a verb; it is an action word. To believe in
a Biblical sense means to take or to grasp."[1] Contemporary faith leaders
tend to view faith as something that all believers have, and just need to
develop. In fact, Frederick Price goes so far as to say, "Anybody [who]
prays for God to give them more faith is stupid. They don't know that
if you're saved you already have it. You just have to develop it."[2] For
these teachers, faith is a force that needs to be activated or released in

order to become operational and effective.[3] Faith comes by hearing the Word of God (Romans 10:17), so words of confession are the key to triggering faith.[4]

CRITICISM OF CONTEMPORARY FAITH TEACHING

The critics of contemporary faith teaching stress faith in a passive sense of trusting God.[5] Hanegraaff views faith as only "a channel of living trust—an assurance."[6] He opposes the contemporary faith stress on the importance of words as spiritual containers, asserting: "The Faith movement would have us believe that everything that happens to us is a direct result of our words."[7] He also declares the idea of faith as a force as a "deadly error."[8] (This issue will be discussed in Chapter 9).

CLASSIC FAITH TEACHING: THE TWO WINGS OF PASSIVE/ ACTIVE FAITH

Balancing the Two Wings. While contemporary faith teachers and their critics represent opposite poles, classic faith teachers recognized the dynamic tension between the poles. Tozer, who taught that truth has two wings, believed in the "rest of faith" as did the mystics, but also stressed, "Real faith must always mean more than passive acceptance."[9] Thomas Upham, who was influenced by both Quietists such as Guyon and Fenelon, as well as activists such as the Methodists, wrote in his philosophical work *The Life of Faith* that faith involves both quietness of spirit and energy of action.[10] Müller both trusted in the Lord, and took action in faith once he had confidence in the Lord's leading. Hudson Taylor, following Müller's example, recognized the validity of both resting in faith and acting in faith. He warned against the danger of emphasizing one to the neglect of the other: "How sadly possible it is . . . to delight in the rest of faith while forgetful to fight the good fight of faith."[11] F.B. Meyer likewise counseled a balance between the two aspects of faith, "We must beware that we do not substitute the active for the contemplative, the valley for the mountain-top. Neither can with safety be divorced from the other."[12]

Hannah Whitall Smith, showing her Quaker heritage, emphasized passive trust.[13] For her, "trust becomes, like breathing, the natural unconscious action of the redeemed soul."[14] Yet in the very next paragraph in the same book she also counsels to exercise one's faith actively: "You must therefore put your will into your believing. Your faith must not be a passive imbecility, but an active energy."[15] Faith thus needs to be exercised, activated, confessed. Smith maintained the "two wings" analogy as a theological truth: "The power to surrender and trust exists in every human soul and only needs to be brought into exercise. With these two wings we *can* 'flee' to God at any moment, but, in order really to reach Him, we must actively use them. . . . We must *do* it definitely and actively. A passive surrender or a passive trust will not do. I mean this practically."[16]

Simpson also believed in the "rest of faith," but also taught that a believer should "act your faith . . . not to show your faith, or display your courage, but because of your faith, begin to act as one that is healed. . . . But it is most important that you should be careful that you do not do this on any other human faith or word."[17] Simpson recognized the dynamic passive-active tension of faith: "This is the other side of the great dual problem, divine sovereignty and human responsibility. Both are true and each in its place is imperative. We must trust as if all depended upon God and we must work as if all depended on us. . . . The blessings which God has to impart to us through the Lord Jesus Christ do not wait upon some sovereign act of His will, but are already granted, completed and prepared and simply awaiting the contact of a believing hand to open all the channels of communication."[18] Likewise, Charles Price explained, "It is part of the economy of God for man to cooperate with the divine in the exercising of faith so that God's power may be manifest."[19] This is key to understanding the classic faith theology. Both are essential in these classic evangelical leaders' theology and praxis. Passive trust is foundational, but active exercise of faith is built upon that foundation of trust.

The Passive Side of Faith

Faith Comes from Waiting on the Lord. Classic faith leaders stressed that faith comes from waiting on the Lord. They cautioned against acting on presumption, getting out ahead of the Lord. Müller sometimes spent a week in prayer and the Word before making a decision and acting in faith. Early faith healing leader Cullis, who based his ministry on Müller's model, testified, "It is only by waiting before the Lord, in the sense of perfect abandonment to his will, that I can know his voice."[20] Contrary to some contemporary faith teaching, Simpson cautioned to wait and be sure before acting in faith and encouraged believers not to feel guilty for waiting for the sure word: "God is not displeased with us for waiting until He gives us ample assurance of His will, so that when we step out it may be irrevocable. . . . The one thing in which Gideon's act is unmistakably clear as a pattern for us is in the fact of his becoming certain before stepping forward. This is the secret of faith and victory, to be sure of our way and then go forward unfalteringly."[21]

Faith Comes from Listening for the Voice of God. For classic faith leaders, waiting on the Lord does not mean doing nothing or emptying one's mind like some contemporary forms of meditation, but rather listening quietly for the voice of God to give an assurance or "a sure word." Simpson counseled, "This is the attitude of blessing; faith must listen to God's voice if it would have anything to rest its confidence upon, and to hear His voice, it must get quiet and separate itself from the discordant and distracting influences around it; and in the deepest humility it must be willing to listen to whatever He may say, willing even to hear the word of humbling reproof and lie down in silence and contrition at His feet."[22] Waiting on the Lord involves not just listening, but also watching—fixing one's gaze on Jesus.

Faith Comes from Looking to Jesus. Classic faith leaders, such as Upham, Cullis, and Murray, all cited Hebrews 12:2: "Looking unto Jesus the author and finisher of our faith." Upham quotes eighteenth-century Methodist Rogers for her understanding of faith: "By constantly looking to Jesus, I receive fresh strength in every time of need."[23] Cullis continued the same theme: "The promises are revealed to those who are 'looking unto Jesus.'. . . If you are constantly 'looking unto Jesus,' you will be kept in perfect peace and safety."[24] Murray likewise wrote, "In the face of Jesus, the light which leads to 'the full assurance of faith' is always found. To gaze upon His face, to sit still at His feet that the light of His love may shine upon the soul is a sure way of obtaining a strong faith."[25] "Looking to Jesus" thus became a common expression of trust among classic faith leaders.

Faith Comes from a Mind Set on Jesus. For classic leaders, faith comes not only through looking to Jesus or quiet listening, but having the mind dwelling on Jesus. Hudson Taylor counseled, "How then to have our faith increased? Only by thinking of all Jesus is and all His is for us: His life, His death, His work, He Himself as revealed to us in the Word to be the subject of our constant thoughts."[26] Chambers similarly exhorted, "Think of the things your are trying to have faith for! Stop thinking of them and think about your station in God through receiving Christ Jesus."[27]

All of these—waiting on the Lord, listening quietly, looking to and thinking of Jesus—are a part of the believer's devotional life and intimate fellowship with God. Müller's biographer Roger Steer commented, "Müller's faith sprang from his delight in God. Throughout his life, God was—for Müller—not a vague impersonal force but a living reality, a friend every moment of the day.[28] Müller preached, "No one ever knew Jehovah without being able to exercise faith in Him. It is when God is not known that difficulty comes. The great point therefore is to acquaint ourselves with God."[29] Murray also taught, "It is only in living in direct fellowship with Him that our faith can increase and triumph. . . . Those who walk with Him learn from Him to exercise faith."[30] Likewise, Moody preached, "The way to get faith is to know who God is."[31] Thus on at least three continents this principle was recognized.

Faith Is Resting, Not Struggling. Classic faith teachers emphasized that faith is resting, not struggling. Understanding faith as resting is an old concept, as seventeenth-century Archbishop of Armaugh, James Ussher, applying faith to justification, considered faith to be resting upon Christ.[32] This "rest of faith" became a common Keswick holiness concept. Cullis, for instance, emphasized that believing God is not struggling to believe, but "a perfect rest of faith."[33] Spurgeon also affirmed, "Faith is the giving up of self-reliance and independence and the resting of the soul upon Him whom God has laid in Zion for a foundation. . . . He that believes shall be quiet, calm, collected, assured, confident."[34]

The Active Side of Faith

Faith Is Exercised by Our Will. Classic faith teaching also believed that there is an active side to faith. Faith is not merely passive trust, but is also exercised by an act of the will. Even though Hannah Whitall Smith's faith principles are rooted in the teachings of Quakerism, Guyon and Fenelon, which, as we have mentioned earlier, tend to stress the passive approach to faith, she herself believed both in resting and in active exercise of faith, saying that faith "must not be a passive imbecility, but an active energy."[35] While faith is not striving to believe, Smith asserted that it may involve persistence and perseverance: "You may have to believe against every seeming; but no matter. Set your face like a flint to say, 'I will believe, and I know I shall not be confounded."[36]

Faith Acts. Classic faith teachers held that faith acts on what it believes. Murray exhorted, "Believe that every blessing of the covenant of grace is yours; by the death of the Testator you are entitled to it all—and on that faith act, knowing that all is yours."[37] Both Cullis and Montgomery taught acting one's faith before receiving healing—"as they went they were cleansed."[38] Based on the teachings of Cullis and Montgomery, Simpson wrote, "This is the secret of every advance in the Christian life. You must take what He gives by simple faith, and then reckon upon His Word and act your reckoning out, and God will make it real."[39]

Faith Takes. While faith implicitly trusts God, classic faith leaders taught that faith does not receive passively, but takes actively. This concept was gleaned, in part, from mystic/scholar Meister Eckhart on the active nature of faith, cited by Tozer: "God's gifts are meted out according to the taker, not according to the giver."[40] Murray wrote on this theme in his classic book *With Christ in the School of Prayer*: "All spiritual blessings must be received, that is, accepted or taken in faith. . . . The Greek word for receiving and taking is the same. When Jesus said, 'Everyone that asketh, *receiveth*,' He used the same verb as at the Supper, 'Take, eat,' or on the Resurrection morning, 'Receive,' accept, take, 'the Holy Spirit.' Receiving not only implies God's bestowment, but our acceptance."[41] Murray is speaking of the Greek word *lambano*, which implies a more active taking, as opposed to *dechomai*, which implies a more passive acceptance. Bosworth, cited by contemporary faith leaders, also wrote of "the faith that takes," building on Murray's teaching.[42]

Faith Is Increased by Exercise. This faith that takes is increased by exercise. Hudson Taylor believed that all faith is a gift from God, but it grows by exercise of the "spiritual muscles of faith,"[43] which, he claims, is impossible without trial.[44] He taught the principle of growth "from faith to faith," that is, "he that hath, to him shall be given."[45] When we exercise the faith we already have, God grants more faith.

Faith Is Increased by Asking for More Faith. Exercising our faith does not mean that faith worked up by our own efforts. Rather, Taylor's mentor George Müller believed that faith is given by God *as we ask for it*. Contrary to Frederick Price, who, as we noted above, claims that asking for more faith is stupid, Müller gives this counsel based on James 1:7: "As the increase of faith is a good gift, it must come from God, and therefore he ought to be asked for this blessing."[46] If Price is to be believed, then Müller, the great apostle of faith, was stupid.

Faith Acts Only When Hearing from God. Classic faith leaders taught that a believer should act on his faith only when God has given a clear indication.

THE NATURE OF FAITH: ACTIVE OR PASSIVE?

A sampling of Simpson's writings demonstrates the emphasis on acting only when hearing a definitive word or assurance from God:

> Faith believes where it cannot see, . . . believes what sight and evidence even seem to contradict, if only God has said it.[47]

> Whenever faith can clearly know that He has spoken, all it has to do is to lay the whole responsibility on Him and go forward.[48]

> This is the faith that receives divine healing. It is not merely a general trust that God will do what is best, but a specific confidence that He will do the thing we ask Him, if that thing is one that He has promised in His word.[49]

> To all who wait upon His will the Master gives some word of faith for the future.[50]

> Faith had a Divine word of unfailing promise to depend on, and to that word it clung in unfaltering confidence through all the years of the wilderness. This is the sure resting place of faith, and when God once gives us His word let us never even allow a shadow of doubt to fall upon the confidence of our faith.[51]

> It is most essential in our conflicts of faith that we have a sure word of prophecy on which to rest, otherwise the struggle will be a very perplexing one. To Moses and Joshua, to David and Gideon, God was pleased to give an unqualified word of promise, so that there was no place for doubt to enter.[52]

> When the Lord opens our eyes, how the promises grow vivid, and become living realities, streams of water, clear as crystal, fountains in the desert and sources of everlasting consolation.[53]

Further, referring to the faith exercised in Mark 11:24 and James 1:6-7, Simpson commented, "This is a special work of the Holy Ghost."[54] As an associate of Simpson, R. Kelso Carter wrote similarly regarding healing: "If the faith is not given or inwrought by the Holy Spirit, no cure will follow."[55] Again, Carter cautioned, "Anyone may be healed who is drawn of the Spirit to seek healing. . . . We may be drawn of our own desire to be free from suffering or drawn by a mistaken notion of the purpose of God. In such cases the 'prayer of faith' simply cannot be offered. It is purely will power to 'act faith' and 'make believe' we are healed. God holds the 'prayer of faith' in His own keeping, and when He 'inworks' it, the result, the positive result, certainly comes."[56] In a similar vein, Murray taught, "Every exhibition of the power of faith was the fruit of a special revelation of God. . . . The spiritual power is wanting [lacking], except as God Himself speaks them [promises] to us. And He speaks to those who walk and live with Him."[57] Chambers likewise admonished, "No man by mere high human wisdom would dare undertake a step for Jesus' sake unless he knows that the Holy Spirit has directly spoken to him."[58] Each of these leaders expressed the need for a special word from the Lord.

Grace of Faith vs. Gift of Faith. Daniel Steele, professor of New Testament at Boston University and friend of Cullis, explained this concept by distinguishing between the "grace of faith, which is given to all" and the "gift of faith, which is only bestowed upon whom the Spirit selects."[59] This idea of making a distinction between the *gift of faith* and the *grace of faith* comes from Müller.[60] Müller described the gift of faith as a special confidence or assurance given by the Lord to act in faith, almost as a command, so that if he failed to take the step of faith, it would be a sin. The grace of faith is based on a clear command or promise of Scripture as a general, universal truth. Such a truth can be acted upon as general principle without having a special word from God.

However, if a person does not have a clear word in Scripture, to act without hearing from God would be presumption. As Pierson explained, "in one case we have no unequivocal command or promise to guide us, and in the other we have. The gift of faith is not always in exercise, but the grace must be, since it has the definite word of God to rest on, and the absence or even weakness of faith in such circumstances implies sin."[61]

As an illustration of faith praxis based on this principle, Müller had a ministry of healing in which he often had the confidence to pray unconditionally for people to be restored and they *were* healed. This he understood to be the exercise of the gift of faith. In other cases, he prayed for healing and the people were not healed. In those situations he was exercising the grace of faith. The grace of faith is based on the general promises of Scripture (such as that it is God's nature and desire to heal). The gift of faith is based on a special word or impression from the Lord giving unconditional confidence that God will answer the prayer. See Chapter 12 on the *logos/rhema* theological construct for further explanation of this concept.

THE NATURE OF FAITH: ACTIVE OR PASSIVE?

Hudson Taylor is another example of one who demonstrated this faith praxis when he had been weakened almost to the point of death due to infectious contact with a cadaver as a medical student. While still weak he had an impression to walk a distance to see about some needed funds. He prayed to see if it was the Lord and was impressed with John 14:15, "Whatsoever ye shall ask in my name, that will I do, that the Father may be glorified in the Son." He acted on that word from the Lord, and was strengthened as he went.[62] Once a believer has a sure word from God he can confidently act and step out in faith, and not let a shadow of doubt creep in. If he does not think he has that faith, he can ask Christ to give him the faith.

Faith Confronts the Forces of Evil. Classic faith leaders believed that faith acts aggressively and authoritatively against the attacks of Satan. Simpson is representative of this teaching: "Faith is contending for its inheritance when the enemy disputes it. . . . When Satan disputes our standing, and puts his foot upon our inheritance, we will arise in the name of he Lord against the most tremendous odds, and claim the victory through Jesus Christ, by that aggressive and authoritative faith which treads on scorpions and serpents, and triumphs over all the power of the enemy; saying even to the mountain, 'Go, throw yourself into the sea' (Matthew 21:21), and withering the fig tree of evil in His name."[63]

MacMillan, with many classic faith leaders, believed that illness and calamity are often the doing of the forces of Satan and are not to be accepted submissively as the will of God:

> It is ours to take hold jointly with the Spirit—for as He takes hold with us we must also cooperate with Him—against the things and the forces which assail our individual lives with a faithful and firm refusal of their right to control our bodies or our circumstances. Too often the Christian passively accepts whatever comes to him as being the will of the Lord, yielding without resistance at times to the wiles of the enemy himself. True faith in conflict is a steadfast and earnest will for victory. . . . That 'God hath spoken' is the ground upon which every forward step in the spiritual life must be taken.[64]

REFLECTIONS AND CONCLUSIONS

Anti-faith Critics' Overemphasis on Passive Faith. We acknowledge, contrary to the critics of the contemporary faith movement, that faith does have an active side, as well as passive. Hanegraaff correctly acknowledges that faith, at its base, involves an implicit trust in God. He does not recognize, however, as do the classic faith leaders, that faith is also active, that as Tozer has aptly put it, "Truth has two wings." Hanegraaff's concerns about contemporary faith's overemphasis on the action of faith have validity, but lack balance, failing to maintain the dynamic tension between the two polarities.

Contemporary Faith's Overemphasis on the Action of Faith. On the other hand, contemporary faith teaching tends to focus almost exclusively on the active side of faith, emphasizing the importance of man's role in exercising his faith. Little is taught about resting, or looking to Jesus, or waiting on the Lord. The stress is on man activating his faith, utilizing faith as a force, tapping into the law of faith. While all of these have a measure of truth, the problem is imbalance—emphasizing one truth to the exclusion or neglect of another truth, thus breaking the dynamic tension of truth. Some contemporary faith teaching commits the opposite error of Quietism. Perhaps in reaction to passive acquiescence, contemporary faith teaching tends toward extreme activism. In stressing man's role, the overemphasis seems to attribute sovereignty to man, rather than to God, thus man becomes the master of his own fate. While some from a strong Reformed background may overemphasize the sovereignty of God, some contemporary faith teaching gives too much authority to man's free will.

Sometimes the overemphasis on man's part to act his faith has resulted in some contemporary faith teaching seeming to advocate a striving or struggling to work up faith. On the contrary, as noted above, real faith rests, not struggles. Taylor's advice needs to be heeded by contemporary faith adherents: "But how to get faith strengthened? Not by striving after faith, but by resting on the Faithful One."[65] Similarly, Charles Price cautioned, "Struggling with mental powers and faculties will never bring [faith], for *faith is a gift of God*. It will never be imparted by God until the spiritual condition of the believer warrants the gift."[66]

A Legalistic View of Faith. As mentioned earlier, contemporary faith father E.W. Kenyon was in agreement with classic faith teachers when he declared, "Faith grows out of continual fellowship with the Father."[67] Wigglesworth, often cited by contemporary faith adherents, also avowed, "Just as we have heart fellowship with our Lord, our faith cannot be daunted."[68] However, contrary to classic faith teachers, as well as these contemporary faith models, contemporary faith teacher Charles Capps teaches that God does not answer prayer out of friendship but because of a legal document—the Scripture.[69] Contrary to classic leaders as well as Kenyon and Wigglesworth, Capps reduces prayer to legalism—God must obey his contract.

Failure to Distinguish Special Faith from General Faith. Kenyon reverts to legalism when he claims, "I cannot see . . . where we need to have any special faith to use the Name of Jesus, because it is legally ours."[70] Although it is true that the Name of Jesus can be legally accessed by believers, they cannot use His name indiscriminately or arbitrarily. A believer can make general claims on the name of Jesus, but often needs to wait to hear a fresh word from God before he or she can act in faith and obedience.

While contemporary faith teachers would teach similar to classic leaders that a believer should act his faith, some fail to heed Simpson's warning to "be careful that you do not do this on any other human faith or word."[71] Assuming that a believer can just act in faith may result in presumptive action, as Charles Price counseled, "Remember that faith acts, but the act comes from the faith rather than the faith from the act. That is why it is very easy to step over the border line from the Faith that God imparts into the realm of presumption."[72] Even Bosworth, who is often cited by contemporary faith teachers, makes this distinction: "Christ first gives faith, then calls it to its wondrous exercise. . . . Concerning anything that God calls us to do, 'All things are possible [not to him that feels able in himself, but] to him that believeth.'"[73] The teaching of these classic leaders that a person should act on faith only when God has given a clear indication has often been ignored. These issues will be pursued further in Chapter 10 on the "faith of God" concept and in Chapter 12 on *logos* and *rhema*.

1. Kenneth E. Hagin, *The Real Faith* (Tulsa, Okla.: Kenneth Hagin Ministries, n.d.), 8.

2. Ed Donally, "He's Still Not Afraid to Confront," *Charisma*, Aug., 2000, 67.

3. Kenneth E. Hagin, *How To Turn Your Faith Loose* (Tulsa, Okla.: Kenneth Hagin Ministries, n.d.); Kenneth Copeland, *The Force of Faith* (Ft. Worth, Tex.: KCP Publications, 1983); Charles Capps, *The Tongue, a Creative Force* (Tulsa, Okla.: Harrison House, 1976).

4. Capps, *The Tongue, a Creative Force*, 23-24, 110, 135-136; Charles Capps, *Authority in Three Worlds* (Tulsa, Okla.: Harrison House, 1982), 24; Hanegraaff, 65-69.

5. Hanegraaff, 69-71.

6. Ibid., 70.

7. Ibid., 66.

8. Ibid., 65.

9. Tozer, *The Divine Conquest*, 63.

10. Thomas Upham, *The Life of Faith* (Boston: Waite, Pierce; New York: Garland, [1845] 1984), 284.

11. J. Hudson Taylor, *Union and Communion with Christ* (Minneapolis: Bethany House, n.d.), 59.

12. Meyer, *The Secret of Guidance*, 58.

13. H.W. Smith, *The Christian's Secret*, 26.

14. Ibid., 55.

15. Ibid.

16. Ibid., 169-170.

17. Simpson, *The Gospel of Healing*, 90.

18. Simpson, *CITB* (1992), 4:247.

19. Charles S. Price, *The Meaning of Faith and the Sick Are Healed: Resolving the Mysteries of Faith* (Shippensburg, Penn.: Destiny Image Publishers, 2002), 50.

20. W.H. Daniels, ed., *Dr. Cullis and His Work* (New York: Garland Publishers, [1885] 1985), 167.

21. Simpson, *In the School of Faith*, 144-145.

22. Ibid., 226.

23. Upham, *The Life of Faith*, 128.

24. Daniels, 151.

25. Murray, *The Blood of the Cross*, 59.

26. Howard Taylor, *Hudson Taylor's Spiritual Secret*, 157.

27. Oswald Chambers, *Still Higher for His Highest* (Grand Rapids: Zondervan, 1970), 20.

28. Roger Steer, *Spiritual Secrets of George Müller* (Wheaton, Ill.: Harold Shaw Publishers, 1985), 17.

29. Ibid.

30. Murray, *The Blood of the Cross*, 59.

31. D.L. Moody, "How To Get Faith," *Triumphs of Faith*, May 1887, 117.

32. McGrath, 236-237.

33. Daniels, 9.

34. Spurgeon, *The Triumph of Faith in a Believer's Life*, 20, 22.

35. H.W. Smith, *The Christian's Secret*, 55.

36. Ibid.

37. Murray, *The Two Covenants*, 74-75.

38. Carrie Judd Montgomery, *The Prayer of Faith* (Chicago: Fleming H. Revell, 1880), 100, 101.

39. Simpson, *The Highest Christian Life*, 31.

THE NATURE OF FAITH: ACTIVE OR PASSIVE?

40. Tozer, *That Incredible Christian,* 66, 77.

41. Murray, *With Christ in the School of Prayer*, 52.

42. Bosworth, 131, 132.

43. Howard Taylor, *Hudson Taylor's Spiritual Secret*, 32.

44. Dr. and Mrs. Howard Taylor, *Hudson Taylor in the Early Years*, 131-132.

45. Ibid., 137.

46. Steer, 76.

47. Simpson, *In the School of Faith*, 14.

48. Ibid., 48.

49. Ibid., 51-52.

50. Ibid., 82.

51. Ibid., 126.

52. Ibid., 161-162.

53. Simpson, *CITB* (1992), 1:121.

54. Simpson, *The Gentle Love of the Holy Spirit*, 135.

55. Carter, *Faith Healing Reviewed*, 101.

56. Ibid., 88-89.

57. Murray, *With Christ in the School of Prayer*, 90-91.

58. McCasland, 51.

59. Carter, *Faith Healing Reviewed*, 93.

60. Arthur T. Pierson, *George Müller of Bristol* (New York: Fleming H. Revell, 1899), 90.

61. Ibid.

62. Phyllis Thompson, *Hudson Taylor: God's Venturer* (Chicago: Moody Press, n.d.), 26-34.

63. Simpson, *CITB* (1992), 1:81.

64. John A. MacMillan, "The Cooperating Spirit," *AW*, May 4, 1936, 275.

65. J. Hudson Taylor, quoted in *World Shapers,* 108.

66. Charles S. Price, *And Signs Followed* (Plainfield, N.J.: Logos, 1972), 123.

67. Kenyon, *The Two Kinds of Faith*, 101.

68. Smith Wigglesworth, *The Ever-Increasing Faith* (Springfield, Mo.: Gospel Publishing House, 1924), 13.

69. Charles Capps, *Releasing the Ability of God* (Tulsa, Okla.: Harrison House, 1978) 65.

70. Kenneth E. Hagin, *In the Name of Jesus* (Tulsa, Okla.: Kenneth Hagin Ministries, 1979), 117.

71. Simpson, *The Gospel of Healing*, 90.

72. Charles S. Price, *The Real Faith* (Plainfield, N.J.: Logos, 1940, 1972), 25.

73. Bosworth, 123-124.

CHAPTER 7

Faith and the Authority of the Believer

The concept of the authority of the believer arose out of Reformation and pietistic belief in the priesthood of the believer and the Higher Life teaching on the believer's inheritance. Teaching on the spiritual authority of the believer is not new with the contemporary day faith teachers, but was taught as a restored truth by classic teachers of faith in the nineteenth and early twentieth-centuries. It is based on such Scriptures as:

> But as many as received Him, to them He gave the right [exousia: authority] to become the children of God, even to those who believe in His Name (John 1:12).

> Behold, I have given you authority to tread upon serpents and scorpions, and over all the power of the enemy, and nothing shall injure you (Luke 10:19).

> . . . He raised Him from the dead, and seated Him at His right hand in the heavenly places, far above all rule and authority and power and dominion, and every name that is named, not only in this age, but also in the one to come. And He put all things in subjection under His feet, and gave Him as head over all things to the church, which is His body, the fullness of Him who fills all in all. . . . and raised us up with Him, and seated us with Him in the heavenly places in Christ Jesus (Ephesians 1:20-23; 2:6).

On the basis of these Scriptures, John MacMillan, the seminal writer on the authority of the believer, defined the concept in this way: "Authority is delegated power. . . . The elevation of His people to the heavenlies has no other meaning than that they are made sharers, potentially for the present, of the authority which is His. They are made to sit with Him; that is, they share His throne. To share a throne means without question to partake of the authority which it represents. . . . They may even now exercise, to the extent of their spiritual apprehension, authority over the powers of the air, and over the conditions which those powers have brought about on the earth and are still creating through their ceaseless manipulations of the minds and circumstances of mankind."[1]

CONTEMPORARY FAITH TEACHING

Contemporary faith teaching on the authority of the believer finds its roots in classic faith teaching, as will be presented below, although it varies from classic faith teaching on some points. Kenneth Hagin, Kenneth Copeland, Charles Capps, and Frederick Price have been the most prominent contemporary faith teachers on the authority of the believer, although the teaching has proliferated throughout the charismatic movement. Among the chief components of contemporary faith teaching on the believer's authority is the authority to bind and loose demonic powers according to Matthew 12:29; 16:19; and 18:18.

However, some also extend teaching on the believer's authority to include such doctrines as transfer and/or abdication of God's authority, authority to be "little gods," and authority to command God. Referring to Matthew 28:18, Hagin teaches, "When Christ ascended, He transferred His authority to the Church."[2] On this basis, Copeland asserts, "Each time you stand on the Word, you are commanding God to a certain extent because it is His Word."[3] He does give a caveat, saying, "Now I don't say, 'Look here, God, You have to do this because I said so!' No, that it ridiculous! I simply go before Him in the name of Jesus and remind Him of His Word."[4] Frederick Price goes even further, teaching that believers are in control, not God: "Now this is a shocker! But God has to be given permission to work in this earth realm on behalf of man. . . . Yes! You are in control! So if man has control, who no longer has it? God. . . . When God gave Adam dominion, that meant God no longer had dominion. So, God cannot do anything in this earth unless we let Him. And the way we let Him or give Him permission is through prayer."[5]

CRITICISM OF CONTEMPORARY FAITH TEACHING

Hanegraaff criticizes contemporary faith teaching on binding and loosing, asserting that application to church discipline is the only valid interpretation.[6] Hence, he believes it is a distortion of Scripture to apply it to binding demonic powers. Hanegraaff also warns about the dangers of misusing the doctrines of the authority of the believer by over-emphasizing the activity of demonic powers. He cites Robert Tilton raging against what he perceives to be demonic powers attacking people physically: "Satan, you demonic spirits of AIDS and AIDS virus—I bind you! You demon spirits of cancer, arthritis, infection, migraine headaches, pain—come out of that body! Come out of that child! Come out of that man. . . . Satan, I bind you! You foul demon-spirits of sickness and disease. Infirmities in the inner ear and the lungs and the back. You demon-spirits of arthritis, sickness, and disease. You tormenting infirm-spirits in the stomach. Satan, I bind you! You nicotine spirits—I bind you! In the name of Jesus!"[7] Hanegraaff considers it foolish to believe that all diseases are demonic and can be dealt with by binding the supposed spirits of infirmity.[8]

McConnell claims that contemporary faith teaching engages in excess and presumption, assuming that Christ has given all His authority to the Church and that His hands are tied unless the Church exercises that authority in Jesus' name, thus denying God's sovereignty. Further, McConnell criticizes Kenyon's concept of "power of attorney" in the name of Jesus, which again, he argues, limits God.[9] Hanegraaff condemns Price's teaching that God has abdicated control to man as a demotion of God and deification of mankind. He warns, "If God could be controlled by positive confessions, He would be reduced to the status of a cosmic servant subject to the formulas of faith. You would be God and He would be your bellhop."[10] The idea of limiting God through a negative confession or "commanding God" is repugnant to Hanegraaff as denigrating the sovereignty of God.

CLASSIC FAITH DEVELOPMENT OF THE CONCEPT OF THE AUTHORITY OF THE BELIEVER

Teaching on the Authority of Believers as Kings and Priests. A.J. Gordon comments that Swiss healing movement leader Dorothy Trudel recognized the authority of the believer in the mid-1800s, claiming that it is the believer's privilege to be kings and priests of God.[11] The Keswick and Higher Life movements picked up the theme in the latter half of the nineteenth century with their emphasis on Covenant theology and the privileges and inheritance of the saints through the Covenant. In 1885, for example, Murray was teaching that believers have authority: "Church of the living God! Thy calling is higher and holier than thou knowest. Through thy members, as kings and priests unto God, would God rule the world; their prayers bestow and withhold the blessings of heaven."[12] He quoted famed Scottish preacher and hymn writer Horatius Bonar, saying, "God is seeking kings. Not out of the ranks of angels. Fallen man must furnish Him with the rulers of His universe. Human hands must wield the sceptre, human hands must wear the crown."[13]

Teaching on the Believer's Position in the Heavenlies. At a China Inland Mission conference in 1897 Penn-Lewis taught on the believer's position in Christ according to Ephesians 1 and 2: "The Cross is the gate into this heavenly sphere, so that if the Holy Spirit reveals to us that when we are submerged into the death of Christ, we are loosed from the claims of sin, the flesh, and the devil, He will as certainly impart to us the life of the Risen Lord. He will lift us in real experience into our place in Him, seated with Him in the heavens far above all principalities and powers . . . far above the powers of darkness."[14] Further she declared on the basis of Luke 10:19, "The soul hidden with Christ in God has authority over all the power of the enemy, for he shares in the victory of Christ. In Him he has power to tread on serpents and scorpions, and power to deliver and loose others from the bonds of the evil one."[15] Later, in 1912 she and Evan Roberts included short sections on the believer's authority in their book *War on the Saints.*[16]

Also about 1897, Simpson began teaching on the believer's position in Christ as well according to Ephesians 2:6: "This is much more than resurrection. It is ascension. It is taking the place of accomplished victory and conceded right, and sitting down in an attitude of completed repose, from henceforth expecting with Him until all our enemies be made our footstool. . . . It is throne life. It is dwelling with Christ on high, your head in the heaven even while your feet still walk the paths of the lower world of sense and time. This is our high privilege."[17] Whether one was influenced by the other, we cannot be sure, but apparently they came to the same basic insight, either through the Holy Spirit independent of one another or perhaps through interchange of ideas. Meyer likewise wrote, "Is Satan under Christ's feet? In God's purpose he is under ours also."[18] Thus this became a common Higher Life/Keswick theme around the turn of the century.

Teaching on the Authority of Faith. In 1895 as interim successor to Spurgeon, A.T. Pierson taught, "Obedience to Him means command over others; in proportion as we are subject to Him, even the demons are subject to us in His name."[19] Pierson also taught "the authority of faith": "This we regard as the central, vital heart of this great lesson on Faith. The Master of all girds the servant with His own power and entrusts him with authority to command. Faith claims not only blessing but power to bless."[20] This concept of the believer's authority was further developed in germinal form by Simpson in an article entitled "The Authority of Faith" based on Luke 10:19:

> He did not promise the disciples power first, but the author-
> ity first; and as they used the authority, the power would be
> made manifest, and the results would follow. Faith steps out
> to act with the authority of God's Word, seeing no sign of the
> promised power, but believing and acting as if it were real. As
> it speaks the word of authority and command, and puts its foot
> without fear upon the head of its conquered foes, lo, their pow-
> er is disarmed, and all the forces of the heavenly world are there
> to make the victory complete.

This was the secret of Christ's power that He spake with authority, prayed with authority, commanded with authority, and the power followed. The reason we do not see more power is because we do not claim the authority Christ has given us. The adversary has no power over us if we do not fear him, but the moment we acknowledge his power, he becomes all that we believe him to be. He is only a braggart if we will dare to defy him, but our unbelief clothes him with an omnipotence he does not rightly possess. God has given us the right to claim deliverance over all his attacks, but we must step out and put our foot upon his neck as Joshua taught the children of Israel to put their feet upon the necks of the conquered Canaanites, and faith will find our adversaries as weak as we believe them to be. Let us claim the authority and the victory of faith for all that Christ has purchased and promised for our bodies, our spirits, or His work.[21]

Teaching on Throne Power. This concept of "throne life" described by Simpson above is one of the foundational principles of classic faith understanding of the authority of the believer. The theme of throne life permeated the Keswick, Higher Life, and Overcomer movements. George Peck, a friend of Gordon and Simpson and a leader in the early C&MA, wrote his book *Throne-Life, or The Highest Christian Life*, in which he wrote concerning "throne-power," or the "command of faith."[22] In 1906, Jessie Penn-Lewis also wrote a booklet entitled *Throne Life of Victory*, which was hailed as "God's answer to powers of darkness."[23]

Also in the late 1800s George Watson wrote on "Steps to the Throne."[24] In another book, *Bridehood Saints*, Watson wrote a chapter entitled "The Hand on the Throne," commenting on Exodus 17: "Because of the hand that was on the throne, that is, because the hands of Moses were held up in prayer, and those hands were laid on the throne of Jehovah and prevailed with God in getting the victory. . . . It is because the hands of the man Christ Jesus are on the throne that His prayer prevails, and through Him we lift up our hands and place them on the same throne, that we may prevail against all our enemies. . . . And when we, like Moses, lift up our hands and through Jesus lay them on the throne of grace, it is then we gain the day, . . . the Amalekites were conquered because the hands of a man were upon the throne."[25] J.A. MacMillan, as we will see below, borrowed from Watson, elaborating on the concept in his book *The Authority of the Believer*.[26] A contemporary revival of this classic faith teaching is found in the book *Destined for the Throne* by Paul Billheimer, who in turn borrowed from MacMillan.[27]

Teaching on the Church as God's Law Enforcement Agency. An article by Simpson posits a policeman analogy of spiritual authority: "'I give you authority.' This is the policeman's badge which makes him mightier than a whole crowd of ruffians because, standing upon his rights, the whole power of the state is behind him. . . . Are we using the authority of the name of Jesus and the faith of God?"[28] Simpson taught on the basis of Luke 10:19, that believers have authority to act as Christ's law enforcement officers, as legal authorities representing the government of the King: "It is not power that He gives us. We do not have the power. He has the power. But He gives us authority to act as if we had the power, and then He backs it up with His power. It is like the officer of the law stepping out before a mob and acting in the name of the government. His single word is stronger than a thousand men because he has authority, and all the power of the government is behind him. So faith steps out in the name of heaven and expects God to stand by it."[29]

Similarly, Meyer wrote, perhaps based on Simpson, "He gives us authority to tread on all the power of the enemy. As a man in uniform is able to regulate the traffic of a crowded street, because he represents the authority of the state, so the weakest child of God, who stands in the victory of Calvary, is able to resist and overcome all the power of the evil spirits, who infect the air. If only you can claim to be in the *feet* of the mystical body of the risen Lord, you can tread on serpents and scorpions and on all the power of the devil."[30]

More recently, Billheimer explains this as a dynamic synergy between God and the believer, in which God decrees in heaven, and the church executes God's decrees as His law enforcement agency on earth: "Heaven holds the key by which decisions governing earthly affairs are made but we hold the key by which those decisions are implemented. . . . It is enforcing His will upon earth."[31]

John A. MacMillan—The Seminal Writer of The Authority of the Believer. The concept of the authority of the believer developed in bits and pieces over several decades. However, MacMillan, a missionary and professor with the C&MA who actively engaged in spiritual warfare, really wrote the seminal book entitled *The Authority of the Believer* in 1932. The book is a more thorough exposition of the position of the believer according to Ephesians 1-3, combining together and expanding upon the ideas of Simpson, Murray, Penn-Lewis, Meyer and Watson. He adapted and further developed Simpson's law enforcement analogy, changing it from a mob to bustling traffic stopped by a policeman at a busy intersection.[32] Alluding to Simpson's exposition of Ephesians entitled *The Highest Christian Life*, MacMillan wrote, "The Epistle to the Ephesians is the manual of the higher life. In a fuller degree perhaps than any of the others its leads the believer up to the heights of fellowship, of authority, and of victory."[33]

MacMillan expanded upon the concept of throne life from Watson's book *Bridehood Saints*. Using one of Watson's chapter titles "The Hand on the Throne," as a subtitle, he declared, like Watson, that the believer can assert "in prayer the power of the Ascended Lord, and the believer's throne union with Him. . . . Where in faith the obedient saint claims his throne-rights in Christ, and boldly asserts his authority, the powers of the air will recognize and obey."[34] Elaborating on Watson's application of Exodus 17, he commented, "The rod [of Moses] symbolizes the authority of God committed to human hands. By it the holder is made a co-ruler with his Lord, sharing His throne-power and reigning with Him. . . . So today, every consecrated hand that lifts the rod of the authority of the Lord against the unseen powers of darkness is directing the throne-power of Christ against Satan and his hosts in a battle that will last until 'the going down of the sun.'"[35]

FEATURES OF CLASSIC FAITH TEACHING
ON THE AUTHORITY OF THE BELIEVER

The doctrine of the authority of the believer has practical consequences for faith praxis. This section will highlight some of the practical features of this doctrine. Teaching and real life illustrations of this doctrine in practice will be cited from various sources, but especially from Mac-Millan, since he is the prime and most extensive writer on the concept. In fact, MacMillan devoted an entire chapter in *The Authority of the Believer* on "The Practical Exercise of Authority."[36]

Authority over Creation. Classic faith leaders taught that believers can exercise authority over nature and the animal kingdom, based on the dominion God has given man over the earth (Gen. 1:26; Ps. 8:5-8). They took the promise of authority to trample on snakes and scorpions in Luke 10:19 not only spiritually, but literally. Simpson, for example, wrote, "The forces of nature and providence are subject to the need and help and blessing and glory of His little flock, His glorious bride."[37] He gave an example from the mission field: "He that went with Daniel into the lion's den has gone many times since then with men like Arnot into the jungles of Africa, and paralyzed the fury of the savage beasts and made them slink away abashed before the keen and fearless yes of His trusting child."[38]

Murray also demonstrated authority over creation, claiming protection from God while walking through a pack of wild dogs.[39] MacMillan likewise discerned that the forces of nature sometimes were directed by demonic powers to reek havoc on mankind. As with Jesus rebuking the storm on the sea (Matt. 8:23-27), MacMillan believed that believers can speak to the powers of the darkness "who were behind the fierce disturbance of nature."[40] He also held that believers can exercise authority over animals, reciting the story of divine protection when a saloon keeper loosed a ferocious dog on a group of Women's Christian Temperance Union protesters.[41]

Authority of Claiming Divine Protection. MacMillan believed, according to Psalm 91, that believers who walk closely to God can claim divine protection:

> The children of the Lord have not been exempt from accident, and some have suffered severely. Do we all fully realize that the element of chance does not exist for the believer? And is it equally clear that the malignity of the enemy is never absent from the environment of those who confess the name of Christ and who carry the message of salvation? True it is that the angel of the Lord encamps round about them that fear Him, with

a view to their deliverance. But the child of God is personally responsible for the definite claiming of such protection, and also for abiding within the circumscribed limits wherein it is effective.

Faith is the channel along which the grace of God flows, consequently, there is the necessity for maintaining a constantly victorious spirit over all the wiles and the attacks of the enemy. . . . More and more, therefore, it is vital that every true servant of God learn the secret of dwelling "in the secret place of the Most High," thereby in all the going out and coming of life, experiencing the security of those who "abide under the shadow of Shaddai."[42]

MacMillan himself practiced what he preached. When the house next door to his home caught fire and threatened to spread to his home, he claimed protection according to Psalm 91 and the fire stopped at the wooden fence between the two houses. On another occasion, while a missionary in South China he claimed the same Scripture as protection for the mission station against a cholera plague engulfing the city. He and the other missionaries were protected, while many outside the compound died.[43] Spurgeon likewise had claimed and received health and protection according to Psalm 91 while ministering to people during a deadly plague.[44]

Covenant Right to Claim Family Salvation. On the basis of Acts 16:31 ("Believe in the Lord Jesus, and you shall be saved, you and your household"—NIV), from the viewpoint of Reformational Covenant theology classic faith leaders believed that salvation of the family can be claimed. MacMillan, an example of such teaching, declared, "Every child born to a Christian family can be claimed for God with full assurance."[45] However, for MacMillan, family salvation is not automatic, for "salvation is not hereditary, but covenant of grace provides for the salvation of the children of believers. The believer must claim the covenant and abide in it; and when he does so, its working will be found to be effectual."[46]

Authority to Open Locked Doors to Evangelism and Missions. From his experiences in China and the Philippines MacMillan recognized that Satan often impedes the advance of the gospel, and must be rebuked: "The enemy has been preternaturally active; he has shut the doors of the lands against the Church's efforts; he presses on her heels as she goes forward. It is a time for those, who know the experience of sitting in heavenly places with the risen Lord, to hold the rod of His authority over the blocked roads before His people that all hindrances may be removed, that the way to the last tribes may be opened and the last individuals of the people for His name may be called out."[47]

MacMillan exercised that authority as Field Director of the C&MA Missions in the Philippines. When he took over as Field Director, the missionaries were demoralized, dissension was rife, and they were ready to close the mission. Within three years, the mission turned around and revival broke forth, resulting in hundreds of conversions in a place that was considered hard, stony soil.[48]

Authority to Influence World Events and Avert War. According to Ephesians 3:10-11, classic faith leaders believed that the church has authority to declare God's purposes to principalities and powers: "His intent was that now, through the church, the manifold wisdom of God should be made known to the rulers and authorities in the heavenly realms, according to his eternal purpose which he accomplished in Christ Jesus our Lord" (NIV). MacMillan understood this to mean, "The Church is to be God's instrument in declaring to these rebellious, and now usurping powers, the divine purpose, and in administering their principalities after they have been unseated and cast down."[49] He explains further, "'Authority' moreover is God's constant offer to His children in every department of spiritual life. . . . To such as yield themselves in full obedience and faith, the mysteries of the kingdom are opened; they are made to share the throne of the risen Lord; principalities and powers are put under their feet; and there is granted an ever-increasing knowledge of the purpose of the ages which the Father has purposed in His dear Son."[50]

With that increasing knowledge of the purposes of God, believers also share in the government of God over the powers of heaven and earth. Classic faith leaders, especially from the Overcomer Movement in which Penn-Lewis was involved, thus believed that the believer's authority can exercise influence in world events.[51] MacMillan summarized that viewpoint:

> As he follows the urges of his spirit, and takes to the throne everything that touches his heart, he becomes a partner with his Lord in the government of the universe. His intercessions become channels along which the divine power is enabled to flow for the alleviation of suffering, the extension of the gospel,

and the control of the activities of the rulers of mankind. At his word the unseen principalities and powers are restrained, wars are hindered or delayed, calamities are averted, and national and individual blessings are bestowed. He may think himself but an infinitesimal factor in all this, but it is the divine purpose that the people of the Lord shall be associated with Him in His administration.[52]

Further, MacMillan declared, "Devastating wars might at times be held back if the Church of Christ realized its authority and privilege."[53] He cited examples: "Even in world matters where war seemed inevitable, there have been times in recent years, when groups of instructed believers, united with one accord against the working of the powers of the air in some great crisis, have seen the problem gradually clear up without coming to the worst. Christians are far from realizing the extent and the reality of their union with Christ in His great task of world authority."[54] Welsh intercessor Rees Howells is an example of one who practiced this with remarkable practical results before and during World War II.[55]

Authority to Overcome Satanic Forces and Set People Free from Demonic Control. Through the nineteenth-century pioneering spiritual warfare ministries of Johannes Blumhardt, John Nevius and Pastor Hsi, awareness of the believer's authority and victory over demonic forces arose. Their teaching and practice in this arena provided a foundation for early twentieth century ministry in spiritual warfare. Simpson and MacMillan especially taught in this vein, citing Luke 10:19.[56] Spiritual and mental depression, MacMillan averred, must often be met with authority because it is many times due to oppression from satanic forces through attacks of deceiving spirits.[57] In his writings, MacMillan cited instances in which he rebuked depression in the name of Jesus with remarkable results.[58]

Authority to Bind and Loose. The concept of binding and loosing according Matthew 12:29; 16:19 and 18:18-20 has a long history in the biblical days and the church. I have written on this extensively elsewhere.[59] While the concept was institutionalized and watered down in the medieval period, the doctrine was gradually restored to the church in the nineteenth century through the ministries and teachings of the Blumhardts, Murray, Spurgeon, Murray, Simpson, and others. Basically, the doctrine teaches that believers have the authority to bind (limit) demonic forces and to loose (set free) people from spiritual oppression or bondage.

Murray, as early as the 1880s in his classic book *With Christ in the School of Prayer*, had prayed, "Grant especially, Blessed Lord, that Thy Church may believe that it is by the power of united prayer that she can bind and loose in heaven; that Satan can be cast out; that souls can be saved; that mountains can be removed; that the Kingdom can be hastened."[60] Spurgeon, like Chrysostom, related binding and loosing to Elijah's authoritative prayer to forbid and allow rain: "Thus are Elijahs trained to handle the keys of heaven, and lock or loose the clouds."[61] Moody, Bounds, and Penn-Lewis all wrote of the believer's authority to lock and loose the heavens.[62] Identifying Matthew 16:19 as Christ giving the believer authority to wage war against demonic powers, Meyer wrote, "This is the secret of the blessed life. Go through the world opening prison-doors, lifting heavy burdens, and giving light, joy, and peace to the oppressed."[63]

Following the Welsh Revival of 1904, teaching on binding and loosing increased. In particular, Montgomery and Penn-Lewis had popularized the concept in their writings.[64] MacMillan, as Associate Editor of *The Alliance Weekly*, reprinted a portion of Penn-Lewis' booklet entitled "How to Pray for Missionaries," which discussed the practice of binding and loosing.[65] He also wrote of the concept in *The Authority of the Believer*: "As we continue to abide closely in Him, our prayers for the advancement of the Kingdom, will become less and less the uttering of petitions, and will increasingly manifest the exercise of a spiritual authority that recognizes no national boundaries, but fearlessly binds the forces of darkness in any part of the world."[66] Watchman Nee, influenced by Penn-Lewis, Murray and Simpson, also taught authoritative prayer and the power of binding and loosing in 1934.[67] Nee also applies it in a broader sense in this way: "Bind all the inordinate activities of brothers and sisters in the meeting; bind all the disturbances to the work that come from people of the world; bind all the evil spirits and demons; and bind Satan and all his activities. We may rule as kings over all things."[68]

Authority over Territorial Spirits. Though the classic faith leaders did not use the contemporary terminology of "territorial spirits," they understood that principalities and powers had established strongholds in certain geographical locations. Penn-Lewis had hinted at the concept as early as 1897 at a China Inland Mission conference in London, declaring on the basis of Daniel 10 that there are "principalities who rule over various lands."[69] C&MA missionary statesman Robert Jaffray discerned a "prince of darkness" over a specific geographical area.[70]

From his own study and experience, MacMillan developed the theological concept further. Some personality trait weaknesses that are usually considered characteristic of a certain nationality or ethnic group, MacMillan suggests, are "quite as likely to be a working of that undercurrent of Satanic force."[71] He posits the atheism of Russia and the unexplainable submissiveness of its people as due to an occult power, which he calls a "hellish counterfeit."[72] For most heathen religions, MacMillan explained, "Every god is confined to definite territorial limits, outside of which his influence does not extend."[73] He called for intercessors "to roll back the powers of the air, and make it possible to bring the Truth to bear on these regions where the devil is blocking the way."[74] Though not nearly so highly developed a strategy as presented today, nonetheless, MacMillan taught and practiced an embryonic form of spiritual mapping, which he called "praying geographically":

> There is among the saints of the Most High a chosen group—perhaps larger than we think—whose divinely appointed ministry is that of the prayer closet. There, on their knees with a world map before them, its members individually and methodically pray out the problems of the advance of the kingdom. They precede missionaries into areas where Christ has not been named; they observe them as they attack firmly-placed barriers, breaking down by the high explosive of authoritative prayer the Satanic opposition that continually impedes the forward progress of the gospel. Because the working of the Spirit of God is everywhere, working through some mysterious law, dependent on intercession, these unseen workers are the real pioneers of Christian missions. Unknown to themselves their word in the heavenlies is mighty through God to the overthrowing of principalities and powers. National boundaries are melting down before the faith and fervor of their supplications.[75]

He spoke out of the authority of his own practical experience, having done battle with such territorial spirits in the Philippines. It should be noted, however, that MacMillan and other early leaders did not advocate commanding territorial spirits as some do today in the strategic level spiritual warfare movement.

Authority to Speak to the Mountain. MacMillan understood the exercise of spiritual authority to be not merely prayer.[76] Rather, prayer paves the way for the exercise of authority, but does not substitute for it. The exercise of authority, then, involves "command of faith" based on Jesus' statement in Mark 11:22-24, exhorting disciples to speak to the mountain: "The question involved is not that of an imposing faith, but that of an all-sufficient Name. . . . As he speaks to the mountain in the name of Christ, he puts his hand on the dynamic force that controls the universe. Heavenly energy is released, and his behest is obeyed."[77] Believers are not merely to pray to God about our problems; but to speak an authoritative word in the name of Jesus directed to the problems. This concept MacMillan clearly gleaned from Pierson. Expounding on Mark 11:22-24 and its parallel passages in Luke 17:5-6 and Matthew 17:20-21, Pierson comments:

> The coincidence is too remarkable to be either accidental or un-important. In all these cases it is not "pray" but "say," not the word of petition but of direction, not as a suppliant but as of a sovereign. This we regard as the central, vital heart of this great lesson on Faith. The Master of all girds the servant with His own power and intrusts him with authority to command. Faith claims not only blessing but power to bless. This lesson is at first sight so astounding as to seem incredible—it passes all understanding, and faith itself staggers at such promises. Let us reverently seek to take in the marvelous thought. Faith in God so unites to God that it passes beyond the privilege of asking to the power of commanding.[78]

Thus this authority to speak to the mountain is not a prayer, but authority to command. Nee put it this way: "Commanding prayer is praying from heaven to earth. . . . We sit in the heavenly places and pour forth commanding prayer. . . . And thus we command what God has already commanded; we decide on that which God has already decided."[79]

Commanding God—Isaiah 45:11. Springing out of the authority to speak a word of commanding faith, the most controversial and misunderstood of the classic faith concepts is that of "commanding God." The idea is based primarily on a prophecy of Isaiah from the King James Version: "Thus saith the Lord, the Holy One of Israel, and his Maker, Ask me of things to come concerning my sons, and concerning the work of my hands command ye me" (Isa. 45:11, KJV). MacMillan discussed this controversy, commenting on this passage of Scripture:

> So unreasonable to the natural mind seems the proposition of Jehovah to His people . . . that they should "command" Him

concerning the work of His hands, that various alternative readings of the passage have been made with the intent of toning down the apparent extravagance of the divine offer. Men are slow to believe that the Almighty really means exactly what He says. They think it a thing incredible that He would share with human hands the throttle of divine power. Nor have they the spiritual understanding to comprehend the purpose of the Father to bring those who have been redeemed with the precious blood of His dear Son into living and practical cooperation with that Son in the administration of His kingdom.[80]

MacMillan is correct that many interpretations of this passage are posited among scholars in attempting to explain the verse, and there is no consensus. It is like the Jewish saying that when four rabbis get together to discuss a passage, they come up with five opinions![81]

However, MacMillan is not alone in his interpretation of the passage, but rather it was typical of evangelical scholars and classic faith leaders who preceded him. For example, Spurgeon declared:

Thou art thyself a decree. . . . Our prayers are God's decrees in another shape. . . . Do not say, "How can my prayers affect the decrees?" They cannot, except in so much as your prayers are decrees, and that as they come out, every prayer that is inspired of the Holy Ghost unto your soul is as omnipotent and eternal as that decree which said, "Let there be light and there was light." . . . The ear of God Himself shall listen, and the hand of God Himself shall yield to thy will. God bids thee cry, "Thy will be done," and thy will shall be done. When thou canst plead His promise, then thy will is His will.[82]

Spurgeon's friend, A.T. Pierson, commented on this Scripture as well, asserting: "Faith in God so unites to God that it passes beyond the privilege of asking to the power of commanding. This language of Christ is not that of a request, however bold, but of a *fiat*. . . . And so—marvelous fact! The child of God, laying hold by faith of the Power of the Omnipotent One, issues his fiat. . . . Obey the Law of the Power and the Power obeys you. Conform to the Laws and modes of the Spirit's operations, and in the work of God's hands you may command the Spirit's Power."[83] Simpson likewise followed in the footsteps of Spurgeon and Pierson: "In the name of Jesus we are to not only ask, but claim and pass in the orders of faith to the bank of heaven."[84] He further supported the interpretation with John 15:7, saying "as one has translated it, 'Ye shall ask what ye command and it shall be done unto you.'" He calls this "the confidence of prayer." [85] Bounds is even stronger in his language, claiming that Isaiah 45:11 is "God's *carte blanche* to prayer."[86] Referring to the faith expressed in the appeal of the Syrophoenician woman, Bounds explains, "Jesus Christ surrenders Himself to the importunity of a great faith."[87] Thus, while the language is controversial, several respected evangelical leaders who believed in the sovereignty of God nonetheless speak of God as responding to the bidding of His consecrated servants who are in close communion with Him.

EVALUATION OF CRITICISMS OF CONTEMPORARY FAITH TEACHING ON THE AUTHORITY OF THE BELIEVER

Criticism of Binding and Loosing. The evidence cited above counters Hanegraaff's claim that binding and loosing does not deal with spiritual warfare, as we have demonstrated that it was considered a sound concept around the world by classic faith teachers. Respected British expositor G. Campbell Morgan, typical of classic faith leaders, asserted that the binding and loosing actions of Matthew 18:18 "have a much wider application than the application Jesus made of them at this point. We are perfectly justified in lifting them out of their setting and using them over a wider area of thought."[88] For example, twice earlier in Matthew Jesus refers to the concept of binding and loosing in relation to exercising spiritual authority over demonic activity (Matt. 12:28-29; 16:18-19; see also Mark 3:27; Luke 11:20-22). In other words, the principle of binding and loosing does not apply merely to discipline, but is an overall function of the spiritual authority of believers that has been delegated to the Church. Morgan thus summarized the accepted classic evangelical faith hermeneutic. The book *Binding and Loosing: Exercising Authority over the Dark Powers*, co-authored by K. Neill Foster and myself further refutes Hanegraaff's thesis, documenting authoritative exegesis of the doctrine of binding and loosing, as well as tracing the record of the doctrine in relationship to demonic powers throughout biblical history, extra-biblical Jewish and Greek writings, the early church fathers and more recent church history.

The Problem of Overemphasis on the Demonic. Hanegraaff does have a valid concern, however, about the dangers of misusing the doctrines of the authority of the believer and binding and loosing by over-emphasizing the activity of demonic powers. He is correct that not all Tilton claims to be demonic is actually demonic. One needs to distinguish between the works of the flesh, the results of the fallen nature of the world, and the realm of Satan. In our book *Binding and Loosing* Foster comments, "Probably the most alarming part of this boisterous prayer is the indiscriminate and ubiquitous use of binding terminology. Confronted with such behavior, along with the supposition that such a procedure is supposedly correct, anyone with less than a bombastic psyche will tend to be driven away from the biblically ordered and Christ adorning doctrine of binding and loosing."[89] At the same time, classic faith teachers recognized from Scripture that *some* illnesses are caused by demonic forces (cf. Acts 10:38; Luke 13:11-12), but may be due to other causes as well.

Misuse of the Authority to Use the Name of Jesus. McConnell validly points out the excess and presumption of some contemporary faith teaching in assuming that Christ has relinquished all His authority to the Church and that His hands are tied unless the Church exercises that authority in Jesus' name, thus denying God's sovereignty. McConnell does not, however, grant that the church has delegated authority through which Christ will not act unless the church acts. Yet this is not a new doctrine invented by contemporary faith teachers, but rather a teaching propagated universally by classic faith advocates. Spurgeon, for example, says, "The Lord can do everything; but when He makes a rule that according to our faith so shall it be unto us, our unbelief ties the hand of His omnipotence."[90]

While McConnell criticizes Kenyon's concept of "power of attorney" in the name of Jesus, he does not recognize that the idea was taught among classic faith leaders as well. Murray wrote of the concept in his classic *With Christ in the School of Prayer* as early as 1885.[91] The C&MA propagated the belief in the 1920s.[92] Other evangelical writers have written that God will not act without man's acts of faith. For example, Spurgeon taught, "Some bank bills require the signature of the person for whom they are drawn, and they would not be payable at the bank, though regularly signed, unless counter-signed by the person to whom they are due: now many of the Lord's promises are drawn in like fashion. Armed with such promises, you go to the bank of prayer, and you ask to have them fulfilled, but your petitions are not granted because they need to be countersigned by the sign-manual of your faith in them; and when God has given you grace to believe his promise, then shall you see the fulfilment of it with your eyes."[93] Spurgeon's entire devotional book

Faith's Checkbook is based on this premise that the promises of God are appropriated by faith as in endorsing and cashing a two-party check.[94]

Similarly, Simpson wrote, "God would have us learn that even His surest promises must be endorsed by faith and presented by prayer at the heavenly bank that the name of Jesus may be specifically honored every time a promise is fulfilled."[95] Conveying the same idea with a different analogy, MacMillan commented, "The Lord [is] Head over all. His position and power are supreme. Why, then, is there not more manifest progress? Because a head is wholly dependent upon its body for the carrying out of its plan. . . . The Lord Jesus, 'Head over all things to the church, which is His body,' is hindered in His mighty plans and working because His body has failed to appreciate the deep meaning of His exaltation, and to respond to the gracious impulses which He is constantly sending for its quickening."[96]

Coming from the Reformed Higher Life/Keswick traditions, these classic faith writers believed strongly in the sovereignty of God, but also recognized that God has limited Himself in these matters. A key difference with the faith teaching is that some contemporary faith teachers seem to say God has given *all* authority to the church, whereas these writers would say God has given delegated co-authority in certain circumstances.

Confusion between Delegation and Transfer of Authority—Who Is in Control? Even though Hagin gets much of his teaching from MacMillan, contrary to Hagin, MacMillan asserts only that Christ has *delegated* authority, not "transferred" authority to the church. Transfer of authority implies the handing over of authority as when one president leaves office and another takes over. Delegation of authority does not imply that Christ has relinquished his authority to the church. While Hagin may not have intended to go that far, the ambiguity of such a statement can cause some to interpret it in such a way. Moreover, Hanegraaff rightly criticizes Frederick Price for teaching that God has abdicated control to man.

Classic faith leaders would repudiate this teaching. On the contrary, God never abdicates authority; He delegates it. God is, was, and always will be in control. MacMillan clearly asserts, "In the world's long history, one Man only, with the unmeasured unction of the Holy Ghost upon Him, has been able to say, 'All authority hath been given unto me in heaven and in earth.'"[97] This delegated authority is only potentially and partially the believer's in this present age, and fully only in the millennial age.[98] Some contemporary faith teachers have thus not understood the distinctiveness of the kingdom of God in this age being manifested as "already, but not yet." It is true that God will not act on some matters unless we pray and take authority in the name of Jesus, but He is still sovereign.

The Controversy of "Commanding God." It is important to understand that while classic faith leaders spoke of commanding God, they did not denigrate the sovereignty of God and thus give sovereignty to man. Rather, when a believer is in such intimate communion with God in the secret place of the Most High, he knows beyond a shadow of a doubt the will of God, and thus can speak with confidence and authority for God to carry it out.[99] MacMillan expressed it this way:

> To them [authoritative intercessors] the Word of God has become a battle chart on which is detailed the plan of campaign of the host of the Lord. They realize that they have been appointed by Him for the oversight of certain sections of the advance, and they have humbly accepted His commission. Deeply conscious of their own personal unworthiness and insufficiency, they yet believe God's statement concerning their identification with Christ in His throne power. . . . Their closet becomes a council chamber from which spiritual commands go forth concerning matters widely varied in character and separated in place. As they speak the word of command, God obeys. His delight is in such co-working.[100]

Classic faith leaders such as MacMillan, Simpson, Pierson, and Spurgeon would all strongly reject the idea that man has sovereignty over God.

There is valid concern, nonetheless, about the misunderstanding and abuse of the idea of commanding God. Regarding the question of the proper exegesis of Isaiah 45:11, while the meaning can be debated, the "commanding God" interpretation has substantial evangelical exposition behind it to uphold the position. Further, these classic faith writers support their understanding by other Scriptures, so that even if the interpretation of Isaiah 45:11 is questioned, the concept is upheld. Perhaps, though, because of the insights of more recent scholarship regarding this verse and the misunderstanding and misuse of the concept, it might be wiser today to use different language than "commanding God." For example, even though, as cited above, Copeland gives a disclaimer to his claim of commanding God, his language makes it sound as though he is giving sovereignty to man, thus liable to misunderstanding and distortion, and thus vulnerable to criticism.

Final Reflection—Avoiding Misuse of the Believer's Authority. I conclude that the doctrine of the authority of the believer is valid and biblical. It was recognized and practiced at various levels and progression of understanding by respected evangelical leaders of the nineteenth and early twentieth centuries. Hence, it is not an aberrational doctrine as claimed by some anti-faith leaders, but sound biblical teaching and practice based on the priesthood of the believer.

As with all authority, however, the authority of the believer can be misused and abused. MacMillan cautions that "the authority of His name could never be efficacious in the mouth of an unspiritual disciple."[101] It is only a "consecrated hand" that can direct throne power of Christ.[102] In all exercise of authority and faith, there is great need for humility. MacMillan's admonition is timely and timeless for faith praxis: "So Jesus says, when you as servants have done all those things which are commanded you; when you have uprooted trees, removed mountains, healed the sick, led multitudes to salvation—remember that you are still servants of God. What you have done is simply what He has endued you with power to do, and what you have engaged to do for Him. You have not done aught of yourselves—all has been of His working."[103]

---

1. MacMillan, *The Authority of the Believer*, 12, 18. See my Doctor of Ministry dissertation, *A Case Study of the Authority of the Believer*, 316-342, for further particulars on this section. See also my book, *A Believer with Authority: The Life and Message of John A. MacMillan* (Camp Hill, Penn.: Christian Publications, 2001), adapted from this dissertation.

2. Kenneth E. Hagin, *The Believer's Authority* (Tulsa, Okla.: Kenneth Hagin Ministries, 1984), 11.

3. Copeland, *Our Covenant with God*, 40-41.

4. Ibid., 41.

5. Frederick Price, cited in Hanegraaff, 85.

6. Hanegraaff, 257-258.

7. Ibid., 257.

8. Ibid., see also K. Neill Foster with Paul L. King, *Binding and Loosing: Exercising Authority over the Dark Powers* (Camp Hill, Penn.: Christian Publications, 1998), 202-203.

9. McConnell, 142-143.

10. Hanegraaff, 85.

11. A.J. Gordon, *The Ministry of Healing*, 149.

12. Murray, *With Christ in the School of Prayer*, 142.

13. Ibid., 142.

14. Jessie Penn-Lewis, *The Warfare with Satan* (Dorset, Eng.: Overcomer Literature Trust, 1963), 63.

15. Ibid., 65.

16. Jessie Penn-Lewis with Evan Roberts, *War on the Saints*—Unabridged Edition, Ninth Edition (New York: Thomas E. Lowe, Ltd., 1973), 22, 32-33, 259-262.

17. Simpson, *CITB* (1992), 5:413-414.

18. Meyer, *The Secret of Guidance*, 47.

19. Pierson, *The Acts of the Holy Spirit*, 92.

20. A.T. Pierson, *Lessons in the School of Prayer* (Dixon, Mo.: Rare Christian Books, n.d.), 59.

21. A.B. Simpson, "The Authority of Faith," *AW*, Apr. 23, 1938, 263.

22. George B. Peck, *Throne-Life, or The Highest Christian Life* (Boston: Watchword Publishing, 1888), 171, 174-175, 177.

23. Brynmor Pierce Jones, *The Trials and Triumphs of Mrs. Jessie Penn-Lewis* (New Brunswick, N.J.: Bridge-Logos Publishers, 1997), 136; see also Penn-Lewis and Roberts, *War on the Saints*, 183.

24. George D. Watson, *Steps to the Throne* (Cincinnati: Bible School Book Room, n.d.).

25. George D. Watson, *Bridehood Saints* (Cincinnati: God's Revivalist, n.d.), 117-118, 120-122.

26. MacMillan, *The Authority of the Believer*, 86-88, 93-96.

27. Paul Billheimer, *Destined for the Throne*; see King, *A Case Study of a Believer with Authority*, 271-276.

28. A.B. Simpson, "Spiritual Talismans," *AW*, June 14, 1919, 178.

29. A.B. Simpson, *Christ in the Bible: Luke* (Harrisburg, Penn.: Christian Publications, n.d.), Vol. XIVB, 183.

30. Meyer, *Five Musts of the Christian Life*, 27-28.

31. Billheimer, *Destined for the Throne*, 52.

32. MacMillan, *The Authority of the Believer*, 11-12.

33. John A. MacMillan, *The Full Gospel Adult Sunday School Quarterly*, Oct. 28, 1934, 12.

34. MacMillan, *The Authority of the Believer*, 49, 55.

35. Ibid., 93, 96. My Doctor of Ministry dissertation, *A Case Study of a Believer with Authority*, documents the significant influence of MacMillan's writings on the contemporary faith teaching on the authority of the believer (pp. 280-286). In particular, Kenneth Hagin made extensive use of MacMillan's material, popularizing the concept in the Pentecostal, charismatic, and contemporary faith movements (pp. 263-294).

36. MacMillan, *The Authority of the Believer*, 45-59.

37. Simpson, *CITB* (1992), 5:408.

38. A.B. Simpson, *Christ in the Bible: Matthew* (Harrisburg, Penn.: Christian Publications, n.d.), Vol. XIII, 326.

39. William Lindner, *Andrew Murray* (Minneapolis: Bethany House, 1996, 41-42.

40. John A. MacMillan, *The Full Gospel Adult Sunday School Quarterly*, Nov. 26, 1939, 28.

41. John A. MacMillan, "Divine Protection," *AW*, Dec. 6, 1947, 770.

42. John A. MacMillan, "Raging Chariots," *AW*, May 15, 1937, 307.

43. King, *A Case Study of a Believer with Authority*, 61-62, 88.

44. Lewis Drummond, 221.

45. John A. MacMillan, "The Family Altar," *AW*, May 5, 1945, 130.

46. John A. MacMillan, *The Full Gospel Adult Sunday School Quarterly*, Dec. 23, 1934, 36.

47. John A. MacMillan, "Go Forward!" *AW*, May 11, 1946, 290.

48. King, *A Case Study of a Believer with Authority*, 101-125, 143-145.

49. MacMillan, *The Authority of the Believer*, 23

50. John A. MacMillan, "Authority," *AW*, June 19, 1937, 386.

51. Jones, 282-283.

52. John A. MacMillan, "Broadening Sympathies," *AW*, Dec. 10, 1938, 787.

53. John A. MacMillan, "The Goodness of God," *AW*, Nov. 20, 1948, 743.

54. John A. MacMillan, *The Full Gospel Adult Sunday School Quarterly*, Oct. 15, 1939, 10.

55. See Norman Grubb, *Rees Howell Intercessor* (Ft. Washington, Penn.: Christian Literature Crusade, [1952] 1984), 221-225, 246-274.

56. Simpson, *CITB* (1992), 4:222; see also *CITB*, 2:34; *CITB*, 3:238-239; MacMillan, *The Authority of the Believer*, 11.

57. John A. MacMillan, "The Oppression of the Enemy," *AW*, June 21, 1947, 386.

58. MacMillan, *The Authority of the Believer*, 49-50; MacMillan, *Encounter with Darkness*, 87-88.

59. A comprehensive discussion of the history of binding and loosing appears in Paul L. King "The Restoration of the Doctrine of Binding and Loosing," *Alliance Academic Review 1997*, Elio Cuccaro, ed. (Camp Hill, Penn.: Christian Publications, 1997), 57-80; and the book *Binding and Loosing* by Foster and King.

60. Murray, *With Christ in the School of Prayer*, 117.

61. Spurgeon, *Faith's Checkbook*, 28; compare Chrysostom, *NPNF*, 1:11: 226.

62. D.L. Moody, cited in Mrs. Charles Cowman, *Springs in the Valley* (Minneapolis: World Wide Publications, [1939] 1968), 63; E.M. Bounds, *The Preacher and Prayer* (Grand Rapids: Zondervan, 1950), 100; Jessie Penn-Lewis, *Soul and Spirit* (Dorset, Eng.: Overcomer Literature Trust; Ft. Washington, Penn.: Christian Literature Crusade, n.d.), 5-6.

63. F.B. Meyer, *Changed by the Master's Touch* (Springdale, Penn.: Whitaker House, 1985), 134-135.

64. Montgomery, *Secrets of Victory*, 67-74; Jessie Penn-Lewis, *Prayer and Evangelism* (Dorset, Eng.: Overcomer Literature Trust, 1921), 53-62.

65. Jessie Penn-Lewis, "How To Pray for Missionaries," *AW*, June 12, 1937, 373-375; June 26, 1937, 406-407.

66. MacMillan, *The Authority of the Believer*, 38; see also pp. 40, 46, 47, 54, 69-71, 81.

67. Watchman Nee, *God's Plan and the Overcomers* (New York: Christian Fellowship Publishers, Inc., 1977), 72-77.

68. Ibid., 76.

69. Penn-Lewis, *The Warfare with Satan*, 20.

70. Foster and King, *Binding and Loosing*, 253-254, 266-267.

71. John A. MacMillan, "The Weakness of Power," *AW*, Apr. 2, 1938, 211.

72. Ibid.

73. John A. MacMillan, "Our Most Stubborn Foe," *AW*, June 27, 1942, 402.

74. John A. MacMillan, "Our Mohammedan Problem in the Philippines," *AW*, June 22, 1929, 404.

75. John A. MacMillan, "Praying Geographically," *AW*, Sept. 14, 1946, 579.

76. John A. MacMillan, "All Authority," *AW*, Mar. 2, 1940, 130.

77. MacMillan, *The Authority of the Believer*, 67-68.

78. Pierson, *Lessons in the School of Prayer*, 59-60.

79. Nee, *God's Plan and the Overcomers*, 74-75.

80. MacMillan, *The Authority of the Believer*, 60; see also John A. MacMillan, "Commanding God," *AW*, Oct. 7, 1939, 626.

81. Matthew Henry gives three different interpretations, apparently preferring the imperative interpretation ("Command Me"), but leaving room for the other possibilities. Matthew Henry, *A Commentary on the Whole Bible* (Old Tappan, N.J.: Fleming H. Revell, 1935), 4:253-254. The more recent exegetes and expositors tend to emend the passage, proposing textual changes of a character or two, or a different word division, etc., to make the clause more palatable. John D.W. Watts, *Word Biblical Commentary*, ed. David A. Hubbard and Glenn W. Barker (Waco, Tex.: Word, 1987), 25:151. Some translators soften the word by changing it "ask" rather than "command," but the word clearly means command, not ask. In fact, it is in the piel conjugation in Hebrew, which is more intensive. Some put it in the form of a question ("Will you command me?), rather than imperative. The piel imperfect can be expressed either as an imperative or a question, although the wording suggests that the imperative is more likely. The LXX translates with an imperative, showing that to be the understanding by Jewish exegetes c. 200 B.C. (ibid., 151-153).

Rawlinson (one of MacMillan's sources) in *The Pulpit Commentary* translates it as an imperative, explaining it in this way: "First learn of Me what in My designs is to be the course of human events, and then (if necessary) give me directions concerning my sons (Israel), who are the work of My hands; but do not presume to give Me directions while you are still in utter ignorance of My design. In any case remember who I am—the Maker of heaven and earth, the Creator of man, One accustomed to give directions to the angelic host." George Rawlinson, *The Pulpit Commentary: Isaiah*, H.D.M. Spence and Joseph S. Exell, eds. (Chicago: Wilcox and Follett, n.d.), 174. Barnes interprets, "This verse is designed . . . especially to show them, that instead of complaining of his designs, or of find fault with his sovereignty, it was their privilege to inquire respecting his dealings, and events. . . . The word 'command' is here to be taken rather as indicating the privilege of his people to present their desires in the language of fervent and respectful petition, and that God here indicates that he would, so to speak, allow them to direct him; that he would hear their prayers, and would conform the events of his administration to their wishes and their welfare. This is the most obvious interpretation." Alfred Barnes, *Barnes Notes on the New Testament*, Robert Frew, ed. (Grand Rapids: Baker [1851, 1884] 1985), 1:154. See also

King, *A Case Study of a Believer with Authority*, 331-334; King, *A Believer with Authority*, 231-235.

82. Charles H. Spurgeon, "True Prayer, True Power," *The New Park Street Pulpit* (Grand Rapids: Zondervan, 1964), Vol. 6, 336. For an updated revised version, see Charles H. Spurgeon, *The Power of Prayer in a Believer's Life*, Robert Hall, comp. and ed. (Lynnwood, Wash.: Emerald Books, 1993), 67.

83. Pierson, *Lessons in the School of Prayer*, 60-61.

84. Simpson, *CITB* (1992), 3:498.

85. Ibid.

86. E.M. Bounds, *Purpose in Prayer* (Chicago: Moody Press, n.d.), 24.

87. Ibid., 45.

88. G. Campbell Morgan, *The Gospel According to Matthew* (Old Tappan, N.J.: Fleming H. Revell, 1929), 233.

89. Foster and King, *Binding and Loosing*, 203.

90. Spurgeon, *Faith's Checkbook*, 172.

91. Murray, *With Christ in the School of Prayer*, 186-188.

92. E.A. Coray, "A Power of Attorney from God," *AW*, Oct. 26, 1929, 689.

93. Charles H. Spurgeon, *1000 Devotional Thoughts* (Grand Rapids: Baker, 1976), 341.

94. See Spurgeon, *Faith's Checkbook*, p. ii.

95. Simpson, *In the School of Faith*, 270.

96. MacMillan, *The Authority of the Believer*, 32, 73.

97. MacMillan, "Praying Geographically," 578.

98. John A. MacMillan, "Mount of Transfiguration," *AW*, July 21, 1934, 450.

99. John A. MacMillan, *The Full Gospel Adult Sunday School Quarterly*, Nov. 22, 1942, 19.

100. MacMillan, *The Authority of the Believer*, 73.

101. John A. MacMillan, "Fasting as an Aid to Prayer, *AW*, Mar. 4, 1950, 130.

102. MacMillan, *The Authority of the Believer*, 96.

103. John A. MacMillan, *The Full Gospel Adult Sunday School Quarterly*, May 3, 1936, 17.

PART 3

**THEOLOGICAL ISSUES OF FAITH TEACHING
AND PRACTICE**

CHAPTER 8

Faith as a Law

The controversy regarding faith as a law begins with the Scripture: "by the law of faith" (Rom. 3:27). It is evident that Scripture teaches a law of faith. The real question is, What is meant by the law of faith? Is the law of faith a rule of law, a principle/axiom of life, or a natural law of cause and effect like the law of gravity? Does God set up laws and let the world run on its own in deistic fashion? How people understand the nature of the law of faith affects their practice of faith.

CONTEMPORARY FAITH TEACHING

The contemporary faith movement interprets this Scripture to mean that God has spiritual laws that govern the universe. Copeland puts it this way: "We must understand that there are spiritual laws governing every single thing in existence. Nothing is by accident. There are laws of the world of the spirit and there are laws of the world of the natural. . . . We need to realize that the spiritual world and its laws are more powerful than the natural world and its laws. Spiritual laws give birth to physical laws. The world and the physical forces governing it were created by the power of faith—a spiritual force. . . . It is that force of faith which makes the spiritual world function."[1] The practical implication of that belief, according to contemporary faith teaching, is: "The same rule is true in prosperity. There are certain laws governing prosperity in God's Word. Faith causes them to function. . . . The success formulas in the Word of God produce results when used as directed."[2]

CRITICISM OF CONTEMPORARY FAITH TEACHING

Hanegraaff and McConnell claim that the idea of a law of faith is of secular metaphysical origin, involving the manipulation of spiritual laws, instead of trust in God.[3] The practical concern expressed by McConnell and Hanegraaff involves the proverbial "tail wagging the dog"—the tendency to maneuver laws and forces for one's own purposes and the danger of deflating God's sovereign will and inflating man's sovereignty.[4]

CLASSIC FAITH TEACHING

Development of Thought on Spiritual Laws. While recognizing the real dangers Hanegraaff and McConnell validly warn about, we must back up and ask the question, "Is the teaching that faith is a spiritual law necessarily from metaphysical cultic sources?" McConnell presupposes that because of the similarity between metaphysical New Thought and contemporary faith teaching regarding spiritual laws such teaching is *ipso facto* metaphysical. On the contrary, many evangelical holiness leaders from the nineteenth and early twentieth centuries taught a law of faith. The idea of spiritual laws corresponding to natural laws was a common theme in nineteenth-century theological writing, such as Henry Drummond's *Natural Law in the Spiritual World* and Horace Bushnell's *Nature and the Supernatural*. As a result of Sir Isaac Newton's studies of natural law and his discovery of the law of gravitation, it became common in religious circles to speak of the existence of spiritual laws as well.

As early as the seventeenth century, French mystic Jean-Nicholas Grou wrote of love as a law.[5] Prefiguring contemporary faith teaching by more than a century, Phoebe Palmer, in the Methodist tradition, indicated there are "laws which govern God's 'moral universe' just as there are laws governing the physical universe."[6] Likewise, Hannah Whitall Smith declared, "Faith is the conquering law of the universe."[7] She explained further, "Divine law is all one with natural law, only working in a higher sphere and with more unhindered power."[8] Spurgeon also preached that God established laws to "govern nature and direct providence."[9] He suggested, "Perhaps there are other forces and laws which He has arranged to bring into action just at the times when prayer also acts, laws just as fixed and forces just as natural as those which our learned theorizers have been able to discover. The wisest men know not all the laws which govern the universe."[10] J.G. Morrison, who was General Superintendent of the Church of the Nazarene in the 1930s, likewise wrote of faith as "governed by law" in his 1926 book *Achieving Faith.*[11]

Faith as a Magnetic Law of Attraction. Classic faith leaders compared the law of faith to magnetism or the law of gravity. Thomas Upham wrote in *The Life of Faith* that "Faith is the one great law of the life of holy beings—like the law of attraction, which is universal and reaches every particle of matter, however minute and however remote, it reaches and keeps in its position every moral being that is united to God as its centre."[12] Similarly, Hannah Whitall Smith called it "a Divine law, 'the law of faith,' a law as certain in its action as the law of gravitation."[13]

Faith like the Law of Lift Overcoming the Law of Gravity. Before the age of the airplane classic faith leaders also envisioned faith as the law of lift spiritually. Smith wrote, "Birds overcome the lower law of gravitation by the higher law of flight; and the soul on wings overcomes the lower law of sin and misery and bondage by the highest law of spiritual flying. The 'law of the spirit of life in Christ Jesus' must necessarily be a higher and more dominant law than the law of sin and death; therefore the soul that has mounted into this upper region of the life in Christ cannot fail to conquer and triumph."[14]

Distinguishing Natural and Supernatural Faith. As early as the fourth century, church father Cyril of Jerusalem wrote of a natural faith, in which "all that are accomplished in the world, even by those who are aliens from the Church, are accomplished by faith," a faith by which "therefore most of men's affairs are held together."[15] Yet he also distinguished this from faith "which is bestowed by Christ as a gift of grace" and is "that faith which worketh things above man."[16] Upham believed there is a law of natural faith that is similar to religious faith, but different as well: "The difference between natural faith and religious faith is a marked and a great one, and . . . it would tend to great complexity and error if they should be confounded together."[17] "Natural faith," Upham wrote, "rests upon natural things; that is to say, faith in man; in man's wisdom and man's capability. Religious faith rests upon religious things; that is to say, it is faith in God's wisdom and God's mighty resources."[18] Similarly, nearly a century later, the Pentecostal apostle of faith, Smith Wigglesworth distinguished between natural faith and supernatural faith, which is the gift of God.[19] Carrie Judd Montgomery, who published Wigglesworth's sermon on faith, also distinguished the two kinds of faith: "Now we have a natural power to exercise faith, but in order to exercise faith God-ward the blood of Jesus must cleanse us from sinful unbelief, and the power of God's Holy Spirit quicken us to believe."[20] Natural faith may be exercised by unbelievers, but supernatural faith can only be exercised by believers.

The Law of Faith as a Principle. Simmon's research demonstrates that holiness leaders also often spoke of laws in the sense of principles, rather than fixed mechanical laws.[21] Simpson wrote of the "law of faith" in this sense.[22] Referring to Romans 3:27, Simpson commented, "Faith is the law of Christianity, the vital principle of the Gospel dispensation. Paul calls it the law of faith in distinction from the law of works."[23]

The Law of the Measure of Faith. Murray wrote that receiving according to the measure of our faith (Matt. 9:29) is one of the "principal laws of the kingdom of heaven," and also that it is the "foundation law of the kingdom of grace."[24] Likewise, Simpson taught that this Scripture "was Christ's law of healing and blessing."[25] Simpson furthers applied this to healing, asserting, "The signs of healing do not follow all believers, but they follow those who believe for the signs. It is the law of the New Testament just as binding as the laws of nature and the great law of the fitness of things."[26] Spurgeon also declared of this Scripture, "It is a standing rule of the kingdom."[27] Spurgeon's interim successor, A.T. Pierson, also recognized this as a spiritual law.[28] Hannah Whitall Smith noted the negative consequences of this law, saying, "It is an inexorable rule in the spiritual life that according to our faith it is to be unto us; and of course this rule must work both ways, and therefore we may fairly expect that it will be also unto us according to our doubts."[29] Phoebe Palmer taught the same principle earlier in the century: "He cannot work where unbelief prevails, consistently with the order of his government."[30]

REFLECTIONS AND CONCLUSIONS

Faith as a Law Is Not Necessarily Metaphysical. This overview of classic faith teaching demonstrates that it is a misconception among contemporary faith critics that the idea of faith as a law is of secular metaphysical origin. These evangelical leaders did not accept metaphysical teaching, yet they used the terminology of faith as a law. Simpson clearly opposed metaphysical philosophy, making a sharp distinction and contrast between Biblical divine healing principles and Christian Science.[31] "Divine healing is not metaphysical healing," Simpson unequivocally avowed.[32] To believe in a law of faith thus can be a valid evangelical principle so long as it is not viewed in a metaphysical or deistic way.

Natural Faith Differs from Believers' Supernatural Faith. Some contemporary faith teaching fails to make a distinction between natural faith and supernatural faith, as do the classic faith leaders, and even contemporary faith forerunner Wigglesworth. Two practical-theological problems arise from this failure to distinguish. First, much teaching is thus devoted to developing and exercising one's own faith, thus relying upon self-effort, rather than viewing faith as a gift that is granted by God.

The second problem is that some contemporary faith teaching (and at least one classic faith leader) claims that anyone can use the law of faith, even unbelievers.[33] In contrast, Simpson stipulated that it is the "law of Christianity."[34] Likewise, as cited above, while Upham believed the law of faith is a universal law, he limited the operation of the law of faith to "holy beings" which are further defined as "moral beings united to God as the center," not to unbelievers.[35] I would thus conclude that Hunt correctly criticizes Pat Robertson, Kenneth Hagin, and David Yonggi Cho for teaching that unbelievers can tap into this law of faith and do great miracles.[36] Most classic faith leaders, on the contrary, do not teach this. Rather than tapping into the law of faith, I would concur with Jessie Penn-Lewis, who believed that unbelievers (and sometimes believers) exercise what she called "soul force," and with Watchman Nee, who called it "the latent power of the soul."[37]

The Law of Faith Does Not Denigrate the Sovereignty of God. Some contemporary faith teaching has given the impression that God is bound by His own laws. Some classic teaching also appears to give that impression. For instance, Simpson, coming from a Reformed heritage stressing the sovereignty of God, nonetheless wrote, "God is bound to act by our faith and our unbelief."[38] By this, however, Simpson is not saying that God is held hostage, but that God in His sovereignty has established this law by which He works and has voluntarily limited Himself to these laws, which are, in fact, a part of His nature. He explained, "Our Lord has announced this as the principle of His throne of grace, the law on which petitions will receive attention and consideration."[39] Spurgeon, also a strong advocate of the sovereignty of God, made a similar statement: "On the throne of grace, sovereignty has placed itself under bonds of love. God will do as He wills, but on the mercy seat, He is under bonds of His own making, for He has entered into covenant with Christ, and so into covenant with His chosen."[40] Spurgeon further noted, "Prayer . . . is coercing the universe, binding the laws of God themselves in fetters, constraining the High and Holy One to listen to the will of His poor but favoured creature-man."[41]

Although some teachers in the contemporary faith movement seem to indicate that believers can dictate to God, at least one, Kenneth Hagin, acknowledges that this is not so: "You cannot make the Spirit of God do anything. Instead of using the Spirit, let the Spirit use you."[42]

I would conclude that if we speak of God being bound or limited by our faith, that we need also to be careful to give these caveats that Spurgeon and Simpson assert, or we are in danger of denigrating the sovereignty of God or being misunderstood. Murray added an important thought that "faith is not a logical reasoning which ought to in some way oblige God to act according to His promises," but rather a confident "attitude of the child who honours His Father, who counts upon His love."[43]

I would agree with the classic leaders, as mentioned above, that on the basis of Matthew 9:29, unbelief can hinder God's will being accomplished. To clarify this, I would distinguish as a general principle, as do grammarians, between the *inclinational* will of God (*thelema*—desire) and the *intentional* will of God (*boule*—determination).[44] God's *boule*, His intentional, determined will, cannot be limited by man's faith or lack thereof. However, God's *thelema*—what He desires to accomplish— works in synergy with man. It should be noted that this distinction is not a hard and fast rule in all biblical passages, but a general principle or theological construct.

So on one hand, God has ordained the law of faith to involve man's action of prayer and faith, not to manipulate God, but as the means of accomplishing His *thelema*. Bounds counseled, "Not that prayer has in it some talismanic force, nor that it is a fetish, but that it moves God to do things that it nominates. Prayer has no magic, no potent charm in itself, but is only all potent because it gets the Omnipotent God to grant its request."[45] On the other hand, we must recognize that God is ultimately sovereign and that His *boule* will be done regardless of man's response. Chambers thus appropriately warned that believers have a tendency to "tie God up in His own laws and allow Him no free will."[46]

The Danger of Making the Law of Faith a Mechanistic Formula. If someone knows about the law of gravity, but does not understand the law of lift, that person may come to the conclusion that the law of gravity is a formula that cannot be over-ridden, thereby allowing for no exceptions. But, as mentioned above, Spurgeon tells us that there are laws we do not know about. We cannot presume that we know all of God's laws, because, as God says, "As the heavens are higher than the earth, so are my ways higher than your ways and my thoughts than your thoughts" (Isa. 55:9, NIV). Hannah Whitall Smith and Simpson, as noted above, recognized that there are higher laws that transcend other laws.[47] Carter likewise recognized: "Even in miracle, God does not actually break His Laws, but uses other laws to remove the cause as well as the effect. I take it that God's law, if law at all, is a truth; and of course God cannot break a truth; for that would be destroying Himself, who *is truth*."[48] Practically speaking, then, no law can be touted as absolute without exceptions. We must not say, for instance, that it is absolutely, always, God's will to heal, and if healing does not come it must be man's sin or lack of faith. Yes, as a general principle, it is God's will to heal; and, yes, sometimes lack of healing may be due to sin or lack of faith, but these are not hard-and-fast rules.

Final Conclusions. None of these classic faith writers were in any way associated with metaphysical cults. These writers speak of spiritual laws, not metaphysically or deistically, but of spiritual principles of life by which God operates or consistent spiritual patterns of working that are designated as laws. On the other hand, God is not controlled by these laws as metaphysical as some contemporary faith teachers seem to imply, but God controls these laws. Contemporary faith teachers need to be careful of the language they use and the practical implications they draw when they speak of faith as a law. Anti-faith critics need to understand that the concept of faith as a law can be validly taught without implying a deistic or metaphysical connection.

---

1. Kenneth Copeland, *The Laws of Prosperity* (Ft. Worth, Tex.: Kenneth Copeland Publications, 1974), 18-20, cited in McConnell, 171.

2. Ibid.

3. Hanegraaff, 73-85; McConnell, 172-173.

4. McConnell, 172-173; Hanegraaff, 105-127.

5. Jean-Nicholas Grou, cited in *AW*, July 2, 1952, 424; Jean-Nicholas Grou, "On Being Truly Spiritual," *AW*, Sept. 10, 1952, 592.

6. Raser, 185.

7. Hannah Whitall Smith, *The Unselfishness of God* (Princeton, N.J.: Littlebrook Publishing Co., 1987), 190; Smith, *The Unselfishness of God and How I Discovered It*, 252.

8. H.W. Smith, *Living Confidently in God's Love*, 258.

9. Spurgeon, *Spiritual Warfare in a Believer's Life* (Lynnwood, Wash.: Emerald Books, 1993), 168.

10. Charles H. Spurgeon, "Conditions of Power in Prayer," *Metropolitan Tabernacle Pulpit*, Vol. 19 (1873), 176. For updated revised version, see Spurgeon, *The Power of Prayer in a Believer's Life*, 114.

11. Simmons, *E.W. Kenyon*, 290.

12. Upham, *The Life of Faith*, 238.

13. H.W. Smith, *The Unselfishness of God and How I Discovered It*, 252; see also Smith, *Living Confidently in God's Love*, 260-261.

14. H.W. Smith, *The Christian's Secret*, 168.

15. Cyril of Jerusalem, "Catechetical Lectures," Lecture V:3; *NFPF*, 2nd Series, Vol. VII, 29.

16. Ibid., Lecture V:11, *NFPF*, 2nd Series, Vol. VII, 31-32.

17. Upham, *The Life of Faith*, 28.

18. Ibid., 36.

19. Smith Wigglesworth, "Faith," *Triumphs of Faith*, Nov. 1922, 249.

20. Montgomery, *Secrets of Victory*, 22.

21. Simmons, *E.W. Kenyon*, 155-156.

22. Simpson, *The Gospel of Healing*, 68.

23. Simpson, *A Larger Christian Life*, 10-11.

24. Murray, *Divine Healing*, 22; Murray, *The Blood of the Cross*, 54.

25. Simpson, *A Larger Christian Life*, 137.

26. Simpson, *Christ in the Bible: Luke* (n.d.), 182.

27. Spurgeon, *The Power of Prayer in a Believer's Life*, 110.

28. Pierson, *The Acts of the Holy Spirit*, 100.

29. H.W. Smith, *The Christian's Secret*, 83; see also H.W. Smith, *The Unselfishness of God*, 190; H.W. Smith, *The Unselfishness of God and How I Discovered It*, 252, 259, 262.

30. Raser, 185.

31. Simpson, *The Gospel of Healing*, 185-191.

32. A.B. Simpson, *The Fourfold Gospel* (Harrisburg, Penn.: Christian Publications, n.d.), 48; see also Carter, *Faith Healing Reviewed*, 5.

33. Simmons notes that Nazarene leader J. G. Morrison also held this position, showing that Kenyon was not the only one in the holiness camp with this belief. Simmons, *E.W. Kenyon*, 290.

34. Simpson, *A Larger Christian Life*, 10.

35. Upham, *The Life of Faith*, 238.

36. Dave Hunt, *The Berean Call*, Sept. 1995, 2.

37. Penn-Lewis, *Life in the Spirit* (Dorset, Eng.: Overcomer Literature Trust, 1910), 62; Jessie Penn-Lewis, *Soul and Spirit* (Dorset, Eng.: Overcomer Literature Trust, n.d.), 62, 68-70, 77-79; Watchman Nee, *The Latent Power of the Soul* (New York: Christian Fellowship Publishers, Inc., 1972).

38. Simpson, *A Larger Christian Life*, 11.

39. Simpson, *The Life of Prayer* (Camp Hill, Penn.: Christian Publications, 1989), 60.

40. Spurgeon, *The Power of Prayer in a Believer's Life*, 27.

41. Spurgeon, "True Prayer, True Power," *The New Park Street Pulpit*, Vol. 6, 337.

42. Hagin, *The Art of Prayer*, 74-75.

43. Murray, *Divine Healing*, 42.

44. See Joseph H. Thayer, *Thayer's Greek-English Lexicon of the New Testament* (Grand Rapids: Baker, 1977), 104, 286; Gerhard Kittel, ed., *Theological Dictionary of the New Testament* (Grand Rapids: Eerdmans, 1964, 1965), 1:629ff; 3:44ff.

45. Bounds, *Prayer and Praying Men* 148.

46. Chambers, *The Place of Help*, 91.

47. Smith, *The Christian's Secret*, 168.

48. Russell Kelso Carter, *The Atonement for Sin and Sickness* (Boston, New York: Willard Tract Repository, 1884), 114-115, cited in Simmons, *E.W. Kenyon*, 157.

CHAPTER 9

Faith as a Force

The concept of faith as a force has developed from an understanding of the role of forces and energy in the Scriptures, as well as understanding faith as a law. The Biblical idea of force is wrapped up primarily in two New Testament Scriptures:

> *From the days of John the Baptist until now, the kingdom of heaven has been forcefully advancing, and forceful men lay hold of it*
> (Matt. 11:12, NIV).

> *For our struggle is not against flesh and blood, but against the rulers, against the authorities, against the powers of this dark world and against the spiritual forces of evil in the heavenly realms*
> (Eph. 6:12, NIV).

Ephesians 6:12 recognizes the reality of demonically-inspired forces. In Greek, the word "forces" does not appear, but most translations insert the word to further explicate the text. The demonic entities are thus universally understood as forces. Logically and theologically, there are spiritual forces of righteousness that oppose the spiritual forces of evil.

Matthew 11:12 has been translated in a variety of ways. Past translations have conveyed the idea that the church has had violence done to it. However, as translated by the *New International Version*, scholars today generally understand this passage to mean that the church itself is exercising force. Young studied the Hebrew roots of this Scripture, concluding, "Jesus viewed the kingdom of heaven as an active force in the world that was energized by God's power."[1] According to Young, the ancient rabbis conceived of "the leaven of the Torah" as a force.[2] Chrysostom also made reference to Matthew 11:12 in reference to the force of using the believer's authority of binding and loosing spiritual forces.[3]

Merriam-Webster's Collegiate Dictionary defines force as "strength or energy brought to bear."[4] Most translations do not use the term "force," but the Greek word which best corresponds to the idea is *energeia*, frequently translated as "working." In secular Greek "the word group is used of cosmic or physical forces at work in man or the world around. In the OT and NT ενεργεια [*energeia*], and in the NT the verb ενεργειν [*energein*], are used almost exclusively for the work of divine or demonic powers."[5] In Colossians 2:12, the phrase "faith in the working (*pistis tes energeias*) of God" could thus be literally translated as "faith in the divine energy or force of God." In James 5:16, "The effective [*energoumene*] prayer of a righteous man can accomplish much" could be translated "the divine energy or force of prayer."

CONTEMPORARY FAITH TEACHING

The idea that faith is a creative force or power is a common concept in contemporary faith teaching. Hagin likens faith to muscular force, teaching, "Faith is a force. To build up faith muscles, you have to use your faith against something. . . . You have got to put the force of faith against that test."[6] Frederick Price also teaches that "faith force" strengthens spiritual muscles to believe for greater things: "Faith is a force. It has power inherent within it. If you will think of faith as a force, you will realize that it can be developed in ability to push or move an object."[7] Copeland writes: "Faith is a power force. It is a conductive force. It will move things. Faith will change things. Faith will change the human body. It will change the human heart. Faith will change circumstances . . . The force of faith is released by words. Faith-filled words put the law of the Spirit of life into operation."[8] Capps takes this thought farther, declaring the tongue "a creative force": "Words governed by spiritual law become spiritual forces working for you. Idle words work against you."[9] To Capps, it is not merely faith that is a force released by words, but speaking faith-filled words have creative force within themselves.

CRITICISM OF CONTEMPORARY FAITH TEACHING

McConnell considers the concept of faith as a force heretical, in that it makes God an "impersonal force that must do man's bidding."[10] He compares it to learning "how to manipulate 'the good side of the Force'" through mind control in the *Star Wars* movies, claiming that Word of faith teaching trains "how to manipulate the Faith god with positive confession."[11] Hanegraaff, drawing upon McConnell, also condemns this concept as metaphysical and cultic, claiming that it is derived from New Thought metaphysics.[12] To them, the idea of forces that correspond to laws, like "the law of attraction," is anti-biblical metaphysics. They view the idea of faith as a force as an impersonal force that manipulates and binds God, making man sovereign by his words of faith.

CLASSIC FAITH TEACHING ON FORCE

Since the anti-faith critics condemn the idea of faith as a force, it is important to know classic evangelical teaching regarding force. Is it really and solely a heretical metaphysical concept as McConnell and Hanegraaff claim? Or is it Scriptural? Does believing in faith as a force necessitate a mechanistic and manipulative view of the force of faith?

Most of the classic faith leaders were knowledgeable of the original languages of the Bible, so they likely associated *energeia* with spiritual force, as discussed above. The nineteenth century evangelical idea of forces in the spiritual realm is derived additionally from an understanding of spiritual laws, as discussed in the previous section. Where there are spiritual laws, they believed, there are spiritual forces corresponding to those laws. Upham wrote of the law of faith being like the "law of attraction," which today we would call "magnetic force."[13] In was during that period of time in the 1800s that great discoveries were being made about magnetic forces. He spoke of the "energy of faith," which differs from natural energy, and also distinguished natural faith, which can be expressed through unbelievers, and "religious faith," which can only be exercised by believers.[14] Upham's "energy of faith" corresponds closely to the Greek phrase *pistis tes energeia* (Col. 2:12), and even may have been derived from it, as Upham would have been familiar with the Bible in the original languages.

Spurgeon also recognized the believer's authority in this Scripture: "You may force your way through anything with the leverage of prayers. . . . The kingdom of heaven still suffereth violence and the violent taketh it by force. Take care that ye work away with the mighty implement of prayer, and nothing can stand against you."[15] A.T. Pierson, Spurgeon's interim successor, similarly affirmed, "No more wonderful fact confronts us in our actual experience of contact with this universe of God than the power He has given to man of commanding and controlling these eternal forces. They all move in obedience to certain conditions or in certain channels or modes of activity, which we call 'laws.'"[16] Similarly, Henry Drummond, the friend of Moody, made comparisons between what he calls "Spiritual Life" or "Vitality" and natural forces, saying, "vitality has much in common with such forces as magnetism and electricity."[17] However, he also made important distinctions: "Spiritual Life is not something outside ourselves. . . . This localization of Life in the individual is precisely the point where Vitality differs from the other forces of nature. . . . Spiritual Life is not a visit from a force, but a resident tenant in the soul. . . . Spiritual life is not an ordinary form of energy or force."[18] Drummond also wrote of spiritual laws and forces in his book *The Changed Life*.[19] Simpson would appear to make reference to this concept of Drummond's when he wrote:

> There is a stronger law than the law of gravitation—my own life and will. So through the operation of this higher law—the law of my vitality—I defy the law of gravitation, and lift my hand and hold it above its former resting place and move it at my will. The law of vitality has made me free from the law of gravitation.
>
> Precisely so the indwelling life of Christ Jesus, operating with the power of the law lifts me above and counteracts the power of sin in my fallen nature. This is the secret of sanctification. It is not so much the expulsion of sin, as the incoming of the Holy Spirit, which has broken the control which sin formerly exercised, lifting me into an entirely new sphere of holy life and victory.[20]

God as a Force. The concept of God as a spiritual force may be traced back at least as far as the writings of Guyon, who referred to God Himself as "The Central Force."[21] Among the classic faith leaders, Bounds wrote, "To a prayerful man God is present in realized force. . . . The driving power, the conquering force in God's cause is God Himself."[22] For F.B. Meyer, to come into contact with God is to encounter a magnetic force, thus he prayed, "Human souls which touch Thee become magnetized, charged with a spiritual force which the world can neither gainsay nor resist. Oh, let me touch Thee! Let me dwell in unbroken contact with Thee, that out of Thee successive tides of Divine energy may pass out into and through my emptied and eager spirit, flowing, but never ebbing, and lifting me into a life of blessed ministry."[23] This was a common analogy among classic faith leaders, as Murray, Spurgeon, Pierson, Penn-Lewis, Simpson, Carmichael, Hannah Whitall Smith, and Tozer all viewed God as a force in some sense.

The entire Trinity was viewed by classic faith leaders as a force. Murray and Tozer spoke of Christ Himself as "a living force."[24] Tozer, perhaps drawing upon Guyon's idea of God as the "central force" combined with the concept of centripetal force, also referred to Christ as "this mysterious Presence and Force that holds all things together."[25] Spurgeon considered Jesus the one ultimate magnetic force.[26] Penn-Lewis and Simpson compared Jesus as a force of power.[27]

Spurgeon wrote of spiritual forces likened to an electrical current, saying that "the influences of the Spirit of God are a force most spiritual."[28] Pierson considered the Holy Spirit as "the one subduing, all-controlling Force, Power or Energy," likening the Spirit's force to electricity or magnetism.[29] He further developed Spurgeon's thought, saying, "The Spirit of God has His chosen channels and methods; and this Supreme Force of the universe offers Himself to serve man for the ends of the Work of God. Is it not still true, and may it not with reverence be said, 'Obey the law of the divine force and the force obeys you?'"[30] Many other classic faith leaders recognized the Holy Spirit as a force including Simpson, Chambers, Carmichael, Hannah Whitall Smith, and Welsh revival leader Evan Roberts.[31]

The Human Spirit as a Force. Penn-Lewis and Nee, drawing from nineteenth-century British scholar Pember, wrote of a "spirit force" in opposition to "soul force" or "psychic force."[32] Penn-Lewis said that the upward move of "spirit victory" is "the overcoming force of the life of Christ in your spirit."[33] She defined "spirit force" as "the energy of the Holy Spirit" and "the power of God Himself as 'Spirit' brought into action through the spiritual man."[34] In other words, being led by the Holy Spirit will cause one's own human spirit to act as a force. Simpson warned that spirit force may be either good or evil.[35] Chambers also devoted an entire chapter to spirit force in his book *Biblical Psychology*.[36] He also wrote that Paul exercised "an amazing force of spirit" in his teaching.[37] Bounds wrote of the gravitational pull of magnetic "forces of godliness" that draw people to Christ.[38]

Prayer as a Force. The concept of prayer as a force dates back in antiquity to Chrysostom in the fourth century. He considered the Lord's Prayer as a force, especially the declaration, "Thy will be done on earth, as it is in heaven."[39] In the seventeenth century, Scougal regarded meditative prayer that flows from love and adoration of God as a force that upholds the soul and propels it toward God. He considered this "the great secret of devotion and one of the most powerful instruments of the divine life."[40] Especially in conjunction with Holy Communion, through contemplative prayer, the soul makes "its most powerful sallies toward heaven and assault it with a holy and acceptable force."[41] Also in the seventeenth century, Grou declared, "Concerted and united prayer . . . creates a force that God will not resist."[42] Similarly, nineteenth-century mystic Therese de Lisieux made a personal declaration, "For me, prayer means launching out of the heart towards God; it means lifting up one's eyes, quite simply, to Heaven, a cry of grateful love from the crest of joy on the trough of despair; its vast, supernatural force which opens out my heart, and binds me close to Jesus."[43]

As mentioned above, Spurgeon also regarded prayer as a force.[44] Bounds taught that not only is God Himself a force, but also believing prayer: "Prayer puts God in full force in the world. . . . Prayer is not a negation. It is a positive force. . . . Prayer puts God in the matter with commanding force."[45] For Bounds, the "wrestling quality of prayer . . . is not an impulse of energy, not a mere earnestness of soul; it is an inwrought force, a faculty implanted and aroused by the Holy Spirit."[46] Determination in prayer, affirmed Murray, will make "the morning watch itself a mighty force in strengthening our character and giving us boldness to resist self-indulgence."[47]

Resembling Scougal's language, Simpson maintained, "Daniel's heart was filled with God's love for his work and kingdom, and his prayers were the mightiest forces of his time. . . . Desire . . . is a necessary element in all spiritual forces. It is one of the secrets of effectual prayer. . . . There is no factor in prayer more effectual than love. If we are intensely interested in an object or an individual, our petitions become like living forces."[48] For Simpson, "Prayer is not only a pleading but a force, a conscious power beating against the forces of evil and claiming their defeat."[49] Moody's associate R.A. Torrey and Samuel Chadwick, who was Principal of Cliff College, Sheffield, England, a friend of Pierson and mentor of evangelist Leonard Ravenhill, both referred to prayer as a force.[50] Penn-Lewis, Nee and S.D. Gordon also called prayer a "spirit force."[51]

The Word of God as a Force. As mentioned earlier, the concept of the Scriptures as a force is very ancient, going back to Jewish rabbis regarding "the leaven of the Torah as a force." Quoting John 15:7, Spurgeon referred to the Word of God as a force: "We must hear Jesus speak if we expect Him to hear us speak. . . . Moreover, what is heard must remain, must live in us, and must abide in our character as a force and a power."[52] For Spurgeon, "In us truth must be a living force, an active energy, and an indwelling reality."[53] He also proclaimed that the word of God spoken from our lips is an electrical force like lightning.[54] Similarly, C&MA leader MacMillan wrote, "The sayings of God have in them a penetrating force which no human philosophy possesses. The preacher who studies the Word on his knees, humbly looking for the illumination from on high, will not himself be deceived, and he will have unusual power with men."[55] Tozer, a colleague of MacMillan, in his classic book *The Pursuit of God*, likewise considered the voice of God as "the most powerful force in nature, indeed the only force in nature, for all energy is here only because the power-filled Word is being spoken."[56]

With this background, it is not surprising that Bosworth and Wigglesworth, two classic leaders involved with the Pentecostal movement and popular with the contemporary faith movement, also considered Scripture as a force. Bosworth wrote, "The Word is lifeless until faith is breathed into it on your lips. Then it becomes a supernatural force."[57] Wigglesworth asserted, "His word had creative force."[58]

Love as a Force. Since mystics understood God as a force, it is natural that His qualities and character would be understood as forces emanating from Him. The concept of love as a force is an ancient one. Medieval mystic William of St. Thierry wrote of faith, hope and love as a "trinity of powers."[59] Scougal referred to love as "a secret force and energy" that transforms the soul.[60] Boardman, reminiscent of William of St. Thierry, wrote in 1858 that faith, hope, and love are "abiding forces": "They are also the great permanent forces wrought and employed by the Spirit of God for the development and progress of the divine life in the soul, and for its outraying influence."[61] Expanding the notion of Scougal, he held that they are the "forces of the life of God in the soul."[62] Like Boardman and William, theologian Herbert Lockyer speaks of the triad of faith, hope, and love as "three abiding forces."[63]

As mentioned above, Simpson understood love to be the most vital factor in making prayer a living force. In other words, the force of love motivates the force of prayer. In similar fashion, Carmichael made reference to "the forces of love" acting as a flowing current of water removing hindrances to the fullness of God.[64] This, too, sounds very much like Scougal's thought.

Faith as a Force. With this kaleidoscope understanding of spiritual forces, it becomes a natural progression to view faith as a force. If God Himself is a force, then as Simpson described it, faith emanates as a force from the character of God, from His omnipotence, as "one of the attributes of God Himself."[65] This appears to be an echo of Clement of Alexandria, who wrote, "Faith is a power of God."[66] Murray also considered faith as "an active power" that is "the breaking out of the divine life within."[67] Boardman, who influenced Simpson, was perhaps the earliest known writer (apart from William of St. Thierry) to include faith specifically as one of the spiritual forces, saying, "Faith is the all inclusive gift of God, as the great force for sustaining and developing the Christian life."[68]

Spurgeon is the next known advocate of the concept, declaring faith is "an all-prevailing force."[69] Again, he proclaimed, "Faith is the great force which is needed by those whose principal work is to overcome sin."[70] In words reminiscent of Scougal and Boardman, Spurgeon proclaimed, "Faith is the hand of the soul, and without it we cannot grasp eternal things. . . . for faith is of the very essence of spiritual life."[71] This last clause sounds very much like Clement of Alexandria's concept of faith as a first principle or essence. According to Spurgeon, "God gives salvation to our faith" and "has taken possession of the inner battery and can send the sacred current of His life to every part of our nature."[72] Such faith "creates peace and joy."[73] "Faith is full of inventions," claimed Spurgeon.[74]

Hannah Whitall Smith echoed Spurgeon, saying, "Faith is an all-conquering force. I believe it is the creative force of the universe. It is the higher law that controls all the lower laws beneath it. What looks like a miracle is simply the working of the higher controlling law of faith."[75] She also called faith "an active energy."[76] Murray, in his classic book *With Christ in the School of Prayer*, combined the forces of prayer and faith together (similar to Bounds), comparing them to the mighty force of water being released from a dam: "Real faith can never be disappointed. It knows how, just as water, to exercise the irresistable power it can have, must be gathered up and accumulated, until the stream can come down in full force, there must often be a heaping up of prayer until God sees that the measure is full, and the answer comes."[77]

Simpson seems to make the most use of the concept of faith as a force, declaring that it is "one of the attributes of God Himself": "There is no doubt that while the soul is exercising, through the power of God, the faith that commands what God commands, a mighty force is operating at that moment upon the obstacle."[78] Simpson's understanding of faith as a force is probably most influenced by Spurgeon, whom he frequently quoted, and Boardman, whose book *The Higher Christian Life* had a strong impact on Simpson's experience and understanding of the crisis of sanctification. For Simpson, like Spurgeon, "faith is a creative force that produces effects and operations of the most important character . . . a resistless force, a divine power that actually moved upon second causes and compelled their obedience. . . . . It is a spiritual force that God requires us to cooperate with, to enter into, to use with Him and for His glory. The mighty forces of nature must have man's cooperation or they are lost and wasted. Electricity goes to waste if we do not constrain it to our will and use it according to its own laws. Even so, by our faith we must take hold of God's omnipotence and actually use it, with deep humility but also with holy confidence, for the carrying through of His own great purposes!"[79]

Likewise, Cowman, who frequently quoted both Spurgeon and Simpson, admonished, "Use all the forces of faith."[80] Others who taught faith as a force and were probably influenced by Simpson include MacMillan and Charles Price. For MacMillan, the "command of faith" in the name of Christ is "the dynamic force that controls the universe."[81] Charles Price, who opposed some of the teachings of the contemporary faith movement, nonetheless wrote: "Faith is the root force from which all things of God spring."[82] Price, a few pages later in the same book, wrote that Simpson had received spiritual revelation.[83] He may have also been alluding to Spurgeon, who also claimed that faith "touches the springs of action,"[84] and to the teachings of the early Church Fathers that faith is one of the "first principles." Amy Carmichael asserts that we "must learn to prevail by force of faith."[85]

Summary of Classic Faith Teaching on Faith and Force. The metaphors used to describe spiritual forces abound among these classic leaders. To summarize, classic evangelical writers conceive of the laws of spiritual forces in these ways: 1) an electrical current (Spurgeon, S.D. Gordon, Drummond, Simpson, Pierson), 2) force of gravity (Simpson, Drummond, Smith), 3) magnetic force (Simpson, Upham, Spurgeon, Bounds, Pierson), 4) an energy force (Smith, Spurgeon, Upham, Drummond, Penn-Lewis, Nee), 5) an initiating force like a spring (Spurgeon, Charles Price) or as a creative force (Spurgeon, Smith, Simpson, Bosworth, Wigglesworth), 6) life forces (Murray, Boardman, Spurgeon, Bosworth), 7) a water current (Smith, Murray, Carmichael), 8) a wind (Carmichael), 9) an overcoming or controlling force (Smith, Bounds, Pierson, Penn-Lewis), 10) spirit force (Penn-Lewis, Nee, Chambers, S.D. Gordon), 11) centripetal force (Tozer). Faith, in particular, is viewed as the force of an electric current (Spurgeon, Simpson), a creative force (Spurgeon, Smith, Simpson), the force of a water current (Murray), an energy force (Smith), and the force of a spring (Spurgeon, Charles Price).

REFLECTIONS AND CONCLUSIONS

Contemporary Force of Faith Is Derived from Classic Teaching. It is obvious through this study that contemporary teaching on faith as a force is derived from classic evangelical faith teaching. Thus McConnell's and Hanegraaff's claim that the concept of faith as a force is derived from New Thought metaphysics, and is thus heretical and cultic, is blatantly false. This does not mean, however, that everything taught by contemporary faith teachers about faith as a force is valid. It should be noted that there are dissimilarities as well as similarities between classic and contemporary faith teaching.

First, we note the similarities. A comparison between Simpson (representing classic faith teaching) and Copeland (representing contemporary faith teaching) shows a remarkable correspondence:

SIMPSON:	COPELAND:
Faith is an actual spiritual force. It is no doubt one of the attributes of God Himself.[87]	Faith is a power force. It is a tangible force. It is a conductive force.[86] This force originates from God, out of His unlimited heart.[88]
Would it seem strange if this law of faith were found to be the principle of the spiritual world as it is of the natural— the underlying force that holds it together.[90]	It is the force of gravity which makes the law of gravity work. . . . It is this force of faith which makes the laws of the spirit world function.[89]
The faith of God must mean the faith that God Himself exercises.[91]	The world was born out of the force of faith that was resident inside the being of God.[92]
Indeed it seems faith is the principle upon which God Himself acts, the secret of His power in creating matter and in commanding the events of providence.[94]	Faith is God's source of power.[93]
God is bound to act upon this principle, and He cannot justly acknowledge our plea if we do not present it according to the prescribed rule.[96]	God cannot do anything for you apart or separate from faith.[95]

In fact, the two are so similar, it would appear that Copeland's teaching is a concise summary of Simpson's teaching. So it can be observed that contemporary faith leaders like Copeland are not teaching a new maverick doctrine, but one derived from and quite similar to classic faith teaching. However, it can also be observed that though they are similar, Copeland's presentation is more simplistic, thus more prone to misunderstanding and error. Recognizing the similarities, we can now identify the dissimilarities.

Faith Is Not an Impersonal Force. It is important to note that the classic faith writers did not believe God is an impersonal force, but a "living force," a force *who* is a living personality. The Holy Spirit is not an "it" as taught by heretical groups like Jehovah's Witnesses. For instance, A.J. Gordon made reference to the Holy Spirit as both a divine person and a "divine force" like an electrical current.[97] Murray cautioned that the work of the Spirit of God is "no blind force."[98] While Spurgeon called the Spirit a force, he also avowed that He is not a mere influence.[99] Chambers also wrote that the Holy Spirit is an influence, but He is a person as well.[100] Tozer also affirmed that the Holy Spirit is not an impersonal force: "The Holy Spirit is a living Person and should be treated as a person. We must never think of Him as a blind energy nor as an impersonal force."[101]

Simpson likewise disavowed that faith is an impersonal force: "It is not a mysterious current which flows into one body from another. . . . Such an influence is repudiated by all who act as true ministers of divine healing."[102] For Simpson, faith is an attribute of God Himself. "Divine healing is not metaphysical healing," which Simpson explains as healing "by mental force."[103] So Simpson distinguishes between forces that are from God, which are living and a part of the very nature of God, and "mental force," which is not from God, but from self.

For these writers faith is not an impersonal universal binding force. Although contemporary faith leaders would probably claim they do not believe God is an impersonal force, their language makes the force of faith appear mechanistic. So if faith originates in God, and faith is a force from a law to which God is bound, then faith and God appear to become impersonal forces.

Unbelievers Cannot Tap into the Biblical Force of Faith. Spurgeon's statement "faith in its natural form is an all-prevailing force" by itself sounds very much like some contemporary faith teaching that faith is a force that non-believers as well as believers can tap into. However,

Spurgeon qualified his statement by adding, "God gives salvation to our faith." In other words, natural faith needs to be saved, redeemed, transformed. Natural faith in and of itself is inadequate. Similarly, Upham said that faith is the basis of all great, active enterprises, but that is in the realm of natural faith.[104] Hanegraaff's charge against the concept that unbelievers can tap into the force of faith is legitimate. Many of these contemporary teachers do not discern the sharp difference between natural and supernatural faith.

Some "Force of Faith" Is Soulish Power, Not God's Force. Penn-Lewis warned against developing mind power, or power within oneself, saying that "your constructive forces, Faith power, or your Inspirational forces" are all counterfeits of spirit force.[105] She quoted Murray saying, "The greatest danger the religion of the Church or the individual has to dread is the inordinate activity of the soul, with its power of mind or will."[106]

Some contemporary faith leaders who teach that the force of faith can be used by believers and non-believers alike have failed to discern between the soulish use of faith as a force, which the old writers such as Spurgeon called "natural faith," and the Spirit-led use of faith as a force. Much of what is called developing one's faith, or using the law of faith as a force, may in reality be soul-force rather than spirit force. Contrary to some contemporary faith teaching, Simpson distinguished between true faith in Christ as a spiritual force and faith as a psychical or physical force that can be exercised by a Hindu, which involves believing a lie.[107]

Also contrary to some contemporary teaching, Penn-Lewis made clear, "The Spirit of God does not use the nature forces of the soul for the carrying out of the purposes of God, though He does use the faculties of the soul in a consecrated man, as a vehicle for expression of the life of God."[108] Penn-Lewis further warned against soul forces being called "divine forces" and cloaked in religious language.[109] Those who teach that unbelievers can use their faith are failing to distinguish soul force and spirit force. Soul force, or, "the development of the 'psychic faculty,'" she cautioned, "is the drawing out into action some of the capabilities lying dormant in the 'natural man.'" Her admonitions are just as practical and relevant, if not more so, today: "In 'warfare' against the Devil himself, there can be an actual development of soul-force, unless there is a deep work of the Cross continually applied to the old Adam life, with a real life-union with the Risen Lord by the Holy Ghost. Soul-force versus Spirit-force is the battleground today."[110] Watchman Nee, drawing on Penn-Lewis and Murray, likewise recognized prayer as a

ONLY BELIEVE

spirit force, but also warned against prayer that uses psychic or soul force rather than spirit force.[111]

Words Are Not the Containers of the Force of Faith. In contrast to contemporary faith teachers, classic faith writers do not believe that words are the containers of the force of faith, nor that those words can create reality. For Boardman, "Faith [is] evidencing to him the invisible realities of the present."[112] Words of faith do not create reality, but give evidence of already existing realities. Wigglesworth, who influenced contemporary faith teaching, taught that God's Word had creative force. Some contemporary faith teaching, though, fails to distinguish that Wigglesworth taught not that *man's* words are a creative force, but rather *God's* words. The danger of attributing such powers to man's words is the use of soul force, or talismanic powers. Chambers warned against using the name of Jesus as a magic word.[113] Tozer likewise admonished against ascribing magical power to words.[114] These classic leaders make it clear that it is faith imparted by God that creates, not man's faith or his words of faith.

Faith Is Not a Force That Binds God. Faith is not a mechanistic force that operates independently of God, nor can it bind God. Grou, as mentioned above, declared that prayer creates a force that God *will not* resist.[115] It is vital to note he says that God *will not* resist, not that God *cannot* resist. In the comparison of Simpson and Copeland above, Copeland simply says, "God cannot do anything for you apart or separate from faith," whereas the gist of Simpson's statement is that God cannot do anything that logically contradicts His nature. This is a crucial difference in understanding that Copeland fails to acknowledge.

CLOSING REFLECTIONS AND CONCLUSIONS

To the ears of many theologians, to speak of God or faith as a "force" sounds like it is depersonalizing God and mechanizing the operation of the Christian life. Like many other faith concepts, there is a counterfeit in metaphysical thought or the possibility of misuse or soul force. However, as mentioned earlier, the idea that faith can exercise creative power finds its roots in the Reformation teaching of Luther.[116] Classic evangelical leaders refer to faith, prayer, love, Scripture, and even God Himself as a force. To say that faith is a force is not inappropriate unless it is considered an independent force that operates apart from God and can be exercised by unbelievers as well as believers.

FAITH AS A FORCE

As a practical faith application, I would conclude that a healthy faith that is strong and sound understands that God is a Person exercising spiritual force. His Word, love, prayer, and faith are all forces that extend out of relationship with Him. When our spirit is in touch with the Holy Spirit, it acts as a spirit force through prayer, Spirit-enlivening of the Word, and the exercise of faith, a faith that comes from God and is a part of His omnipotent character. However, we must be careful not to use our own soul power as a force, because it is not divine or pure, but is human, corrupted and tainted by sin, the world and Satan. Faith as a force should never be used to manipulate people, circumstances or God. It is not a magical or mechanistic formula. Tozer's counsel against formulas is appropriate here: "God wants you to get your eyes away from the gifts, the formulas, the techniques. He wants your gaze to be on the Giver, Christ Himself."[117]

---

1. Brad Young, *Jesus the Jewish Theologian* (Peabody, Mass.: Hendrickson, 1995), 49.

2. Ibid., 79-80.

3. Chrysostom, *Homilies on Timothy*, Homily 10," *NPNF*, 1:13:516-518.

4. *Merriam-Webster's Collegiate Dictionary*, 445.

5. Kittel, 2:652.

6. Kenneth E. Hagin, *Must Christians Suffer?* (Tulsa, Okla.: Kenneth Hagin Ministries, 1982), 31.

7. Frederick K.C. Price, *Faith, Foolishness or Presumption?* (Tulsa, Okla.: Harrison House, 1979), 41, 46-47.

8. Copeland, *The Force of Faith*, 10, 16.

9. Capps, *The Tongue, a Creative Force*, 8-9.

10. McConnell, 143.

11. Ibid.; see also pp. 141-145.

12. Hanegraaff, 65-71.

13. Upham, 238.

14. Ibid., 281, 283.

15. Charles H. Spurgeon, "Golden Key of Prayer," Sermon #619, *The Metropolitan Tabernacle Pulpit*, Vol. 11 (1865), 152. For updated version, see Spurgeon, *The Power of Prayer in a Believer's Life*, 55. As cited earlier, Chrysostom made reference to Matthew 11:12 in reference to the force of using the believer's authority of binding and loosing spiritual forces. Spurgeon may possibly have gleaning the concept from Chrysostom whom he studied.

16. Pierson, *The New Acts of the Apostles*, 193.

17. Henry Drummond, *Natural Law and the Spiritual World* (New York: H.M. Caldwell Co., n.d.), 99-100.

18. Ibid.

19. Henry Drummond, *The Changed Life* (Westwood, N.J.: Fleming H. Revell, n.d.), 4-25, 60.

20. Simpson, *Christ the Bible*, 5:84.

21. Madame Guyon, *Experiencing God through Prayer* (Springdale, Penn.: Whitaker, 1984), 41-42.

22. Bounds, *Purpose in Prayer*, 9, 24.

23. Meyer, *The Secret of Guidance*, 101-102.

24. Andrew Murray, *God's Best Secrets* (Grand Rapids: Zondervan, 1971), Nov. 12; A.W. Tozer, *Jesus, The Author of Our Faith* (Camp Hill, Penn.: Christian Publications, 1988), 142.

25. Tozer, *Who Put Jesus on the Cross?*, 127.

26. Spurgeon, *Faith's Checkbook*, 139.

27. Penn-Lewis, *Life in the Spirit*, 35; A.B. Simpson, "Two Stages of Divine Healing," *AW*, Jan. 28, 1953, 6.

28. Spurgeon, *1000 Devotional Thoughts*, 443.

29. Pierson, *Lessons in the School of Prayer*, 61.

30. Pierson, *The New Acts of the Apostles*, 194; see also p. 192; Pierson, *The Acts of the Holy Spirit*, 92.

31. See Cowman, *Springs in the Valley*, 95; A.B. Simpson, *Friday Meeting Talks: Series # 3* (Nyack, N.Y.: Christian Alliance Publishing Co., 1900), 82-87; Simpson, "Two Stages of Divine Healing," 5; Elliot, 126-127; Jack R. Taylor, *The Key to Triumphant Living* (Nashville: Broadman Press, 1971), 98; Chambers, *Biblical Psychology*, 194.

32. Penn-Lewis, *Soul and Spirit*, 77; Nee, *The Latent Power of the Soul,* 35, 37-86; George H. Pember, *Earth's Earliest Ages and Their Connection with Contemporary Spiritualism and Theosophy* (Toronto, Ontario: A. Sims, Publisher, n.d.), 253.

33. Penn-Lewis, *Life in the Spirit*, 35.

34. Penn-Lewis, *Soul and Spirit*, 58, 77.

35. Simpson, *CITB* (1992), 4:220.

36. Chambers, *Biblical Psychology*, 193-203.

37. Chambers, *Still Higher for His Highest*, 48.

38. Dorsett, *E.M. Bounds*, 161.

39. Chrysostom, *Homilies on Timothy*: Homily 6," *NPNF*, 1:13:428.

40. Scougal, 92.

41. Ibid., 93-94.

42. Grou, *How To Pray*, 88.

43. Kenneth J. Collins, "Abiding in the Kingdom of God: The Disciplines of the Liberated Life," *The Asbury Herald*, (Spring 1997), 108:2:3.

44. Spurgeon, "Golden Key of Prayer," Sermon #619, *Metropolitan Tabernacle Pulpit*, Vol. 11 (1865), 152.

45. Bounds, *Purpose in Prayer*, 9, 78, 80.

46. Bounds, *The Complete Works of E.M. Bounds: Book 1: The Necessity of Prayer* (Grand Rapids: Baker, 1990), 39.

47. Murray, *The Inner Life* (Springdale, Penn.: Whitaker, 1984), 11.

48. Simpson, *Days of Heaven on Earth* (Nyack, N.Y.: Christian Alliance Publishing Co., 1897), Nov. 13, Nov. 15.

49. Simpson, "Two Stages of Divine Healing," 5.

50. Torrey, *The Power of Prayer*, 27; Samuel Chadwick, *The Path of Prayer* (London: Hodder & Stoughton, 1931), 86-87.

51. Penn-Lewis, *Prayer and Evangelism*, 52; Nee, *The Latent Power of the Soul*, 46-48; S.D. Gordon, *Quiet Talks on Prayer* (Chicago: Fleming H. Revell, 1911), 32.

52. Spurgeon, *Faith's Checkbook*, 28.

53. Spurgeon, *Morning by Morning*, 335.

54. Charles H. Spurgeon, *The Treasury of the Bible: Matthew to Luke 15* (London: Marshall, Morgan and Scott, 1952), 1:547.

55. John A. MacMillan, "Self-Deception," *AW*, July 24, 1937, 467.

56. Tozer, *The Pursuit of God*, 68.

57. Bosworth, 145.

58. Wigglesworth, *The Ever-Increasing Faith*, 141.

59. William of St. Thierry, 7.

60. Scougal, 49; Robert G. Tuttle, Jr., *John Wesley: His Life and Theology* (Grand Rapids: Zondervan, 1978), 48-49.

61. William E. Boardman, *The Higher Christian Life* (Boston: H. Hoyt; Chicago: William Tomlinson; New York: Garland, [1858] 1984), 247-248.

62. Ibid., 248.

63. Herbert Lockyer, "Three Abiding Forces," *AW*, Sept. 2, 1953, 10.

64. Amy Carmichael, *Thou Givest . . . They Gather*, 96.

65. Simpson, *A Larger Christian Life*, 13.

66. Clement, *Stromata*, 2:11, *ANF*, 2:358.

67. Andrew Murray, *The Holiest of All* (New Kensington, Penn.: Whitaker, 1996), 422, 465; see also pp. 438, 440, 441, 443, 446, 464, 466.

68. Boardman, *The Higher Christian Life*, 256.

69. Spurgeon, *All of Grace*, 65.

70. Charles H. Spurgeon, "The Best Strengthening Medicine," Sermon #2209, June 21, 1891, *Metropolitan Tabernacle Pulpit*, Vol. 37 (1891), 329.

71. Spurgeon, *The Triumph of Faith in a Believer's Life*, 43.

72. Ibid., 36.

73. Ibid., 36.

74. Spurgeon, *Morning by Morning*, 253.

75. Smith, *Living Confidently in God's Love*, 261.

76. Smith, *The Christian's Secret*, 55.

77. Murray, *With Christ in the School of Prayer*, 119.

78. Simpson, *A Larger Christian Life*, 13.

79. Simpson, *The Life of Prayer*, 60-62; see also Simpson, *CITB* (1992), 4:199.

80. Cowman, *Streams in the Desert*, July 7.

81. MacMillan, *The Authority of the Believer*, 67-68.

82. Charles S. Price, *Two Worlds* (Pasadena, Calif.: Charles S. Price Publishing Co., 1946), 13.

83. Ibid., 19.

84. Spurgeon, *The Triumph of Faith in a Believer's Life*, 36.

85. Amy Carmichael, *Mountain Breezes: The Collected Poems of Amy Carmichael* (Ft. Washington, Penn.: Christian Literature Crusade, 1999), 372.

86. Copeland, *The Force of Faith*, 10.

87. Simpson, *A Larger Christian Life*, 11.

88. Kenneth Copeland, *Forces of the Recreated Human Spirit* (Ft. Worth, Tex.: Kenneth Copeland Ministries, 1982), 8.

89. Copeland, *The Laws of Prosperity*, 18-19.

90. Simpson, *The Life of Prayer*, 57.

91. Ibid., 60.

92. Copeland, cited in Hanegraaff, 65.

93. Kenneth Copeland, *Freedom from Fear* (Ft. Worth, Tex.: KCP Publications, 1983), 12.

94. Simpson, *The Life of Prayer*, 60.

95. Copeland, *Freedom from Fear*, 11.

96. Simpson, *The Life of Prayer*, 59.

97. A.J. Gordon, *How Christ Came to Church*, 43.

98. Murray, *The Inner Life*, 115.

99. Spurgeon, *What the Holy Spirit Does in a Believer's Life*, 120, 127, 131.

100. Chambers, *Biblical Psychology*, 193.

101. Tozer, *The Divine Conquest*, 126.

102. Simpson, *The Fourfold Gospel*, 51.

103. Ibid., 48ff.

104. Upham, *The Life of Faith*, 24, 25.

105. Penn-Lewis, *Soul and Spirit*, 68, 69.

106. Ibid., 62.

107. Simpson, *CITB* (1992), 4:200.

108. Penn-Lewis, *Soul and Spirit*, 62.

109. Ibid., 77-79.

110. Ibid., 70.

111. Nee, *The Latent Power of the Soul*, 46-48.

FAITH AS A FORCE

112. Boardman, *The Higher Christian Life*, 254.

113. Chambers, *My Utmost for His Highest*, 150.

114. Tozer, *Of God and Men*, 85-88.

115. Grou, *How To Pray*, 88.

116. Lederle, *Systematic Theology*, 4.

117. A.W. Tozer, *Whatever Happened to Worship?* (Camp Hill, Penn.: Christian Publications, 1985), 115.

— *169* —

Faith in What? Faith from Where?—
The Object and Source of Faith

Several questions need to be addressed regarding the object and source of faith: 1) From where does faith come? 2) In what is our faith based? 3) Does God have faith, or is it something that just man can exercise? The answers contemporary faith leaders give in answer to these questions is a source of great controversy. We want first to identify contemporary faith teaching on these issues and criticism of these teachings. Then we will examine how the classic faith teachers answered these questions and evaluate and reflect practically upon these issues in order to provide sound faith praxis.

CONTEMPORARY FAITH TEACHING ON THE OBJECT AND SOURCE OF FAITH

Have Faith in Your Self. One version of contemporary faith teaching is "positive thinking" or "possibility thinking," which encourages people to have faith in themselves. This has been promoted by twentieth-century contemporary leaders not usually associated with the contemporary faith movement, such as Norman Vincent Peale's *The Power of Positive Thinking* and Robert Schuller's *You Can Become the Person You Want to Be* and *Self Esteem: The New Reformation.*[1] Other contemporary faith leaders would not normally say that a person should have faith in one's self. However, they do claim that a person should have faith in his/her own faith, which critics maintain is a form of faith in one's self.

Have Faith in Your Faith. Contemporary faith theology teaches that you should have faith in your own faith. Kenyon is usually credited with the concept of having faith in your own faith, although the concept probably arose earlier.[2] Kenyon claimed, "You believe in your own rights in Christ," encouraging believers to have faith in legal standing in Christ and resultant "sonship rights and privileges."[3] Kenyon initially was concerned that a believer should learn to operate on his or her own faith, rather than depending upon the faith of someone else: "The largest percentage of those who are healed in mass meetings, where they have mass faith, seldom ever maintain their healing. The reason is obvious. They have no personal faith. It is just faith in other people's faith. . . . Those people who have been healed by someone else's faith for yours, have reached a place where God demands that they have faith of their own."[4]

However, he went further, asserting that a person who asked for prayer for healing through the laying on of hands and anointing with oil according to James 5 was depending upon the faith of another person.[5] He believed that the superior form of faith was claiming healing according to the Word of God for one's self, rather than depending the prayers and faith of others. Hagin picked up on Kenyon's teaching, declaring, "Having faith in your words is having faith in your own faith. That's what you have got to learn to do to get things from God: Have faith in your faith."[6]

Have Faith in the Word. Kenyon placed strong emphasis on faith in the Bible as the Word of God: "The Word is the source of all faith."[7] Hagin likewise writes, "Faith in God is simply faith in His Word. . . . Real faith in God is based upon the Word of God. Real faith says, 'If God says it is true, it is.' Believing God is believing His Word."[8] As Knight observes, for contemporary faith teachers, "Faith is essentially trusting in God's promises in Scripture rather than trusting in God."[9]

Have Faith in the Name of Jesus. Kenyon asserted that the name of Jesus is a substitute for the presence of Jesus Himself: "When we pray in Jesus' name, we are taking the place of the absent Christ; we are using his name, his authority, to carry out his will on earth."[10] Further, he taught, "We use His Name representatively. The sick and afflicted come to us, and healing virtue that is in Christ—that is in His finished work, is available to the sick one in that Name. Then—it is not healing through Christ;—that Name becomes Christ, the healer."[11]

Faith Heals, Not God. In several passages of Scripture Jesus told people, "Your faith has healed you" (Matt. 9:22; Mark 10:52; Luke 7:50; 17:19;

18:42). On the basis of these statements, one contemporary faith teacher, Frederick Price, has interpreted this to mean that faith is the source and origin of healing, claiming, "It's not God who heals you, it's your faith!"[12] Hagin also appears to teach a form of this when he says, "Your own faith can initiate healing. . . . You don't have to wait for God to move."[13]

Have the God-kind of Faith. Kenyon taught that God is a "faith God," who exercises faith and that believers can develop a "God-kind of faith": "We have God's faith produced in us by His living Word, by His nature that is imparted to us."[14] He called it having "faith in my Father's faith."[15] This is based on interpretation of two particular verses of Scripture:

> *Have faith in* (lit., *of*) *God* (Mark 11:22).

> *I live by the faith of the Son of God* (Gal. 2:20, KJV).

These verses are interpreted by contemporary faith leaders as subjective genitives to mean that God Himself and His Son Jesus Christ themselves possess and exercise the quality of faith, and thus that believers can develop this God-like quality of faith. Hagin goes even further, claiming, "*Every* believer has a measure of this kind of faith. You don't have to get it; you've already got it."[16]

CRITICISM OF CONTEMPORARY FAITH TEACHING

Critics of the contemporary faith movement are adamant in condemning these contemporary faith beliefs. Regarding having faith in one's self or one's own faith, McConnell contends that the contemporary faith view is humanistic or anthropocentric in nature, rather than a Scriptural theocentric faith.[17] McConnell also criticizes Kenyon's assertion that the church has power of attorney through the name of Jesus, claiming that it makes God bound to answer whenever a believer uses the name of Jesus, which is the Christian's "carte blanche with God. It confers unconditional authority on the believer."[18]

McConnell, Hanegraaff, and Bowman also declare the "faith of God" or the "God kind of faith" concept as false teaching, asserting that interpreting the phrase as a subjective genitive is not accepted by scholars.[19] McConnell cites commentator Cranfield calling such interpretation "a monstrosity of exegesis." McConnell claims "is always translated as an objective genitive" and that "This is yet another example of the disturbing tendency of Faith theology to reduce faith to an abstract human concept, . . . thereby divorcing it from God.[20]

Hanegraaff considers the interpretation a "perversion," adding, "In order for their rendering of Mark 11:22 to be accurate, they would have to violate more than one principle of biblical interpretation. A Faith reading of the text dethrones God as Sovereign of the universe and makes Him subject to the impersonal laws of faith."[21] Bowman concludes, "The claim that God exercises faith is disastrous theologically. It implies that God is bound by the constraints of time and does not see or know the future until it has happened to him. It implies that God has hopes of his own that he is seeking to realize."[22]

Classic Faith Teaching on the Object and Source of Faith

Do the classic faith leaders agree with the contemporary faith movement or with its critics? The classic evangelical position is crucial in this debate. If they speak to either side of this controversy, their teachings need to be considered strongly. Examining these classic faith writers can give us a clear picture of truth and error in this teaching, and a balance between these two opposing poles.

Not Faith in One's Self. Although the positive thinking movement tends to encourage people to put their faith in themselves, this is not the teaching of the classic evangelical leaders. As early as the seventeenth century Moravian leader Zinzendorf declared, "No man can create faith in himself."[23] Similarly, Blumhardt, known as a pioneering nineteenth century Lutheran faith healer, proclaimed, "Our pitiful faith doesn't accomplish anything anyway. . . . I can't hear such prattle about 'faith,' because it produces the most self-loving of people. They pay attention only to themselves. I, too, know what faith is. But a faith which we create, in which we wish to see things go according to our own ideas, such a faith I don't want. . . . Who among us would stand up and say, 'Look, I have the right faith!'? That is delusion. . . . A person must know whether his faith is on the right track or not."[24]

Other classic faith leaders, such as Montgomery, Spurgeon, and Hannah Whitall Smith, agreed as well. Smith avowed, "You are not asked to have faith in yourself, and would be in a very wrong condition of soul if you had."[25] Spurgeon agreed, "It must be faith in the finished work of Christ; you must have no confidence in yourself or any man, but rest wholly and entirely upon Christ, else your shield will be of no use."[26]

Again Spurgeon explained, "When you have no faith in yourself, there is more room in the soul for faith in Jesus."[27] Montgomery warned against starting in the Spirit and resorting to the flesh (Gal. 3:3): "You say, 'This is wonderful; Jesus has begun a new faith in me.' But perhaps there is another struggle now; the Devil tries to get you to finish the work that God has begun. You forget that Jesus is the Finisher as well as the Author of your faith, and so you try to add your works to His."[28] Chambers summed up the position of the classic faith writers: "If we have faith at all, it must be faith in Almighty God."[29]

Not Faith in One's Own Faith. While some contemporary faith teachers advocate having faith in one's own faith, the classic leaders of faith speak against this. Spurgeon warned, "Faith must not be above the divine source of all blessing that lies in the grace of God. Never make a Christ of your faith. . . . Our life is found in looking unto Jesus (Heb. 12:2), not in looking to our own faith. By faith all things become possible to us, yet the power is not in the faith but in the God upon whom faith relies."[30] Again Spurgeon counseled, "Your faith must be of heaven's forging, or your shield will certainly fail you."[31] Simpson likewise counseled, "Faith is hindered most of all by what we call 'our faith,'"[32] advising, "Jesus does not say to us, 'Have great faith yourselves.' But He does say, 'have the faith of God.'"[33]

In fact, the classic faith leaders are united in directing against having faith in one's own faith, among whom were Otto Stockmayer, Boardman, S.D. Gordon, Chambers, Meyer, Torrey, Charles Price, and Montgomery. Stockmayer, writing in Montgomery's *Triumphs of Faith*, advised, "Faith ignores itself, that it may see and possess only its object. The moment a believer contemplates himself or his faith, he ceases to believe."[34] Mrs. William Boardman similarly advised, "So we cease to think of our faith by being absorbed in the Object of faith."[35] Practically speaking, Müller stated regarding a healing he received: "The Lord gave me faith to get out of bed. I would consider it great presumption if the Lord had not given me the faith to do it."[36]

S.D. Gordon added, "This is what faith means; not thinking about your faith, but thinking about Him. It's not looking in, it's looking up to Him."[37] Chambers quoted Hudson Taylor, saying, "Have faith in the faithfulness of God, not your own faithfulness."[38] Again, referring to Galatians 2:20, Chambers commented, "This faith is not Paul's faith in Jesus Christ, but the faith that the Son of God has imparted to him. . . . It is no longer faith in faith."[39] Further he counseled, "Stick steadfastly, not to your faith, but to the one who gives you the faith."[40] In fact, he goes so far as to assert that unless faith is in God alone, it is an illusion.[41] Additionally, Meyer wrote, "All faith that turns toward Jesus is the right faith," explaining that he would pray, "My faith is flickering out. Its hand seems paralyzed, its eye blinded, its old glad song silenced forever. But Thou are faithful, and I am reckoning on Thee."[42]

Torrey, who believed in divine healing, nonetheless cautioned about the wrong kind of faith: "The kind of healing that is only temporary and dependent upon the continued faith of the one healed is not divine healing, not God's healing, but it is a faith healing, an entirely different matter, a purely psychological process. . . . Here lies one of the saddest and most dangerous errors of the day on this whole subject of divine healing, substituting man's faith for God's power, substituting a mental process for the work of the Holy Spirit on the body."[43] Charles Price, as a healing evangelist, also cautioned against faith in one's own faith: "Struggling with mental powers and faculties will never bring [faith], for FAITH IS A GIFT OF GOD. It will never be imparted by God until the spiritual condition of the believer warrants the gift."[44] Again he wrote, "Faith . . . the weight of a grain of mustard seed . . . will do more than a ton of will or a mind full of determination."[45]

Price also warned, similar to McConnell and Hanegraaff, against metaphysical influence: "When we try to believe ourselves into an experience we are getting into a metaphysical realm."[46] He admonished further, "With many people the wrong has been that they have mistaken their own ability to believe for the faith which is of God. . . . The belief that is genuine scriptural faith is not our ability to 'count it done,' intellectually and mentally, but the deep consciousness in the heart that it is done, born of the faith that only God can give. . . . To many, many Christians faith is still their own ability to believe a promise or a truth, and is often based on their struggles to drive away doubt and unbelief through a process of affirmations."[47]

Montgomery advised, "Jesus is the author and finisher of our faith, and He will work *His own faith* in our hearts. Let us give up our own poor attempts at faith and take the faith of the Son of God. The Lord Jesus has faith in His own power to make good all His promises."[48] She quoted a poem that countered the "faith in your faith" belief:

> The Shepherd does not ask of thee
> Faith in thy faith, but only faith in Him.
> And in this He meant in saying, "Come to Me"

In light or darkness seek to do His will
And leave the work of faith to Jesus still.[49]

More recently, Tozer admonished: "Faith in faith is faith astray,"[50] counseling, "I cannot recommend that anyone have faith in faith. . . . Our confidence must not be in the power of faith but in the Person and work of the Savior Jesus Christ. . . . I have been memorizing the Scripture ever since I was converted, but my faith does not rest on God's promises. My faith rests upon God's character. Faith must rest in confidence upon the One who made the promises."[51]

Even Wigglesworth, frequently cited by contemporary faith teachers, is in opposition to their position of having faith in their faith: "Oh, this wonderful faith of the Lord Jesus. Your faith comes to an end. How many times I have been to the place where I have had to tell the Lord, 'I have used all the faith I have,' and then He has placed His own faith within me."[52] Further, referring to Acts 26:19, Wigglesworth questioned, "Is that the faith of Paul? No, it is the faith that the Holy Ghost is giving."[53] Again Wigglesworth counseled, "We have got to get rid of our small measure of faith, because God's measure is so much greater than ours."[54]

It Is Not Faith That Heals, But Christ. The writings of classic faith leaders refute Frederick Price's claim above that it is not God who heals, but rather one's own faith. Contrary to Price, Spurgeon wrote, "Faith does not heal; that is the work of the atonement of Christ."[55] Moreover, Spurgeon, as cited above, warned that faith must not be exalted above the divine source of all blessing in the grace of God, warning, "Never make a Christ of your faith."[56] This is exactly what Price has done—he has exalted faith above the divine source of all blessing; he has made a Christ of faith. As mentioned earlier, Price was once a pastor in the C&MA, founded by Simpson. But Price did not follow the C&MA founder's counsel, for Simpson himself taught, "It is not the faith that heals. God heals, but faith receives it."[57] It is significant that even Wigglesworth, the Pentecostal "Apostle of Faith" who is frequently cited by contemporary faith teachers, would strongly disagree with Price's claim, saying, "Faith is the open door through which the Lord comes. Do not say, 'I was healed by faith.' . . . I am here because God healed me when I was dying."[58]

The classic leaders understood that the origin of healing is not faith, but personal contact with God Himself. Healing and spiritual warfare pioneer Blumhardt "insisted there could be no cure unless there was believing contact of the person's spirit with God."[59] Echoing Blumhardt,

Simpson taught, "There is no power in prayer unless it is the prayer of God Himself. Unless you are in contact with Christ the living Healer, there is no healing. . . . Faith is more than believing; it is a living contact with a living Savior."[60] Building on the thought of both Blumhardt and Simpson, Charles Price proclaimed, "Healing is the supernatural life of God."[61]

Secondary Faith in the Word of God. The classic leaders would agree with contemporary faith teachers that there is a sense in which we are to have faith in the word of God, but they would stress that it is a secondary sense. Contrary to contemporary faith teaching, trusting God Himself is to be distinguished from trusting God's promises. Simpson, for example, wrote, "True faith is not believing in words merely, even divine words, but believing ON the Lord Jesus Christ."[62] Chambers wrote in similar fashion, "Faith is not in what Jesus says, but in Himself; if we only look at what He says we shall never believe."[63]

Expounding further, Murray taught, "Have faith in God. This word precedes the other, Have faith in the promise of an answer to prayer. The power to believe a promise depends entirely, but only, on faith in the promiser. . . . Faith in the promise is the fruit of faith in the promiser. . . . Let faith look to God more than the thing promised. . . . His love, His power, His living presence will awaken and work the faith. . . . Faith in God begets faith in the promise."[64] Meyer echoed Murray, speaking of Abraham's faith: "He [Abraham] leant not so much upon the promise as upon the Promiser."[65] Hannah Whitall Smith, in her old age while reflecting back on her life, wrote in similar fashion, "I had found that God, just God alone, without anything else, was enough. Even the comfort of His promises paled before the comfort of Himself. What difference did it make if I could not find a promise to fit my case? I had found the Promiser, and He was infinitely more than all His promises."[66] Likewise, in opposition to contemporary faith teaching, Bounds asserted, "Primarily it is not trust in the Word of God, but rather trust in the person of God. For trust in the person of God must precede trust in the Word of God."[67]

In agreement with these classic faith leaders, Spurgeon preached, "And above all, you must mind that your faith is fixed in the person of Christ, for nothing but faith in Christ's divine person and in His proper manhood when as the Lamb of God's passover He was sacrificed for us—no other faith will be able to stand against the tremendous shock and the innumerable attacks that you must receive in the great battle of spiritual life."[68] Here Spurgeon was speaking of the practical implications of making Christ the source of faith.

ONLY BELIEVE

Tozer, approaching it from a different angle, wrote, "Now the theological rationalist understands [1 Corinthians 2:4-5] in this way: He says that your faith should stand not in the wisdom of men but the Word of God. But that is not what Paul said. He said that your faith should stand in the power of God. . . . Your faith can stand in the text and you can be as dead as the proverbial doornail."[69] While it sounds spiritual to put faith in the Word, Tozer considered this as mere theological rationalism.

As we have seen again and again, the classic teaching is that faith must be focused primarily on Christ. For classic evangelical leaders, the Scriptural emphasis is not dependency upon God's Word, but upon God Himself. We do believe His Word—it is true, it is sure. We take Him at His Word, we rest on His Word, as R. Kelso Carter wrote in his gospel song, "we are standing on the promises of God," but our faith is in *Himself*. We believe upon *Him*; we lean upon *Him*, not His Word.

This is not to say that the Word of God has no significant part in the walk of faith. Classic leaders, such as Simpson, taught that there is creative power in the Scripture: "The Word of God creates what it commands. When Christ says to any of us, 'Now are ye clean through the word which I have spoken to you' (John 15:3), ye are clean. When He says, 'no condemnation' [Rom. 8:1] there is none, though there has been a lifetime of sin before. And when He says, 'mighty through God to the pulling down of strongholds' [2 Corinthians 10:4], then the weak are strong. This is the part of faith to take God at His word and then expect Him to make it real."[70] Simpson's friend, Wheaton College president Charles Blanchard, wrote of the healing power of Scripture, describing how a physician prescribed to a depressed, nervous, sick woman to read the Bible an hour for thirty days then come back and see him. She eventually obtained an appetite for the Word and came back to the doctor a different woman. He told her, "I saw as soon as you came into the room that what you needed was not medicine nor anything else that man could give or do. What you needed was God. You have now come in touch with Him. Keep in touch with Him and you will be well."[71] Murray likewise believed in the creative power of the Scriptures: "Let the Word create around you, create within you a holy atmosphere, a holy, heavenly light, in which your soul will be refreshed and strengthened for the work of daily life."[72] Howard Taylor, the son of Hudson Taylor found Murray's exhortation meaningful, and cited the statement as a description of his father's way of life.

Faith in the Atonement—The Finished Work of Christ. Classic leaders believed faith must be based upon the work of redemption or atonement, the finished work of Christ on the cross. Spurgeon taught, "It must be faith in the finished work of Christ; you must have no confidence in yourself or any man, but rest wholly and entirely upon Christ, else your shield will be of no use."[73] Chambers, as well, wrote of "faith in the Great Redemption," saying, "Unless we have faith in the Redemption, all our activities are fussy impertinences which tell God He is doing nothing."[74]

The Faith of God—Mark 11:22. As mentioned above, Hanegraaff claims "faith of God" interpretation is a "perversion," citing several Greek grammarians in support.[75] McConnell asserts that Kenyon is the originator of this interpretation.[76] However, he ignores the fact that his own mentor and critic of the contemporary faith movement, Oral Roberts University professor Charles Farah (Ph.D., University of Edinburgh), validated this interpretation from the Greek New Testament, citing Pentecostal evangelist Charles Price, who also was knowledgeable of Greek grammar and wrote of the concept before Kenyon.[77] They, in turn, were preceded by many others taking this viewpoint in some form. Even in ancient times church father Jerome, in his Latin Vulgate translation of the Bible, rendered the phrase *habete fidem Dei.*[78] In 1380, Wyclif, in one of the earliest English translations, following Jerome, translated it "haue ye the feith of God."[79] Commentator John Gill notes that the Syriac and Ethiopic versions also translate the passage as "the faith of God."[80]

Though "faith in God," as an objective genitive may generally seem to be the favored interpretation today, the idea of "faith of God" as a secondary or alternative translation is by no means uncommon among evangelical leaders and scholars, and is found in some form in several eighteenth and nineteenth century commentaries.[81] Contrary to the claims of McConnell, Hanegraaff, and Bowman, this apparently was an acceptable interpretation among many scholarly evangelical circles by the nineteenth century. Variations of the "faith of God" translation of Mark 11:22 were interpreted in at least six ways among classic faith leaders: 1) God as the source or author of faith, 2) the faithfulness of God, 3) the faith of Jesus Christ, 4) God's own faith—the faith that God possesses and exercises as a part of His nature, 5) special mountain-moving faith, not everyday faith, and 6) a dual or multiple interpretations, such as both an objective genitive, with a secondary "faith of God" interpretation, or some other combination of two or more of the first five interpretations.

1. God as the source or author of faith. As early as 1852, *Gill's Commentary* translated "have the faith of God," meaning "make use of that faith which has God for its author, which is the work of God, and of his operation, a free grace-gift of his."[82] Spurgeon preached a sermon in 1879 on Mark 11:22 in which he used both interpretations, saying that we should have faith in God as the object of our faith and the faith of God as the source of faith: "It is literally, 'Have the faith of God'—the faith which is wrought in us by God, and sustained by God, for that is the only faith that is worth the living. . . . He is the author, the giver, and the nourisher of faith."[83] Other evangelical leaders likewise followed this interpretation that it is faith imparted by God, including Chambers and McCrossan.

Referring to Galatians 2:20, Chambers asserted that Paul's faith was not in his faith in Christ, "but the faith that the Son of God has imparted to him."[84] Greek professor T.J. McCrossan taught the validity of the "faith of God" interpretation: "This 'faith of God' is the faith the Holy Ghost imparts to God's saints, just in proportion as we allow Him to control our lives. 1 Corinthians 12:9 tells us that 'faith' is one of the gifts of the Spirit, and this 'Spirit-imparted faith' is the faith of God."[85] The Scofield Reference Bible notes in the margin, "Have the faith of God, i.e. the faith that God gives."[86]

2. *The faithfulness of God.* Writing in Montgomery's *Triumphs of Faith*, Hudson Taylor understood the "faith of God" as the faithfulness of God, God's covenant loyalty. He interpreted Mark 11:22 as "Reckon on God's faithfulness," commenting, "I could not reckon on my faith but I could reckon on God's faithfulness."[87] Chambers, Meyer, and Bosworth also evidently alluded to Taylor, using the same expression, "reckon on God's faithfulness."[88] Similarly, Murray, referred to Sarah as cited in Hebrews 11:11, "By faith Sarah . . . counted him [God] faithful who had promised, commenting, "The faithfulness of God was . . . her faith."[89] This appears to be the meaning of the same phrase in Romans 3:3.

3. *The Faith of Jesus Christ.* Several early evangelical leaders related Mark 11:22 with Galatians 2:20, interpreting "the faith of the Son of God" as faith that Jesus exercised in His human nature. Donald Bloesch acknowledges, "Reformed theology has always affirmed the reality of faith and hope in Jesus. One of the early Puritans described Jesus as 'the greatest and best Believer that ever lived.'"[90] Reformed theologian Abraham Kuyper affirmed, "With our Reformed Church we confess that according to His human nature our Mediator has really and factually believed. Faith is that expression of the soul which clearly seizes hold of God's

Word and through this Word again possesses its God. . . . Of such a faith we now say that it was also in Jesus."[91]

In this same Reformed tradition, Andrew Murray in 1885 regarded Mark 11:22 as "faith in God," yet he also made reference to "the faith *of* the Beloved Master," the faith that belongs to Christ, which He Himself exercised on earth and continues to exercise in His continuing role of intercession.[92] Referring to Galatians 2:20, Chambers wrote, "Literally, the faith that was in Christ Jesus is now in me."[93] Nee commented on this Scripture, "When we believe and receive the Son of God, not only His life but His faith too enters into us. Hence we may live by *His* faith."[94] Charles Price also wrote of "faith of the Lord Jesus Christ."[95]

Some current scholarship also acknowledges that Jesus Christ exercised faith as part of His human nature. Systematic theology scholar Veli-Matti Kärkkäinen states in relationship to Galatians 2:15-21 that the "faith of Christ" or "the covenant-faithfulness of the author of salvation" interpretation "is gaining more and more support among New Testament scholars."[96]

4. *God's own faith.* Though the most controversial interpretation, several classic leaders understood that if "the faith of God" is imparted by God it must be a faith that God Himself possesses and manifests as part of His divine nature, and that Jesus Christ manifested that faith of God on earth through His human nature. It is likely that they connected this with the doctrine of *communicatio idiomatum,* the mutual communication of the attributes of the divine and human natures of Christ. This concept was established out of the Christological formulations of the Calcedonian Definition of A.D. 451 regarding the inseparableness of the divine and human natures of Christ, and the Trinitarian concept of *perichoresis,* the mutual interpenetration and reciprocal interrelation of the two natures and attributes.[97]

Simpson, in the Reformed tradition, held this interpretation in 1890: "The divine pattern of faith is the faith of God."[98] Again he wrote, "We must claim the faith of God, letting the Spirit of Jesus sustain our faith with His strong faith."[99] Charles Price also interchanged the terminology of "faith of the Lord Jesus Christ and the "faith of God," counseling, "Get some of God's faith. . . . You simply cannot believe without the alloy of doubt until you have the faith of God. It takes God's faith to clean up these human hearts of ours of all the debris, the fears, misgivings and doubts."[100] Likewise, Greek scholar A.S. Worrell connected Jesus' faith with God's faith: "Have the faith of God; translators generally render this, 'Have faith in God;' but, if this had been the thought, it would have been easy to have expressed it in Greek. Faith originates with God; and those who have real faith have His faith; the same perhaps as 'the faith which is of the Son of God' (Gal. 2:20)."[101]

Other leaders also considered the faith of God to be God's own faith. Meyer, mentioned above, contrasted his faith with God's faith.[102] Greek scholar and translator W.B. Godbey rendered the passage, "Have God's faith."[103] Renowned Methodist missionary and devotional writer E. Stanley Jones wrote that having faith in God's faith is better than faith in our faith.[104]

These leaders would argue against Bowman that the concept of God having faith does not limit Him in any way so that He does not know the future or that He needs to hope for something.[105] Rather, they would contend that the faith of God is an exercise of faith as the very power of God, similar to that taught by Clement of Alexandria. Faith to them is not trust or hope in some unknown future, but confidently seeing the unseen.

5. *Special mountain-moving faith.* Classic faith leaders recognized that this faith in Mark 11:22-24 is a "mountain-moving faith," that is, a gift of faith from God, not the ordinary everyday exercise of faith, as claimed by some contemporary faith teachers. Contrary to some contemporary faith teachers who make a blanket application of Jesus' statement to all situations, early commentators and classic faith teachers recognized that this type of faith is given by God only on special occasions. As early as the fourth-century, church father Cyril of Jerusalem identified this mountain-moving faith of which Jesus speaks with 1 Corinthians 12:9, designating it as "bestowed by Christ as a gift of grace."[106] Likewise, connecting these two Scripture passages Chrysostom differentiates between dogmatic faith and faith that is "the mother of miracles."[107] Murray identified mountain-moving faith as "great faith."[108] The *Scofield Reference Bible* cross-referenced Mark 11:22 with 1 Corinthians 12:9, indicating a connection between the faith of God and the gift of faith.[109]

As mentioned earlier in Chapter 10, Simpson explained that the faith that does not doubt in Mark 11:22-24 and James 1:6-7 is "a special work of the Holy Ghost."[110] Practically applying this understanding to the abandoning of medical treatment, Simpson cautioned, "If you have any question about your faith for this, make it a special matter of preparation and prayer. Ask God to give you special faith for this act. All our graces must come from Him, and faith among the rest. We have nothing of our own, and even our very faith is but the grace of Christ Himself within us. We can exercise it, and thus far our responsibility extends; but He must impart it, and we simply put it on and wear it as from Him."[111]

Others evangelical leaders also distinguished this kind of faith as special, mountain-moving faith. Similar to Simpson, Torrey taught that the prayer of faith of Mark 11:22-24 is "prayer that the Holy Spirit inspires."[112] Alluding to James 5:15, Torrey wrote, "It is not always possible to pray 'the prayer of faith,' only when God makes it possible by the leading of the Holy Spirit."[113] Regarding Galatians 2:20, Chambers comments that the "faith of the Son of God" is "not elementary faith in Jesus," but rather "the faith which is in the Son of God," "the very faith which governed Jesus Christ."[114]

6. *Dual or multiple interpretations.* We have already seen that Spurgeon regarded Mark 11:22 as both an objective faith in God and God as the source of faith. Murray spoke of both faith in God and the faith of the Son of God. Meyer wrote of both God's faith and God's faithfulness.

Some identified mountain-moving faith as the very faith of God, or perfect faith, the ultimate or zenith of faith. *The Pulpit Commentary* interpreted Mark 11:22 as "literally, have the faith of God—full, perfect, effectual faith in him."[115] Nee commented on these verses, "Only with perfect faith may one speak to the mountain."[116] While Bounds did not use the term "faith of God," he nonetheless identified such mountain-moving faith in God, not as ordinary, everyday faith, but as the summit of a peak: "When a Christian believer attains to faith of such magnificent proportions as these, he steps into the realm of implicit trust. He stands without a tremor on the apex of his spiritual outreaching. He has attained faith's veritable topstone which is unswerving, unalterable, unalienable trust in the power of the living God."[117]

Rawlinson similarly viewed Mark 11:22-24 as a "'supernatural' degree of faith."[118] Clarke interpreted it as "have strong faith, or the strongest faith."[119] Robertson, though translating the passage as an objective genitive (of genus or kind), nevertheless called it "the God kind of faith,"[120] the very term which McConnell and Hanegraaff criticize contemporary faith teachers for using.

Some regarded mountain-moving faith as also the faith imparted by God. Classic devotional writer, Mrs. Charles Cowman, echoes this teaching: "The faith of God is in-wrought within our hearts by the Holy Ghost. And that is the faith that will say to the mountains, 'Be removed!' And they will melt like wax at His spoken word through us."[121]

Significantly, McCrossan, one of Hagin's own sources, contradicts Hagin's interpretation of Mark 11:22, saying, "This 'faith of God' is the faith the Holy Ghost imparts to God's saints, just in proportion as we allow Him to control our lives. . . . This Spirit-imparted faith is the faith of God."[122] Charles Price combined four interpretations of Mark 11:22 together, identifying the faith of God as God's own faith, the faith of Jesus Christ, mountain-moving faith and faith that is imparted by God.

Wigglesworth, whom contemporary faith teachers love to quote, like other classic faith teachers, distinguished between natural faith, and supernatural faith that is a gift from God.[123] He recognized that hearing from God is needed to exercise this special faith, which is the faith of God:

> All lack of faith is due to not feeding on God's Word. . . . Feed on the living Christ of whom this Word is full. As you get taken up with the glorious fact and the wondrous presence of the living Christ, the faith of God will spring up within you. "Faith cometh by hearing and hearing by the word of Christ.". . . . Seek God until you get from Him a mighty revelation of the Son, until that inward revelation moves you on to the place where you are always steadfast, unmovable, and always abounding in the work of the Lord.[124]

While this is a special, supernatural faith, some faith leaders recognized that such faith, through exercise, could become what we might today call "supernaturally natural." Referring to Mark 11:22-24, Müller recorded early in his journal that he had a special gift of faith.[125] However, years later he reversed his earlier statement: "I do not have the gift of faith mentioned in 1 Corinthians 12:9 along with the gifts of healing, the working of miracles and prophecy."[126] Why this apparent contradiction?—because he wanted people to understand that this special faith was not out of reach, but is available for every believer to receive, that as we exercise the faith God grants us, God will bestow upon us more faith. Montgomery similarly commented of this commanding, mountain-moving faith of Mark 11:2-24, "God wants us all to have this faith. He desires to bring His children up to an every-day, working faith for all the difficulties that arise."[127] For these leaders, unlike some contemporary faith teachers, this faith is not developing the God-kind of faith that we already have, but God imparting to us more faith as we use the faith we have.

Summary of Classic Faith Teaching. To summarize, early commentators and classic faith teachers understood Mark 11:22 and Galatians 2:20 to refer to the faith of God in six ways: 1) faith imparted from God—God as the source of faith; 2) the faithfulness of God; 3) the faith of Christ; 4) God's own faith; 5) special mountain-moving faith; 6) a combination of two or more of these meanings, so that the faith imparted by God is God's own faith or faithfulness or that the supernatural faith was the very faith of God Himself, part of His omnipotent character, which was also exercised by the human Jesus.

So then, Kenyon was no maverick in his interpretation of Mark 11:22, nor was he the originator of the concept. Kenyon may have gleaned his interpretation from Bibles of the time, one of several commentaries or evangelical leaders, such as Spurgeon or Simpson, or perhaps more immediately from Charles Price's book, which was published two years before Kenyon's *Two Kinds of Faith.*

The difference between classic understanding of the faith of God and contemporary faith teaching is that contemporary faith teachers assert that believers should develop and exercise this "God-kind of faith," whereas classic faith leaders who taught the "faith of God" maintained that believers receive as a special gift from God the faith of God Himself. So it is not a matter of faith in God vs. faith of God, but both. They made it clear that having the faith of God does not mean having faith in one's own faith.[128]

REFLECTIONS AND CONCLUSIONS

God Is Ultimately the Object of Faith. While secondarily believers may exercise faith in the Word of God and Name of Jesus and the Work of Christ, as the classic faith leaders have shown, ultimately God is the object of faith. As mentioned above, Chambers indicated that if we have any faith at all, it should be faith in God Himself. Faith in any other object, such as one's self, or one's own faith, is misplaced. The sound counsel of the classic faith leaders is summed up by Tozer's admonition, as cited earlier: "Faith in faith is faith astray," thus a faith that is unhealthy. To be fair and accurate, it should be noted that Hagin's earlier booklet *Having Faith in Your Faith* is no longer in print. I had opportunity to talk with one of the editors of Hagin's material who told me I would never see it in print again. Although I know of no statement where Hagin has publicly renounced the concept, it is obvious that he recognized his error and dropped the teaching.

God Is Also the Subject and Source of Faith. One may argue interpretations of grammar, but for Hanegraaff to say that the "faith of God" interpretation held by Alexander, Spurgeon, Murray, Chambers, Taylor, Meyer, Price, McCrossan, and a host of other evangelical scholars and leaders is a "perversion" obviously goes too far. Either all of these respected evangelical leaders teach a perversion, or Hanegraaff is teaching error. McIntyre exposes the fact that Hanegraaff actually interprets Greek scholar A.T. Robertson's comments on Mark 11:22 incorrectly: "Now here is the irony. Robertson was quoted correctly, but incompletely. The whole quote was not given because it would prove embarrassing to the argument."[129] He then cites Robertson's commentary completely in its full context: "Thus in Mk 11:22 εχετε πιστιν θεου [*echete pistin theou*] we rightly translate 'have faith in God,' though the genitive does not mean 'in,' but only the God kind of faith."[130] McIntyre comments further: "This is amazing! The scholar who is being quoted to disprove the "faith of God" is actually the source of that very phrase that has drawn tremendous criticism to the Faith movement, 'Have the God kind of faith.'"[131]

While McConnell cites one commentator, Cranfield, who considers the faith of God interpretation "a monstrosity of exegesis," other commentators and translators believe the opposite, such C.S. Mann in *The Anchor Bible*, who argues, "The phrase 'Have faith in God' (Greek *pistis theou*) is found nowhere else and is grammatically barely defensible."[132] David Stern, translator of the *Jewish New Testament*, renders the passage, "Have the kind of trust that comes from God."[133] There is thus great debate among scholars regarding the appropriate translation as an objective or a subjective genitive, or some kind of a combination of the two. One Greek scholar friend remarked that such passages are "divinely ambiguous" so as to allow both interpretations. Since Alexander, Robertson, Spurgeon, Murray, and others give both translations or a combination of interpretations, it would appear that they viewed these Scriptures as intended to be a *double entendre*. Kenyon himself recognized both interpretations: "We have both. We have God's faith reproduced in us by His living Word, by His nature that is imparted to us. We have faith in God, because it is a normal, natural thing for a child to have faith in its parent."[134]

McConnell, Hanegraaff, Bowman, and others who accepted their claims, are in error claiming that all scholarship agrees that this cannot be a subjective genitive because God cannot have faith. Certainly, if the nature of faith is understood solely as a human quality with the pole of passive trust in someone human or something else, then obviously God cannot have faith. However, with the elliptical nature of truth, there is also a pole of active faith (as discussed in Chapter 6). If faith is understood as a force or energy or power emanating out of the very nature of God's omnipotence (as taught by many leaders throughout church history from Clement of Alexandria to the present), then God can exercise faith. This does not limit God in any way.

Further, in Trinitarian thought as an extension of the concept of *perichoresis*, the three Persons of the Trinity can be understood in their Triune relational nature as a Divine Community of Faith. In other words, stemming from their mutual love for and interdependence with one another, each member of the Trinity has complete faith in the other members of the Trinity. Love and interdependence imply implicit trust. The Father and Son have complete faith in each other; the Father and the Spirit have complete faith in each other; the Spirit and the Son have complete faith in each other. The Three-in-One model perfect trust, which flows out of perfect love.

Thus I would conclude, when faith is defined not merely as trust in a human person or thing, but mutual trust within the Trinity and also then from that as an active spiritual force that originates in the very nature of God, as do classic faith leaders, it is therefore legitimate to say that God has faith. Therefore, one can say that a person can both have faith in God and receive from God the very faith of God.

God Is the Source of Healing; Faith Is the Agent. Classic faith teaching has shown that Frederick Price errs when he claims that God does not heal, but rather one's faith. Price has confused the agent of healing with the source of healing. God must always be acknowledged as the source of the healing. Faith is the channel, the conduit, the agency through which the healing comes. As cited above, Spurgeon warned against making a Christ of our faith.

Final Reflections and Conclusions. Through this investigation, we have seen that classic faith leaders have sometimes been, along with anti-faith critics, in disagreement with contemporary faith leaders (regarding teaching on faith in one's self, one's own faith, and faith as the source of healing), while at other times they have been in agreement with contemporary faith teachers against faith critics (regarding the "faith of God" interpretation). Classic faith leaders thus, for the most part, present a sound balance between the two extremes. They would teach us that we should not have faith in ourselves or in our own faith, that God is the source of faith, and that such faith of God is not a type of faith that believers automatically have or can develop, but rather is specially imparted by God. God thus remains sovereign and receives all the glory for the provision of faith, though man has the responsibility to work in synergy with God to exercise the faith that He imparts. This maintains a healthy dynamic tension of a practical walk of faith.

---

1   Norman Vincent Peale, *The Power of Positive Thinking* (Englewood Cliffs, N.J.: Prentice-Hall, Inc., 1952); Robert H. Schuller, *You Can Become the Person You Want to Be* (Old Tappan, N.J.: Fleming H. Revell, 1973); Robert H. Schuller, *Self Esteem: The New Reformation* (Waco, Tex.: Word Books, 1982).

2. As I show in this chapter, some earlier classic faith leaders addressed this issue, so some form of the concept must have occurred earlier than Kenyon's teaching.

3. Kenyon, *In His Presence*, 57.

4. Kenyon, *The Two Kinds of Faith*, 38-39.

5. E.W. Kenyon, *Jesus the Healer* (Seattle: Kenyon's Gospel Publishing Co., [1940] 1943), 37.

6. Kenneth E. Hagin, *Having Faith in Your Faith* (Tulsa, Okla.: Faith Library Publications, 1980), 5.

7. Kenyon, *In His Presence*, 33.

8. Kenneth E. Hagin, *New Thresholds of Faith* (Tulsa, Okla.: Kenneth Hagin Ministries, 1985), 5, 23.

9. Henry H. Knight III, "God's Faithfulness and God's Freedom: A Comparison of Contemporary Theologies of Healing," *Journal of Pentecostal Theology*, 1993, 2:69.

10. E.W. Kenyon, *The Wonderful Name of Jesus* (Seattle: Kenyon's Gospel Publishing Co., [1927] 1963), 20, cited in McConnell, 142.

11. Kenyon, *The Wonderful Name of Jesus*, 62.

12. Frederick Price, cited in McConnell, 97.

13. Kenneth E. Hagin, *Seven Things You Should Know About Divine Healing* (Tulsa, Okla.: Kenneth Hagin Ministries, 1979), 61.

14. Kenyon, *The Two Kinds of Faith*, 103.

15. Kenyon, *In His Presence*, 56.

16. Kenneth E. Hagin, *Mountain Moving Faith* (Tulsa, Okla.: Kenneth Hagin Ministries, 1993), 5.

17. McConnell, 146

18. Ibid., 142.

19. Ibid., 145; Hanegraaff, 87-95, 390; Bowman, *The Word-Faith Controversy*, 70, 107-109.

20. McConnell, 145.

21. Hanegraaff, 91.

22. Bowman, *The Word-Faith Controversy*, 112.

23. McGrath, 238.

24. Vernard Eller, ed., *Thy Kingdom Come: A Blumhardt Reader* (Grand Rapids: Eerdmans, 1980), 173, 175.

25. H.W. Smith, *The Christian's Secret*, 52

26. Charles H. Spurgeon, *The Metropolitan Tabernacle Pulpit* (Pasadena, Tex.: Pilgrim Publications, 1979), Vol. 7, 548.

27. Ibid., Vol. 36, 478.

28. Montgomery, *Secrets of Victory*, 119-120.

29. Chambers, *The Place of Help*, 49.

30. Spurgeon, *All of Grace*, 45.

31. Spurgeon, *Spiritual Warfare in a Believer's Life*, 156.

32. Simpson, *A Larger Christian Life*, 19.

33. Simpson, *The Gospel of Healing*, 89; see also p. 54.

34. Otto Stockmayer, "Faith Opposed to Sight," *Triumphs of Faith*, June 1891, 124.

35. Mrs. William Boardman, "Simple Truths about Faith," *Triumphs of Faith*, Nov. 1890, 242.

36. George Müller, *The Autobiography of George Müller* (Springdale, Penn.: Whitaker, 1984), 44.

37. S.D. Gordon, *The Healing Christ* (New York: Fleming H. Revell; Ann Arbor, Mich.: Vine Books, [1924] 1985), 105.

38. Oswald Chambers, *Oswald Chambers: His Life and Work* (London: Simpkin Marshall, 1941), 53.

39. Chambers, *My Utmost for His Highest*, 81.

40. Chambers, *The Place of Help*, 210.

41. Ibid., 63.

42. Meyer, *The Secret of Guidance*, 50, 51.

43. Torrey, *Divine Healing*, 24-25.

44. Charles Price, *And Signs Followed*, 123.

45. Charles Price, *The Real Faith*, 8.

46. Ibid., 12.

47. Ibid., 16, 18, 103.

48. Montgomery, *Secrets of Victory*, 28.

49. Montgomery, *The Prayer of Faith*, 50.

50. Tozer, *Of God and Men*, 57.

51. A.W. Tozer, *Faith Beyond Reason* (Camp Hill, Penn.: Christian Publications, 1989), 34, 42.

52. Wigglesworth, *The Ever-Increasing Faith*, 136.

53. Wigglesworth, *Faith That Prevails* (Springfield, Mo.: Gospel Publishing House, 1938), 6.

54. Albert Hibbert, *Smith Wigglesworth—The Secret of His Power* (Tulsa, Okla.: Harrison House, 1993), 103.

55. Charles H. Spurgeon, *Power in the Blood* (New Kensington, Penn.: Whitaker, 1996), 22.

56. Spurgeon, *All of Grace*, 45.

57. Simpson, *The Fourfold Gospel*, 62.

58. Wigglesworth, *The Ever-Increasing Faith*, 46.

59. Chappell, 355-356.

60. Simpson, *The Gospel of Healing*, 54, 127.

61. Charles S. Price, *Spiritual and Physical Health* (Pasadena, Calif.: Charles S. Price Publishing Co., 1946), 66.

62. Simpson, *CITB* (1992), 1:79.

63. Chambers, *My Utmost for His Highest*, 60.

64. Murray, *With Christ in the School of Prayer*, 86, 89, 90, 92.

65. Meyer, *Abraham or the Obedience of Faith*, 26.

66. H.W. Smith, *The Unselfishness of God*, 216.

67. Bounds, *The Complete Works of E.M. Bounds: Book 1: The Necessity of Prayer*, 25.

68. Spurgeon, *Spiritual Warfare in a Believer's Life*, 157.

69. Tozer, *Faith Beyond Reason*, 25-26.

70. Simpson, *In the School of Faith*, 110.

71. Blanchard, 145-146.

72. Andrew Murray, cited in Howard Taylor, *Hudson Taylor's Spiritual Secret*, 236.

73. Spurgeon, *The Metropolitan Tabernacle Pulpit*, Vol. 7, 548.

74. Chambers, *Still Higher for His Highest*, 69.

75. Hanegraaff, 87-95, 390.

76. McConnell, 141.

77. Farah, *From the Pinnacle of the Temple*, 100-103; cf. Charles S. Price, *The Real Faith*, 52-60.

78. Jerome, *Biblia Sacra: Iuxta Vulgatam Versionem* (Stuttgart, Germany: Württembergische Bibelanstalt, 1969), 2:1595.

79. John Wyclif, *The Holy Bible Containing the Old and New Testaments with the Apocryphal Books* (London: Oxford University Press, 1850).

80. John Gill, *Gill's Commentary* (Grand Rapids: Baker, [1852] 1980), 377.

81. See Barnes, 372-373; Princeton scholar J.A. Alexander's commentary, *The Gospel According to Mark* (Grand Rapids: Baker, [1885] 1980), 310; H.D.M. Spence, and Joseph S. Exell, eds., *The Pulpit Commentary* (Chicago: Wilcox & Follett Co., n.d.), 36:123; A.E.J. Rawlinson, *Westminster Commentaries* (London: Methuen & Co., Ltd., 1925), 38:158; F.C. Cook, ed., *The Bible Commentary: Matthew to Luke* (Grand Rapids: Baker, [1871] 1981), 7:270; Charles John Ellicott, ed., *Ellicott's Commentary on the Whole Bible* (Grand Rapids: Zondervan, 1959), 6:220; Matthew Henry, and Thomas Scott, *A Commentary on the Whole Bible* (Nashville: Thomas Nelson, [1710, 1792] 1979), 3:192; Adam Clarke, *Clarke's Commentary on the New Testament* (New York: Abingdon Press, 1830), 1:327; Gill, *Gill's Commentary*, 5:377; Robert Young, *Young's Literal Translation of the Holy Bible* (Grand Rapids: Baker, 1898). Montgomery pointed out that Bibles printed in 1921 give "faith of God" as an alternative translation, indicating that it was an acceptable interpretation by biblical scholars. *Secrets of Victory*, 28. For more examples including the 1599 Geneva Bible, Douay-Rheims Bible, Wilbur M. Smith, and R.A. Torrey, see Troy J. Edwards, "The God-Kind of Faith—A Biblical, Historical, and Theological Defense" (n.d.), available on the Internet at www.100megspop2.com/victoryword.

82. Gill, 5:377.

83. Spurgeon, *The Metropolitan Tabernacle Pulpit*, Vol. 24, 645.

84. Chambers, *My Utmost for His Highest*, 81.

85. McCrossan, *Christ's Paralyzed Church X-Rayed*, 320-321.

86. C.I. Scofield, ed., *The Scofield Reference Bible* (New York: Oxford University Press, 1917), 1061.

87. J. Hudson Taylor, "Reckon on God's Faithfulness," *Triumphs of Faith*, July 1902, 159.

88. Chambers, *Oswald Chambers: His Life and Work*, 53; Meyer, *Five Musts of the Christian Life*, 91ff. Meyer, *The Secret of Guidance*, 51; Bosworth, 185.

89. Murray, *The Holiest of All*, 441.

90. Donald G. Bloesch, *Jesus Christ: Savior and Lord* (Downers Grove, Ill.: IVP, 1997), 63.

91. Abraham Kuyper, cited in Bloesch, 63.

92. Murray, *With Christ in the School of Prayer*, 1, 84, 86.

93. Chambers, *The Place of Help*, 160.

94. Nee, *God's Plan and the Overcomers*, 29.

95. Charles Price, *The Real Faith*, 83, see also pp. 31, 38, 57, 63, 111, 125.

96. Veli-Matti Kärkäinen, *Christology: A Global Introduction* (Grand Rapids: Baker, 2003), 52-53. See also *The Interpreter's Bible: Mark*, ed. George Arthur Buttrick (New York, Nashville: Abingdon, 1951), 7:831-832, where it interprets Mark 11:22 as Jesus' faith in God.

97. Drickamer explains, "The communication of attributes means that whatever can be attributed to (said about) either the divine or the human nature in Christ is to be attributed to the entire person. Whatever is true of either nature is true of the person." J. M. Drickamer, "Communication of Attributes, Communicatio Idiomatum," *Evangelical Dictionary of Theology*, 2nd Edition, ed. Walter A. Elwell (Grand Rapids: Baker Academic, 2001), 277. Further, C.W. Mitchell comments, "Because of the strength of the union of the two natures of Christ, 'what Christ is or does according to the divine nature the whole Christ is said to be or do; and . . . what he is and does or has suffered according to the human nature the whole Christ, the Son of God, God is said . . . to be, to do or to have suffered." C.W. Mitchell, "Communicatio Operationum," *Evangelical Dictionary of Theology*, 277. Drickamer notes that "this doctrine is more characteristic of Lutheran than Reformed theology. . . . Reformed theologians have tended to designate Christ's acts as the acts of one nature or the other." Drickamer, 277. Though the classic faith leaders of the Keswick/Higher tradition tended to be Reformed in background, they appear to have accepted the more Lutheran Christology. On *perichoresis*, see S.M. Smith, Perichoresis," *Evangelical Dictionary of Theology*, 906-907.

98. Simpson, *A Larger Christian Life*, 54.

99. Simpson, *The Life of Prayer*, 70. In his commentary on the Book of Acts, Simpson referred to Alexander, so his interpretation may have been based on Alexander's exegesis. Simpson, *CITB* (1992), 4:591. See also Simpson, *The Life of Prayer*, 60; *A Larger Christian Life*, 137-38; *The Gospel of Healing*, 89, 142-143; *In the School of Faith*, 34.

100. Charles Price, *The Real Faith*, 54; see also pp. 4, 37, 39, 52, 53.

101. A.S. Worrell, *The Worrell New Testament* (Springfield, Mo.: Gospel Publishing House, [1904], 1980.

102. Meyer, *The Secret of Guidance*, 50. He used the terms "God's faith" and "God's faithfulness" interchangeably.

103. W.B. Godbey, *Translation of the New Testament from the Original Greek* (Cincinnati: God's Revivalist, n.d.), 102.

104. E. Stanley Jones, *Abundant Living* (New York, Nashville: Abingdon-Cokesbury Press, 1942), 79. See also *The Basic Bible* (New York: E.P. Dutton & Co., 1950).

105. Bowman also argues that such a view means that God must hope for what He does not know. Bowman, *The Word-Faith Controversy*, 112. He does not realize that the Greek word for hope (*elpis*) does not mean wishful thinking, but confident expectation. God can hope in the sense of confidently expecting what he has willed and exercised through the power of His faith will indeed come about without any possibility of failure.

106. Cyril of Jerusalem, *Catechetical Lectures*, Lecture 5:11; *NPNF*, 2:7:31.

107. Chrysostom, *Homilies on First Corinthians*, Homily 29, *NPNF*, 1:12:172.

108. Murray, *The Secret of the Faith Life*, 69.

109. *The Scofield Reference Bible*, 1061.

110. Simpson, *The Gentle Love of the Holy Spirit*, 135.

111. Simpson, *The Gospel of Healing*, 88-89.

112. Torrey, *The Power of Prayer*, 140.

113. Ibid., 126.

114. Chambers, *Biblical Psychology*, 43.

115. Spence and Exell, *The Pulpit Commentary*, 36:123.

116. Nee, *God's Plan and the Overcomers*, 75.

117. Bounds, *The Complete Works of E.M. Bounds: Book 1: The Necessity of Prayer*, 38.

118. A.E.J. Rawlinson, *Westminster Commentaries*, 38:158.

119. Clarke, 1:327.

120. A.T. Robertson, *A Grammar of the Greek New Testament in Light of Historical Research*, 2nd Edition (New York: George H. Doran Co., 1915), 500.

121. Cowman, *Streams in the Desert*, July 7.

122. McCrossan, *Christ's Paralyzed Church X-Rayed*, 321.

123. Wigglesworth, *Faith That Prevails*, 6.

124. Ibid., 18-19.

125. Müller, *Autobiography*, 85.

126. Ibid., 154-155.

127. Montgomery, *Secrets of Victory*, 46.

128. See also Montgomery, *The Prayer of Faith*, 50; Montgomery, *Secrets of Victory*, 28.

129. McIntyre, 257.

130. Robertson, 500.

131. McIntyre, 257.

132. C.S. Mann, *The Anchor Bible: Mark* (Garden City, N.Y.: Doubleday, 1986), 27:453.

133. David H. Stern, *Jewish New Testament* (Clarksville, MD: Jewish New Testament Publications, 1979, 1989, 1990).

134. Kenyon, *The Two Kinds of Faith*, 103.

CHAPTER 11

———◆·◆·◆———

Faith and the Will of God

The relationship between the operation of faith and the will of God is a matter of controversy, not only in regard to contemporary faith teaching, but also historically between the theological positions of Calvinism and Arminianism. Typically, Calvinists emphasize the sovereignty of God and Arminians emphasize man's free will. Also interrelated is whether or not the nature of faith is passive or active, as discussed in Chapter 6. Calvinists would tend to view faith as a passive trust in the sovereign will of God, while Arminians would tend to view faith as an active participation in synergy with God. Contemporary faith teaching tends to be more Arminian in its approach to the will of God. Here again, the elliptical nature of truth needs to be recognized.

CONTEMPORARY FAITH TEACHING ON FAITH AND THE WILL OF GOD

On Praying, "If It Is God's Will." A common teaching in the contemporary word of faith movement is that to pray "if it be God's will" or "Thy will be done" demonstrates a lack of faith. Hagin wrote in relationship to the prayer of faith, "It is unscriptural to pray 'if it is the will of God.' When you put an 'if' in your prayer, you are praying in doubt."[1] However, he also acknowledges that there are appropriate times and types of prayer in which it is appropriate to pray "if it is your will."[2] Frederick Price goes so far as to say the Lord's Prayer does not apply to believers today because of the clause "Thy will be done."[3] Moreover, Price declares, "If you have to say, 'If it be Thy will,' or 'Thy will be done,' . . . then you're calling God a fool."[4]

On Healing as God's Will for All. Some in the contemporary faith movement claim it is always God's will to heal, and if healing does not take place, it is not God's fault—it is due to sin or lack of faith. Hagin, for example, declares, "I believe it the plan of God our Father that no believer should ever be sick. That every believer should live his full length of time and actually wear out, if Jesus tarries, and fall asleep in Jesus. It is not—I state boldly—it is not the will of God my Father that we should suffer with cancer and other dread diseases which bring pain and anguish. No! It is God's will that we be healed."[5]

CRITICISM OF CONTEMPORARY FAITH TEACHING

Hanegraaff criticizes the Faith teaching on praying "if it be Thy will":

> Frederick Price, for example, instructed his followers that praying for the Lord's will to be done is "really stupidity." He calls such prayers a "farce" and "an insult to God's intelligence."
>
> In the real world, however, Jesus Christ contradicts these statements in the strongest terms possible. . . . If Price is right, Jesus Himself would be "stupid," because in His passionate prayer in the Garden of Gethsemane He prayed, "My Father, if it is possible, may this cup be taken away from Me. Yet *not as I will, but as You will*" (Matthew 6:39, emphasis added).[6]

Hanegraaff and MacArthur cite additional biblical examples (Matt. 6:10; James 4:15; 1 John 5:14; Rom. 8:27; 10:10; 15:32) to demonstrate the scriptural validity of praying "if it be Thy will."[7]

Critics also oppose contemporary faith teaching on healing as God's will for all. McConnell maintains that similar to metaphysical religions contemporary faith leaders make absolutes out of experiences As a result they claim a cause-and-effect power for their healing formulas, and since it is impossible that God would fail to comply with these Scripture formulas, the believer has only himself to blame for sickness. Thus, healing is not a sovereign miracle bestowed by a merciful God. Healing is a cause-and-effect formula that works every time the Christian applies it in 'faith.' . . . Those who use healing formulas to claim that God heals *all* our diseases *every* time are denying reality.[8]

CLASSIC FAITH TEACHING ON FAITH AND THE WILL OF GOD

On Praying, "If It Is Thy Will." Several classic leaders do indicate that there are times when it is inappropriate to pray "if it be Thy will." For instance, referring to Matthew 7:7-11, Finney wrote: "You have no right to put an *if* and say, 'Lord, *if it be Thy will*, give us Thy Holy Spirit.' This is to insult God. To put an *if* into God's promise, where God has put none, is tantamount to charging God with being insincere. It is like saying: 'O God, if Thou art in earnest in making these promises, grant us the blessing we pray for.'"[9] Murray, though coming from a Reformed theology, nonetheless made a similar statement: "The tendency of human reason is to interpose here, and with certain qualifying clauses, 'if expedient,' 'if according to God's will.'. . . Beware of dealing thus with the Master's words."[10] Simpson, likewise from Reformed background, also wrote, "The prayer for healing, 'if it be His will,' carries with it no claim for which Satan will quit his hold. . . . There is much subtle unbelief often in the prayer, 'Thy will be done.'"[11]

Further Simpson wrote, "Submission to sickness is not always submission to God."[12] C&MA evangelist Bosworth stated that saying "if it be Thy will" can be "faith-destroying words,"[13] a phrase that Hanegraaff attacks.[14] Greek professor and fellow C&MA leader McCrossan, a friend of Bosworth, likewise used the same phrase.[15] This documentation demonstrates that, contrary to Hanegraaff's claim, this belief did not come from metaphysics, Kenyon, or contemporary faith teachers, but it is consistent with classic holiness teaching, such as what Kenyon received from Murray and Simpson.

It should be noted, however, that classic faith teachers do not go so far as to say that believers should *never* pray "if it be Thy will." On the contrary, they also teach that there are appropriate times for a prayer of seeking the will of God or of relinquishment and submission. For Spurgeon, submission to God's will must be implicit in spirit, even if it is not spoken: "We can only pray without an 'if' when we are quite sure that that our will must be God's will, because God's will is fully our will."[16] Spurgeon further counseled:

> If that man at any time has a desire which is not according to God's will, . . . but he provides for this defect by this addendum at the end of it, "Lord, if I have asked, in this my prayer, for anything which is not according to Thy mind, I beseech thee do not regard me. And if any wish which I have expressed to Thee—even though it is the desire which burns in my bosom above all other wishes—be a wish that is not right in Thy sight, regard me not, my Father, but in Thy infinite love and compassion, do something better for Thy servant than Thy servant

knows how to ask." Now, when a prayer is after that fashion, how can it fail?[17]

Simpson also gave a caveat to his earlier statement, saying that when we have no clear warrant or promise from Scripture or clear leading of the Holy Spirit, "we ought ever to refer the matter to the arbitration of that unknown will."[18] Similarly, Hannah Whitall Smith found joy in submissively praying, "Thy will be done": "If I were lost in a track-less wilderness and could see no way out, and a skillful guide should offer to lead me to safety, would I consider it a hard thing to surrender myself into his hands, and say, 'Thy will be done' to His guidance? And can it be a hard thing to surrender myself to my Heavenly Guide, and say, 'Thy will be done' to His guidance? No, a thousand times no!"[19] For her it was a matter of delightful consecration or surrender to God.

This goes back to the foundation of faith that views the active and passive aspects of faith as two sides of the same coin or two polarities of truth. There are appropriate times to trust God passively and pray, "Thy will be done," and also appropriate times to act on that trust and claim actively by faith. This leads to the classic faith understanding of the role of man in accomplishing the will of God.

Man's Role in Accomplishing God's Will. Murray, from a Dutch Reformed background that was also strongly pietistic, emphasized the sovereign fulfillment of God's will, but nonetheless believed that man plays a vital role in accomplishing God's will:

> There is often great confusion as to the will of God. People think that what God wills must inevitably take place. This is by no means the case. . . . God has made the execution of His will, in many things, dependent upon the will of man. Of God's will revealed in His promises, so much will be fulfilled as our faith accepts. Prayer is the power by which that comes to pass which otherwise would not take place. And faith, the power which it is decided how much of God's will shall be done in us. When once God reveals to a soul what He is willing to do for it, the responsibility for the execution of that will rests with us.[20]

MacMillan, likewise from a Reformed background, recognized man's role and advised:

How many believers content themselves with the uttering of the words "Thy will be done," in all matters they bring to the Lord. Their spirits assume a passive attitude that accepts anything that comes to them as the will of the Father. This is not Scriptural, and very far from the desire of God for His children. The Holy Spirit teaches a hearty cooperation rather than mere resignation; an active entering into God's plan instead of a vague yielding to circumstances; a definite claiming and appropriating of the promises which are set before us in the Word, as being the expression of the Father's will for His children. We are to positively will the will of God; to seek it out as He willed it; and to maintain our place of quiet assurance before Him until it has been fully accomplished.[21]

Oral Roberts has likewise carried on this classic faith belief through repeating a popular motto: "Without God I cannot; without us God will not."

Is Healing for All?—Faith and the Sovereignty of God. The question of praying for the will of God in relationship to healing is also a thorny practical issue that arises from this teaching. Some in the contemporary faith movement claim it is always God's will to heal, and if healing does not take place, it is not God's fault—it is due to sin or lack of faith. What is the teaching of the classic leaders?

Simpson wrote, "Is it the will of God to heal all? It is the will of God to heal all who believe," indicating that faith is a key element in God's will to heal.[22] Simpson also wrote similarly that healing is "His normal provision for the believer. It is something that is included in our redemption rights, something that is part of the gospel of His grace, something that is already recognized as within His will and not requiring a special revelation to justify us claiming it."[23] Further, Simpson explained:

The prayer for healing, "If it be His will," carries with it no claim for which Satan will quit his hold. This is a matter about which we ought to know His will before we ask, and then will and claim it because it is His will. Has He given us any means by which we may know His will? Most assuredly . . . the Word of God is for evermore the standard of His will, and that Word has declared immutably that it is God's greatest desire and unalterable principle of action and will to render to every man according as he will believe, and especially to save all who will receive Christ by faith, and to heal all who will receive healing by similar faith. No one thinks of asking for forgiveness "if the Lord will." Nor should we throw any stronger doubt on His promise of physical redemption.[24]

This sounds very much like the contemporary faith teaching. Yet Simpson and other classic leaders did not make an absolute out of this principle, as do some contemporary faith leaders, but made room for exceptions in the sovereignty of God: "Divine healing fully recognizes the sovereignty of God and the state and spiritual attitude of the individual."[25]

Citing Paul's thorn, Simpson taught: "Paul certainly prayed until he got an answer from heaven, and so we should claim deliverance at the very least until we get a refusal as clear and divine as he did."[26] Other evangelical leaders such as Torrey echoed the same teaching: "Healing is to be expected. Paul himself expected healing in his own case [his thorn in the flesh] *until God definitely revealed to him that it was not His will in that particular instance.*"[27] Similarly, Carter, an associate of Simpson, wrote on Paul's thorn, indicating that the source of this teaching came from Boardman and Cullis: "We have Paul's example for steadfastly praying in faith for its removal, until we get an answer from the Lord about which there can be no mistake."[28]

It was then the belief of the classic leaders of faith that while healing is generally provided for all believers through the atonement, God in His sovereignty may not heal all. Simpson also wrote, "We are not told that He healed all the sick, but He healed many of them. It was not universal, and it was not special. He does not heal all the sick yet, but He heals without distinction or respect of persons all that are able to touch Him and take His help according to the conditions of the gospel."[29] Carter explained further the practical implications, "Mr. Simpson has always allowed that one's time may come and the faith not be given, but the point here is that practically the position [of Simpson and the C&MA] has been one of special answers in the will of God, not a broad Atonement for all at any time."[30] Carter also wrote of Cullis, "The practical position occupied by Dr. Cullis was that of special healing in the will of the Lord. . . . He never was given to preach the matter doctrinally, but urged all to come to God in faith and be guided by the Spirit."[31]

Likewise, Chambers, while believing that healing is a provision in the Atonement, also believed in the sovereignty of God:

When it comes to healing it is not a question of God's will, but of His sovereignty, that is, whether the pre-dispensational efficacy of the Atonement is active on our behalf just now. There is no case of healing in the Bible that did not come from a direct intervention of the sovereign touch of God. We make the mistake of putting an abstract truth deduced from the Word of God in the place of God Himself. When God does not heal it is time we got down to close quarters with God and asked Him why. There is a deep lesson behind; we cannot lay down a general law for everyone, we can only find out the reason by going to God.[32]

Chambers believed that the Atonement is only effective for healing when God deems it so.

A.J. Gordon summed up the dynamic tension and balance between the healing promises of God and the sovereignty of God: "While we recognize the doctrine of the Divine Sovereignty, . . . this should no more prevent our asking in faith for the healing of our bodies, than the doctrine of election should prevent our asking with the fullest assurance for the salvation of our souls."[33] Simpson also advised that a believer needs to be totally surrendered to the ultimate will of God before claiming healing: "No man can take it [divine healing] rightly until he has surrendered his will to the will of God, either to live or die, and then accepts the blessing because it is God's highest will. There is a way of wanting healing because we want it, and this will only defeat itself, but there is a blessed surrender of our will, which is followed immediately be the revelation of His will and the acceptance of the blessing, not because we wish, but because God wills it. Our first attitude is a surrendered will, our second attitude is a persistent will in harmony with the Divine will."[34]

This question of whether or not it is God's will to heal also involves the question of whether sickness comes from God. Classic faith leaders did not believe as a general premise that God wills or causes sickness. They would trace the causes of sickness and suffering to the Fall and Satan's part in the matter.[35] Yet Simpson also cautioned, "We must not carry this too far by concluding that all sickness comes directly from Satanic power. Sickness may come from a physical cause, and it may come from the direct stroke of God Himself in judgment."[36] Bounds likewise attributed much sickness to the power of the devil, but did not blame sickness on sin or lack of faith: "The great power and malignity of Satan is seen in that among the most distressing cases [of sickness or demonization] were those who were not noted for great sins, but the young and comparative innocent ones were the victims of his dread power."[37]

REFLECTIONS AND CONCLUSIONS

On Praying, "If It Be Thy Will." The anti-faith critics condemn the contemporary faith teaching against praying "if it be Thy will," but do not allow for times when it would be inappropriate to pray in that way. Some contemporary faith teaching (but not Hagin, as noted above) criticizes the belief that it is ever appropriate to pray "if it be Thy will." Both positions represent opposite extremes in the contra-polarity of truth. Classic faith teaching demonstrates a balance between the two polarities, maintaining that there are times when it is appropriate to pray "if it be Thy will," and there are also times in which praying that type of prayer would not be appropriate, but would indeed hinder or destroy faith. So it is not a case of "either-or," but rather "both-and," in different contexts, as A.J. Gordon expressed the dynamic tension: "Because we find both sides of this truth distinctly expressed in scripture, we must be sure to emphasize both."[38]

On God's Will for Healing for All. The contemporary faith position maintains that it is God's will for all to be healed, without exception. The anti-faith critics maintain that it is up to God's sovereignty, and that healing is not provided for in the atonement. Again, neither camp is totally right, nor totally wrong. Both camps represent the contra-polarities of faith. There is validity to McConnell's charge of setting up fixed cause-and-effect formulas. While cause-and-effect relationships *can* exist in the operation of faith, they are not absolute. McConnell observes the most serious flaws of contemporary faith teaching regarding healing are found in their faith praxis.[39] Three particular errors of practice McConnell mentions are denial of sickness, refusing medical care, and lack of encouraging pastoral care and proper treatment of the chronically or terminally ill.[40]

However, it should also be noted that there has been a more recent move in some contemporary faith circles to move away from formulistic thinking and practice. Kenneth Hagin, Jr., son of the famed contemporary faith leader, has more recently disavowed the "faith as a formula" practice that his father avowed years earlier, saying, "Faith is not a set of legalistic formulas. . . . God doesn't respond to formulas but He does respond to faith in His Word (Isa. 55:11; Ps. 138:2; Heb. 11:6)."[41] Kenneth Hagin, Sr., had written years earlier, "A formula for faith is: (1) Find a promise in God's Word for whatever you are seeking. (2) Believe God's Word. (3) Do not consider contradictory circumstances. (4) Praise God for the answer."[42]

Faith and the Will of God

Again, the classic faith teachers have demonstrated that a sound and strong practical faith lies between these two extremes. They show us that it is possible for a person to believe in the sovereignty of God and yet also believe that it is generally God's will to heal. Practically speaking, a person can pray for healing in confidence, because it is God's general will unless He reveals otherwise.

---

1. Kenneth E. Hagin, *Exceedingly Growing Faith* (Tulsa, Okla.: Faith Library, 1983), 10, cited in MacArthur, 349.

2. Kenneth E. Hagin, *The Art of Intercession* (Tulsa, Okla.: Kenneth Hagin Ministries, 1980), 5-7; Kenneth E. Hagin, *The Art of Prayer* (Tulsa, Okla.: Kenneth Hagin Ministries, 1991), 71-75.

3. Frederick Price, cited in Hanegraaff, 34, 271, 286.

4. Frederick Price, cited in Hanegraaff, 271.

5. Kenneth E. Hagin, "Healing: The Father's Provision," *Word of Faith*, Aug., 1977, 9.

6. Hanegraaff, 271.

7. Ibid.; MacArthur, 349-350.

8. McConnell, 158-159.

9. Charles G. Finney, *Revivals of Religion* (Virginia Beach, Va.: CBN University Press, 1978), 71.

10. Murray, *With Christ in the School of Prayer*, 79; see also p. 230ff.

11. Simpson, *The Gospel of Healing*, 76, 79.

12. Simpson, *CITB: Luke* (n.d.), 176.

13. Bosworth, 165.

14. Hanegraaff, 271.

15. McCrossan, *Christ's Paralyzed Church X-Rayed*, 317.

16. Spurgeon, "Golden Key of Prayer," Sermon #619, *Metropolitan Tabernacle Pulpit*, Vol. 11, 151.

17. Spurgeon, "Conditions of Power in Prayer," Sermon #1103, *Metropolitan Tabernacle Pulpit*, Vol. 19, 178. For an updated version, see Spurgeon, *The Power of Prayer in a Believer's Life*, 116.

18. Simpson, *The Gospel of Healing*, 61.

19. Smith, *The Unselfishness of God*, 224.

20. Murray, *With Christ in the School of Prayer*, 237-238.

21. MacMillan, *The Authority of the Believer*, 64.

22. Simpson, *The Gospel of Healing*, 120-121; see also pp. 60ff.

23. Simpson, *CITB: Luke* (n.d.), 178.

24. Simpson, *The Gospel of Healing*, 76-78.

25. A.B. Simpson, "Inquiries and Answers," *The Word, Work and World*, Nov. 1886, 294; "Inquiries and Answers" was published later in A.B. Simpson's book, *The Lord for the Body* (New York: Christian Alliance Publishing Co., n.d.), accessed via Internet, Alliance Studies website: http://online.cbccts.sk.ca/alliancestudies/simpson/LORDBODY.HTM For an updated edition of this book, see A.B. Simpson, *The Lord for the Body*, revised edition (Camp Hill, Penn.: Christian Publications, 1996).

26. Simpson, "Inquiries and Answers," *Word, Work and World*, Nov. 1886, 292-293.

27. Torrey, *Divine Healing*, 19.

28. Carter, *The Atonement for Sin and Sickness*, 126; see also pp. 124-133.

29. Simpson, *CITB* (1992), 4:197.

30. Carter, *Faith Healing Reviewed*, 113.

31. Ibid., 112.

32. Oswald Chambers, *The Servant as His Lord*, (United Kingdom: Marshall Morgan & Scott, 1959), accessed on *The Complete Works of Oswald Chambers*, CD-ROM (Grand Rapids: Discovery House, 2000).

33. A.J. Gordon, *The Ministry of Healing*, 234-235.

34. A.B. Simpson, "The Connection Between Spiritual and Physical Life," *AW*, Aug. 2, 1919, 292.

35. See Simpson, *The Gospel of Healing*, 28-29, 96-99, 105; Carter, 6, 227.

36. Simpson, *CITB: Luke* (n.d.), 175.

37. Dorsett, *E.M. Bounds*, 230. See also Chapter 27 for related discussion.

38. A.J. Gordon, *The Ministry of Healing*, 213.

39. McConnell, 164.

40. Ibid., 164-169.

41. Kenneth Hagin, Jr., *Another Look at Faith* (Tulsa, Okla.: Kenneth Hagin Ministries, 1996), 74.

42. Kenneth Hagin, Sr., *New Thresholds of Faith*, 23.

CHAPTER 12

Logos and Rhema

The concept of distinguishing between the objective Word of God (*logos*) and a subjective word from the Lord (*rhema*) is common in contemporary charismatic teaching. It is usually based on two main passages of Scripture that are interpreted to use the term *rhema* to refer to a special, specific word from God:

> *But what does it say? 'The word* [rhema] *is near you, in your mouth and in your heart'—that is, the word* [rhema] *of faith which we are preaching. . . . So faith comes from hearing, and hearing by the word of Christ* (Rom. 10:8, 17).

> *And take the helmet of salvation, and the sword of the Spirit, which is the word* [rhema] *of God* (Eph. 6:17).

Oral Roberts University theologian Charles Farah explains the typical teaching, describing it as a theological construct:

> There is a difference between the Word of God in general and the word of God which is spoken specifically to you. In the Greek New Testament this is sometimes expressed by two different words for "word": *logos* and *rhema*.
>
> *Logos* denotes the expression of thought, not the mere name of an object, but the body, conception, or an idea, like God. In other words, we may think of *logos* as a sort of universal, at least in the Gospel of John. . . . *Rhema* was a specific statement whereas *logos* tended to be general. *Rhema* was more precise and definite. The particular is *rhema*. . . . The *logos* is objective, while the *rhema* is often subjective, a word spoken for a particular occasion to a

particular person. The *logos* is eternal, while the *rhema* is often contemporary.[1]

CONTEMPORARY FAITH TEACHING

Hagin's understanding of the *logos/rhema* distinction is derived initially from *Vine's Expository Dictionary of New Testament Words*, which he quotes: "The significance of *rhema* (as distinct from *logos*) is exemplified in the injunction to take 'the sword of the Spirit, which is the word of God,' Eph. 6:17; here the reference is not to the whole Bible as such, but to the individual Scripture that the Spirit brings to our remembrance for use in time of need, a prerequisite being the regular storing of the mind with Scripture."[2]

However, his son Kenneth Hagin, Jr., gives an interpretation beyond Vine's definition when he teaches, "The Word of God that is spoken out in faith becomes the 'rhema' word—*the spoken Word*."[3] Lovett , a former Oral Roberts University professor, thus summarizes the contemporary faith teaching on *rhema* and *logos*: "The Rhema doctrine is the primary key to the Positive Confession theology. Romans 10:8 is the primary passage or archtext of the Rhema doctrine. In its classical Greek usage, the word *rhema* has to do with stating something specifically. The major premise of Rhema doctrine is that whatever is spoken by faith becomes immediately inspired and therefore dynamic in the particular situation or event to which it is addressed."[4]

CRITICISM OF CONTEMPORARY FAITH TEACHING

The Rhema Teaching Is Neo-orthodox. MacArthur directs his criticism toward Farah (even though Farah was a critic of the contemporary faith movement), claiming the teaching on *logos* and *rhema* is neo-orthodox: "The historic, objective *logos*, in Farah's system, has no transforming impact until it becomes *rhema*—your own personal word from God. That sounds dangerously close to what neo-orthodox theologians have been saying for years: that the Bible only becomes God's Word when it speaks to you."[5] It is true that neo-orthodox theologian Karl Barth is one source for the concept that the Bible becomes God's Word when it speaks to the believer,[6] but Barth did not link this to the two Greek terms. Further, having known and studied under Farah personally, I can attest to the fact the Farah was not neo-orthodox in his theology.

The Logos/Rhema Distinction Is Not Biblical. An official statement from the Assemblies of God entitled "The Believer and Positive

Confession" opposes the *logos/rhema* distinction by contemporary faith teaching: "The distinction is not justified by usage either in the Greek New Testament or in the Septuagint. . . . The words are used synonymously in both. . . . The distinctions between *logos* and *rhema* cannot be sustained by Biblical evidence."[7] Further, the Assemblies statement admonishes, "Passages of Scripture are sometimes selected without regard to the context or analogy of faith which they claim to speak by faith. In this kind of application of the so-called *rhema* principle, adherents are more concerned with making the Word mean what they want it to mean than in becoming what the Word wants them to become. In some instances it becomes they love God more for what He does than for who He is."[8] Likewise, MacArthur claims, "The problem with that idea is that neither the Greek meaning nor the New Testament usage make any such distinction."[9]

There Is No Direct Leading of the Holy Spirit. Yet another attack comes from critics who claim a believer cannot receive a word, an impression, a leading from the Lord. For example, Gary Friesen in *Decision Making and the Will of God* claims, "The way of wisdom does not consider peace or lack of peace as a direct message communicating specific guidance into the individual will of God."[10] He downplays the role of the Holy Spirit in giving guidance, declaring "leadings of the Spirit" as invalid, and saying that "impressions are just impressions."[11] He puts a high premium on common sense as the wisdom from God for guidance: "With the wisdom view, the believer may confidently apply common sense to every single decision. . . . The only time common sense is to be set aside is when it contradicts God's revealed (moral) will."[12]

Classic Faith Teaching

The Antiquity of Distinguishing the Objective and Subjective Word. However, while the *logos/rhema* terminology may be a more recent theological construct, contrary to MacArthur's claim that the teaching is neo-orthodox, this concept of distinguishing the general word from the specific word in season, as we will see, is not original with Barthian neo-orthodoxy, but was taught by classic leaders of faith. In fact, the concept of distinguishing between the objective Word of God and a subjective word from the Lord is ancient in church history. According to commentator Marcus Dods, early church father Theophilis was the first to distinguish the word internal and the word external or emitted.[13]

An Immediate Word Near in the Heart. The nineteenth-century writers did not refer specifically to the Greek terms *logos* and *rhema*, but they did acknowledge the need to receive a special, personal word from the Lord, which is distinguished from the Word of God in general. Alluding to Romans 10:8, Hannah Whitall Smith wrote of this concept in her earlier Quaker heritage: "[I] would rather recommend him to the immediate teaching of the word nigh in the heart, even the Spirit of God."[14] This idea is characteristic of early Quaker thought.

A Word of Promise in Due Season. Spurgeon described the process of receiving this *rhema*, this fresh word of God as a promise in due season:

> Often you cannot get at a difficulty so as to deal with it aright and find your way to a happy result. You pray, but have not the liberty in prayer which you desire. A definite promise is what you want. You try one and another of the inspired words, but they do not fit. You try again, and in due season a promise presents itself which seems to have been made for the occasion; it fits exactly as a well-made key fits the lock for which it was prepared. Having found the identical word of the living God you hasten to plead it at the throne of grace, saying, "Oh Lord, Thou hast promised this good thing unto Thy servant; be pleased to grant it!" The matter is ended; sorrow is turned to joy; prayer is heard.[15]

Spurgeon's Baptist friend, F.B. Meyer, likewise wrote about reckoning on God's "sure word of promise."[16]

A Definite Leading of the Holy Spirit. This fresh word from the Lord could come through a direct leading of the Spirit. Murray explained: "The personal application of the general promises of the word to our special personal needs—it is for this that the leading of the Holy Spirit is given to us. . . . Not from without, but from within, comes the quickening of the Word by the Spirit."[17] Murray believed that every demonstration of the power of faith is "the fruit of a special revelation of God. . . . The spiritual power is wanting, except as God Himself speaking them [promises] to us. And He speaks to those who walk and live with Him."[18] Torrey shared his own experience, commenting on Mark 11:24, "I used to say, 'The way to get anything I want is to believe that I am going to get it.' I would kneel down and pray, trying to believe, but I did not get the things I asked for. I had no real faith. Real faith must have a guarantee. Before I can really believe I am to receive what I ask for, I must have a definite promise from God's Word, or a definite leading of the Holy Spirit, to rest my faith on."[19]

A Prophetic "Thus Saith the Lord" or Special Word of Faith. Simpson expressed it is this way: "We must have a 'Thus saith the Lord' about things before we act."[20] As mentioned in Chapter 10, Simpson, along with other classic faith leaders, believed that faith acts on a special word from God. Also as pointed out earlier, Müller described the gift of faith as a special confidence or assurance given by the Lord to act in faith, almost as a command, so that if he failed to take the step of faith, it would be a sin.[21] The grace of faith is based on a clear command or promise of Scripture as a general, universal truth (what today is called *logos*). Such a truth can be acted upon as general principle without having a special word from God. However, if a person does not have a clear word in Scripture, to act without hearing from God would be presumption. The grace of faith is based on the general promises of Scripture (such as that it is God's nature and desire to heal). The gift of faith is based on a special word or impression from the Lord giving unconditional confidence that God will answer the prayer (what today is called *rhema*).

An Impression of a Word of Scripture. As mentioned earlier, when Hudson Taylor had been weakened with a life-threatening infection due contact with a cadaver as a medical student, he stated that he had an *impression* to walk a distance to check on needed funds. Then he prayed for confirmation to know if it was from the Lord and was *impressed* with John 14:15. Acting on that word from the Lord, he found his strength increasing as he went.

Chambers, though by no means neo-orthodox, nevertheless makes a statement similar to Barth: "The written Word became a Living Word."[22] Yet he differs from neo-orthodoxy in that he regards Scripture as the written Word of God. He believed that the words of Scripture, though they are the Word of God, "do not give us life unless Jesus speaks them to us."[23] Chambers explained that the Holy Spirit "will frequently take a text out of its Bible context and put it into the context of our lives. We have all had the experience of a verse coming to us right out of its Bible setting and becoming alive in the settings of our own lives, and that word becomes a sacred, secret possession."[24] Tozer, who was also far from neo-orthodoxy, in his classic book *The Pursuit of God*, similarly asserted against MacArthur that "all energy is here only because the power-filled Word is being spoken. . . . It is the present Voice which makes the written Word all-powerful."[25]

Carmichael was woman of faith who believed in receiving a "word from the Lord": "This 'word' might be something remembered at the crucial moment, or a direct command. Such commands, in the days of the apostles, came when the Holy Spirit spoke or when an angel appeared. Amy admitted that she had never been vouchsafed an angel visit, but all other methods of guidance she knew well. If there was neither inward assurance nor the visible opening of circumstances, a token was asked for and not refused."[26] She believed in and received "a word that cannot be mistaken" which "doth in a way known to Himself twine and bind the heart which way He pleaseth."[27] She received what she called "shewings," "things revealed in special ways."[28] One of these ways was through the special enlivening of Scripture in what Carmichael called a *durbar*, an Indian word for a special personal audience with a high official, which she relates to the Hebrew word *dabar*, to speak a word, used in Genesis 18:33 of the Lord communing with Abraham: "When reading your Bible, have you not often noticed that some word has shone out in a new, direct, clear way to you? It has been as though you have never read it before. You cannot explain the vivid freshness, the life, in it, the extraordinary way it has leapt to your eye—to your heart. It just was so. That was the 'durbar'; you were in the very presence of your King at that moment. He was speaking to you. His word was spirit and life."[29] Carmichael added, "This special word may be given through another child of God,"[30] sounding much like the giving of a prophecy.

Logos vs. Rhema. Eventually, the *logos/rhema* terminology became recognized and utilized by later scholars (see Reflections and Conclusions below). In the classic faith camp, evangelical expositor G. Campbell Morgan in his book *The Teaching of Christ* noted in a rudimentary form the distinction between *logos* and *rhema*:

> Those who read the New Testament in the Greek will be careful to distinguish between the words *logos* and *rhema*; for such distinction may make all the difference in the interpretation of a particular passage. . . . [*Logos*] suggests words so set together and framed as to express thought; and therefore it refers to the thought itself, orderly and sequential, which is put together and expressed. . . . The word *rhema* simply means articulate speech,

something beyond a mere sound; a sound which is a method of expression, or a sound conveying a meaning. . . . when Jesus spoke of His own sayings, and described them by the word *rhema*. . . . In this study I shall indicate the distinction between *logos* and *rhema* by translating the former, *word* or *words*; and the latter, *sayings*.[31]

Reflections and Conclusions

The Logos/Rhema Distinction Has Biblical Precedence. A number of scholarly sources recognize the *logos/rhema* distinction. As early as the nineteenth-century, Thayer's *Greek-English Lexicon of the New Testament* distinguished *logos* from *rhema*, defining *logos* as: "a word which, uttered by the living voice, embodies a conception or idea; (hence it differs from ῥῆμα [*rhema*] and ἔπος [*epos*])."[32] As mentioned above, *Vine's Expository Dictionary of New Testament Words* likewise defined the distinction between the two terms.[33] Moreover, *The New International Dictionary of New Testament Theology* distinguishes *logos* from *rhema*: "Whereas *logos* can often designate the Christian proclamation as a whole in the New Testament, *rhema* usually relates to individual words and utterances" [citing as examples Matt. 12:36; 27:14; 2 Cor. 12:4].[34]

According to Kittel's *Theological Dictionary of the New Testament, rhema* is "what is definitely stated."[35] *Logos* is the more rational element in speech "in contrast to ῥῆμα [*rhema*] as the individual and more emotional expression or saying. . . . ῥῆμα [*rhema*] thus denotes the word as expressed will, as distinct from the explicatory element in λόγος [*logos*]," although it is also noted they can often be used synonymously.[36] The phrases *rhema theou* (word of God) or *rhema kuriou* (word of the Lord) frequently refer to a special word of God to an individual, especially in the New Testament (cf. Matt. 4:4; 26:75; Luke 2:29; 3:2; 4:4; John 3:34; Acts 11:16; Rom. 10:8, 17; Eph. 6:17; Rev. 17:17; see also LXX: 1 Kings 15:10; 2 Kings 24:11).[37]

Therefore, claims that the distinction has no biblical basis are clearly false. Farah acknowledges that the dichotomy cannot be pressed too far, and that not all passages of Scripture can sustain the *logos/rhema* distinction. He views it more as a theological construct, which helps to explain a theological concept, rather than a consistent across-the-board exegetical differentiation.[38]

Many of these scholarly and classic evangelical interpretations of Scripture predated neo-orthodox teaching, and demonstrate that the concept of distinguishing *logos* and *rhema* is indeed biblical, but not to be taken to extremes or forced on all Scripture passages using the terms.

They do not support the contemporary faith idea that speaking a word turns it into a *rhema* from God. In fact, Farah cautions, "*Rhema* is not always divine in origin."[39] Practically speaking, we can speak the *logos* in faith and let God cause it to become a *rhema*, a fresh word in due season, but we cannot cause a *logos* to become a *rhema* by our confession.[40]

God Does Lead Subjectively through the Holy Spirit. In contrast to Friesen's claim that God leads only by common sense and wisdom, rather than a special leading from the Holy Spirit, the testimonies of these holy men and women of faith have amply demonstrated that his interpretation of Scripture is invalid. Chambers gave testimony of God's working in his own life that God blessed him and made him a blessing to others only as "I am bold enough to trust His leading and not the dictates of my own wisdom and common sense."[41] For Chambers, common sense is not always the "sense of my Father"), because "God is not a fact of common sense, but of revelation."[42] When the Spirit of God was near him, writes Chambers, "all the lower common-sense things have dwindled away down into their proper proportions."[43] Contrary to Friesen, who asserts believers can find their place and calling in life just through common sense,[44] Chambers intimated that he would not have entered the ministry if he had followed common sense, for he was on his way to a great career in the field of art. I would concur with Chambers, that while God can and does use common sense in our lives, He often transcends the understanding that common sense provides.

Practical Cautions about a Special Word Are Necessary. Chambers did warn that "the way we are renewed is not by impulses or impressions, but by being gripped by the Word of God. The habit of getting a word from God is right; don't give up till you get one. Never go on an impression, that will pass, there is nothing in it; there is nothing lasting until a word becomes living; when it does it is the Holy Spirit bringing back to your remembrance some word of Jesus Christ."[45] Again Chambers admonished, "Beware of impressions and impulses unless they wed themselves to the standards given by Jesus Christ."[46] So an impression or impulse is not to be acted upon unless it is assured to be from Christ or until it is confirmed by a "rhema," but contrary to Friessen, Chambers considered it as often a leading of the Holy Spirit. Impressions and the need for discernment will be discussed further in Chapter 19.

Logos and Rhema

1. Farah, *From the Pinnacle of the Temple*, 25-26, 29.

2. W.E. Vine, *Vine's Expository Dictionary of New Testament Words* (McLean, Va.: Mac-Donald Publishing Co., n.d.), 1253.

3. Kenneth Hagin, Jr., *Another Look at Faith*, 14.

4. L. Lovett, "Positive Confession Theology," *DPCM*, 719.

5. MacArthur, *Charismatic Chaos*, 46; see pp. 45-46, 93-94 for his full discussion.

6. David L. Smith, *A Handbook of Contemporary Theology* (Wheaton, Ill.: Bridgepoint/Victor Books, 1992), 29.

7. Assemblies of God, "The Believer and Positive Confession," an official statement as approved by the General Presbytery on Aug. 19, 1980. *Pentecostal Evangel*, Nov. 16, 1980, 19.

8. Ibid., 19-20.

9. MacArthur, *Charismatic Chaos*, 45.

10. Gary Friesen with Robin Maxson, *Decision Making and the Will of God* (Portland, Ore.: Multnomah, 1980), 276.

11. Ibid., 127-147.

12. Ibid., 269.

13. Theophilis, *To Autolycus*, 22, *NPNF*, 2:103, note 5.

14. H.W. Smith, *The Unselfishness of God*, 128.

15. Spurgeon, cited in Cowman, *Streams in the Desert*, Jan. 13

16. Meyer, *Five Musts of the Christian Life*, 93.

17. Murray, *With Christ in the School of Prayer*, 234.

18. Ibid., 90-91.

19. R.A. Torrey, *How to Obtain Fullness of Power* (New Kensington, Penn.: Whitaker, [1982] 1984), 77-78.

20. Simpson, *The Land of Promise*, 72.

21. Steer, *Spiritual Secrets of George Müller*, 29; Pierson, *George Müller of Bristol*, 90.

22. Chambers, *Oswald Chambers: His Life and Work*, 152.

23. Chambers, *The Place of Help*, 146.

24. Chambers, *Biblical Psychology*, 200.

25. Tozer, *The Pursuit of God*, 68.

26. Elliot, 253.

27. Ibid.

28. Ibid.

29. Carmichael, *Thou Givest . . . They Gather*, 9, see also pp. 12-14, 16. Carmichael says the Hebrew word is "darbar," which is either a typographical error or a mistake on her part.

30. Ibid., 14.

31. G. Campbell Morgan, *The Teaching of Christ* (New York: Fleming H. Revell, 1913), 4-5.

32. Joseph H. Thayer, *Thayer's Greek-English Lexicon of the New Testament* (Grand Rapids: Baker, 1977), 380.

33. Vine, 1253.

34. Colin Brown, ed., *The New International Dictionary of New Testament Theology* (Grand Rapids: Zondervan, [1971] 1978), 3:1121.

35. Kittel, 4:75.

36. Ibid., 4:79-80.

37. Ibid., 4:113.

38. Farah, *From the Pinnacle of the Temple*, 49-50.

39. Ibid.

40. Ibid., 29.

41. McCasland, 109.

42. Ibid, 110, 141.

43. Ibid., 57.

44. Friesen, 311-322, 335-354.

45. Chambers, *Biblical Psychology*, 200.

46. Ibid., 145.

CHAPTER 13

Revelation and Sense Knowledge

Related to the *rhema/logos* distinction is the differentiation between revelation (or faith) knowledge and sense knowledge. The concepts of revelation knowledge and sense knowledge are based on such Scriptures as:

> For to us God revealed them through the Spirit; for the Spirit search-es all things, even the depths of God. For who among men knows the thoughts of a man except the spirit of the man, which is in him? Even so the thoughts of God no one knows except the Spirit of God. Now we have received, not the spirit of the world, but the Spirit who is from God, that we might know the things freely given to us by God, which things we also speak, not in words taught by hu-man wisdom, but in those taught by the Spirit, combining spiritual thoughts with spiritual words. But a natural man does not accept the things of the Spirit of God; for they are foolishness to him, and he cannot understand them, because they are spiritually appraised (1 Cor. 2:10-14).

This concept is based on the idea that sense knowledge is knowledge received through the five senses, and is limited in scope, because the natural man (of the senses) cannot understand or accept the things of the Spirit (revelation knowledge). Revelation knowledge transcends sense knowledge, as knowledge that is received from the Bible and/or illumi-nation of the Holy Spirit by faith.

CONTEMPORARY FAITH TEACHING

Contemporary faith teaching on revelation and sense knowledge origi-nates chiefly through E.W. Kenyon. He distinguished "sense knowledge facts" from "revelation knowledge," which for Kenyon is the Bible: "There are two kinds of Knowledge. One kind of Knowledge has to do with the spirit of man and the other has to do with his senses."[1] He explained further, "Just as Sense Knowledge is developed by reading Sense Knowledge literature, so the spirit grows by reading and meditating in the Revelation that was designed to be its food, for 'Man shall not live by bread alone, but by every Word that proceedeth out of the mouth of God.' . . . You cannot develop faith through the reasoning faculties, no matter how much you try to do it. Faith is the law in the human spirit."[2] Copeland takes the concept further, maintaining, "We are not even to be led by good sense. . . . The ministry of Jesus was never governed by logic or reason. . . . We are talking about being led by the Spirit, not by the common sense world."[3] Contemporary faith leaders tend to believe that sense knowledge is in conflict with revelation knowledge.

CRITICISM OF CONTEMPORARY FAITH TEACHING

Revelation Does Not Occur Today. Some cessationist contemporary faith critics such as MacArthur equate revelation with canonical inspiration and thus insist that because the canon of Scripture is closed there can be no revelation today. He argues that to believe that revelation can be received today puts such revelation on par with Scripture.[4] MacArthur criticizes Presbyterian charismatic theologian J. Rodman Williams, claiming, "He is alleging that the Bible is not our final source of God's revelation but simply a 'witness' to additional revelation that God is giving today. Williams is declaring that Christians can add to the Bible—and that they can accept others' additions to Scripture as normal and conventional."[5] On the other hand, Williams, himself disavows this: "I do not intend in any way to place contemporary experience on the same level of authority as the Bible. Rather do I vigorously affirm the decisive authority of Scripture; hence, God does not speak just as authoritatively today as he spoke to the biblical authors."[6] MacArthur does not accept his explanation, however, claiming that William's distinction is artificial.

The Revelation Knowledge Concept Is Gnostic. McConnell claims Kenyon's concept is a rebirth of the ancient heresy of gnosticism in a different form with parallels to metaphysical cults.[7] He goes into detail, citing these parallels and errors as dualism, sensory denial, perfect knowledge of God, transcending human limitations, anti-rationalism, and classification of levels of spirituality.[8]

Hanegraaff castigates the revelation knowledge concept as a cover-up for misinterpreting Scripture by claiming revelation from God: "The Faith teachers seem to implicitly recognize that their Scripture-twisting alone will not convince anyone of their claims. That's when they call in a second wave of artillery. It's called 'revelation knowledge,' which supposedly bypasses the mind and goes directly into the spirit."[9] He cites examples of heretical teaching passed off as revelation knowledge.[10]

CLASSIC FAITH TEACHING ON REVELATION AND SENSE KNOWLEDGE

For the purposes of this study, we cannot investigate all of the areas of conflict regarding revelation and sense knowledge, but will limit our study to the practical implications of the following concepts in classic faith teaching: spiritual sensing; the concepts of revelation and sense knowledge through church history, especially among the classic faith leaders; and the relationships and/or conflicts between faith, revelation, reason and sense. The theological questions McConnell raises, such as dualism and fideism in Kenyon's theology and their relationship to the Keswick/Higher Life holiness movements, are addressed by Simmons, McIntyre, and DeArteaga, so I will not repeat them here.[11]

Spiritual Sensing. The concept of spiritual senses, as distinguished from natural senses, can be found in embryonic form as early as the church father Cyril of Jerusalem: "Faith is an eye that enlightens every conscience. . . . For, when enlightened by faith, the soul hath visions of God."[12] The concept of spiritual senses became prevalent among the classic faith leaders. Spurgeon, for example, appears to have expanded upon Cyril's metaphor when he preached, "Faith is to the Christian all the spiritual senses. . . . The natural man has his eyes, but by faith we see Him who is invisible. The natural man has his hand and his feeling. We live not by feeling, but our faith is the hand by which we take fast hold upon eternal realities. The natural man has his ear and is delighted with sweet sounds. Our faith is the ear through which we hear the voice of God and sometimes catch stray notes from the harps of the angels. The natural man hath the nostril with which he is aware of sweet perfumes; and to our faith the name of Jesus is as the choicest ointment poured forth."[13] His interim successor, A.T. Pierson, likewise wrote of a "new sense of divine realities."[14] Their contemporary, F.B. Meyer, wrote similarly of faith and feeling, distinguishing the life of faith from "the superficial life of sense."[15] These are quite similar to Kenyon's statement:

"We know that he can reveal Himself to our spirits so that we are as sure of spiritual realities as we are of the realities of the Senses."[16] It is thus likely, as McIntyre has suggested, that he may have adapted his teaching from these classic leaders.[17]

Other classic leaders taught the concept of spiritual senses as well. Murray taught, "Faith is the spiritual sense of the soul, being to it what the senses are to the body."[18] Further, Murray explained, "Faith is the spiritual sense by which man recognizes and accepts the revelation of His God—a spiritual sense awakened by that revelation."[19] He also spoke of "exercising faith as an organ of the Spirit, as a spiritual sense."[20] In a similar vein, Simpson wrote, "The spiritual life has a set of senses corresponding to the outward senses of touch, taste, smell, sight and hearing."[21] Charles Price echoed Murray, Simpson and Spurgeon, making mention of "spiritual senses" saying, "The born again Christian possesses a duplicate set of faculties and all of them operate in the spiritual realm."[22] More recently, Tozer likewise acknowledged, "Faith is an organ of knowledge."[23] Further, Tozer maintained, "Faith enables our spiritual sense to function."[24] It should be noted, however, that these classic leaders do not follow the dualistic gnostic tendency that pits "sense knowledge" against "revelation knowledge."

Revelation and Sense Knowledge in Church History. Today many evangelical leaders, as does MacArthur above, distinguish between revelation and illumination, defining revelation as pertaining only to authoritative inspiration from God. However, classic writers often used the term "revelation" more broadly in the sense that illumination is used today, or in the sense of receiving a special word from the Lord, like a prophecy or a *rhema*, as discussed in Chapter 12. The concept of distinguishing sense knowledge and revelation knowledge is thus is not derived from Kenyon or metaphysics or Gnosticism, but is in reality an ancient concept, predating metaphysical philosophy by many centuries. As mentioned in Chapter 1, the second century theologian Clement of Alexandria, when refuting Gnosticism, distinguished between knowledge by reasoning or the senses and knowledge by faith or revelation. Although Clement does not use the term "revelation," the idea is implicit in his language. An excerpt from Clement entitled "First Principles of Faith," paraphrased by Hazard, elucidates this implicit idea:

> This type of *reasoning knowledge* is *dependent upon our senses*— that is, our abilities to see, feel, hear, touch, and taste. Through

sensing we are led to reasoning and understanding. From understanding, to knowledge. And then we form our opinions. But far above this way of knowing are the first principles of our knowledge—the *knowledge of God, given to us by revelation.* For the principles of our faith were revealed to us by God, from above, by the Spirit. . . . For whatever your human senses insist that you believe must be brought under the spirit.[25]

This citation from Clement is significant because it demonstrates, contrary to McConnell, that the seemingly dualistic notions of revelation and sense knowledge are not inherently Gnostic since Clement uses the concepts in refutation of Gnosticism.[26]

About 500 A.D. Dionysius the Areopagite taught that a glimpse of eternity cannot be comprehended by sense and reason: "For the beholding of the hidden things of God, shalt thou forsake sense and the things of the flesh, and all that the senses can apprehend, and that reason of her own powers can bring forth, and all things created and uncreated that reason is able to comprehend and know, and shall take thy stand upon an utter abandonment of thyself."[27] Citing this statement centuries later (c. 1350), the *Theologia Germanica* added that a person cannot perceive spiritual matters or insight from God regarding oneself "so long as the man is holding converse with outward things through his senses and reason."[28]

Concurrently, the pre-Reformation Czech reformer Jan Hus remarkably similar to Clement also distinguished between the senses and "the faith which comes from divine knowledge," explaining, "This faith is the foundation of other virtues which the church of Christ practices. . . . Faith is not of things which appear to the senses but of hidden things."[29] In the same time frame, the anonymous fourteenth century writing *The Cloud of Unknowing* similarly distinguished "sense knowledge" and "spiritual knowledge": "As we begin to understand the spiritual where our sense-knowledge ends, so we most easily come to the highest understanding of God possible in this life with the help of grace, where our spiritual knowledge ends. . . . Do not try to use your interior or exterior senses to grasp the spiritual. . . . Nature designed the senses to acquire knowledge of the material world, not to understand the inner realities of the spirit."[30]

In the eighteenth century, English theologian William Law, citing German Lutheran Pietist and mystic Jacob Böhme, also distinguished between divine knowledge, which is beyond reason, and natural knowledge, which involves sense and reason.[31] Moving to the nine-teenth century, Pierson believed God is known only through spiritual sensing: "[God's] subtle essence evades all carnal approach or analysis. He must be otherwise known, if at all: the spirit alone has the higher senses which, being exercised to discern good and evil, can enable us to perceive God and hold communication with Him."[32] He related "revela-tion of God" through prayer and Scripture with the "fundamental laws or first principles," possibly alluding to Clement's use of Aristotle in de-scribing faith or revelation knowledge.[33]

In the early twentieth century, Chambers, in language strikingly similar to (yet predating) Kenyon, used a variant, but similar, terminol-ogy, in which he differentiated between revelation and sense as well. Rather than Kenyon's "revelation knowledge" he used the terms "rev-elation sense" or "revelation facts;" and rather than Kenyon's "sense knowledge" he used "common sense" or "common-sense facts."[34] Ke-nyon's phraseology is so similar that one may wonder if he may have borrowed it from *The Cloud of Unknowing* and/or Chambers.

More recently, in her books, Corrie Ten Boom distinguished between "faith knowledge and "sense knowledge."[35] According to Norwegian Kenyon scholar Geir Lie, she had contact with the writings of Kenyon, serving as a distributor of Kenyon's *Herald of Life* in the 1940s.[36] Hence, it is probable that she gleaned the concept from Kenyon. Tozer, mov-ing away from a dualistic view, differentiated between "three degrees of religious knowledge," similar to Eckhart (see Chapter 1): by senses and reason, by faith and revelation, and by direct spiritual experience, the third being the highest form of knowledge.[37] His latter two degrees would encompass Kenyon's "revelation knowledge" concept. His con-cept is quite similar to Kenyon's (though he would differ in some of Ke-nyon's interpretations and applications), but he derived his ideas from the mystics and classic faith writers, rather than Kenyon or metaphys-ics. Thus we see that similar terminology and concepts differentiating between revelation knowledge and sense knowledge have been in use in some form throughout church history. Hence, the concepts are not a recent dualistic anomaly derived from metaphysical cults, as claimed by McConnell, nor are they gnostic in their origin or nature.

The Relationship of Faith, Revelation, and Reason. Classic faith lead-ers were not opposed to reason; in fact, most of them had been highly educated, and were knowledgeable in Greek, Hebrew, and the classic writings, both religious and secular. Bounds taught that faith and reason work hand-in-hand while asserting the preeminence of faith: "Faith makes brain, educates God's leaders, gives them courage, conviction, bone, and muscle. It of itself makes God's leaders, and must be the sovereign of all. Faith must be stronger than the brain, must curb and direct the brain."[38] Further, Bounds wrote, "Bible revelations are not against reason, but above reason, for the uses of faith, man's highest faculty. The powers of reason are not able to discover these Bible facts, and yet they are for reason's use, its light, strength, and higher elevation, but more essentially to form, to nourish and to perfect faith."[39]

Spurgeon likewise explained the symbiotic relationship of faith and reason, commenting on 1 John 5:4: "Christians do not triumph over the world by reason. Reason is a very good thing, and no one should find fault with it. Reason is a candle, but faith is the sun. While I prefer the sun, I do not put out the candle. I use my reason constantly, but when I come to real warfare, reason is a wooden sword. It breaks, it snaps, while faith, that sword of true Jerusalem metal, cuts to the dividing of soul and body."[40] To Tozer this is "faith beyond reason,"[41] or as some unidentified person has said, "Faith has reasons reason knows nothing of." A similar saying dates back to A.J. Gordon, who quoted some anonymous person: "Faith has its reasons, which reason cannot understand."[42] Noted twentieth-century writer and thinker, Malcolm Muggeridge, likewise calls faith "a form of knowledge which transcends the intellect."[43] These classic leaders exalt faith over reason, similar to Kenyon, but give greater place to reason than does Kenyon.

Faith and Sense. Classic faith leaders acknowledged the value of sense knowledge, particularly common sense, but they also indicated that it is inferior to, and *sometimes* contrary to faith or revelation knowledge (but not always, as some contemporary faith teaching seems to imply). Hannah Whitall Smith, for example, indicated that there are times when faith is contrary to all the evidences of human sense and emotion.[44] As mentioned earlier, Simpson counseled that faith can be hindered by sight, sense, and dependence on external evidences.[45] Simpson also asserted, "Faith always speaks its message before sense confirms it."[46] Spurgeon similarly wrote, "Faith always sees the bow of covenant promise whenever sense sees the cloud of affliction."[47] For Spurgeon, sometimes, "The testimony of sense may be false, but the testimony of the Spirit must be true."[48]

Chambers, more than any other, addressed the relationship of revelation knowledge and common sense: "The Bible does not deal in common-sense facts; the natural universe deals in common-sense facts, and we get at these by our senses. The Bible deals with revelation facts, facts we cannot get at by our common sense, facts we may be pleased to make light of by our common sense."[49] In a statement strikingly similar to Kenyon and Copeland he wrote, "The Bible is the universe of revelation facts; the natural world is the universe of common sense facts."[50] Contrary to some contemporary faith teaching, though, he warned against pitting faith and sense against each other: "Faith in antagonism to common sense is fanatical, and common sense in antagonism to faith is rationalism. The life of faith brings the two into a right relation. . . . Nothing Jesus Christ ever said is common sense, it is revelation sense, and it reaches the shores where common sense fails."[51] Similarly, he again wrote, "God is not a fact of common sense but of revelation."[52] A comparison with Copeland's quote earlier shows them to be almost identical in thought:

> Chambers: "Nothing Jesus Christ ever said is common sense, it is revelation sense, and it reaches the shores where common sense fails."

> Copeland: "We are not even to be led by good sense. . . . The ministry of Jesus was never governed by logic or reason. . . . We are talking about being led by the Spirit, not by the common sense world."

The statements are so close in wording, it may be possible that Copeland is paraphrasing Chambers. However, in contrast to Copeland, Chambers believed very strongly in the use of reason as long as it was subordinated to revelation.

To Chambers, common sense is a gift of God, not to be denigrated;[53] however, it is not "supernatural sense" or "the sense of my Father," which is a higher gift of God.[54] Again, however, in contrast to some contemporary faith teaching, Chambers did not pit sense knowledge against revelation knowledge, but rather believed that revelation knowledge transcends sense knowledge. Common sense is lower and the leading of the Spirit of God is higher.[55] Chambers was not opposed to common sense, for he believed, "Common sense is a gift which God gave to human nature."[56] He also advised that common sense can be a positive thing when regarded in its proper place: "When you are rightly related to God, it is a life of freedom and liberty and delight, you *are* God's will, and all your common-sense decisions are God's will for you unless He checks. . . . God instructs us in what we choose, that is, He guides our common sense."[57] In fact, contrary to some contemporary faith teaching, Chambers believed "the spirit can operate through the senses."[58] Nonetheless, he also warned, "Never enthrone common sense."[59] Likewise, Tozer agreed, "I have never been against reason. . . . In every area where human reason is qualified, I say, 'Turn human reason loose.' . . . But there are some things human reason cannot do—things that are beyond its capacity."[60]

Spirit-Sense vs. Satan's Use of Sense. According to church leaders throughout history, as well as classic faith leaders, there are also times when human sense is used by Satan. In antiquity, one of the early Church Fathers, Minucius Felix, asserted that demons can deceive the senses in that they "feign diseases, alarm the minds, wrench about the limbs."[61] Centuries later, the author of *The Cloud of Unknowing* also taught that Satan can use the senses deceptively: "Let us be clear about this: the fiend must be taken into account. Anyone beginning this work (I do not care who he is) is liable to feel, smell, taste, or hear some surprising effects concocted by this enemy in one or other of his senses. So do not be astonished if it happens. There is nothing he will not try in order to drag you down from the heights of such valuable work."[62] In the early twentieth-century, Penn-Lewis, typical of many classic faith leaders, maintained a difference between body or physical sense and "spirit-sense," particularly in distinguishing genuine and counterfeit supernatural manifestations.[63] Classic faith leaders believed the senses can be used by God, but cannot always be trusted, recognizing that manifestations of illness may be feigned by demonic forces or manifestations of the supernatural involving bodily sensations may be spurious.

REFLECTIONS AND CONCLUSIONS

Revelation and Sense Knowledge Are Not Necessarily Gnostic. Just because some have used the concepts of revelation and sense knowledge in seemingly gnostic ways does not invalidate the concept of revelation and sense knowledge altogether. This investigation has shown that the idea has existed throughout church history in some form. The distinction between the two kinds of knowledge has valid theological history. Practically speaking, sense knowledge through reason, the senses, common sense, etc., has a valid place in the believer's life, contrary to what some contemporary faith teaching implies. Yet the contemporary faith elevation of revelation knowledge above and beyond sense knowledge has solid support from classic faith leaders, so long as sense knowledge is not denied altogether.

Elitist/Gnostic Tendencies Should Be Avoided. Some people tend to exalt revelation knowledge as equal to or above Scripture. This is not what Kenyon intended, for he understood revelation knowledge to be the Spirit's illumination of Scripture. However, there have been abuses of the revelation knowledge concept. Hanegraaff is correct that some leaders have erroneously passed off their pet (sometimes false) doctrines as revelation knowledge. There is thus a real danger of regarding revelation knowledge in an elitist revelation from God, therefore a Gnostic way of knowing. The need for discernment of impressions and revelations from the Lord is discussed in Chapter 19. As counsel to both contemporary faith teaching and evangelical rationalistic thinking, Tozer cautions that revelation may actually lack illumination from the Holy Spirit: "Revelation is not enough! There must be illumination before revelation can get to a person's soul."[64] Typical of Tozer, he believes there is a balance between what he calls "evangelical rationalism" and "evangelical mysticism."[65]

Believers Should Use Their Senses, But Ultimately Depend on the Revelation Knowledge of God's Word. I would conclude regarding the use of reason and our senses as Spurgeon counseled, "Prefer the sun, but do not put out the candle." Spurgeon's counsel not to find fault with reason but to use it constantly is especially practical and relevant to those in the contemporary faith movement. On the other hand, Spurgeon's admonition not to enthrone reason and common sense is just as practical and relevant to those opposing the idea of revelation knowledge. So again it is not "either/or," but "both/and": Use your mind and sense to its fullest, but recognize that knowledge by faith or revelation is higher and may sometimes seem to contravene reason.

1. Kenyon, *The Two Kinds of Knowledge*, 19.
2. Ibid., 16, 17, 36.
3. Copeland, *The Force of Faith*, 7-8.
4. MacArthur, *Charismatic Chaos*, 54-77.
5. Ibid., 58.

6. J. Rodman Williams, "Opinion," *Logos Journal*, May-June 1977, 35, cited in MacArthur, *Charismatic Chaos*, 65.

7. McConnell, 109.

8. Ibid. See Thomas Smail, Andrew Walker, and Nigel Wright, "'Revelation Knowledge' and Knowledge of Revelation: The Faith Movement and the Question of Heresy," *Journal of Pentecostal Theology* 1994, 5:57-77, for a critique of the revelation knowledge concept by British charismatic scholars.

9. Hanegraaff, 172.

10. Ibid., 123, 124, 133, 159, 172, 173, 283.

11. Simmons, *E.W. Kenyon*, 96-109; McIntyre, 211-224; William DeArteaga, *Quenching the Spirit* (Lake Mary, Fla.: Creation House, 1996), 223-227.

12. Cyril of Jerusalem, *Catechetical Lectures*, Lecture V, 4, 11; *NPNF*, 2:7:29, 32.

13. Spurgeon, "Faith Tried and Triumphing," Sermon #3265, *Metropolitan Tabernacle Pulpit*, Vol. 57 (1911), 410.

14. Pierson, *Lessons in the School of Prayer*, 32.

15. Meyer, *The Secret of Guidance*, 35.

16. Kenyon, *The Two Kinds of Knowledge*, 17.

17. Cf. McIntyre, 87, 216-222.

18. Andrew Murray, *Holy in Christ* (Toronto: Willard Tract Depot, 1888), 158.

19. Andrew Murray, *The Spirit of Christ* (Springdale, Penn.: Whitaker, 1984), 216.

20. William M. Douglas, *Andrew Murray and His Message* (Grand Rapids: Baker, 1984), 300; see also Murray, *The Holiest of All*, 422, 429-430.

21. Simpson, *CITB* (1992), 1:43.

22. Charles S. Price, *See God!* (Pasadena, Calif.: Charles S. Price Publishing Co., 1943), 60, 61.

23. Tozer, *Man: The Dwelling Place of God*, 24.

24. Tozer, *The Pursuit of God*, 47.

25. Clement of Alexandria, "First Principles of Faith," cited in *You Give Me New Life*, ed. David Hazard (Minneapolis: Bethany House, 1995), 36-38. Italics mine.

26. Farah, a mentor of McConnell and myself, had presented a paper in 1980, in which he viewed the revelation knowledge concept of the contemporary faith movement as a new Gnosticism. (Farah, "A Critical Analysis: The 'Roots and Fruits' of Faith Formula Theology"). However, when I discovered and shared with him the citation from Clement in refutation of Gnosticism, we mutually came to the conclusion that the concepts of revelation and sense knowledge are not inherently Gnostic after all, but can be applied in Gnostic ways.

27. Cited in *Theologia Germanica*, Chapter 8, 51-52.

28. Ibid., Chapter 9, 54.

29. Hus, 33.

30. *The Cloud of Unknowing*, 138-139.

31. William Law, *The Way of Divine Knowledge* (Albany, Ore.: AGES Software, 1997).

32. Pierson, *Lessons in the School of Prayer*, 23.

33. Ibid., 30-32.

34. Chambers, *The Psychology of Redemption*, 20.

35. Corrie Ten Boom, *Defeated Enemies* (Ft. Washington, Penn.: Christian Literature Crusade, [1963] 1970), 23; Corrie Ten Boom, *Plenty for Everyone* (Ft. Washington, Penn.: Christian Literature Crusade, 1967), 47, 65; Corrie Ten Boom, *Not Good If Detached* (Ft. Washington, Penn.: Christian Literature Crusade, 1957), 88.

36. Conversation with Geir Lie, 2002. See also Ten Boom, *Plenty for Everyone*, 93, where she mentions Kenyon.

37. Tozer, *Man: The Dwelling Place of God*, 49-52; 1992:120-122; Tozer, *Faith Beyond Reason*, 1989), 39-40.

38. Dorsett, *E.M. Bounds*, 152.

39. Ibid., 191.

40. Charles H. Spurgeon, "The Victory of Faith," Mar. 18, 1855, Sermon 14, *Sermons from New York Street Pulpit, 1855-1860*, Deep Worship CD-ROM.

41. Tozer, *Faith Beyond Reason*, 35.

42. A.J. Gordon, *The Ministry of Healing*, 51.

43. Malcolm Muggeridge, cited in A.W. Tozer, *The Pursuit of God: A 31-Day Experience*, compiled by Edythe Draper (Camp Hill, Penn.: Christian Publications, 1995), 79.

44. Smith, *The Christian's Secret*, 59.

45. Simpson, *A Larger Christian Life*, 18.

46. Simpson, *In the School of Faith*, 183.

47. Spurgeon, *Faith's Checkbook*, 6.

48. Spurgeon, quoted in D. Martyn Lloyd-Jones, *Revival* (Wheaton, Ill.: Crossway Books, 1987), 223.

49. Chambers, *The Psychology of Redemption*, 20.

50. Ibid.

51. Chambers, *My Utmost for His Highest*, 304.

52. McCasland, 141.

53. Ibid., 222.

54. Ibid., 110.

55. Ibid., 57.

56. Chambers, *My Utmost for His Highest*, 222.

57. Ibid., 80, 155.

58. Chambers, *Biblical Psychology*, 223.

59. Chambers, *My Utmost for His Highest*, 222.

60. Tozer, *Faith Beyond Reason*, 38-39.

61. Minucius Felix, *Octavius*, 27; *ANF*, 4: 190.

62. *The Cloud of Unknowing*, 163-164.

63. Penn-Lewis and Roberts, *War on the Saints*, unabridged edition, 58, 59, 153, 157, 159.

64. Tozer, *Faith Beyond Reason*, 23.

65. Ibid., 22.

CHAPTER 14

Faith and Healing in the
Atonement

The doctrine of healing in the atonement is based upon three chief
passages of Scriptures:

> *Surely our griefs* [margin, "sickness"] *He Himself bore,*
> *And our sorrows* [margin, "pains"] *He carried;*
> *Yet we ourselves esteemed Him stricken,*
> *Smitten of God, and afflicted.*
> *But He was pierced through for our transgressions,*
> *He was crushed for our iniquities;*
> *The chastening for our well-being fell upon Him,*
> *And by His scourging we are healed* (Isa. 53:4-5)

> *And when evening had come, they brought to Him many who were*
> *demon-possessed; and He cast out the spirits with a word, and healed*
> *all who were ill; in order that what was spoken through Isaiah the*
> *prophet might be fulfilled, saying, "He Himself took our infirmities,*
> *and carried away our diseases"* (Matt. 8:16-17).

> *He Himself bore our sins in His body on the cross, that we might die*
> *to sin and live to righteousness; for by His wounds you were healed*
> (1 Pet. 2:24).

This teaching recognizes that the Hebrew words for griefs and sorrows
can carry the meaning of sicknesses and pains, and thus believes that
healing is a privilege of believers through the Atonement, and can be
claimed as a redemption right according to these passages of Scripture.

CONTEMPORARY FAITH TEACHING

Contemporary faith teachers all believe that healing is a provision of the atonement, as was taught among the early Pentecostals and many holiness groups. Kenyon taught a unique form of this doctrine, which has been carried on by other faith leaders. According to his interpretation of the doctrine, "sickness was healed spiritually. God did not deal with sickness physically. Disease today is spiritual. . . . As long as we think that disease is purely physical, we will not get our deliverance. But when we know it is spiritual, and it must be healed by the Word of God, for you remember He said, 'He sent his Word and healed them,' then healing becomes a reality."[1] Kenyon believes that all sickness is spiritual and must be healed spiritually. Thus, as McConnell summarizes the teaching, "Christ had to suffer spiritually in hell to provide healing because all diseases are but a physical effect of a spiritual cause."[2] Additionally, Kenneth Hagin, Jr. considers healing in the atonement as absolute, declaring healing "a forever settled subject. . . . Jesus Christ settled it—and healing *is* the will of God."[3] The implication is that God makes no exceptions, and that if healing does not come it cannot be that it was not God's will.

CRITICISM OF CONTEMPORARY FAITH TEACHING

Criticism of contemporary faith teaching on healing in the atonement usually takes one of two forms: 1) Denial that healing is provided for in the atonement in this life, or 2) criticism of contemporary faith interpretation of the doctrine. MacArthur in *Charismatic Chaos* and Hanegraaff in *Christianity in Crisis* write against the doctrine of healing in the atonement as if it is a cultic misinterpretation of Scripture by charismatic faith teachers.[4] As a cessationist, MacArthur criticizes the belief in healing as a provision of the atonement in this age, claiming, "There is healing in the atonement, but only in its ultimate aspect of eternal glory in heaven (cf. Rev. 21:4)."[5] Hanegraaff disparages a claim by Copeland that healing is one of the covenant rights of a believer.[6] Both MacArthur and Hanegraaff argue that it is twisting of Scripture to apply these passages of Scripture to physical healing.

McConnell does not denigrate the concept of healing in the atonement, recognizing that classical Pentecostals often cite Isaiah 53:4-5, Matthew 8:17, and 1 Peter 2:24. Rather, he is concerned about the contemporary faith interpretation and application of the doctrine, which deviates from classic Pentecostalism. Contemporary faith leaders, he claims, teach "that diseases are healed by Christ's *spiritual* atonement in hell, not his physical death on the cross."[7] Further, McConnell asserts that contemporary faith teaching is parallel to metaphysical New Thought: "Both systems of thought deny that disease has any physical or organic causes, teaching instead that disease is entirely the physical effect of a spiritual cause."[8]

CLASSIC FAITH TEACHING

Evangelical Leaders Who Believe in Healing in the Atonement. Contrary to MacArthur's position that healing in the atonement is not a provision for the believer in this life, there are a host of evangelical scholars, ministers, and classic faith leaders who attest to the doctrine. In fact, there are so many that we can only list in summary fashion this "great cloud of witnesses." Although Spurgeon did not work out a clear systematic theology of healing and did not fully adopt the doctrine of healing in the atonement as taught by some classic faith leaders, he implicitly connected healing with the atonement when he made reference to Isaiah 53:4-5, commenting, "The Church on earth is full of souls healed by our beloved Physician."[9] While Spurgeon's emphasis was on spiritual healing, the implication is nonetheless evident. Keith Bailey, in his book *Healing: The Children's Bread*, documents that this doctrine is not uniquely charismatic or word of faith teaching, but was also held by non-charismatic evangelical leaders of various denominations such as Presbyterian/C&MA Simpson, German Lutheran Stockmayer, Baptist A.J. Gordon; and Congregationalist Torrey. He also cites Princeton scholars A.A. Hodge and J.A. Alexander, as well as Franz Delitzsch, Hebrew professor at the University of Leipzig, Germany, as supporters of the doctrine.[10]

To these can be added Murray and Chambers.[11] Murray, for example, asserted on the basis of Reformed Covenant theology, "It is His Word which promises us healing. The promise of James 5 is so absolute that it is impossible to deny it. This promise only confirms other passages, equally strong, which tell us that Jesus Christ has obtained for us the healing of our diseases, because He has borne our sicknesses. According to this promise, we have right to healing, because it is a part of the salvation which we have in Christ."[12] Hanegraaff criticizes Copeland for virtually the same assertion as Murray: "You have a Covenant with Almighty God and one of your covenant rights is the right to a healthy body."[13] Greek scholar T.J. McCrossan's book, *Bodily Healing and the Atonement* ([1930] 1982), presented an in-depth study of the Greek and Hebrew passages in defense of the doctrine of healing in the atonement. In addition to

Delitzsch, he cited additional scholars in support of the interpretation, including Young, Leeser, MacLaren, Gaebelein, and Calvin. [14] It should be noted that while Hagin has reprinted and used McCrossan's book in his teaching, McCrossan does not go as far as Hagin in his beliefs on healing and the atonement (in particular, the belief of the atonement of the devil, which Hanegraaff and McConnell discuss).

Healing in the Atonement Not an Absolute. Carter's early teaching in *The Atonement for Sin and Sickness* took a more radical viewpoint, similar to some of the criticized contemporary faith teaching and practice. However, his later book, *Faith Healing Reviewed After 20 Years*, moderated his earlier position, disavowing that the doctrine means that all will be healed and that medicine and doctors should not be used. Chambers taught similarly, "The Redemption of our Lord Jesus Christ mirrored in the Atonement embraces everything. Sin, sickness, limitation and death are all done away with in Redemption; but we have to remember the Atonement works under God's dispensational sovereignty." [15] He believed that the Atonement is only efficacious for healing when God sovereignly deems it so, not as an absolute law.

While these evangelical leaders believed in healing as a provision of the atonement, in contrast to contemporary faith teachers, they did not consider it a given in all circumstances. Carter explained the emerging view of Simpson and The Christian and Missionary Alliance: "Mr. Simpson has always allowed that one's time may come and the faith not be given, but the point here is that practically the position [of the C&MA] has been one of special answers in the will of God, not a broad atonement for all at any time." [16]

Torrey believed that physical healing is in the atonement, but also recognized it is not automatic or absolute, saying: "While we do not get the full benefits for the body secured for us by the atoning death of Jesus Christ in the life that now is but when Jesus comes again, nevertheless, just as one gets the first fruits of his spiritual salvation in the life that now is, so we get the first fruits of our physical salvation in the life that now is. We do get in many, many, many cases of physical healing through the atoning death of Jesus Christ even in the life that now is." [17]

Most of the classic faith leaders do not appear to espouse the "spiritual atonement of the devil" theory Kenyon is alleged by McConnell to have been teaching, but, as McIntyre's research shows, similar concepts were not totally absent from classic faith teaching. [18] Many would hold that Christ's atonement was both physical and spiritual in nature, including Calvin, Luther and Spurgeon.[19] Hence, although there may be similarities in Kenyon's teaching to New Thought metaphysics, McIntyre shows that there are even closer affinities to some of the classic faith leaders with whom Kenyon had contact. So while the interpretation may be questioned, it is not necessarily cultic or heretical in origin. It should be noted, however, that there is a vast difference between Calvin's concept that Jesus suffered spiritually (specifically that the descent into hell refers to the suffering of His soul in addition to bodily torment) and the flamboyant "demonizing" and the "rebirth" of Jesus in hell that Hanegraaff critiques.[20] It is possible, however that someone might read Calvin and misinterpret his statements.

REFLECTIONS AND CONCLUSIONS

Various interpretations and applications of the doctrine of healing in the atonement abound both in contemporary and classic faith teaching. Confusion and misunderstanding of healing in the atonement have caused some charismatic leaders such as Wimber to back off from the teaching, preferring instead to call it "healing through the atonement" or an "outcome of the atonement."[21] Wimber does acknowledge, "Not all of those who believe physical healing is in the atonement conclude healing is automatic and immediate."[22] Simpson, Murray, Torrey, Carter, Chambers, and Gordon would all be examples of that statement. However, Wimber misinterprets Torrey's statements on healing in the atonement, asserting: "What he means is that based on what Jesus experienced on the cross we as a consequence may experience one hundred percent healing here on earth."[23] On the contrary, Wimber is misinformed, for Torrey also declared, "Sometimes it is God's will to heal, usually it is God's will to heal, if the conditions are met; but it is not always God's will to heal. . . . It is not always possible to pray 'the prayer of faith,' only when God makes it possible by the leading of the Holy Spirit."[24]

The C&MA realized the ideal of healing in the atonement, but that not all are automatically healed. C&MA theologian and historian G.P. Pardington, noted that many who died in the first twenty-five years of the C&MA, died of illnesses, yet there is no claim that they were sick or died from disobedience or lack of faith. Rather, they are regarded as "Our Honored Dead."[25] He also wrote with insight of some who have not received divine healing, but receive strength in their infirmities:

Whatever the explanation, it is a fact that of those who take Christ as their Healer some are not healed of their diseases or delivered from their infirmities in the sense that the diseases wholly disappear or the infirmities are entirely removed. They could not get a doctor's certificate of good health nor, because of physical unsoundness, could they take out a life insurance policy. Yet such persons daily experience a supernatural quickening of their bodies which gives them freshness and strength and in some instances extraordinary physical endurance. Indeed, they seem to have something more than Divine Healing; they have Divine Life. Theirs indeed is a paradoxical experience. Instead of being bedridden or helpless invalids they keep going in the strength of Jesus, not only carrying their own burdens but stretching out a helping hand to others. Surely it is one thing to sink down under the power of disease or the weight of infirmity; but it is quite another thing to rise above the power of disease and the weight of infirmity and in the strength of the ascended and glorified Christ not only have a victorious spirit but bear fruit, yea, the 'much fruit' that shall abide the day of His coming.[26]

This shows a more balanced approach, understanding that healing is provided for in the atonement, but not all receive the fullness of healing in this life. Many times it is a partial healing, or a supernatural enabling in the midst of weakness that is imparted from God.

Cessationists such as MacArthur relegate healing in the atonement solely to the age to come. Contemporary faith leaders tend to insist that healing in the atonement is absolutely and fully available now. Classic faith leaders view healing in the atonement as a provision that begins in this age, but is not fully consummated until the age to come. This maintains the "already, but not yet" principle of Cullmann and Ladd, and strikes a balance between the two polarities. I would conclude, like Murray, Simpson, Carter, and Torrey, that it is valid to consider healing as a provision of the atonement in this life, but not as automatic or complete healing in this life. Nor is it through an "atonement of the devil." As the classic faith leaders believed, it is generally God's will to heal, but there may be exceptions. God's sovereignty rules over all His promises and provisions. We can pray expectantly for healing, but leave room for God's greater purposes, which are higher and greater than our understanding.

Faith and Healing in the Atonement

1. Kenyon, *Jesus the Healer*, 31.

2. McConnell, 150.

3. Kenneth Hagin, Jr., *Healing: A Forever Settled Subject* (Tulsa, Okla.: Kenneth Hagin Ministries, 1981), 1, 4.

4. MacArthur, *Charismatic Chaos*, 124-125, 268; Hanegraaff, 249-251.

5. MacArthur, *Charismatic Chaos*, 125.

6. Hanegraaff, 241.

7. McConnell, 150.

8. Ibid., 150.

9. Spurgeon, *Morning by Morning*, 130.

10. Keith Bailey, *The Children's Bread* (Harrisburg, Penn.: Christian Publications, 1977), 43-57.

11. Murray, *Divine Healing*, 54ff.; Oswald Chambers, *If Ye Shall Ask*, (United Kingdom: Marshall Morgan & Scott, 1937), accessed on *The Complete Works of Oswald Chambers*, CD-ROM (Grand Rapids: Discovery House, 2000).

12. Murray, *Divine Healing*, 72; see also p. 17; Douglas, 330.

13. Cited in Hanegraaff, 241.

14. McCrossan, *Bodily Healing and the Atonement*, 13, 21, 38, 39.

15. Chambers, *If Ye Shall Ask*, accessed on *The Complete Works of Oswald Chambers*, CD-ROM.

16. Carter, *Faith Healing Reviewed*, 113.

17. Torrey, *Divine Healing*, 28-29.

18. McIntyre, 183-197.

19. Ibid., 186-190.

20. For an in-depth scholarly study of the "Jesus Died Spiritually" teaching, see William P. Atkinson, "A Theological Appraisal of the Doctrine that Jesus Died Spiritually, as Taught by Kenyon, Hagin and Copeland," Ph.D. dissertation, University of Edinburgh, Edinburgh, Scotland, 2007. For a discussion of various views of the Apostles Creed statement about Jesus, "He descended into hell," see Alan E. Lewis, *Between the Cross and the Resurrection: A Theology of Holy Saturday* (Grand Rapids: Eerdmans, 2001), especially pp. 37-40.

21. Wimber and Springer, 155-156.

22. Ibid., 156.

23. Ibid., 154.

24. Torrey, *The Power of Prayer*, 126.

25. G.P. Pardington, *Twenty-five Wonderful Years* (New York: Christian Alliance Publishing Co., 1912; New York: Garland, 1984), 160-238.

26. Ibid., 59-60.

CHAPTER 15

Faith, Evidence, and the Baptism in the Spirit

One of the basic foundations for both classic and contemporary faith teaching is the concept of "walking by faith" without seeing the external evidences. Jesus advanced the concept when He said to Thomas, "Blessed are those who believe and have not seen." The apostle Paul declared, "For we walk by faith, not by sight" (2 Cor. 5:7). Further, the author of Hebrews 11:1 states that "faith is the substance of things hoped for, the evidence of things not seen" (KJV). Medieval theologian Anselm expanded upon this concept, teaching that we believe in order to know, rather than seeking knowledge in order to believe. Interpretation of these verses lays the foundation for faith and evidences, particularly as it relates to the experience of the baptism in the Spirit.

CONTEMPORARY FAITH TEACHING

Contemporary faith teaching emphasizes the importance of walking by faith, not by sight. Yet there is an anomaly in contemporary faith teaching, in which the "walking by faith, not by sight" teaching is not held consistently. This is in regard to the "evidence doctrine," the belief that speaking in tongues is the initial evidence of the baptism in the Spirit. Contemporary faith teachers believe in the baptism in the Spirit as an experience of empowerment with the Holy Spirit subsequent to conversion. They generally hold the American classical Pentecostal position that the baptism in the Holy Spirit is an experience of empowering subsequent to conversion and also that speaking in tongues is the initial evidence of the baptism in the Holy Spirit.

Curiously, however, Kenyon, the acknowledged founder of the contemporary faith movement, did not hold to the typical contemporary faith position of tongues as the initial evidence of the baptism in the Spirit. Rather, Kenyon asserted, "They declare that no one ever received the Holy Spirit unless he has received a physical manifestation. They do not believe that God is in the midst of people unless there is sense evidence. . . . You do not need Sense Knowledge evidence to prove that you have received the Holy Spirit. . . . Your confidence is not in any physical manifestation or physical evidence. It is always in the Word of God."[1] This teaching of Kenyon, though ignored by contemporary faith teachers, exposes the inconsistency of teaching people not to trust sense knowledge, on one hand, and requiring physical evidences, on the other.

CRITICISM OF CONTEMPORARY FAITH TEACHING

Criticism of contemporary faith teaching on tongues as the initial evidence of the baptism in the Spirit comes in two main forms. First is criticism of its belief in a subsequent baptism in the Spirit, what MacArthur calls the "charismatic doctrine of subsequence."[2] He considers it an elitist doctrine in which those who have not received are considered second-class Christians. Second is criticism of belief in tongues as the evidence of the baptism with the Spirit. While cessationists such as MacArthur would deny the validity of speaking in tongues occurring at all today, more often criticism is leveled against making tongues the initial evidence, a view not held by (and opposed by) most of the classic faith leaders.

CLASSIC FAITH TEACHING

Regarding Subsequence. Most of the classic faith leaders believed in an empowering experience of the Holy Spirit subsequent to conversion, often referred to as baptism or filling of the Holy Spirit.[3] Their beliefs differed in terminology of the experience, and regarding the relationship of sanctification to the experience, but almost uniformly they believed that this experience included full surrender, an enduement with power and some sort of intensification of the work of sanctification.[4] It might variously be called the baptism of the Spirit, filling of the Spirit, crisis of sanctification, witness of the Spirit, sealing of the Spirit, and many other terms. Examples of classic leaders of various theological stripes who maintain a subsequent empowering of the Spirit include Moody, Finney, Torrey, Chambers, Murray, Meyer, Simpson, Spurgeon, Hannah Whitall Smith, Hudson Taylor, Martyn Lloyd-Jones, John Wesley, John Fletcher,

Phoebe Palmer, and the list could go on and on. Although some contemporary scholars and leaders like John Stott, Third Waver John Wimber, and others define the "baptism in the Spirit" as occurring at conversion, while still believing in a subsequent experience of sanctifying and/or empowering, for the purposes of this study, I will use the term "baptism in the Spirit" to designate this subsequent experience.

Regarding the Evidence of a Subsequent Baptism in the Spirit. For most classic faith leaders, the chief evidence of this subsequent experience of the Spirit was regarded as a changed life, an intensified manifestation of the fruit of the Spirit. For some no evidence was necessarily expected initially although results were expected eventually. For example, Hannah Whitall Smith believed that she had received the baptism of the Spirit, even though she did not feel different for some time: "By faith I claim that I have the baptism of the Spirit. And it really does seem to me that if the Bible is true, I must have it."[5]

However, at times people looked for other evidences—some looked for a manifestation of extreme joy such as holy laughter or holy dance, others bodily sensations of heat or chills, others a manifestation of swooning or trembling. Synan notes, "Many of the holiness people had felt that some physical evidence would often accompany sanctification to prove that a person had 'prayed through.' Some thought that the best proof of being baptized with the Holy Ghost was the ability to perform the 'holy dance.' Others taught that 'hallelujah earthquakes' would be felt by the newly-baptized, while some thought the best evidence was a shouting in drunken ecstasy, like the disciples on the day of Pentecost. Tongues had been experienced by a number of holiness people over the years, but they were considered to be only one of many 'evidences' or 'proofs' of sanctification."[6] Alma White's holiness group, which was anti-tongues movement, nevertheless expected a "holy dance" as an evidence of the baptism in the Spirit.[7]

One of the distinctions between classic and contemporary faith teaching is its view of tongues as the initial evidence of the baptism in the Holy Spirit (with the exception of the Pentecostals of the classic faith teaching). Many of the classic faith teachers after the Pentecostal revival of 1906 who taught various aspects of the faith message taught today agree that the gift of tongues is available to believers today, but did not believe tongues is necessarily the initial evidence of the baptism in the Spirit. Simpson, who had been vocal about the reality and validity of supernatural gifts today, including tongues, was just as vocal about tongues not being the evidence of the baptism in the Spirit: "One of these greatest errors is a disposition to make special manifestations an evidence of the baptism of the Holy Ghost, giving to them the name of Pentecost, as though none had received the Spirit of Pentecost but those who had the power to speak in tongues, thus leading many sincere Christians to cast away their confidence, plunging them in perplexity and darkness or causing them to seek after special manifestations of other than God Himself. . . . When we seek anything less than God, we are sure to miss His highest blessing and likely to fall into side issues and serious errors."[8]

For Simpson, requiring tongues as the evidence of the Holy Spirit's empowering was a hindrance to the operation of faith, for "a faith that is going to wait for signs and evidence will never be strong."[9] Simpson opposed the emphasis upon external evidences, considering them as an obstacle to walking by faith: "Faith is hindered by sight and sense, and our foolish dependence upon external evidences."[10] German faith healing and holiness pastor/theologian Otto Stockmayer held essentially the same position as Simpson, and his views were published in *The C&MA Weekly*.[11] Paul Rader, in his hymn "Old Time Power," proclaimed the classic teaching of claiming by faith the baptism in the Spirit:

> Bring us low in prayer before Thee,
> And with faith our souls inspire,
> Till we claim, by faith, the promise
> Of the Holy Ghost and fire.[12]

McCrossan, though often cited by contemporary faith leaders for his teaching on healing in the atonement, in his book *Speaking in Tongues: Sign or Gift—Which?* gave virtually the same testimony as Simpson and Rader: "Today hundreds of God's saints really speak with other tongues when baptized or filled with the Holy Ghost, just as the hundred and twenty Galileans spoke on the day of Pentecost. . . . We have also heard many good people speak with other tongues when we felt absolutely sure that the Holy Spirit had nothing whatever to do with the speaking. . . . We have known several saints who at the time of their baptism [in the Spirit], did not receive the gift of tongues, who today have that gift; but they all know well that their baptism or infilling really occurred without the speaking in tongues."[13] MacMillan, frequently cited by Hagin, also believed that while tongues may be given from God, they are not necessarily the initial evidence.[14] Other classic faith leaders who were not cessationists but disavowed the "evidence doctrine" included Penn-Lewis, Nee, Torrey, and Chambers.

Pentecostalism and the Evidence Doctrine. Charles Parham first taught tongues as the evidence of the baptism in the Spirit in 1901. Seymour, mentored by Parham, propagated the doctrine in the Azusa Street Pentecostal revival of 1906. The Assemblies of God officially adopted the "evidence doctrine" in 1918. Wigglesworth is reputed to have said, "If I don't receive what the apostles received, I won't know if I got what they got." Not all Pentecostals, however, continued to maintain the evidence doctrine. A few years after Azusa Street, Seymour recanted the teaching, admonishing, "Wherever the doctrine of the baptism in the Holy Spirit will only be known as the evidence of speaking in tongues, that work will be an open door for witches and spiritualists, and free loveism. . . . When we leave the word of God and begin to go by signs and voices we will wind up in Spiritualism."[15]

Bosworth, cited frequently by contemporary faith leaders, was actively involved in Pentecostal circles, with many people receiving the gift of tongues under his ministry. However, in 1918 when the Assemblies of God took a firm position endorsing the evidence doctrine, Bosworth left the Assemblies of God and rejoined the C&MA. Bosworth gave this testimony: "Many thousands have spoken in supernatural tongues as on the Day of Pentecost, as a result of the same mighty Baptism that came upon that waiting company in the upper room. . . . After some time in the work on the Pentecostal lines (during which it has been my privilege to see thousands receive the precious baptism in the Holy Spirit) I am certain that many who receive the most powerful Baptism for service do not receive the manifestation of speaking in tongues. And I am just as certain that many who *seemingly* speak in tongues are not, or ever have been Baptized in the Spirit."[16] He argued strongly that physical evidences are not to be sought after:

> If made a sign to the seeker for the Baptism, it not only leaves no place for faith, but on the other hand destroys faith already Divinely given. After God has most powerfully Baptized the seeker, and, with perfect faith Divinely inwrought, he is rejoicing with joy unspeakable and full of glory, with every ounce of his flesh quivering under the power of the indwelling Spirit, some one will tell him that he has not yet received the Holy Ghost because he did not speak in tongues. This destroys his faith, which . . . is

both "the evidence" and "the substance,". . . . Everywhere I have gone I have met hungry souls who seemingly speak in tongues, but who have not this assuring faith that they are Baptized in the Spirit. Nothing short of real faith can satisfy the heart and put the soul at rest. The word "evidence" in the Scriptures is never used in connection with a spiritual gift, or manifestation, making faith to depend upon any sign or physical manifestation, but the Apostle distinctly states that *faith* is the evidence. . . . Where any sign is placed before faith, it hinders the Spirit, and lessens the power. Jesus taught that "these signs shall follow" faith, and not "faith shall follow these signs."[17]

Thus Bosworth agreed with Simpson, McCrossan, Rader, Seymour and Kenyon that tongues is not necessarily the initial evidence.

Further, Montgomery, who circulated in Pentecostal as well as C&MA circles, was said to have accepted the evidence doctrine and maintained credentials with the Assemblies of God. Nevertheless, she maintained friendship with Simpson, and recorded that she received the Spirit many years before she spoke in tongues.[18] Additionally, though known as an independent Pentecostal pastor and evangelist, Charles Price held a position similar to his friends Bosworth and McCrossan, and to Simpson, whom he revered. C&MA churches were even started out of some of his meetings.[19] Woodworth-Etter, a friend of Bosworth's and prominent in both Pentecostal and holiness circles, also warned about the dangers of receiving spurious tongues when seeking tongues as the initial evidence.[20]

One time Canadian C&MA pastor Oswald J. Smith indicated that Aimie Semple McPherson was not firm in the evidence doctrine though she leaned that way.[21] Rader preached for three months at McPherson's Angelus Temple, and Walter Turnbull, pastor of Simpson's Gospel Tabernacle and foreign missionary secretary of the C&MA, also preached for McPherson.[22] There was evidently openness on the part of McPherson to a more moderate stance such as the C&MA's regarding the evidence doctrine, as well as a receptivity on the part of C&MA leaders to the Pentecostal movement, as long as the evidence doctrine was not emphasized. European Pentecostals also were less dogmatic about teaching an initial evidence doctrine, making the teaching more of an American phenomenon.[23]

REFLECTIONS AND CONCLUSIONS

The Problem of Elitism. There is a valid point in warning of the danger of elitism, particularly among those who insist on tongues as the initial evidence of such a baptism. However, MacArthur's characterization of the doctrine of subsequence as distinctly charismatic ignores and opposes the views and experiences of great classic evangelical non-charismatic leaders of faith: Spurgeon, Müller, Taylor, Murray, Simpson, Carmichael, Smith, Torrey, Gordon, Moody, etc. The doctrine of subsequence is not originally or distinctly a charismatic or contemporary faith doctrine, but is rooted in the theology and experiences of the Reformed "sealers," Wesleyan holiness, and Higher Life/Keswick movements.[24] A case could also be made for the existence of the doctrine of subsequence in antiquity, but that is not germane to the discussion here.

The Problem of the Doctrine of Evidence. This is an area in which contemporary faith leaders are inconsistent and contradictory in their teaching on faith. While they claim that a believer is to walk by faith and not by sight, they insist on tongues being the evidence of receiving the fullness of the Spirit, not faith. As Simpson, Kenyon and Bosworth have shown, it is a theological and logical inconsistency to say that one is walking by faith, not by sight, and then require a physical sign as the evidence. Requiring a physical sign for evidence is the antithesis of walking by faith. Contemporary faith teachers have substantially accepted the faith and healing teachings of Kenyon, MacMillan, Bosworth, Simpson, and McCrossan, but have not accepted their balanced position on tongues. While contemporary faith teachers have disseminated their writings on faith, they have taken their positions to an extreme and gone farther than these men would teach.

More recently, Jack Hayford, one of McPherson's contemporary-day successors in the Foursquare Church and a leader in the charismatic movement, has expressed a similar doubt that the evidence doctrine can be legitimately taught: "If you wish to proof text an initial-physical-evidence-as-tongues proposition, a case can be made and argued on biblical grounds. However, I was coming to see—integrity with the Word forcing me to confess—that it is equally true that a conclusive airtight case could not be categorically proven."[25] Other contemporary charismatics and Pentecostals of the classic faith orientation have also backed away from insistence on tongues as the evidence of the baptism in the Spirit, including former *Charisma* editor Jamie Buckingham, Teen Challenge founder David Wilkerson, Lutheran charismatic renewal leader Larry Christensen, Assembly of God scholar Gordon Fee, and numerous Oral Roberts University theology professors.[26]

FAITH, EVIDENCE, AND THE BAPTISM IN THE SPIRIT

Lederle concludes, "Few charismatics accept that glossolalia is the condition *sine qua non* for Spirit baptism. . . . The hesitancy among charismatics to embrace a full-fledged doctrine of initial evidence as sole condition for Spirit baptism rests not only on the lack of explicit or conclusive support for it in Scripture, but also on a general uneasiness about the 'proof mentality' which may harbor and which may lead to triumphalism and elitism."[27] I would likewise conclude that contemporary faith, Pentecostal, and charismatic churches today need to revisit the "evidence doctrine" and revise their theology.[28] The practical-theological concerns expressed by Simpson, Bosworth and others, especially that the evidence doctrine actually discourages faith and often results in confusion, lack of confidence, seeking the gift rather than the Giver and even opening the door to false manifestations, need to be taken seriously.

---

1. Kenyon, *The Two Kinds of Faith*, 15-16, 31; see also McIntyre, 34-35, 132, 144, 289, 355.

2. MacArthur, *Charismatic Chaos*, 209.

3. See V. Raymond Edman, *They Found the Secret* (Grand Rapids: Zondervan, 1960); James Gilchrist Lawson, *Deeper Experiences of Famous Christians* (Anderson, Ind.: Warner Press, [1911] 1970).

4. The three chief viewpoints on sanctification were: 1) eradication—the old man of sin is eradicated, done away with (Wesleyan); 2) suppression—the old man is suppressed (Keswickian); 3) habitation—the old man of sin is overcome by the habitation of Christ within the believer (Higher Life/Simpson).

5. Marie Henry, *Hannah Whitall Smith* (Minneapolis: Bethany House, 1984), 88.

6. Synan, *The Holiness-Pentecostal Tradition*, 108-109.

7. Ibid., 95.

8. A.B. Simpson, *Annual Report, The Christian and Missionary Alliance*, May 1908. For more on the history, theology, and practice of the early C&MA regarding tongues, evidence, the baptism in the Spirit, and *charismata*, see Paul L. King, *Genuine Gold: The Cautiously Charismatic Story of the Early Christian and Missionary Alliance* (Tulsa, Okla.: Word & Spirit Press, 2006).

9. Simpson, *The Gospel of Healing*, 41.

10. Simpson, *A Larger Christian Life*, 18.

11. *CMAW*, Mar. 9, 1909, 397; see also Nienkirchen, 92.

12. Paul Rader, "Old Time Power," *Hymns of the Christian Life* (Harrisburg, Penn.: Christian Publications, 1978), 145.

13. T.J. McCrossan, *Speaking with Other Tongues: Sign or Gift—Which?* (Harrisburg, Penn.: Christian Publications, 1927), 3-4, 26.

14. King, *A Case Study of a Believer with Authority*, 254-255; 358-359.

15. Seymour, *The Doctrines and Disciplines of the Azusa St. Apostolic Faith Mission*, 3.

16. Perkins, 53, 57.

17. Ibid., 66-67, 70.

18. Montgomery, *Secrets of Victory*, 58.

19. Charles S. Price, *Golden Grain*, Aug. 1932, 10; Lindsey Reynolds, *Rebirth* (Beaverlodge, Alberta: Evangelistic Enterprises, 1992), 214-218, 226-228.

20. Woodworth-Etter, *Marvels and Miracles*, 503-505, 507-508.

21. Nienkirchen, 39, note 60.

22. Ibid, 39.

23. Lederle, *Treasures Old and New*, 47-48.

24. Ibid., 5-9; D. Martyn Lloyd-Jones, *God's Ultimate Purpose: An Exposition of Ephesians 1:1-23* (Edinburgh: Banner of Truth, 1978), 243-311.

25. Jack Hayford, *The Beauty of Spiritual Language* (Dallas: Word, 1992), 93-94; see pp. 92-99 for a fuller discussion.

26. Personal conversations with several professors. See also James B. Shelton, *Mighty in Word and Deed: The Role of the Holy Spirit in Luke-Acts* (Peabody, Mass.: Hendrickson, 1991), 130, 159-162. For a discussion of various viewpoints on the evidence doctrine, see *Initial Evidence*, Gary B. McGee, ed. (Peabody, Mass.: Hendrickson, 1991), especially the following articles: H.I. Lederle, "Initial Evidence and the Charismatic Movement: An Ecumenical Appraisal," 131-141; Cecil M. Robeck, Jr., "William J. Seymour and 'the Bible Evidence,'" 72-95; and Larry W. Hurtado, "Normal, but Not a Norm: Initial Evidence and the New Testament," 189-201.

27. Lederle, "Initial Evidence and the Charismatic Movement," 132, 136.

28. For recent studies on revisiting the "Tongues as Evidence" doctrine, see Paul L. King, "Why Not Tongues without Controversy?—A.B. Simpson's Model and Appeal for Pentecostal Ecumenicity." Paper presented at the 35th Annual Meeting of the Society for Pentecostal Studies, Fuller Theological Seminary, Pasadena, California, Mar. 23-25, 2006.

PART 4

PRACTICAL ISSUES OF FAITH TEACHING AND PRACTICE

CHAPTER 16

Faith and Positive Mental Attitude

Positive mental attitude (PMA) is a concept taught in both secular and Christian circles in which it is believed that positive attitudes affect positively health, relationships, prosperity, and success in life. In secular teaching it is often association with the human potential movement or mind science, sometimes taking on an occult flavor. In Christian circles, the concept is usually related to Christian principles of joy, peace, and the mind of Christ. Proverbs 23:7 is often cited as a basis for the concept: "For as he thinks within himself, so he is." Before the days of cognitive theories of psychology, Tozer explained it this way: "To be right we must think right."[1] Many Scriptures are quoted to uphold the idea, among which these are the prime passages:

A joyful heart is good medicine,
But a broken spirit dries up the bones (Prov. 17:22).

For those who are according to the flesh set their minds on the things of the flesh, but those who are according to the Spirit, the things of the Spirit. For the mind set on the flesh is death, but the mind set on the Spirit is life and peace (Rom. 8:5-6).

Finally, brethren, whatever is true, whatever is right, whatever is pure, whatever is lovely, whatever is of good repute, if there is any excellence and if anything worthy of praise, let your mind dwell on these things (Phil. 4:8).

Thus, the Bible teaches a concept of positive mental attitude, but it is not the same as the secular concept, even though they may appear to be similar. The distinctions will become apparent as the issue is pursued further.

CONTEMPORARY FAITH TEACHING

The concept of PMA is taught broadly in Christian circles, both in the contemporary 'Word of Faith' movement and through other Christian leaders as illustrated by Norman Vincent Peale's book *The Power of Positive Thinking* and Robert Schuller's concept of "possibility thinking," which he relates to the exercise of faith.[2] Peale has declared, "Change your thought and you change everything."[3] Similarly, Hagin teaches, "What we believe is a result of our thinking. If we think wrong we will believe wrong."[4] His son, Kenneth Hagin, Jr., asserts, "I am acquainted with the greatest Positive Thinker who ever was: God!"[5]

Conversely, contemporary faith teaching cites Job as an example of fear bringing negative results. According to Capps, "The thing you fear will come upon you. Fear will activate satan [sic]. Job activated satan by his fear. '. . . the thing which greatly I feared is come upon me' (Job 3:25). Active faith brings God on the scene. Fear brings satan on the scene."[6] On the basis of 2 Corinthians 10:4-5, Hagin counsels against letting doubts and fears and negative thought occupy one's mind: "Never permit a mental picture of failure to remain in your mind. Never doubt for one minute that you have the answer. . . . Eradicate every image, suggestion, vision, dream, impression, feeling, and all thoughts that do not contribute to your faith that you have what you ask. . . . Thoughts are governed by observation, association, and teachings. Guard against every evil thought that comes into the mind. Stay away from all places and things that do not support your affirmation that God has answered prayer. You may even have to stay away from some churches—those that put out more unbelief than anything else."[7]

CRITICISM OF CONTEMPORARY FAITH TEACHING

Hunt and McMahon warn of PMA being "paganism in Christian dress."[8] They particularly associate the ideas of positive confession and faith in one's own faith with secular PMA. Likewise, McConnell considers these concepts as a type of "charismatic humanism" in that "they confer upon man unrestrained power to meet his own self-defined 'needs.'"[9] According to McConnell, the contemporary faith concept of positive and negative mindsets comes from cultic metaphysical belief "that *fear* as well as *faith* creates reality."[10] He relates this to the New Thought belief in the power of impersonal forces.

CLASSIC FAITH TEACHING

"A Scriptural State of Mind." Contrary to the claims of contemporary faith critics, the concept of a positive mental attitude is found throughout the writings of "deeper life" devotional writers. As early as the seventeenth century, Fenelon was teaching the concept, encouraging his readers to cultivate peace of mind.[11] Upham, who was influenced by Fenelon writes in *The Life of Faith* about rejoicing in the Lord as a "scriptural state of mind" and that faith is expressed by rejoicing in the Lord.[12]

A positive mental attitude became of utmost importance to Müller's faith: "I saw more clearly than ever that the first great and primary business to which I ought to attend every day was to have my soul happy in the Lord."[13] To Müller, renewing and strengthening this positive attitude of the inner man daily is an essential prerequisite to witnessing and helping others in the right spirit.[14] He accomplished this by establishing a habit of walking and meditating on the Word of God before breakfast each morning. Considering it food as nourishment for the inner man, Müller claimed this practice was also beneficial to his health.[15] His own testimony after forty years of this faith walk was: "I cannot tell you how happy this service makes me. Instead of being the anxious, careworn man many persons think me to be, I have no anxieties and no cares at all. Faith in God leads me to roll all my burdens upon Him."[16] One of his biographers, Roger Steer, noted, "Müller's longevity (he died when he was ninety-two) surely confirms his insistence that he was not worn out by worry."[17] Spurgeon, friend of both Müller and Pierson, also advised, "Let your conscious feebleness provoke you to seek the means of strength: and that means of strength is to be found in a pleasant medicine, sweet as it is profitable—the delicious and effectual medicine of 'the joy of the Lord.'"[18]

Drawing from Fenelon, Upham, Müller, and Spurgeon, Simpson further developed this line of thought in regard to sickness and healing: "A flash of ill temper, a cloud of despondency, an impure thought or desire can poison your blood, inflame your tissues, disturb your nerves and interrupt the whole process of God's life in your body! On the other hand, the spirit of joy, freedom from anxious care and worry, a generous and loving heart, the sedative of peace, the uplifting influence of hope and confidence—these are better than pills, stimulants and sedatives, and the very nature of things will exercise the most benign influence over your physical functions, making it true in a literal as well as a spiritual sense, that 'the joy of the Lord is your strength.'"[19] Simpson, referring to Proverbs 17:22, counseled out of his own experience, "Joy is the great restorer and healer. Gladness of spirit will bring health to the bones and vitality to the nerves when all other tonics fail, and all other sedatives cease to quiet. Sick one, begin to rejoice in the Lord, and your bones will flourish like an herb, and your cheeks will glow with the bloom of health and freshness. . . . Joy is balm and healing; and if you will but rejoice, God will give power."[20]

S.D. Gordon used the term "right mental attitude" in relation to health and healing, rather than positive mental attitude, meaning that one is thinking on Christ, not circumstances: "A right mental attitude exerts enormous influence. . . . Incidently, this is the process of faith at work, a simple faith in Christ, in-breathed by the Holy Spirit. The objective mind lays hold of Christ's promises and accepts unquestioningly the result as already assured."[21] In a statement strikingly similar to Peale, Gordon wrote, "That mental attitude [thinking on Christ] will vitally and radically affect your body."[22] Bosworth also used Gordon's term "right mental attitude" in his book *Christ the Healer* to describe a criterion for healing.[23]

Also drawing on Müller's faith principles, Hudson Taylor had similarly advocated years earlier the need for the mind to dwell on Christ: "How then to have our faith increased? Only by thinking of all that Jesus is and all He is for us: His life, His death, His work, He Himself as revealed to us in the Word to be the subject of our constant thought."[24] Thus the classic faith writers taught that a positive mental attitude *can* affect one's health and outcome of life. However, it is not by one's own mental effort, but by letting one's thoughts dwell on Jesus and His Word.

An Atmosphere of Faith. The concept of faith homes developed by Blumhardt, Trudel, Simpson, Montgomery, and others in the 1800s, was intended to provide a positive atmosphere of faith in which a person could receive healing, not unlike today's retreat centers. Carter indicates that more than thirty faith homes had been established in the latter part of the nineteenth century.[25] Murray was healed after spending three weeks at Baxter's Bethshan Home. Montgomery founded "Faith Rest Cottage," explaining, "The peace and quietness which pervade our little Home, and communion with those of like precious faith, will often aid the dear, struggling ones to come into the place of victory."[26]

Avoiding Negative Attitudes of Fear, Doubt, and Anxiety. Just as a positive mental attitude may result in positive effects such as healing, so classic faith leaders believed that negative attitudes may result in negative effects. Fenelon warned about the consequences of a negative mental attitude: "The strivings of the human mind not only impair the health of your body, but also bring dryness to the soul. You can actually consume yourself by too much inner striving. . . . Your peace and inner sweetness can be destroyed by a restless mind."[27] Hannah Whitall Smith, influenced by Fenelon, expanded upon his thought: "A desponding person is apt to fail in everything he undertakes, while a cheerful, courageous person seems to succeed without any effort. Our mental conditions are far more powerful to affect material things than we know, and I believe that there is here a secret of enormous power, if human beings once understood it."[28] She wrote out of personal experience with her husband's nervous breakdowns and doubts, leading to his loss of faith. Spurgeon suffered much pain from his gout and fell into deep depressions, but also found the importance of this principle, testifying, "Worry kills, but confidence in God is like healing medicine."[29] Spurgeon's friend F.B. Meyer avowed that negative thinking can even cause illness: "The healthiest people do not think about their health; the weak induce disease by morbid introspection."[30]

For Simpson, an optimistic attitude, rather than pessimism, can have a positive effect on health. In his pamphlet *How To Receive Divine Healing,* he counseled not to expect sickness: "Don't expect to have a spell of weariness and reaction," but rather "just go calmly forward, . . . expecting Him to give you the necessary strength to carry you thru [sic]."[31] Moreover, Simpson warned, "Worry, fear, distrust, care—all are poisonous!"[32]

Some may be surprised that classic faith teaching, just as contemporary faith teaching, cites Job 3:25 as fear bringing negative results. Simpson warned, "Fear is dangerous. It turns into fact the things we fear. It creates the evil just as faith creates the good. 'What I feared has come upon me' (Job 3:25), is the solemn warning of Job. Let us therefore be afraid of our fears lest they should become our worst foes. The remedy for fear is faith and love."[33] He further stressed that fear will paralyze faith.[34] Other classic faith leaders such as S.D. Gordon and Carter also viewed this Scripture as a principle of the consequences of negative thinking.[35] Unlike some contemporary faith preachers that would castigate "Poor Old Job" for his lack of faith, however, they did not view Job so negatively.[36] Carter put the correct perspective and balance into the teaching when he wrote, "Job, although perfect in heart, was not mature, and God wanted him to grow."[37]

REFLECTIONS AND CONCLUSIONS

The Legitimacy of Biblical PMA. The classic faith writers have demonstrated that PMA can be a valid Christian concept, so long as it is stressed that it is a mind centered on Christ and the things of Christ. Biblical PMA is therefore not "mind over matter," but Christ over mind and matter. An atmosphere of faith can contribute to health, healing and success, and attitudes or an atmosphere of negativism, pessimism, doubt, or fear can indeed have negative consequences if persisted in. On the other hand, I would share with Hunt and McMahon their concern for humanistic or New Age types of thinking creeping into Christian belief on PMA.

Dangers in Mystical Use of Visualization and Imagination. I would agree with Hunt and McMahon that many aspects of such PMA techniques as visualization and imaging are questionable from a biblical standpoint. Yet I also do acknowledge that some legitimate biblical forms of the techniques have been practiced throughout church history, particularly among the mystics. Hunt is logically and theologically inconsistent here for he argues against all mysticism, yet he himself has been influenced by writers who have in turn been deeply influenced by the mystics: John Calvin, William Law, and classic faith leaders such as Murray, Chambers, and Tozer.[38]

Hunt criticizes Richard Foster, yet Foster's use of the mystics and advocacy for use of the imagination seems to be very similar to Tozer's. Foster cites Teresa of Avila, Francis de Sales, and Julian of Norwich (also quoted by Tozer) as examples of those who advocate use of the imagination and visualizing or picturing.[39] As mentioned earlier, this does not mean Tozer would approve of all that mystics taught.

Foster also cautions against the perils of the contemplative tradition and writes of need for "sanctifying the imagination."[40] He clarifies that what he means by visualizing is not creating something: "We are not trying to conjure up something in our imagination that is not so. Nor are we trying to manipulate God and tell him what to do. Quite the opposite. . . . The ideas, the pictures, the words are of no avail unless they proceed from the Holy Spirit."[41] Hunt quotes Tozer as an authority against Foster's support for use of imagination: "The ability to visualize is found among vigorous-minded persons, whatever their moral or spiritual condition may be. . . . The wise Christian will not let his assurance depend upon his powers of imagination."[42] Tozer does warn (as Foster also does) against over-dependency upon or misuse of the imagination. However, Hunt does not understand Tozer in context. His statement does not mean that he is opposed to use of the imagination. In fact, decades before Foster uses the term, Tozer also wrote positively about "the value of a sanctified imagination":

> That the imagination is of great value in the service of God may be denied by some persons who have erroneously confused the word "imaginative" with the word "imaginary.". . . The value of the cleansed imagination in the sphere of religion lies in its power to perceive in natural things shadows of things spiritual. . . . The imagination, since it is a faculty of the natural mind, must necessarily suffer both from its intrinsic limitations and from an inherent bent toward evil. . . . A purified and Spirit-controlled imagination is, however, quite another thing, and it is this I have in mind here. I long to see the imagination released from its prison and given to its proper place among the sons of the new creation. What I am trying to describe here is the sacred gift of seeing, the ability to peer beyond the veil and gaze with astonished wonder upon the beauties and mysteries of things holy and eternal.[43]

By his own words, Tozer *longs* for release of sanctified, Spirit-led imagination, which is precisely what Foster advocates.

Final Conclusions. I would conclude that on the one hand, Hunt's concerns about the humanistic and occultic use of positive mental attitude, imagination, and visualization are valid to a degree. We must always be on alert for counterfeits. However, a counterfeit presupposes the genuine. Hunt does not appear to acknowledge the genuine. He does not leave any room for the possibility of a biblical expression of PMA and Spirit-directed and purified use of the imagination and visualizing by faith such as Tozer and Foster support. Additionally, though McConnell has legitimate questions about what contemporary faith leaders may teach about PMA, his assertion that the concept of a positive or negative mindset comes from the metaphysical cults has been shown by reference to classic evangelical faith teaching to be erroneous. Faith critics should be careful not to brand everything that has some similarities to cultic and heretical teaching as actually originating in cultic ideas. On the other hand, contemporary faith teachers need to be careful that their language, thought, and practice regarding PMA do not cross the line into cultic or heretical concepts, but stay within the bounds of orthodoxy and orthopraxy.

---

1. A.W. Tozer, *Born After Midnight* (Harrisburg, Penn.: Christian Publications, 1959), 44.

2. Robert H. Schuller, *You Can Become the Person You Want to Be* (Old Tappan, N.J.: Fleming H. Revell, 1973), 12.

3. Norman Vincent Peale, quoted in Hunt and McMahon, *Seduction of Christianity*, 152.

4. Kenneth E. Hagin, *Right and Wrong Thinking* (Tulsa, Okla.: Faith Library Publications, 1977), 3.

5. Kenneth Hagin, Jr., *Word of Faith*, Nov. 1984, 3, cited in Hunt and McMahon, *Seduction of Christianity*, 152.

6. Capps, *The Tongue—A Creative Force*, 92. Some contemporary Word of Faith writers, as in some other evangelical circles, often do not capitalize the name of "Satan" because they believe it gives him too much honor.

7. Hagin, *Seven Things You Should Know About Divine Healing*, 95-97.

8. Hunt and McMahon, *Seduction of Christianity*, 19-20, 23-25.

9. McConnell, 146.

10. McConnell, 139-140.

11. Fenelon, 9.

12. Upham, *The Life of Faith*, 319-324.

13. Steer, 60.

14. Ibid.

15. Ibid., 61.

16. Ibid., 23.

17. Ibid.

18. Spurgeon, *1000 Devotional Thoughts*, 470.

19. A.B. Simpson, *Christ for the Body* (Nyack, N.Y.: The Christian and Missionary Alliance, n.d.), n.p.

20. Simpson, *Days of Heaven on Earth,* Apr. 8.

21. S.D. Gordon, *The Healing Christ*, 104, 108.

22. Ibid., 62-63, 104, 108.

23. Bosworth, 136.

24. Howard Taylor, *Hudson Taylor's Spiritual Secret*, 156.

25. Carter, *Faith Healing Reviewed*, 35.

26. Carrie Judd, "Faith Rest Cottage," *Triumphs of Faith*, Apr. 1888, 96.

27. Fenelon, 9.

28. Strachey, 264.

29. Spurgeon, *Faith's Checkbook*, 87.

30. Meyer, *The Secret of Guidance*, 27.

31. A.B. Simpson, *How To Receive Divine Healing* (Harrisburg, Penn.: Christian Publications, n.d.), 12.

32. Simpson, *Days of Heaven on Earth,* Apr. 8.

33. Simpson, *CITB* (1992), 3:485; see also A.B. Simpson, "Inquiries and Answers," *Word, Work and World*, Dec. 1886, 341.

34. Simpson, *CITB* (1992), 2:23.

35. S.D. Gordon, *The Healing Christ*, 105; Carter, *The Atonement for Sin and Sickness*, 72.

36. I once heard a contemporary Word of Faith pastor who preached a sermon entitled "Poor Old Job," claiming that Job wrongly "feared God" (Job 1:1, 8, 9; 2:3) interpreting that Scripture to mean that Job was afraid of God and thus in sin. This preacher totally ignored the fact that Job was also considered blameless, upright, and turning away from evil, and that the word for fear in the context means reverence.

37. Carter, *The Atonement for Sin and Sickness*, 72.

38. Hunt and McMahon, *Seduction of Christianity*, 147, 165, 197, 200-202; Dave Hunt, *Beyond Seduction* (Eugene, Ore.: Harvest House Publishers, 1987), 14-15, 42, 47, 119, 153-154, 163.

39. Richard J. Foster, *Celebration of Discipline* (San Francisco: HarperSanFrancisco, [1978] 1988), 25, 42.

40. Richard J. Foster, *Streams of Living Water: Celebrating the Great Traditions of the Christian Faith* (San Francisco: HarperSanFrancisco, 1998), 53-56: Richard Foster, *Celebration of Discipline*, 25-26.

41. Foster, *Celebration of Discipline*, 42.

42. A.W. Tozer, *That Incredible Christian*, 69, cited in Hunt and McMahon, *Seduction of Christianity*, 165.

43. Tozer, *Born After Midnight*, 93-95. Richard Foster makes use of Tozer's writings, so he may have borrowed the phrase from Tozer. See Richard Foster, *Celebration of Discipline*, 159; Richard J. Foster, *Prayer: Finding the Heart's True Home* (San Francisco: HarperSanFrancisco, 1992), 54, 71; Richard J. Foster and Emilie Griffin, eds., *Spiritual Classics* (San Francisco: Harper SanFrancisco, 2000), 111-118.

CHAPTER 17

Positive Confession

The concept of positive confession naturally flows out of the idea of a positive mental attitude. Many Scriptures are cited to point to the biblical basis of confessing one's faith in positive manner:

> But what does it say? "The word is near you, in your mouth and in your heart"—that is, the word of faith which we are preaching, that if you confess with your mouth Jesus as Lord, and believe in your heart that God raised Him from the dead, you shall be saved. . . . So faith comes from hearing, and hearing by the word of Christ (Rom. 10:8, 9, 17).

> Therefore, holy brethren, partakers of a heavenly calling, consider Jesus, the Apostle and High Priest of our confession (Heb. 3:1).

> Since then we have a great high priest who has passed through the heavens, Jesus the Son of God, let us hold fast our confession (Heb. 4:14).

> Let us hold fast the confession of our hope without wavering, for He who promised is faithful (Heb. 10:23).

> "Life and death are in the power of the tongue" (Prov. 18:21).

These and other Scriptures point to the importance of how the tongue is used and form a foundation for both classic and contemporary faith teaching on positive confession.

CONTEMPORARY FAITH TEACHING ON POSITIVE CONFESSION

Contemporary faith teaching on positive confession is based primarily on the teaching of Kenyon, and propagated further by Hagin, Copeland,

Frederick Price, Capps, and others. Kenyon taught, "Faith's confessions create realities."[1] According to Kenyon, since faith is a law and a force, there is a cause-and-effect relationship, or law of sowing and reaping (Gal. 6:7, 8), intrinsic in confession. A positive confession creates positive realties; a negative confession creates negative realities. Hagin believes on the basis of Romans 4:17 that believers can create realities through their word by "calling the things that are not as though they are."[2] In fact, Hagin teaches that believers can "write your own ticket with God" through these confessions.[3] Copeland claims that words are the containers of faith: "Words are spiritual containers, and the force of faith is released by words."[4]

By the same token, a negative confession brings about a negative effect. According to Proverbs 6:2, a person can be snared or defeated by the words of their mouth.[5] Kenyon taught, "We unconsciously go down to our level of confession. No one ever rises above it. If you confess sickness, it develops sickness in your system. If you confess doubt, the doubt becomes stronger. If you confess lack of finances, it stops the money from coming in."[6] Capps asserts that according to Mark 11:22-24, "You can have what you say," both positive and negative.[7] He claims that if a person says, "I am taking the flu," that he will have exactly what he says—he will have the flu. He declares that a person should deny the symptoms and say, "I am not sick. I'll not have the flu—by the stripes of Jesus, I am healed."[8]

CRITICISM OF CONTEMPORARY FAITH TEACHING

McConnell claims that teaching on positive confession is suspect because it originates with Kenyon and is rooted in the metaphysical cults. Additionally, he considers the idea that spoken words have the power to create reality as cultic.[9] Hunt and McMahon disparage the Christian psychological concept of "self-talk" as just another form of secular positive thinking and confession.[10] Hanegraaff particularly opposes the contemporary faith concept that words are containers for faith, claiming that it is associated with activating negative or positive impersonal forces.[11] Hunt and McMahon associate this concept with shamanism and Hindu occultism. Hanegraaff and MacArthur warn against self-centeredness that can result through teaching that believers can have whatever they say, or "write their own ticket with God."[12]

CLASSIC FAITH TEACHING ON POSITIVE CONFESSION

Ancient Roots of Positive Confession Teaching and Practice. Taking exception to McConnell, Bruce Barron notes in his book *The Health and*

Wealth Gospel, "The beginnings of positive confession with regard to healing can be spotted as far back as the work of A.B. Simpson, who wrote, 'We believe that God is healing before any evidence is given. It is to be believed as a present reality and then ventured on. We are to act as if it were already true.'"[13] Actually, both McConnell and Barron are wrong, for the idea is not original with Kenyon or even Simpson.

The roots of the concept of confessing one's faith, in actuality, are very ancient. They are found in the basic confession of the Creeds such as the Apostle's Creed and Nicene Creed. Augustine recognized two types of confession: 1) Confession of sin (which he called "accusing one's self") and 2) confession of praise.[14] "In either case," writes Augustine, "it is a godly confession."[15] Through Jesus' confession of praise to the Father, Augustine asserted, Lazarus came forth alive: "He was alive already through confession."[16] By the confession of praise, "the Christian hereby provided protection for himself against his enemies, not those that may be seen."[17] In other words, according to Augustine, confessions of praise can provide defensive armor in spiritual warfare.

Again, making reference to Lazarus on another occasion, he says, "When thou makest confession, thou comest forth. For what is this coming forth, but the open acknowledgement thou makest of the state, in quitting, as it were, the old refuges of darkness? But the confession thou makest is effected by God."[18] Similar to contemporary faith teaching, according to Augustine, the believer's confession can effect a supernatural working, as in the resurrection of Lazarus. But he is also careful to note that it is not our own power of confession, but rather that our confession is made effectual by God.

Puritan and Pietist Roots. The more recent roots of the principle of confessing one's faith are found in seventeenth and eighteenth century Puritans and Pietists. Puritan leader William Gurnall exhorted believers to "boldly profess your faith" and "maintain a steadfast profession of truth."[19] Pietists August Hermann Francke and Friedrich Christoph Oetinger wrote Scripture-based personal confessions of faith strikingly similar to contemporary faith confessions.[20] These Pietists passed on the principles of faith confessions to the Moravians, who, in turn, passed them on to the Methodist movement. It was Moravian missionary Peter Bohler who counseled John Wesley, "Preach faith until you have it, then preach faith," which is similar to contemporary faith teaching on confession.

Phoebe Palmer—Professing the Blessing. Eighteenth century Methodist leaders such as John Fletcher, Hester Ann Rogers, and William Corvosso, also taught these faith principles of confession, which were expanded upon and popularized by early nineteenth century Methodist leader Phoebe Palmer.[21] Referring to Romans 10:9-10 in *Faith and Its Effects* she commented:

> Do not forget that believing with the heart, and confessing with the mouth, stand closely connected (p. 113).

> Your heart has believed, but your lips have not fully, freely, and habitually made confession. And thus your part of the work has been left in part unfulfilled (p. 296).

> The one who initially "claims the blessing," but who does not persevere in regular testimony, loses the blessing (p. 327).

> You became "cautious in professing the blessing," and have "ceased to comply with the condition" laid down by God (p. 327).

> We pronounce our own blessings and curses (p. 31).[22]

These statements appear virtually identical to contemporary faith slogans. It is important to note here, however, that Palmer is making these statements in relation to the blessings of the sanctified life, not necessarily applying them to material blessings, as contemporary faith leaders often do.

Reformed Higher Life/Keswick Teaching. Presbyterian W.E. Boardman wrote *The Higher Christian Life*, a book on holiness from a Reformed perspective, modifying Wesleyan concepts of sanctification, but retaining the idea of "speaking out the faith."[23] Hannah Whitall Smith, who with her husband Pearsall Smith joined with Boardman and others to found the Keswick movement, taught principles of repeated "assertions of faith" in her 1870s classic. Smith wrote:

> Put your will, then, over on the believing side. Say, "Lord, I will believe, I do believe," and continue to say it. . . . I have begun to assert over and over, my faith in Him, in the simple words, "God is my Father; I am His forgiven child; He does love me; Jesus saves me; Jesus saves me now!" The victory has

always been complete. . . . Let your unchanging declaration be from henceforth, "Though He slay me, yet will I trust in Him." When doubts come, meet them, not with arguments, but with assertions of faith. . . . Go at once and confess your faith, in the strongest language possible, somewhere or to someone. If you cannot do this by word of mouth, write it in a letter, or repeat it over and over in your heart to the Lord.[24]

In 1880 Charles Cullis, who began his faith walk and healing ministry after visiting Müller's faith works, recorded his practice of taking the promises of God from the Bible after spending some time in prayer, pasting them on a sheet of paper, and repeating those promises several times during the day.[25] In 1885 Murray continued the faith confession teaching, saying, "It is necessary to testify to the faith one has," and in relation to healing a person should give a testimony of faith "before feeling its effect on the body."[26] Likewise Murray exhorted, "Praise the Lord without waiting to feel better, or to have more faith. Praise Him, and say with David, 'O Lord, my God, I cried unto Thee and Thou hast healed me' (Psalm 30:2)."[27] In a statement resembling some contemporary faith teaching he also declared, "Through Him also you will learn to speak out your desires in the name of Christ."[28] But the key difference from apparently similar contemporary faith teaching is that Murray teaches that before a believer can speak out his desires in Jesus' name, he must not presume that his desires are God's desires, but submit his desires to the leading of the Holy Spirit.[29]

Baptists and Positive Confession—Spurgeon and Meyer. Spurgeon also taught the importance of hearing the Word of God repetitively in order to bolster faith: "God will enable you to believe if you hear very frequently and sincerely that which you are commanded to believe. We believe many things because we have heard them so often. If you hear a thing fifty times a day, at last you come to believe it. God often blesses this method in working faith concerning what is true, for it is written, 'Faith cometh by hearing.' . . . Faith has the daily practice of pleading promises with God, speaking to Him face to face as a man speaks to his friend, and receiving favors from the right hand of the Most High."[30] He thus advocated a habit of claiming God's promises daily by faith, similar to the practice of Müller and Cullis. Spurgeon gave this testimony of confession and positive mental attitude from his own experience of life, particularly in his times of deep depression to which he was prone: "I find that if I can lay a promise under my tongue, like a sweet lozenge, and keep it in my mouth or mind all day long, I am happy enough."[31] He further taught we are to use the shield of faith by quoting the promises of God, speaking the great doctrines of the faith, claiming observations from examples in Scripture, and recalling what God has done in our life in the past.[32]

Spurgeon's Baptist colleague F.B. Meyer (also a leader in the Keswick movement) likewise advised making faith concrete through repeated confessions even when there is no feeling or evidence: "Dare to repeat it often, though you do not feel it, and though Satan insists that God has left you, 'Thou art with me.' Mention His name again and again, 'Jesus, Jesus, Thou art with me.' So you will be conscious that He is there. . . . Say over and over, 'I thank thee, O my God, that Thou hast kept Thy word with me. I opened my mouth, and Thou hast filled it; though as yet I am not aware of any change.'"[33]

Simpson on Positive Confession. The evidence cited above demonstrates that contrary to Barron, Simpson did not begin the positive confession teaching. By the time he began declaring the concept, it had been well established in the evangelical community, though it would appear that he developed the concept more fully, combining his Reformed theology with the accepted teachings on faith, healing and holiness. In several of his writings he strongly advocates confession of faith, saying, "Faith will die without confession."[34] Like Meyer, Murray, Spurgeon, and Smith, he taught that a person must believe first, and confess it regardless of feelings. Speaking of the woman who touched Jesus' garment, he commented, "She did not feel first and then believe, but she believed and then she felt. But her blessing must be confessed. Christ will not allow us to hold His gifts without acknowledgement."[35] Echoing Phoebe Palmer, in the 1890s Simpson used the phrase "confessing our blessings."[36] The popular phrase "confessing your blessing" is thus not original with contemporary faith teachers, but finds its origin with Palmer and Simpson.

Perhaps more than any classic faith leader Simpson stressed confession of faith. For Simpson, positive thinking by itself is not adequate: "It is not enough to think it, to feel it, to resolve it; we must say it. . . . We must confess Him in order to be saved; so we must receive and keep our sanctification, our healing, and the answers to our prayers by acknowledging God, even before we see His working."[37] It is noteworthy that Simpson's confessions of faith are almost always quotes from Scripture. Among the things Simpson teaches that believers should confess include: Christ as

Lord and Savior, as Guardian and Deliverer, and as Helper and Keeper, the promises of God, blessings, healing, and confidence of faith.[38] For Simpson, confession is not claiming personal wealth and self-centered blessing, but confessing the truths and promises of the Word of God.

Simpson's friend and associate Carrie Judd Montgomery developed these concepts further, applying the idea of positive confession to Proverbs 18:21, "Death and life is in the power of the tongue." While this is similar to some contemporary faith teaching and she may have been one of the earliest to make this connection, she did not take it as far as some in the current movement who see the Scripture passage as an absolute formula. Rather, she taught that there is a "connection between a sanctified tongue and divine health in body."[39]

Chambers on Confessing with Our Mouth. Chambers is still another who taught the importance of positive confession of our faith according to Romans 10:9-10: "In the Bible confession and testimony are put in a prominent place, and the test of a person's moral character is his 'say so.' I may try and make myself believe a hundred and one things, but it will never be mine until I 'say so.' If I say with myself what I believe and confess it with my mouth, I am lifted into the domain of that thing."[40] Here, like Augustine (and contemporary faith teaching), Chambers taught that one's confession can have an effect on the outcome, establishing some kinds of a cause and effect relationship.

Avoiding Negative Confessions. Classic faith leaders also stressed the importance of avoiding negative confessions. Hannah Whitall Smith avowed, "It is an inexorable rule in the spiritual life that according to our faith it is to be unto us; and of course this rule must work both ways, and therefore we may fairly expect that it will be also unto us according to our doubts."[41] Murray advised, "Do not lose time in deploring your unbelief, but look to Jesus," but confessing and getting rid of it.[42] He indicates that time should not be spend dwelling on one's problems, but in speaking by faith and confessing the Word of God.

Citing Job 3:25 and other Scriptures, Simpson repeatedly cautioned about the dangers of unbelief, doubt and worry.[43] He admonished, "We must not give place to the devil. Nothing encourages him so much as fear, and nothing dwarfs him and drives him away so quickly as audacity. If you for a moment acknowledge his power, you give him that power. If you for a moment recognized that he is in you, you will find that he is in you. If you let the thought or consciousness of evil into your spirit, you have lost your purity."[44] He was especially concerned about how our thoughts and words affect our health:

> If you want to keep the health of Christ, keep from all spiritual sores, from all heart-wounds and irritations. One hour of fretting will wear out more vitality than a week of work, and one minute of malignity, or rangling jealousy or envy will hurt more than a drink of poison. Sweetness of spirit and joyousness of heart are essential to full health. . . . We do not wonder that some people have poor health when we hear them talk for half an hour. They have enough dislikes, prejudices, doubts and fears to exhaust the strongest constitution. Beloved, if you would keep God's life and strength, keep out of the things that kill it.[45]

Likewise, Montgomery warned against people with negative confessions.[46] She cited a practical illustration in which a man went to the Healing Home in England to receive prayer for healing:

> He talked continually about himself and his symptoms, and this prevented him from getting hold on the Lord for healing. At last those who had charge of the Home told him that he would have to leave the Home unless he stopped talking about himself, and his bad feelings. They said, "You can talk about the Lord Jesus, but you must not say anything more about yourself." So when he would forget, and begin to say something about himself, they would lift a warning finger, and he would manage to change the sentence, before it was finished, into some word of praise or exaltation of the Lord Jesus. Not long after this the man was healed.[47]

Reflections and Conclusions

The Legitimacy of a Form of Positive Confession. Contrary to claims of the contemporary faith critics, the concepts of positive and negative confession are not confined to the metaphysical cults, but were also taught in some form by classic faith leaders and considered to be valid biblical truth. Some respected contemporary evangelical leaders who would not want to be identified with contemporary faith teaching or Schuller and Peale's positive thinking, nevertheless teach a form of positive confession. For example, Neil T. Anderson, former professor at Talbot Theological Seminary (Biola University), advocates making assertions of faith affirming the believer's identity in Christ, similar to those given by both classic and contemporary faith leaders.[48] He also speaks of "the power of positive believing."[49] These leaders show us that we can affirm the concept of positive confession without accepting all of the practical applications found in contemporary faith belief and practice.

The Problem of "Name It and Claim It" Faith Formula. Phoebe Palmer's teaching sounds almost identical to contemporary faith theology, and most certainly forms their foundation for the concept of positive confession, contrary to the claims of McConnell and Hanegraaff that it comes from the metaphysical cults. However, Palmer would not accept the teaching that a believer can "name and claim," "confess and possess," or "have what you say." She warned against those who taught what she called "faithism," which she defined as "telling others to 'only believe you have it, and you have got it.'"[50] Apparently a form of "name it and claim it" was being taught in her day as well. Likewise, a few decades later, Simpson encountered a similar problem and admonished, "Some people seem to think all that is necessary is to have faith and they can claim anything they please. Nay, the will must be surrendered to God, and His Word must be accepted about all things before we shall be able to believe them. We cannot risk our faith on the whims or caprices of ourselves or others."[51]

Nearly a century after Palmer, the "name it and claim it" practice persisted, and Carmichael also issued a similar warning: "It is not a case of 'Believe that you have it, and you have it'. . . . Believe it will come, yes, if you are sure your order is to go forward and buy land or building or save children. But woe unto you if you imagine you have been told to do such things and then find the order has not been signed above. But the sign, the very impress of the signet ring . . . is a solemn thing to see."[52]

While Simpson, Palmer and others taught that we should make confessions of faith, there is no evidence that they taught "confession is possession," and did not teach any kind of a "faith formula." Although some contemporary faith teachers interpret Mark 11:23 to mean that the believer can have whatever he confesses, this was not the claim of classic faith teachers. Murray interpreted this verse to mean, "This is the blessing of the prayer of faith of which Jesus speaks."[53] In other words, the believer can have what *Jesus* says, not what merely the believer himself says. If what the believer says is clearly the will of God, and God has spoken that word to him, then he or she can have whatever that person says because it is what Jesus says. This is a crucial misunderstanding of some contemporary faith teaching. When Jesus speaks a *rhema* to us, then we can have what He says, not merely what we say. There is a danger of presuming that what we desire and speak is what God desires.

Torrey tells of his experience of misinterpreting this Scripture as a young Christian and misapplying it in his prayer life:

> Not long after my conversion I got hold of this promise of our Lord Jesus in Mark 11:24. . . . I said to myself, 'All that I need to do if I want anything is to ask God for it and then make myself believe that I am going to get it, and I'll have it.' So whenever I wanted anything I asked God for it and tried to make myself believe I was going to get it, but I didn't get it, for it was only 'make believe,' and I did not really believe at all. . . . George Mueller never prayed for a thing just because he wanted it, or even just because he felt it was greatly needed for God's work. When it was laid upon George Mueller's heart to pray for anything, he would search the Scriptures to find if there was some promise that covered the case. Sometimes he would search the Scriptures for days before he presented his petition to God.[54]

The classic faith leaders show us that while there can often be a cause-and-effect relationship in one's confession positively or negatively, it is not absolute. The law of sowing and reaping is a general principle, not a legalistic formula that implicitly denies God's control and authority. Maintaining the dynamic tension of truth, they show us that we can legitimately exercise positive confession, but without naming and claiming anything we desire.

The Question of Vain Repetition. Also contrary to contemporary positive confession teaching, for Simpson confessing one's faith is not merely repeating a Scripture or formula, but consistently bearing witness of Christ and God's faithfulness.[55] Later faith healing evangelist Charles Price, who emulated Simpson, warned of mere rote repetition: "To sit down and repeat over and over, 'I am healed—I am healed—I am healed,' is not only unscriptural but spiritually dangerous in the extreme. I admit such an unsound procedure might help a few neurotics, but it would never remove the mountains of which the Master spoke."[56] This is valuable counsel from a classic faith leader to contemporary faith leaders. Hannah Whitall Smith, while strongly advocating repeated declarations of our faith, nevertheless also gives a warning: "But we must not say it with our lips only, and then by our actions deny our words. We must say it with our whole being, with thought, word, and action."[57] Similarly, Tozer avowed, "The Gospel is more than a formula," warning against what he called "religious bookkeeping," just making repeated confessions without really believing.[58] When real faith is exercised, Tozer stressed, there is a change of natures, desires, and instincts.

The Question of Self-talk. Regarding Hunt and McMahon's criticism of the Christian psychological use of the concept of self-talk, we acknowledge that it can lead to psychological manipulation, self-fulfilling prophecy, or self-centered narcissism. Nonetheless, we can see that the psalmist practiced a form of self-talk in the Old Testament:

> *Why are you in despair, O my soul?*
> *And why have you become disturbed within me?*
> *Hope in God, for I shall again praise Him*
> *For the help of His presence* (Ps. 42:5, NIV; see also 42:11; 43:5).

Moreover, David speaks to his soul, exhorting himself, "Bless the Lord, O my soul, and all that is within me, bless His holy name" (Ps. 103:1, KJV). The Bible would appear to support the concept of speaking to oneself in order to awaken oneself to spiritual truth and action.

The Question of "Calling Things That Are Not as Though They Are"-Romans 4:17. Citing this verse in regarding to speaking in faith creatively is not limited to contemporary faith teachers. Hannah Whitall Smith appears to be one of the earliest to make reference to this Scripture: "Faith, we are told, 'calleth those things which be not as though they were.' Calling them brings them into being."[59] For her, such exercise of faith is "the law of creation."[60] Simpson also made use of this Scripture: "We must not merely believe, but we must even call the 'things that are not as though they were,' and take the witnessing stand for God in all that He has called us to."[61] While this would on the surface seem to say that man has power to create out of nothing through his words, like some contemporary faith leaders teach, Simpson earlier in the same book wrote: "Faith 'calleth the things that are not as though they were' . . . for it believes in a God who can make all things out of nothing, and therefore it can step out into the seeming void and speak it full of the mighty creations of His power."[62]

This underscores the importance of taking both a person's statements, and Scripture verses in their proper context and in tandem with other statements. Montgomery taught the same: "At the moment of prayer, as we plead God's promises, we are to believe that God gives the answer, and *that He causes the thing which does not exist to come into existence in answer to our faith.*"[63] Her own italicizing of her words demonstrate she wants to make it emphatically clear to the reader that it is *God* who is creating into existence, not man.

Curiously, however, Nuzum, a friend and colleague of Montgomery, made a seemingly subtle, but potentially significant, omission from classic faith teaching on confession of faith. Referring to this verse, she says "Let *us* call the things that are not as though they are."[64] She did indicate, however, as did Simpson, that God does "create in us and for us whatever He has promised as we meet the conditions, ask, take it and call it as though it were."[65] She is not as clear as Simpson and Montgomery, however, in her wording, and, not read carefully or taken out of context, one could get the impression that she was exhorting the believer himself to create out of nothing.

While some contemporary faith teachers take this verse to mean that man's words have creative power, this is not what Simpson and Montgomery were claiming. Simpson is saying rather that *God* does the creating as a believer speaks in faith, and that *God's words* have creative power.[66] Even Kenyon taught that it is God who is calling into being.[67] It is these seemingly subtle differences which are crucial and which contemporary faith teachers often fail to distinguish. In what might seem to be a contradiction of Smith, Simpson, and Montgomery, Tozer counseled, "Faith creates nothing; it simply reckons on that which is already *there.*"[68] However, what he is saying is consistent with the earlier classic faith writers, for they all are saying that faith creates, not *ex nihilo*, but out of the realities that God has already created. This distinction is vital to maintain.

The Problem of Legalism Regarding Negative Confessions. I conclude that the concept that death and life are in the power of the tongue is a valid biblical concept, supported by classic faith leaders. Montgomery devoted an entire chapter in her book *Secrets of Victory* to "Divine Healing as Related to Our Tongue" based on Proverbs 18:21, asserting that our words can heal or harm ourselves and others.[69] However, this concept is also susceptible to misuse and imbalance. Nuzum, for example, went beyond her friend Montgomery when she exhorted, "Never say, 'I have pain, disease, doubt, or other evil.'"[70] This appears very similar to contemporary faith teachers who warn against never making a negative confession. Capps, for example, warns, "Quit talking foolishness, sickness and disease and saying 'that tickles me to death.'"[71] That generalized kind of counsel causes bondage, by making a person fearful that any negative word can have negative consequences. Yes, if there is a prevailing attitude behind a negative statement or habitual repetition of negative thoughts, it can lead to negative consequences. But just using a figure of speech or making a statement of fact is not going to have a negative effect. If that were so, Paul's statement "Satan thwarted me" (1 Thess. 2:18) would have been a negative confession.

Classic faith teachers differ here, in that they acknowledge that a negative confession may actually be a positive thing when it causes the believer to deal with reality. Murray, for example, advised, "Confess to the Lord all the difficulty you have to believe Him on the ground of His Word."[72] Contrary to contemporary faith teaching, part of proper confession is admitting to the Lord your unbelief, then asking the Lord to give you faith. Murray recommended speaking this confession: "Lord, I am still aware of the unbelief which is in me. I find it difficult to believe that I am assured of my healing just because I possess Him who works it in me. And, nevertheless, I want to conquer the unbelief. You, Lord, will give me the victory. I *desire* to believe, I *will* believe, and by Your grace, I *can* believe. Yes, Lord, I believe, for You help me with my unbelief."[73] Here, then, in Murray we find a healthy progression in confession:

1. Confess unbelief.
2. Express desire to conquer unbelief.
3. Confess that the Lord will give victory.
4. Confess your desire to believe.
5. Confess that you will believe.
6. Confess that you can believe by God's grace.
7. Confess that you do believe with God's help.

Kenneth Hagin, Jr. has come to recognize the overemphasis on fearing a negative confession in the contemporary faith movement, admonishing people not to deny their circumstances:

> Some people think that as long as they don't speak about a problem, that means they are in faith. . . . Some people even say, "I will not admit that I have a problem because I don't want to confess it into existence." But by admitting the problem, they aren't confessing the problem into existence—the problem is already there!

> For example, suppose you have all the symptoms of a cold—your nose is running, your eyes are watering, you have a fever, and you are sneezing and coughing. But instead of admitting you have a cold, you confess, "I don't have any symptoms. I'm fine. Nothing is the matter with me." That's not faith—that's lying.[74]

This is a much-needed statement from a contemporary faith leader in order to restore balance in contemporary faith praxis.

Final Reflections on Positive Confession. According to Romans 10:8-10, faith must be both in the heart and in the mouth to be effective. The classic faith leaders, along with the contemporary, affirm correctly that it is not enough just to believe it in the heart; faith must be expressed verbally. At the same time, that confession cannot be a mere formula, speaking by rote, but must come from the heart. Proper faith confessions come from personal relationship and fellowship with Christ, and are Christ-centered, not self-centered. As Simpson put it: "We must get under His very wings and in the bosom of His love before faith can claim its highest victories in our inmost being."[75] Applying this truth to healing, Simpson wrote, "This is the secret of divine healing. It is union with the One who is our physical Head as well as the source of our spiritual life."[76]

---

1. Kenyon, *In His Presence*, 51.

2. Hagin, *Mountain Moving Faith*, 74, 75, 84, 85.

3. Kenneth E. Hagin, *How to Write Your Own Ticket with God* (Tulsa, Okla.: Kenneth Hagin Ministries, 1979).

4. Copeland, *Forces of the Recreated Human Spirit*, 15.

5. See Kenyon, *In His Presence*, 50.

6. Ibid., 45.

7. Capps, *The Tongue—A Creative Force*, 30.

8. Ibid., 54.

9. McConnell, 137-139.

10. Hunt and McMahon, 154-155.

11. Hanegraaff, 66.

12. Hunt and McMahon, 157-158.

13. Barron, 60, quoting Simpson in *The Four-fold Gospel*, 62.

14. Augustine, *Sermons on New Testament Lessons*, 17:1-4, *NPNF*, 1:6:310-312.

15. Ibid., 311.

16. Ibid.

17. Ibid., see also p. 312.

18. Augustine, *On the Gospel of John*, Tractate 49:24, *NPNF*, 1:7:277.

19. William Gurnall, *The Christian in Complete Armour*, James S. Bell, Jr., ed. (Chicago: Moody Press, [1655] 1994), June 1.

20. Peter C. Erb, ed., *Pietists: Selected Writings* (New York: Paulist Press, 1983), 239-241.

21. For additional information, see Dale Simmons, "Say You Have It and You Have It: The Expanding Role of Positive Confession from Phoebe Palmer to Peter Popoff," paper presented at the Society for Pentecostal Studies, 1998.

22. Phoebe Palmer, *Faith and Its Effects* (New York: Palmer and Hughes, [1848] 1867), 31, 113, 296, 327.

23. Boardman, *The Higher Christian Life*, 261, 263.

24. Smith, *The Christian's Secret*, 53, 81-83.

25. Daniels, 149.

26. Murray, *Divine Healing*, 26, 27.

27. Ibid., 26-27.

28. Andrew Murray, *The Prayer Life* (Basingstoke, Hants, U.K.: Marshall, Morgan and Scott, 1968), 53.

29. Ibid.

30. Spurgeon, *The Triumph of Faith in a Believer's Life*, 37, 100.

31. Spurgeon, *Spiritual Warfare in a Believer's Life*, 176.

32. Ibid., 157-159.

33. Meyer, *The Secret of Guidance*, 89-90, 123.

34. Simpson, *In the School of Faith*, 51; see also Simpson, *The Gospel of Healing*, 128, 142; Simpson, *How To Receive Divine Healing*, 6, 7, 10, 11-12; Simpson, *CITB* (1992), 2:22, 24.

35. Simpson, *The Gospel of Healing*, 128.

36. Simpson, *CITB* (1992), 1:80.

37. Simpson, *CITB* (1992), 3:241.

38. See Simpson, *Friday Meeting Talks*, 108-110; see also Simpson, *The Lord for the Body* (1996), 64-65; Simpson, *CITB* (1992), 3:241; Simpson, *CITB*, 1:80, Simpson, *The Gospel of Healing*, 128.

39. Carrie Judd Montgomery, "The Power of the Tongue," *CMAW*, Sept. 4, 1909, 376.

40. Oswald Chambers, *Daily Thoughts for Disciples* (Grand Rapids: Discovery House, [1976] 1994), Apr. 20.

41. Smith, *The Christian's Secret*, 83.

42. Murray, *Divine Healing*, 26.

43. Simpson, *Days of Heaven on Earth*, Aug. 18; Simpson, *The Gospel of Healing*, 98; Simpson, *In the School of Faith*, 266.

44. Simpson, *CITB* (1992), 2:34-35.

45. A.B. Simpson, *Triumphs of Faith*, Nov. 1921, 253.

46. Montgomery, *Secrets of Victory*, 65.

47. Ibid., 31-32.

48. Neil T. Anderson, *Victory over the Darkness* (Ventura, Calif.: Regal Books, 1990), 45-47, 57-59; see also Neil T. Anderson, *Living Free in Christ* (Ventura, Calif.: Regal Books, 1993). This book is an expansion of these faith assertions.

49. Anderson, *Victory over the Darkness*, 107.

50. Palmer, 189-190.

51. Simpson, *The Land of Promise*, 72.

52. Elliot, 190-191.

53. Murray, *With Christ in the School of Prayer*, 82.

54. Torrey, *The Power of Prayer*, 124.

55. Simpson, *In the School of Faith*, 127.

56. Charles Price, *The Real Faith*, 15.

57. Smith, *Living Confidently in God's Love*, 113.

58. Tozer, *Faith Beyond Reason*, 98-99.

59. Smith, *Living Confidently in God's Love*, 261.

60. Ibid.

61. Simpson, *In the School of Faith*, 51-52.

62. Ibid., 14; see also pp. 50, 253; Simpson, "Inquiries and Answers," Dec. 1886, 342; Simpson, *The Gospel of Healing*, 42; Simpson, *CITB* (1992), 1:80.

63. Montgomery, *Secrets of Victory*, 23.

64. C. Nuzum, *The Life of Faith* (Springfield, Mo.: Gospel Publishing House, [1928] 1956), 82; see also p. 80.

65. Ibid., 81.

66. Simpson, *Present Truths or the Supernatural*, 17.

67. Kenyon, *In His Presence*, 178.

68. Tozer, *The Pursuit of God*, 53.

69. Montgomery, *Secrets of Victory*, 47-53. She also supported this teaching with several additional Scriptures: Proverbs 10:19, 20, 31; 11:13; 12:18; 13:3; 14:25; 15:1, 4, 23, 28; 18:4, 8.

70. Nuzum, 64.

71. Capps, *Releasing the Ability of God*, 85.

72. Murray, *Divine Healing*, 26.

73. Ibid.

74. Kenneth Hagin, Jr., *Another Look at Faith*, 28-29.

75. Simpson, *The Lord for the Body* (1996), 105.

76. Ibid., 115.

CHAPTER 18

Practical Issues of Prayer and Faith:
Praying Once and Point of Contact

Though not closely related to each other, two practical issues of prayer and faith involve how long to keep praying and the use of a point of contact to aid faith. Teaching on these areas has become controversial. Some believe that a person should continually persevere in prayer. Others avow that a believer should only pray once, and that it is a confession of unbelief to pray again. This principle is also important in understanding when to continue praying and when to cease praying for a particular request.

The concept of a point of contact as an expression of faith is rooted in two Biblical passages, especially in relationship to healing: 1) James 5—anointing with oil and laying on hands, and 2) Mark 5:27-28—the woman touching the hem of Jesus' garment. In these Scriptures, touch or physical contact appears to be an aid or accompaniment to faith.

CONTEMPORARY FAITH TEACHING

In one of his books Hagin teaches that believers should pray in faith only once, saying, "Many people undo their prayers. They get into unbelief and stay there. I am convinced that if most Christians would quit praying and start praising God, the answer would materialize right away."[1] He cites Wigglesworth and Murray as support for his teaching: "Smith Wigglesworth said, 'If you pray seven times for any one thing, you prayed six times in unbelief.' Andrew Murray said, 'It is not good taste to ask God for the same thing over and over again. If, when you do pray again, what you have prayed for has not materialized, don't pray for it again in the same way. That would be unbelief. Remind God that you asked for it and what His Word says, and tell Him that you are expecting it. Then thank Him for it.'"[2] Yet in other writings, Hagin acknowledges that there are different kinds of prayer, and some prayers, especially intercession, require repeated praying.[3]

On the other hand, Capps goes far beyond Hagin, claiming, "Faith makes prayer work. Faith will work without prayer."[4] He believes that praying the same thing over and over again is a form of vain repetition.[5] He comments that a footnote on Matthew 7:7 in the Amplified Bible that says prayer is repeated often is in error.[6] He claims that this verse cannot mean that prayer is to be repeated "because that would be contrary to other scriptures concerning prayer (such as Mark 11:24; John 15:7-8; 1 John 5:14-15)."[7]

Many charismatic and contemporary faith leaders use the concept of a point of contact as a reinforcement to acting in faith. Oral Roberts is usually considered the originator of the concept. Although, as mentioned earlier, the ministry and teaching of Oral Roberts falls under the classification of classic faith teaching, some have categorized him as a contemporary faith teacher and the concept of a "point of contact" of faith as a contemporary faith teaching. Hence this concept is treated here.

Points of contact that aid faith might include laying on of hands, holding hands with another, application of anointing oil or blessed water, or touching certain items such as a prayer cloth, or a television screen. Sometimes it may be a touch that conveys heat or shivers, a sense of excitement, electrical impulse, or peace, or a touch of power that causes a person to fall down (sometimes popularly called being "slain in the Spirit").

CRITICISM OF CONTEMPORARY FAITH TEACHING

Critics assert the belief that praying once flies in the face of sound exegesis of Scripture. First of all, the testimony of Scripture indicates that prayer is to be repeated. Against Capps, a literal Greek translation of the iterative present tense of the verbs in Matthew 7:7 would be, "Keep on asking, and it shall be given unto you; keep on seeking, and you will find; keep on knocking and it shall be opened unto you." Additional Scripture illustrations include the repeated prayers of Elijah on the mountain, Jesus in the Garden of Gethsemane, Jesus' parable about persevering in prayer (Luke 18:1-5), and Paul praying to be relieved of his thorn in the flesh.

The idea of using items as a point of contact for faith has come under fire by Kurt Koch as advocating an occult practice. Koch considers the "hot hand" or use of prayer handkerchiefs as mediumistic fetishes,[8] warning, "Even believing Christians can possess or be carriers of mediumistic abilities."[9] In particular, Koch questions the healing abilities of charismatic faith healer William Branham, who possessed mediumistic-like powers such as clairvoyance and a "hot hand."[10] Koch notes that Branham's parents believed in fortune-telling and that he experienced visionary and clairvoyant powers as a child before he became a Christian. He calls into question a wide variety of other faith healing ministries including Kathryn Kuhlman, Oral Roberts, T.L. Osborn, and others.[11] Likewise, MacArthur considers a healing phenomenon like prayer cloths to be limited to the apostles in the New Testament.[12] Hanegraaff scoffs at the point of contact concept, viewing it merely as a gimmick for raising money.[13]

CLASSIC FAITH TEACHING

On Praying Once. Classic faith leaders emphasized the importance of persevering in prayer. Faith and spiritual warfare pioneer Blumhardt believed that repeated prayer was especially effective: "How many attacks does it take before the walls of a well-entrenched city are breached? Our prayers, it might be said, are hammer-strokes against the bulwark of the princes of darkness; they must oft be repeated. Many years can pass by, even a number of generations die away. However, not a single hit is wasted; and if they are continued, then even the most secure wall must finally fall. Then the glory of the Lord will have a clear path upon which to stride forth with healing and blessing for the wasted fields of mankind."[14]

Müller avowed that he had prayed for some things thousands of times over the years, yet maintaining an attitude of trust and thankfulness.[15] In opposition to Capps, who believes that faith can work without prayer, Müller's friend Spurgeon admonished, "He who has true faith in his heart is praying all the day long. . . . If your faith does not make you pray, get rid of it, and God help you to begin again in true faith."[16] Apparently there were some in the early twentieth century who taught that it is wrong to pray more than once, for Charles Blanchard, President of Wheaton College, answered their arguments, saying:

> It is helpful to remember about our Lord's praying in Gethsemane. He prayed once, He prayed twice, He prayed the third time, and it is interesting to note that the Word says, in speaking of these repeated petitions, "saying the same words" (Matt.

26:44). How can one reconcile this fact with the teaching of some who say that when we have once proffered a petition, it is an exhibition of distrust or rebellious spirit if we make the same request again. . . . The fact is that we must be taught by the Spirit how to pray. Sometimes He will teach us to pray once and to look upon the transaction as completed. Sometimes He will bid us pray more than once and when He does so, we must persevere in prayer.[17]

Regarding the same Scripture, Torrey sarcastically spoke of those who insisted on praying only once, saying that they "have either gotten beyond our Master, our Lord and Savior Jesus Christ, or else they have not gotten up to Him."[18]

Hagin did quote Murray accurately in defense of praying only once. In fact, Murray also affirmed, "Will it be needful to pray longer if once we know we have been heard and have received what we asked? There are cases in which such prayer will not be needful, in which the blessing is ready to break through at once, if we but hold fast our confidence, and prove our faith by praising for what we have received, in the face of our not yet having it in experience."[19] However, Hagin did not quote Murray fully in light of his other writings, for Murray also asserted that there are times to continue in repetitive prayer: "There are other cases in which the faith that has received needs to be still further tried and strengthened in persevering prayer. . . . Elijah knew for certain that rain would come; God had promised it; and yet he had to pray the seven times."[20] Hagin does believe, like Murray, that there are appropriate times and types of prayer to be repeated, although he does not cite Murray on this. In addition to Murray, Spurgeon, Müller, Blumhardt, Blanchard, Simpson, and Torrey all speak of persevering in prayer. The prayer lives of Praying Hyde, Bounds, and others could be cited as well. The overwhelming testimony of Scripture and the lives of men of faith is that repeated prayer is vital to the operation of faith and receiving answers to prayer.

But are there legitimate times when praying once can be appropriate? In addition to Murray and Hagin, other classic faith leaders believed so. Müller, when asked this question in his day, replied that when he had clear assurance of something to be the mind of God, he would ask once, then thank Him even hundreds of times for the answer before it was received.[21] Sometimes he had to wait four, six, even eleven years, but still had confidence to give thanks rather than pray. Like Murray, Simpson taught that there were such appropriate times. He counseled:

> The Holy Spirit will also teach us when to cease from prayer and turn our petition into thanksgiving. . . . When we truly believe we shall cease to ask as we asked before, and then our prayers shall simply be in the attitude of waiting for our answer, or holding up God's promise to Him in the Spirit of praise and expectation.
>
> This does not mean that we shall never think any more about that for which we asked, but we shall not think of it in a doubtful manner; we shall think of it only with thanksgiving and restful expectation. We may often remind God of it, but it will always be in the spirit of trust and confidence.[22]

Torrey also agreed, "Doubtless there are times when we are able through faith in the Word, or through the clear leading of the Holy Spirit, to claim a thing the first time we have asked it of God."[23] Pierson and MacMillan taught that there are times in the exercise of the authority of the believer when one speaks a word of faith or command, rather than a request.[24] Once again, for each of these classic faith leaders the key for the appropriate action is receiving an assurance from the Holy Spirit, not just praying once and assuming there is no need to pray again.

On Point of Contact. Although in recent years Oral Roberts has especially been known for teaching the exercise of one's faith by reaching out in a "point of contact," the concept and terminology is not original with him. As early as the seventeenth-century, Zinzendorf taught the aspect of touch in relationship to faith. Referring to Matthew 9:21, "If only I would touch the man's clothes. . .", Zinzendorf described this as "faith-in-distress."[25] Similarly of the faith of this woman who touched the hem of Jesus' garment, Spurgeon called it "faith in its 'touch.'"[26]

The terminology "point of contact" does not originate with Oral Roberts, but is as least as old as Murray's 1884 book on healing.[27] He taught that the laying on of hands and anointing with oil should be regarded "not as a remedy, but as a pledge of the mighty virtue of the Holy Spirit, as a means of strengthening faith, a *point of contact* and of communion between the sick one and members of the Church who are called to anoint him with oil."[28] James McConkey used the image of maintaining a constant point of contact with a live wire (Jesus Christ) in order to maintain the life of abiding in Christ.[29]

Simpson called it the "touch of faith," explaining, "There is a touch of faith as well as a touch of God. . . . The blessings which God has to impart to us through the Lord Jesus Christ . . . are already granted, completed and prepared and simply awaiting the contact of a believing hand to open all the channels of communication."[30] Like McConkey, he compared the power of contact to the contact of two wires completing an electrical circuit.[31] Simpson later wrote about faith in connection with healing, calling such faith "this point of contact, this organ of receptiveness, this open mouth of the soul—confidence in God, appropriating faith."[32]

Referring to Mark 5 and Matthew 18:19-20, popular prayer teacher Rosalind Rinker taught the same concept in her book *Prayer: Conversing with God*: "Your point of contact is when you touch Jesus Christ, whether you are alone or with someone else. . . . Jesus Christ is our 'point of contact,' and as we touch Him, alone or with others, power is released and our prayers are answered."[33] Though a contemporary of Oral Roberts, it is not likely that she gleaned the concept from Roberts, but from other classic faith sources, for she was influenced by people in that stream such as Paris Reidhead of the C&MA (a friend and colleague of Tozer) and the Keswick Conferences.

It is not magic or mere human contact, though, but human contact in faith that touches Christ. Human contact is the *act* of faith through which contact with Christ is made. Spurgeon wrote that faith brings a person into "vital contact with Christ."[34] Simpson explained further: "It involves not only our hand but His personality. Faith must recognize the Lord Jesus Himself and come into immediate contact with Him before it can draw His healing virtue or His comforting love."[35] Likewise, Murray exhorted that power goes forth when coming in touch with the hem of Jesus' garment, symbolic of touching Christ Himself: "Let each contact with the blood be contact with the Lamb, more particularly with His gentleness and meekness. Let your faith touch just the hem of His garment and power will go out from Him."[36] For the most part, these writers do not deal with the question of an object such as a prayer cloth being used as an aid to faith, but they do indicate that power can be transmitted through a physical touch when done in faith and when contact has been made with Christ.

REFLECTIONS AND CONCLUSIONS

The belief that prayer is not to be repeated is based on lack of knowledge of the Scriptures in the original language. Capps' claim regarding

Matthew 7:7 is based on his presuppositions and misinterpretation of the other passages of Scripture. As noted above, he is ignorant of the fact that this verse in the original Greek does indeed mean "ask and keep on asking, . . . seek and keep on seeking, . . . knock and keep on knocking." He does not realize that rather than a contradiction, the seeming paradoxes are really the two wings of truth, two sides of the same coin. Thus he and some other contemporary faith teachers err in locking the principles of faith into an "either-or" absolute, rather than maintaining the dynamic tension of the polarities. I conclude with the classic faith teachers that believers should continue to persevere in prayer unless God gives assurance. In those cases, believers can stop praying and starting praising.

This research also shows that the classic faith teachers taught the principle of point of contact as a valid expression of faith. Their source is not occultic, for they are solidly in the evangelical camp. Such a point of contact is not magical, automatic, or absolute, but is dependent upon true contact with Christ Himself. Laying on of hands and anointing with oil are legitimate biblical uses of point of contact.

Even though the C&MA believed in acts of faith as a point of contact, Alliance leader William T. MacArthur was also concerned about excessive emphasis and almost magical regard for supernatural points of contact. In an article entitled "Fabrics Filled with Power" he affirmed that there is some "semblance of truth" to "the charging of clothing with the power of the Holy Ghost" for healing, but warned that those who have gone into the "handkerchief business" are "charlatans and pretenders." Such conduct, MacArthur advised, cannot be reconciled with the "unostentatious behavior of the apostles." It is an "unwholesome love for the spectacular."[37] On one hand, this Alliance leader affirmed that there is an appropriate place for using such articles as a point of contact of faith and that they could be used by the Lord to transmit the healing power of the Spirit. On the other hand, he stressed that these means were not emphasized by the apostles, nor were they performed in a showy manner.

It would appear from Scripture that such points of contact as prayer cloths may be appropriate on some occasions as aids to faith, but cannot be used indiscriminately or magically. Nor should they be used as fundraising gimmicks. A touch in faith may at times result in physical manifestations from the Holy Spirit such as heat, electrical impulse, falling or swooning, etc., but they are not always to be expected or sought. Such phenomena can also be of the flesh or even a demonic counterfeit.[38]

Practical Issues of Prayer and Faith: Praying Once and Point of Contact

1. Kenneth E. Hagin, *What To Do When Faith Seems Weak & Victory Lost* (Tulsa, Okla.: Kenneth Hagin Ministries, 1979), 113.

2. Ibid.

3. Hagin, *The Art of Prayer*, 74-75.

4. Capps, *Releasing the Ability of God*, 27.

5. Ibid., 29-33.

6. Ibid., 61.

7. Ibid.

8. Kurt Koch, *Demonology Past and Present* (Grand Rapids: Kregel Publications, 1973), 57-70, 110, 122, 124-125.

9. Ibid., 67.

10. Kurt Koch, *Between Christ and Satan* (Western Germany: Evangelization Publishers, n.d.), 150-151.

11. Ibid., 149-152; Koch, *Demonology Past and Present*, 105-106; Kurt Koch, *Occult Bondage and Deliverance* (Western Germany: Evangelization Publishers, 1970), 48-55.

12. MacArthur, *Charismatic Chaos*, 241-242.

13. Hanegraaff, 31, 36, 201-204, 207, 351.

14. Eller, 84-85.

15. Steer, 92.

16. Spurgeon, *The Triumph of Faith in a Believer's Life*, 63.

17. Blanchard, 136.

18. Torrey, *The Power of Prayer*, 133.

19. Murray, *With Christ in the School of Prayer*, 83.

20. Ibid.

21. Steer, 92.

22. Simpson, *The Gentle Love of the Holy Spirit*, 135.

23. Torrey, *The Power of Prayer*, 133.

24. Pierson, *Lessons in the School of Prayer*, 59-60; MacMillan, *The Authority of the Believer*, 38, 60, 67-68.

25. McGrath, 238.

26. Spurgeon, *Morning by Morning*, 240.

27. Murray, *Divine Healing*, 133-134.

28. Italics mine. Ibid., 84.

29. James H. McConkey, *The Three-fold Secret of the Holy Spirit* (Chicago: Moody Press, 1897), 106-107.

30. Simpson, *CITB* (1992), 4:247.

31. Ibid., 204.

32. A.B. Simpson, "According to Your Faith," *CMAW*, Sept. 8, 1906, 146.

33. Rosalind Rinker, *Prayer: Conversing with God* (Grand Rapids: Zondervan, 1959), 60-61.

34. Spurgeon, *The Power of Prayer in a Believer's Life*, 43.

35. A.B. Simpson, *CITB* (1992), 4:427 (originally *John-Acts*, v. 10, 1891).

36. Murray, *The Blood of the Cross*, 78.

37. W.T. MacArthur, "Fabrics Filled with Power," *AW*, Sept. 14, 1912, 390.

38. See Paul L. King, "Holy Laughter and Other Phenomena in Evangelical and Holiness Revival Movements." *Alliance Academic Review 1996*, Elio Cuccaro, ed. (Camp Hill, Penn.: Christian Publications, 1998), 107-122.

CHAPTER 19

Faith, Impressions, and Revelation:
Issues of Discernment

It was established in Chapter 13 that revelation knowledge can be a valid concept when used with discretion. Practical questions arise out of faith praxis of this concept: "How do you know when a revelation, impression, 'rhema,' prophecy, or 'word of the Lord,' is really from the Lord?" "How does one discern?" "Is it lack of faith not to act on such an impression or revelation?" "Can such impressions be from other sources than God?"

CONTEMPORARY FAITH TEACHING

Contemporary faith teaching tends to be dualistic regarding impressions and revelations. On one hand, impressions through sense knowledge are denigrated, but on the other hand, revelation knowledge is exalted. However, there is no clear differentiation between what is considered revelation knowledge and what is an impression, except that impressions are often associated with feelings or reasonings of the mind. Revelation knowledge is often associated with novel interpretations of Scripture, especially when it counters traditional beliefs or teachings.[1] Such revelation is considered to be above traditional understandings of Scripture.[2] Kenyon taught that those who walk in revelation knowledge are "supermen": "We are not common folk. This [revelation knowledge] lifts us out of the common place into the super-realm. You are the real supermen and superwomen. You have gone outside of the realm of the senses, outside of the realm of Sense Knowledge, and you have passed over into the realm of God, the spirit realm."[3]

Some contemporary faith teachers do recognize that supposed revelations can come from other sources, and thus insist that revelations must be judged. For instance, Hagin stresses that revelations must line up with Scripture: "If you get any revelation from God, friends, check it in line with the Word, and then put it into practice for yourself before you start preaching it."[4] Capps likewise teaches, "Many people are deceived by supernatural visitations. Everything supernatural is not of God. Compare all that is said by any supernatural being with what the Word of God has to say."[5] Yet there is no set standard as to what constitutes a proper interpretation of a Scripture.[6] This will be discussed in Chapter 24 on "Faith and Hermeneutics."

CRITICISM OF CONTEMPORARY FAITH TEACHING

Criticism of teaching on revelation and impressions come in varied forms. Against what he calls the "traditional view," Friesen asserts that there are no such things as impressions from the Lord, avowing, "Impressions are just impressions."[7] He believes that anything subjective such as impressions are not a form of revelation, though direct revelation from God can occur upon rare occasions.[8] MacArthur, from a cessationist point of view, avows that any revelation today sets itself up against the authority of the Bible.[9] K. Neill Foster, though not a cessationist, finds fault with prophetic words and revelations that are inaccurate, yet accepted as essentially true. He claims they must be, like Old Testament prophecy, either totally true or else false.[10] Hanegraaff cites several examples of claims of revelation knowledge that are heretical, poor interpretation, or just plain silly.[11] He points out, for example, that Hinn claimed revelation knowledge about the Trinity, which appeared to be a form of heretical tritheism.[12] Though Hinn later retracted the belief as "a dumb statement," still he had claimed it as a revelation from God. These critics are also appalled by what seems to them to be the claiming of divine revelation superseding Scripture. McConnell further warns that those who possess revelation knowledge consider themselves as a higher class of Christians.[13] Some have even placed themselves beyond reproof and warned people to "touch not God's anointed" when their teachings have been criticized.[14]

CLASSIC FAITH TEACHING

The Validity of Impressions and Revelations. Contrary to Friesen, respected classic evangelical faith leaders, by and large, believed in the validity of receiving impressions and subjective revelations from God.

"Müller cultivated habits of life which made his whole nature more and more open to divine impression, and so his sense of God became more and more keen and constant."[15] Müller's walk of faith was based on expecting God to work through impressions: "I had repeatedly asked the Lord for the money but received nothing. But when I prayed that the Lord would impress it on the brother that we needed money, he opened the box and gave it to me." On many occasions he was "led" to ask the Lord for money.[16] He expected people to be "moved" by the Lord to give.[17] Murray believed that at times God may lead by the Spirit through "sudden impulses or strong impressions or heavenly voices" which may involve our thoughts and feelings, but they are not expected to be the ordinary leading of the Spirit.[18] Simpson counseled that believers should rely upon "divine impulses instead of even our best attainments."[19]

Fundamentalists are often known, like MacArthur, to be cessationists, and opposed to the idea of receiving a subjective revelation from the Lord today. However, even respected fundamentalist leader John R. Rice acknowledged the legitimacy of such impulses: "Faith may be based upon a clear and tested impression give by the Holy Spirit that God wants us to do a certain thing and that He will lead us and bless us."[20] Contrary to Foster's claims that New Testament prophecy is the same as Old Testament prophecy, many classic faith leaders understood New Testament prophecy to be different from Old Testament prophecy. Typical of much classic faith teaching, MacMillan averred:

> Prophecy is no longer the receiving of direct messages from on high for the instruction and guidance of the whole congregation. The complete Word of the Lord is in the hands of His people, and from its pages, through the illumination of the Spirit, is received by the prophets and teachers of our day the spiritual food of the flock of God. Guidance is no longer openly spoken from above, but as the Lord is waited upon, gracious intimations of His will are given in various ways, and He unifies the minds and hearts of His servants to understand and carry out His purposes. One of the sweet revelations of the supernatural in the Church is the impressing of many with the same thought, or the bringing of them to one accord over some question of policy or ministry.[21]

Such classic faith teaching believed that revelation often comes through subjective impressions or illuminations from the Holy Spirit, rather than cut-and-dried direct revelations.

The Need for Testing and Verifying Impressions. As mentioned earlier, Wesley declared that visions, revelations, dreams and impressions can be from God, from nature, or from Satan. Murray advised against the "danger of being led away by the imaginings of our own hearts," cautioning that what we may consider to be a leading of the Spirit sometimes proves to be a delusion of the flesh.[22] The safeguard against such error, according to Murray, is "the Word of God as taught by the Spirit of God."[23] Meyer, along with many others of his day, taught a three-fold process of guidance: 1) internal impressions, 2) external Word of God, 3) corroboration by circumstances or providence, waiting quietly "until these three focus into one point."[24]

While Simpson believed we should depend on divine impulses, he also cautioned: "God does give us impressions but not that we should act on them as impressions. If the impression be from God, He will Himself give sufficient evidence to establish it beyond the possibility of a doubt."[25] In other words, we should not act on impressions without some other evidence. Speaking of the prophetic "word of the Lord" Jeremiah received to purchase a field (Jer. 32), Simpson remarked, "He waited until God seconded the impression by a providence."[26] He also illustrated the point from the New Testament: "We are not to ignore the Shepherd's personal voice, but like Paul and his companions at Troas, we are to listen to all the voices that speak, and 'gather' from all the circumstances, as they did, the full mind of the Lord."[27] Simpson further warned against trusting in someone else's supposed word of faith in matters of healing: "Do not rise from your bed or walk on your lame foot because somebody tells you to do so. That is not faith, but impression."[28]

According to Simpson, trusting in impressions and the like can actually sometimes be a superficial walk of faith: "The shallow nature lives in its impulses, its impressions, its intuitions, its instincts and very largely in its surroundings. The profound character looks beyond all these and moves steadily on. . . . When God has deepened us, then He can give us His deeper truths, His profoundest secrets, and His mightier trusts."[29] Simpson's reference to "profoundest secrets" sounds similar to Kenyon's description of revelation knowledge, while the former sounds like Kenyon's understanding of sense knowledge.

As a Quaker, Hannah Whitall Smith adhered to the typical Quaker practice of listening for the inner voice of God. However, she cautioned against trusting the inner voice rather than Scripture and the need for discernment: "If we fail to search out and obey the Scripture rule, where there is one, and look instead for an inward voice, we shall open ourselves to delusions, and shall almost inevitably get into error."[30] Similar to Meyer, she recognized that God does sometimes lead through impressions, but those impressions must be in harmony with the Scripture, providential circumstances, and the conviction of our own higher judgment.[31] She warned, "we must never forget that 'impressions' can come from other sources as well as the Holy Spirit."[32] They can come from strong personalities around us, from our physical conditions, or from spiritual enemies. "It is not enough to have a leading," she cautions, "we must find out the source of that leading before we give ourselves up to follow it."[33] There are times when human sense and emotion are contrary to faith, so faith must come before feeling.[34]

Ironically, at the very time her book was released, her husband did not abide by her counsel, but was involved with a gnostic-like "secret doctrine" being taught in some holiness circles in which it was believed that the Holy Spirit sends thrills up and down the body (some believed that this was the evidence of the baptism or filling of the Holy Spirit).[35] Her words warning of delusion became sadly prophetic of her own husband.

It should be noted, on the other hand, that as wary as she was of impressions, Smith also advised, "Just as our impressions must be tested, . . . so must these other voices be tested by our inward impressions; and if we feel a 'stop in our minds' about anything, we must wait before that is removed before acting. . . . 'I always mind the checks.' We must not ignore the voice of our inward impressions, nor ride roughshod over them, any more than we must over the other three voices of which I have spoken."[36] She maintains that delicate balance or dynamic tension of the two wings.

Prophecy as Impressions and the Need for Judging. Prophecy in the late nineteenth century and early twentieth century was also identified with receiving impressions from the Lord. In 1898 when Carrie Judd Montgomery had been very ill, she testified at the C&MA convention about prophecies that she had received from three women, two of which said she would die, one of which said she would recover: "The Lord spoke to her and told her that I would be raised up speedily and that I would be able to attend the Christian Alliance [C&MA] convention, which would take place in a few days. I was so very weak and ill that her prophecy seemed incredible, but, praise God, it came true." Of the two other women she commented, "Two Christian women thought they had it from the Lord that I was going to die. . . . How this shows us that we must not depend on *impressions* that do not harmonize with the word of God. . . . Dear readers, always stand firmly upon God's Word, and not upon the *impressions* of those around you (italics mine)."[37] Montgomery believed that while prophecy could contain predictive elements, it was still regarded as an impression.

According to early classic faith leaders, prophecy can also be counterfeited and may need to be tested. Simpson alluded to the need of testing prophecy, which he calls *"inward visions and revelations,"* by "the simple test" of "the Word of God [particularly 1 John 4:1-3], and the practical test of righteousness and holiness."[38] He exhorted, "Let us be prepared for false spirits and let us not fear to try them, for if God is giving us any *message or revelation,* He will always give us ample time to be quite sure that it is God" (italics mine).[39] Robert Jaffray, later field chairman of the C&MA mission in China referred to the 1 John 4:1-3 procedure of testing spirits Simpson mentioned and approved its use as needed specifically for the testing of tongues and prophecy, declaring, "Only by a God-given supernatural instinct, only by 'trying the spirits in the Scriptural way, may we be saved from evil influences that fill the 'air' in these last days."[40] He avowed that "a God-given, supernatural instinct" was needed with the test. He also cautioned that those testing a spirit need to take care that they "be separated from and not in any sense under the influence of the spirit at the time of the trial . . . . It is no light or trifling thing thus to come into the very presence of supernatural beings."[41] According to these leaders, Scripture in conjunction with spiritual fruit and spiritual discernment are the standards for judging prophetic content.

Contrary to Neill Foster, C&MA leader Jaffray also warned against considering prophecy as infallible, continuing Simpson's emphasis and interpretation and citing the same incidents as Simpson: "There is a subtle danger of attaching too much importance to supernatural utterances and interpretations of tongues, considering that they are the very infallible Word of the Spirit of God. It is easy to say, 'The Spirit says,' etc. 'The Lord told me so and so' when it is quite possible that it is a matter of our own self-wilfulness. The Apostle Paul did not accept such leadings as the infallible will of the Lord for him (see Acts 21). Some would make the prophets of the Lord mere fortune-tellers."[42] Ironically, Foster, a more recent leader in the C&MA, claimed this view of the fallibility of prophecy is accommodational and cultural, ignoring sixty years of this teaching earlier in his own denomination.[43] My own research verifies this teaching in the C&MA and nineteenth and early twentieth century evangelical leadership in my unpublished paper "The Historic C&MA View of the Fallibility of Prophecy."[44]

Simpson also became concerned about accepting prophecies as authoritative, quite similar to Jaffray: "One of the most alarming tendencies of this [Pentecostal] movement has recently developed in several places in the form of a prophetic authority which certain persons are claiming over the consciences of others and men and women are seeking counsel and guidance from them in the practical matters of private duty, instead of looking directly to the Anointing which they have received of him and obeying God rather than men."[45] Both Simpson and Jaffray warn that in some instances Christians seek out prophetic words almost as the world goes to the clairvoyant and fortuneteller.

Early classic faith leaders also believed that some prophecies may not be from God or Satan, but a mistaken impulse or impression of the flesh. May Mabette Anderson presented the typical classic faith viewpoint in the *C&MA Weekly*:

> The basic principle underlying all such cases of mistaken judgment . . . is always . . . when closely scanned, an undue exaltation given to personal "impressions" and "assurances" believed to be from God.
>
> So infallible are these "impressions" and "revelations" supposed to be, that the one believing them truly believes he will be unfaithful to God should he question them. And when, in the course of events, these "revelations" do not round out into actualities, there are but two courses open: either to admit that he was mistaken in his impressions, or find some "scapegoat" on whom to place the failure. These dear ones are wholly sincere in their course, and, what is still sadder, they are usually very spiritual and lovely souls. So earnest are they, and so assured that their "revelations" have been from above, that they are ready to denounce all who do not accept their view—even though such may be the most Christ-like and spiritually intelligent souls with whom they are bringing in contact—as "under Satanic power."[46]

While classic faith leaders recognized prophecy could be counterfeited by Satan, they also recognized that there could be elements of the flesh in what apparently is a leading of the Spirit, as can be noted in Anderson's quote above. Simpson, commenting on the partially mistaken prophecies Paul had received warning him about going to Jerusalem (Acts 21:4, 10-14), remarked, "We must learn to distinguish between mere impressions and the deeper convictions of the entire judgment under the light of the Spirit, and between the voice of the Shepherd and the spirit of error. This He will teach us, and teach us more and more perfectly through experience."[47]

He notes that prophecies may range from being mere impressions or they may be more surely from the Spirit, but that these prophecies are imperfect and can be discerned more perfectly over time through experience. This idea was promulgated in the evangelical holiness community, for Martin Wells Knapp taught the same idea about three years later, taking his cue from earlier writers such as Wesley, Müller, G.D. Watson, Thomas Upham, Hannah Whitall Smith, and perhaps also Simpson, explaining that "impressions which are of God ripen into convictions."[48] It is evident that the concept of fallible or imperfect prophecy ranging from impressions to "direct convictions" was a part of evangelical holiness theology for at least the latter half of the nineteenth-century and first half of the twentieth-century.

REFLECTIONS AND CONCLUSIONS

I conclude with the classic faith leaders cited above that God continues to give revelation, but it is not on the same level as biblical revelation. If it is not on the same level, then logically it cannot be infallible. Such revelation may range from impressions to clear direct messages, but in all cases needs to be judged and tested. Some may be from the Lord, others from demonic sources, and some from the flesh. Still others may be essentially from the Lord, but containing some inaccurate human elements.

At the same time, I agree that MacArthur and Foster have a valid point that much false prophecy is passed off as merely being impure or imperfect. Some claim to hear from the Lord, and thus their words are considered authoritative. But when they fail, they are not held accountable. People who believe they are hearing from the Lord need to be sure that it is really the Lord they are hearing from. Thus they must be cautious about speaking authoritatively. Many leaders claim too cavalierly that they are hearing from God. There is a contradiction in the logic of some faith teachers: Though such revelation is often considered to come as a hotline from the Spirit, yet revelation knowledge also enters the mind as spontaneous thoughts and is often also associated with feelings, which are supposed to be associated with sense knowledge. Hence, no clear criteria exists for what constitutes revelation vs. what comes from the mind or feeling.

Hanegraaff points out that Hinn temporarily claimed revelation about the Trinity, which was really quite unorthodox. Hinn, to his credit, later recanted his teaching, admitting that he was wrong. Many more leaders who claim revelation knowledge of matters that are really unorthodox need to follow Hinn's example and admit their errors. However, the fact that Hinn claimed revelation knowledge that turned out to be deeply erroneous accentuates the problem. Hanegraaff explains: "I am glad to see that Hinn admits his statement was dumb, but this raises a serious dilemma: Hinn explicitly claimed that his statement was a revelation from God."[49] The fact that he believed it was a revelation from the Lord shows lack of discernment and the need for being more cautious about claiming revelation. Even though Hagin and Capps say that revelations need to be submitted to the Scriptures, they fail to recognize that some of their own revelations can be questioned scripturally, hermeneutically, and theologically. The danger is that many cults also claim revelation, and also claim their revelations are scriptural. Yes, Scripture is a vital standard, but it is not the only standard, especially when it is used as a pretext. Revelation must also be based on sound interpretation of Scripture, and the confirmation of other mature discerning leaders in the church (see Chapters 24 and 28).

Even the most anointed, Spirit-led leader needs to follow the practical classic faith counsel of Anderson regarding the fallibility of impressions, revelations, visions, and inner voices:

> Beloved, let us understand and admit once for all, that we are exceedingly fallible creatures. So very fallible, in fact, that, though our Father may be very desirous of imparting to us some truth and though He may breathe into the soul in all His Divine purity, yet when we undertake to give it voice and pour it out in verbal phrase to others, we are more than apt—unless we lie low at His feet in deepest humility—to so tarnish and becloud it by our clumsy touch and exaggerated language, as will place it beyond the Divine recognition.
>
> A revelation may be truly from God. Yet, being such imperfect transmitters and interpreters of the Divine thought as is true of each one of us, one may easily be mistaken in the interpretation given to such revelation. Those who confidently aver that marvelous experiences have been given them, accompanied by visions and repeated assurance that a certain one who is ill has been already healed or is to be healed in the future, and then following such assurance the sick one dies without healing having been experienced—such persons either misinterpreted God's revelation, or have mistaken the voice of the Adversary for that of the Holy Spirit.[50]

1. See examples in Hanegraaff, 123, 133, 157-159, 172, 173.

2. For an example, see Gloria Copeland, *God's Will for Your Healing* (Ft. Worth, Tex.: Kenneth Copeland Ministries, 1972), 8.

3. E.W. Kenyon, *The Hidden Man: An Unveiling of the Subconscious Mind* (Seattle: Kenyon's Gospel Publishing Co., 1970), 158; see also Kenyon, *The Two Kinds of Faith*, 87.

4. Hagin, *The Midas Touch: A Balanced Approach to Biblical Prosperity* (Tulsa, Okla.: Faith Library Publications, 2000), 37.

5. Charles Capps, *How You Can Avoid Tragedy and Live a Better Life* (Tulsa, Okla.: Harrison House, 1980), 96.

6. Fee, 3.

7. Friesen, 127-131.

8. Ibid., 131, 139.

9. MacArthur, *Charismatic Chaos*, 78-86.

10. K. Neill Foster, *Sorting Out the Supernatural* (Camp Hill, Penn.: Christian Publications, 2001), 67-81.

11. Hanegraaff, 80, 123, 124, 133, 159, 172, 173, 283.

12. Ibid., 123-124.

13. McConnell, 108-109.

14. Hanegraaff, 39, 344, 345, 360, 363-365.

15. Pierson, *George Müller of Bristol*, 134-135.

16. Ibid., 37, 38.

17. Ibid., 7.

18. Murray, *The Spirit of Christ*, 161.

19. Simpson, *Days of Heaven on Earth*, May 16.

20. John R. Rice, *Prayer: Asking and Receiving* (Murfreesboro, Tenn.: Sword of the Lord Publishers, 1942), 168.

21. John A. MacMillan, "Contacting God," *AW*, Nov. 9, 1940, 706.

22. Murray, *The Spirit of Christ*, 162.

23. Ibid.

24. Meyer, *The Secret of Guidance*, 14.

25. Simpson, *Days of Heaven on Earth*, Nov. 17.

26. Ibid.

27. Ibid.

28. Simpson, *Gospel of Healing*, 90.

29. Simpson, *Days of Heaven on Earth*, Dec. 3.

30. Smith, *The Christian's Secret*, 67.

31. Ibid., 67-69.

32. Ibid., 69.

33. Ibid.

34. Ibid.

35. Marie Henry, 82.

36. Smith, *The Christian's Secret*, 70-71.

37. Montgomery, *Secrets of Victory*, 159-161.

38. Simpson, *CITB* (1992), 6:374-375.

39. Ibid.

40. Gilbertson, 348-349.

41. Ibid.

42. Ibid., 343.

43. Foster, *Sorting Out the Supernatural*, 77-79. Though Foster, who died in 2006, was a personal friend and I helped him to research and write his book cited here, we disagreed on this matter, and so we mutually agreed to leave my name off the book.

44. Paul L. King, "The Historic C&MA View of the Fallibility of Prophecy," unpublished paper, 2001.

45. Simpson, *Annual Report, The Christian and Missionary Alliance*, May 1908, 12-13.

46. May Mabette Anderson, "The Prayer of Faith," *CMAW*, Feb. 17, 1906, 98.

47. Simpson, *The Gentle Love of the Holy Spirit*, 48; see also *CITB* (1992), 4:581, where Simpson expounds on this further.

48. Martin Wells Knapp, *Impressions* (Cincinnati: Revivalist Publishing House, 1892), 109; see also p. 56-57, 62-64, 78, 91, 113, 114, 117.

49. Hanegraaff, 124.

50. May Mabette Anderson, "The Prayer of Faith: Part II," *CMAW*, Feb. 24, 1906, 106-107.

CHAPTER 20

Faith, Doctors and Medicine

Debate over the use of medicines and doctors by believers has fo-
mented throughout the centuries of church history. Keith Bailey
notes that while some church fathers allowed the use of medicine in some
cases, "other church fathers protested the materialistic approach of medicine. The controversy became so heated that the church pressured Justin-
ian (A.D. 527-567) to close the medical schools at Athens and Alexandria.
In the year 1215 Pope Innocent III condemned surgery, and in 1248 the
church determined that the dissection of the human body was a sacrilege.
The church's controversy with the science of medicine prevailed until contemporary times."[1] On the other hand, Origen allowed, "When one seeks
help in illness it is possible to use the usual and simple method of medicine. It is also possible to use the higher and better way and seek blessing
from Him who is God above all, and seek Him in devotion and prayer."[2]

Controversy in faith teaching and practice still brews today over
whether or not a Christian should use doctors and medicines if he is
attempting to walk by faith. Many people have sincerely asked the
question, "Do I not show a lack of faith if I take medicine or go to see
a doctor?" Practical counsel is needed on when it is appropriate to use
doctors and medicine and when they should be abandoned in relation
to walking by faith.

CONTEMPORARY FAITH TEACHING

Contemporary faith teachers, for the most part, are not opposed to the
use of medicine and doctors. However, some imply that needing to use
medicine is a lack of faith on man's part, that a person's faith is not strong
enough or not developed enough. For instance, Frederick Price avows,
"I don't have anything against medicine, because medicine is not against

divine healing. Medicine can work with divine healing. Medicine is not God's highest or best. There is a better way when you know how to use your faith. When you have developed your faith to such an extent that you can stand on the promises of God, then you won't need medicine."[3] He believes that people can develop their faith by using their faith little by little to the point of no longer needing medicine. Further, Price views medicine as a crutch for those who have not developed their faith: "If you need a crutch or something to help you get along, then praise God, hobble along until you get your faith moving to the point that you don't need a crutch."[4] The implication is that the weak in faith need medicine, but the strong in faith do not.

CRITICISM OF CONTEMPORARY FAITH TEACHING

McConnell cites the ambiguity in contemporary faith teaching, on the one hand not forbidding doctors and medicine, but on the other hand, regarding them as crutches for those who are not strongly developed in faith. He believes that this haziness in contemporary faith teaching is cultic at its roots, based on metaphysical understanding of physical symptoms.[5] He warns of the practical consequences of such teaching in the contemporary faith movement, such as delaying medical treatment, feelings of guilt and failure for lack of faith, and hesitation to fully cooperate with doctors. In other words, "their 'faith' inhibits medical healing rather than promotes it."[6] With a similar criticism, Hanegraaff cites examples of people who have been made to feel guilty by being told that their sicknesses were due to sin or lack of faith.[7] Critics point out that in some extreme cases, people have died or that serious illnesses have progressed to become life-threatening due to refusal to seek medical treatment.[8]

CLASSIC FAITH TEACHING AND PRACTICE

Radical Teaching Against Doctors and Medicine. The range of belief regarding doctors and medicine varied widely among classic faith leaders. Mary Gill Moise was one of the most extreme teachers of faith with her belief that Christians need never die.[9] John Dowie adamantly opposed the use of doctors and medicine and publicly vilified more moderate faith healing teachers such as Simpson, A.J. Gordon, Torrey and Woodworth-Etter.[10] Woodworth-Etter was less antagonistic toward the use of doctors and medicine than Dowie, but still viewed them negatively.[11]

Divine Healing by Faith—God's Highest and Best Way. Simpson's views on medicine are perhaps the most misunderstood of his faith teachings.

Chappell, Dayton, and Bowman characterize him as a radical.[12] However, his position was more moderate than Woodworth-Etter and Dowie, and was very close to that of Murray. In what appears on the surface to be a position similar to contemporary faith teaching (which may have been derived from it), Simpson taught:

> God has nowhere prescribed medical 'means,' and we have no right to infer that drugs are ordinarily his "means." . . . But for the trusting and obedient child of God there is the more excellent way which His word has clearly prescribed, and by which His name will be ever glorified afresh, and our spiritual life continually renewed. This age is one of increasing rationalism; and unbelief is constantly endeavoring to eliminate all traces of direct supernatural working from the universe, and to explain everything by second causes and natural development; and God, for this very reason, wants to show His immediate working wherever our faith will afford Him an opportunity.[13]

Chappell and Bowman consider this an extreme position, opposed to most use of doctors and medicine.[14] However, they misunderstand Simpson's teaching. While Simpson's statement may seem radical out of its proper context, his teaching was not really considered a unique or extreme position, except by those who opposed divine healing by faith. As another example, Andrew Murray taught similarly: "It is Jesus Himself who is always the first, the best, the greatest Physician."[15] The statements of Simpson and Murray echo Origen's ancient counsel. Actually, a comparison of Murray's and Simpson's teachings, even though their books were written at the same time continents apart without collaboration or influence from each other, shows that their teaching on healing is remarkably the same—virtually identical. And they both would agree with Fred Price (and Origen) that medicine is not God's highest or best.

However, that is where their agreement with Price would end. There is a subtle, but important, difference between contemporary faith teaching and what Simpson and Murray taught. Contrary to Price, Simpson and Murray do not consider medicine a crutch for those who have not developed their faith. Rather, such faith has to be imparted by God, not developed. For Simpson, abandoning the use of medicine (what he calls "means") is not a step to be taken to *prove* one's faith, but a step to be taken only when God clearly gives a word or conviction of faith. It is at that point, and only at that point, that medicine is properly abandoned. Only when God has given faith for healing without medicine does resorting to medicine become a sin: "From that moment doubt should be regarded as absolutely out of the question, and even the very thought of retreating or resorting to old 'means' inadmissible. Of course, such a person will at once abandon all remedies and medical treatment."[16] As cited earlier, Simpson also warned against trusting in someone else's supposed word of faith to rise from bed or walk on a lame foot.[17]

It is important to understand that the concern of Simpson and Murray was that using medicines (means or remedies) might not give the glory to God. They were also concerned that one can become preoccupied with the body and medicines, and thus hinder healing or spiritual blessing. Murray wrote:

> Here is another physician who is a believer, and who prays God's blessing on the remedies which he employs. In this case, also a large number are healed, but neither in one case nor the other does the healing bring with it any spiritual blessing. They will be preoccupied, even the believing among them, with the remedies which they use, much more than with what the Lord may be doing with them, and in such a case, their healing will be more hurtful than beneficial. On the contrary, when it is Jesus only to whom the sick person applies for healing, he learns to reckon no longer upon remedies, but to put himself into direct relation with His love and His almightiness. . . .
>
> When we have recourse to remedies for healing, all the attention of the sick one is on the body. Divine healing, however, calls us to turn our attention from the body, and to abandon ourselves, soul and body, to the Lord's care, occupying ourselves with Him alone.[18]

C&MA healing evangelist F.F. Bosworth picked up this concept from Murray, virtually quoting him though not mentioning him by name.[19] Murray believed that healing by a physician misses the greater blessing: "The healing which is wrought by our Lord Jesus brings with it and leaves behind it more real blessing than the healing which is obtained through physicians."[20] Simpson also makes similar statements.[21]

Likewise, to the question, "Is it okay to pray for God to bless medicine?", Simpson replied, "Yes, but that is not divine healing through the name of Jesus alone, as He has prescribed. That is Esau's blessing. There is a blessing even for Esau; but give me Jacob's."[22] Murray essentially agreed, saying, "Does the use of remedies exclude the prayer of faith?

To this we believe our reply should be: No, for the experience of a large number of believers testifies that in answer to their prayers God has often blest the use of remedies, and made them a means of healing."[23] He goes on to say that the prayer of faith without remedies "best obtains the grace of God."[24] Simpson and Murray are not saying that a person's faith is somehow inferior or their spirituality is lacking if they use medicines, but rather that greater blessing and enduement of God's grace can come through healing without medicine.

Examples of Divine Health and Healing without Medicine. To our knowledge, Simpson never resorted to medical care (except for cough drops and eyeglasses) for nearly forty years after his miraculous healing, even in the last two years of his life after suffering a stroke and depression. Murray usually did not take medicine, except when prodded by his family to do so. Margaret E. Kinney (1831-1897), an evangelist with the C&MA, is an example of one who exercised the kind of faith Simpson and Murray wrote about: "She was influenced by Boardman's lectures on holiness and faith and Cullis' teaching on faith healing. She refused 'to take a drop of medicine from man' up to the time of her death."[25] As another example, one of my first mentors, a retired C&MA evangelist, had not taken medicine in thirty years, until he suffered a broken arm in his late seventies.

Pioneer missionary C.T. Studd, who followed in the faith footsteps of Müller and Hudson Taylor, also frequently practiced divine healing without doctors (trusting in "Dr. Jesus"), although he did make use of medical advice and treated others medically.[26] Mrs. Studd testified: "I had five children and I never saw a doctor. God did wonderfully."[27] Rees Howells, Welsh Bible College founder known for his strong intercessory prayer ministry, was influenced by Simpson and also used no medicines for many years, except for relief from pain in his last dying days.[28] However, he also studied medicine, and his counsel to others was to seek the Lord for guidance to abandon medical means, but in the meantime, "Do what the doctor tells you, and if that fails, you will have a chance then for the Lord to heal you."[29]

When It Is Appropriate to Ignore Symptoms or Abandon Medicine. Simpson also advised those who had received faith from God to ignore symptoms of illness which return or fail to go away: "When you do go forth to act your faith, be careful not to begin to watch the result or look at the symptoms, or see if you stand. You must ignore all symptoms, and see only Him there before you, almighty to sustain you and save you from falling."[30] While this is similar to contemporary faith teaching, two important differences should be noted: (1) Simpson does not counsel to deny symptoms, as some contemporary faith leaders appear to teach; and (2) it is only when God has imparted special faith that the Christian is to disregard the symptoms—again, it is not a matter of developing your faith or having faith in your own faith. For Simpson, it is not a matter of denial; it is a matter of focus: "Keep your eyes off your symptoms and on Christ. He is your life."[31] He also indicated that sometimes symptoms may be from Satan, for "he has the power even to simulate all symptoms," recalling the words of early church father Theophilus that demons may feign diseases.[32] Likewise, Montgomery wrote that once a person has heard from the Lord, "If the Devil brings his symptoms, *when the Lord has declared you to be free,* if he tries to put his tags of different diseases upon you, you have a right to refuse those tags" (italics mine).[33]

Contrary to the mistaken assertions of Chappell, Dayton and Bowman, Simpson did not disdain the use of doctors and medicine. In fact, in the same book cited by Chappell, Simpson clarifies his position and counsels against presumptuous abandonment of medical treatment: "We do not mean to imply . . . that the medical profession is sinful, or the use of means always wrong. There may be, there always will be, innumerable cases in which faith cannot be exercised," and there is "ample room for employment" of such "natural means."[34] In another writing, he taught that unless a believer has been specifically led "to trust Christ entirely for something higher and stronger than their natural life, they had better stick to natural remedies."[35] Further, Simpson explains, "We do believe God heals His sick and suffering children when they can fully trust Him. At the same time we believe that no one should act precipitously or presumptuously in this matter, or abandon natural remedies unless they have an intelligent, Scriptural and unquestioning trust in Him alone and really know Him well enough to touch Him in living contact as their Healer."[36] Actually, Simpson spoke on a positive note that "medical Science has a place in the Natural Economy."[37] He encouraged the development and perfecting of "every possible human remedy against all forms of disease so long as they do not exclude or antagonize His higher way."[38] Against extreme faith leaders like Dowie, Simpson avowed that "it would be most un-Christlike for us to denounce it or oppose it wherever it has its true place."[39]

When Use of Medicine Is OK. Bounds, who believed both in divine healing through prayer and in the use of medicine, explained that using medicine may actually be an act of faith: "Sickness dies before prayer. Health comes in answer to prayer. . . . God often uses remedies in answering prayer. . . . It frequently takes a stronger faith to rise above means and not to trust in them, than it does to wholly reject all means."[40] Similarly, Hudson Taylor also came to believe that using means could be an act of faith, testifying:

> I was a very young believer, and had not sufficient faith in God to see him in and through the use of means. Ever since, I have seen clearly the mistake I made; a mistake that is very common in these days, when erroneous teaching on faith-healing does much harm, misleading some as to the purposes of God, shaking the faith of others, and distressing the minds of many. The use of means ought not to lessen our faith, and our faith in God ought not to hinder whatever means He has given us for accomplishment of his own purposes. . . . (T)o me it would appear as presumptuous and wrong to neglect the use of those measures which He Himself has put within our reach, as to neglect to take daily food, and suppose that life and health might be maintained by prayer alone.[41]

In a significant practical-theological paradigm shift, Simpson associate R.K. Carter, who earlier in life opposed medicine, like Howells, later trained to become a physician. Carter gave further practical examples of this position from the life of Charles Cullis, the physician whose teaching and prayer brought healing to Simpson: "Dr. Cullis believed in setting broken bones and in taking medicine except where faith was perfectly free and spontaneous, notably in incurable cases."[42] Again he noted of Cullis: "Taking a little bottle from his pocket, [Cullis] said, 'Now I know that this will stop my headache in a few minutes. Knowing that, I think it would be wrong to trouble the Lord about it, or expect Him to effect the cure in any unusual way.'"[43]

Carter also gave examples from the life of Simpson and the ministry of the C&MA, indicating that Simpson had moderated his earlier teaching, just as Carter himself had: "A few years ago, Mr. Simpson was attacked with the grippe [flu], and suffered greatly, though refusing to give up and go to bed. The disease ran a reasonable course, and then abated. There was no phenomenal healing. Of course prayer was offered by many and of course it is Christian and just to claim an 'answer,' but nothing more. . . . Most of the [C&MA] missionaries have used quinine and other remedies freely and are instructed to observe most carefully the rules of the climate for rest and food and clothing."[44] It should be noted that some of the earliest missionaries to Africa supported by the C&MA (though not officially sponsored by the C&MA) in 1890 died from fever that same year after not seeking medical treatment. While such practice was voluntary on the part of the missionaries and not sanctioned by the C&MA, Simpson came under criticism because of the association.[45] Hence, it may have had a sobering practical effect of influencing and moderating Simpson and the C&MA position on medicine and doctors.

In 1898 Montgomery had been deathly sick for six months with intense pain from tuberculosis of the spine, but was led by the Lord not to use medicine. Rather, repeated laying on of hands and rebuking the devil brought a degrees of relief from time to time. Eventually, she experienced a dramatic, complete healing. Writing in Simpson's periodical, she testified about her miraculous healing. Yet she also stated that she would not vow never to use medicine again. She understood that the assurance from the Lord not to use medicine was not to be presumed upon in all situations.[46] In printing this caveat from Montgomery, Simpson was implicitly agreeing with the statement.

Carter himself testified that he went several years without medicine, but on one occasion when he continued to have illness without relief he did take medicine without any sense of guilt.[47] He mentioned that Cullis, who had a great anointed healing ministry died "in faith" of heart problems.[48] The same could be said of Kathryn Kuhlman, who had a contemporary day healing ministry similar to Cullis, nonetheless, died of heart problems stemming from rheumatic fever as a child. These anointed leaders did not lack great faith, yet were not healed.

Simpson's friend, S.D. Gordon, also appeared to be positive and accommodating in the use of medicine: "Christ heals human bodies today by his own direct supernatural touch, sometimes through the physician and medicine, sometimes without medicine, sometimes when medicine is confessedly powerless, and sometimes overcoming the unwise use of medicine. The Holy Spirit's leading is the touchstone."[49] Gordon taught that healing may come through natural means, supernatural means, or a blend of both, depending upon the Holy Spirit's leading: "What about the use of means? . . . The answer is this: Ask Christ. Get in touch, if you are not already. Then when the need comes, ask him. He will tell you. . . . He is a true physician, for he advises."[50]

The State of Nineteenth and Early Twentieth-Century Medicine. It must also be noted that classic faith views of doctors and medicine are based on the understanding that the effectiveness of medical treatment then was often questionable, sometimes even harmful. Simmons gives an extensive description of the questionable status of nineteenth-century medicine, commenting, "It was truly a period when the cure could often be worse than the illness."[51] S.D. Gordon pointed out that even medical science in that day recognized and leaned toward using means other than drugs for healing and health: "It is striking that some in science today put the greatest emphasis on the non-use of drugs, on the sort and preparation and quantity of food, on the general habit of life, and on the mental attitude as the proper means of healing and avoiding illness."[52] Woodworth-Etter likewise asserted, "The greater portion of the physicians of the land are ungodly people, many of them professed infidels, and were never designed of God to administer drugs and poisons to anyone, much less the people of God, whose bodies are the sacred temples of the Holy Spirit."[53] She cited medical authorities of the day who acknowledged that medicines sometimes brought more harm than good.[54]

Natural Treatments and Nutritional Supplements. Simpson would agree that treatment we today call nutritional or herbal supplements does not fall under the category of drugs because it is "like food."[55] Pierson, another friend of Simpson and Murray, says similarly, "No use of natural means can be proven improper, provided dependence be on God. The most marked cases of healing have been, like that of the 'woman with the issue of blood,' where ordinary means have failed."[56] He considered ignoring common sense precautions, abandoning "harmless remedies," and "using prayer as the only antidote to poison, the only healer of broken bones, the only preventive of smallpox" as "extreme positions" and "fanaticism." He advised holding "the truth within spiritual and rational and sensible limits."[57]

Further, he believed that antagonism between divine healing and human healing is not necessary and that "the discoveries, achievements and advances of medical science are wonderful. . . . But such science is neither omniscient nor omnipotent; at best, in many things uncertain and experimental, if not blind and powerless, even by the confession of experts."[58] Kenneth MacKenzie, Episcopalian associate of Simpson, similarly wrote in Montgomery's *Triumphs of Faith,* "Let us avail ourselves of all that science has revealed as contributory to our best estate. Let us use these things thankfully. But never forget that they only help the natural."[59] Obviously, Simpson must have had a similar belief or he would not have been such good friends and colleagues with Pierson and MacKenzie.

Presbyterian missionaries Jonathan and Rosalind Goforth also believed in the divine healing power of God through divine wisdom given for natural treatment. Rosalind Goforth recounted a particular incident of healing through a supernatural word of wisdom given for appropriate treatment:

> I told this incident to a medical doctor, and he said: "Why, there is no miracle in that! It was just up-to-date hygiene—giving nature a chance by cleanliness!"
>
> I replied: "Doctor, to me the miracle lay, not in the poultice, but in God's telling me what to use; and now it is to me all the more a miracle of prayer, since you say it was up-to-date hygienic treatment."[60]

REFLECTIONS AND CONCLUSIONS

In actuality, Oral Roberts' concept of merging the healing streams of medicine and prayer would appear to be more moderate than the positions of Murray and Simpson, and closer to the position of S.D. Gordon of blending medicine and faith. Since the medical profession in their time lacked the knowledge and technology and was much less a science than it is today, perhaps with the advances in medical technology today and studies showing the effectiveness of prayer in hospital settings, they would be more receptive to the idea of merging medicine and prayer. The C&MA today, for the most part, blends medicine and prayer, unlike its founder.

It is my conclusion that the classic and contemporary faith teaching of divine healing without the use of medicine and doctors can still be held up as an ideal, as long as one does not become dogmatic about it. The abandoning of medical treatment should not be done to prove one's faith, nor should it be done without seeking the Lord's will about abandoning treatment in specific cases, and receiving from the Lord special faith or a clear assurance (*rhema*) to do so. The important factor is to get the leading of the Lord and to give God all the glory regardless of whether medicine is used or not.

Simpson provides an apt summary of the classic faith view of healing, which is sound counsel for today: "Divine Healing is not giving up medicines, or fighting with physicians, or against remedies. It is not even believing in prayer, or the prayer of faith, or in the men and women who teach Divine Healing. . . . But it is really receiving the personal life of Christ to be in us as the supernatural strength of our body, and the supply of our life."[61]

---

1. Keith Bailey, *The Children's Bread*, 177.

2. Cited in Bailey, *The Children's Bread*, 178; see Origen, *Against Celsus*, 8:60, *ANF*, 4:662.

3. Frederick Price *Faith, Foolishness or Presumption?*, 88.

4. Frederick Price, *Is Healing for All?*, 92-93.

5. McConnell, 154-156.

6. Ibid., 166.

7. Hanegraaff, 262-263.

8. McConnell, 165, 166, 169; Farah, *From the Pinnacle of the Temple*, 1-7; Larry Parker, *We Let Our Son Die* (Irvine, Calif.: Harvest House, 1980).

9. W.E. Warner, "Moise, Mary Gill," *DPCM*, 626.

10. Chappell, 367.

11. Maria Woodworth-Etter, *Acts of the Holy Ghost: The Life, Work and Experience of Mrs. M.B. Woodworth Etter* (Dallas: John F. Worley Printing Co., [1915]), 420-424.

12. Chappell, 363; Dayton, 128; Bowman, *The Word-Faith Controversy*, 61, 69, 75-77, 91, 244.

13. Simpson, *The Gospel of Healing*, 64, 68-69; see also pp. 65-69, 88-89.

14. Chappell, 363-364; Bowman, *The Word-Faith Controversy*, 61, 69, 75-77, 91, 244.

15. Murray, *Divine Healing*, 14.

16. Simpson, *The Gospel of Healing*, 88.

17. Ibid., 90.

18. Murray, *Divine Healing*, 15, 35.

19. Bosworth, 120.

20. Murray, *Divine Healing*, 15.

21. Simpson, *The Gospel of Healing*, 67.

22. Simpson, "Inquiries and Answers," *Word, Work and World*, Dec. 1886, 340.

23. Murray, *Divine Healing*, 80.

24. Ibid., 81.

25. Leslie A. Andrews, "Alliance Practice and Cultural Diversity in Relation to Women in Ministry," Report of the Committee to Study the Role of Women in Ministry, C&MA General Council, May 1995, 109.

26. Grubb, *C.T. Studd*, 90-92, 123-124, 216-217.

27. Ibid., 92.

28. Grubb, *Rees Howell Intercessor*, 160-161, 277-278.

29. Ibid., 138.

30. Simpson, *The Gospel of Healing*, 91.

31. Simpson, "Inquiries and Answers," *Word, Work and World*, Dec. 1886, 340.

32. Ibid., 342.

33. Montgomery, *Secrets of Victory*, 32-33, see also 40-41.

34. Simpson, *The Gospel of Healing*, 68.

35. Simpson, *The Four-fold Gospel*, 48.

36. A.B. Simpson, "Editorial," *Christian Alliance and Missionary Weekly*, Nov. 1890, 274.

37. A.B. Simpson, *The Old Faith and the New Gospels* (Harrisburg, Penn.: Christian Publications, 1966), 59.

38. Ibid.

39. Ibid.

40. E.M. Bounds, *Prayer and Praying Men* (Grand Rapids: Baker, 1977), 62.

41. Dr. and Mrs. Howard Taylor, *Hudson Taylor in the Early Years* (London: China Inland Mission, [1911] 1930), 191.

42. Carter, *Faith Healing Reviewed*, 112.

43. Ibid., 110.

44. Ibid., 112-114.

45. Niklaus, et al., 88.

46. Carrie Judd Montgomery, "Miracle of Healing," *Christian Alliance and Missionary Weekly*, Sept. 28, 1898, 298. Dayton cited Carter saying about Montgomery that she "does not like anyone to attempt much modification of the theory," but also noted that "her husband had ill health and she continued to wear glasses." Dayton, 132.

47. Carter, *Faith Healing Reviewed*, 128.

48. Ibid., 110-111.

49. S.D. Gordon, *The Healing Christ*, xi.

50. Ibid., 65-66.

51. Simmons, *E.W. Kenyon*, 199-207.

52. S.D. Gordon, *The Healing Christ*, 61.

53. Woodworth-Etter, *Acts of the Holy Ghost*, 420.

54. Ibid., 421-424.

55. Simpson, *The Gospel of Healing*, 65.

56. A.T. Pierson, *Forward Movements of the Last Half Century* (New York: Funk and Wagnalls, 1900), 402.

57. Ibid.

58. Ibid., 404-405.

59. Kenneth MacKenzie, "Healing or Helping?," *Triumphs of Faith*, Jan. 1903, 11.

60. Rosalind Goforth, cited in *World Shapers: A Treasury of Quotes from Great Missionaries* (Wheaton, Ill.: Harold Shaw Publishers, 1991), 10.

61. A.B. Simpson, *Triumphs of Faith*, Nov. 1922, 252.

CHAPTER 21

Faith, Death and a Long,
Healthy Life

This chapter addresses practical-theological issues of faith regarding death and living a long, healthy life. Pertinent questions discussed here include: Can people increase the length of their lives by faith and decrease it by lack of faith? If a person dies young or dies of a sickness, does that indicate sin or lack of faith? Can a person expect to die healthy at an old age?

CONTEMPORARY FAITH TEACHING

Often cited by contemporary faith teachers, Psalm 90:10 states, "As for the days of our life, they contain seventy years, or if due to strength, eighty years." Contemporary faith teaching professes on the basis of this Scripture that believers should claim seventy to eighty years of health by faith. It is often implied that a Christian who dies earlier than seventy years old or dies in sickness lacked faith and let the devil steal life. Kenyon taught, "I believe it is the plan of the Father that no believer should ever be sick, that he should live his full length of time and actually wear out and fall asleep."[1] Hagin believes likewise[2] and teaches further:

> The Name of Jesus and faith in that Name always works! It is possible, though, for someone else to nullify the effects of your prayer. Some of our RHEMA Bible Training Center students asked me about the death of a relative. They said, "Brother Hagin, we laid hands on him. We prayed for him. We had all the faith in the world, but he died. Where did we fail?" I said, "You didn't fail. God heard you." You see, the other person can nullify the effects of my faith. I would let them cut off my head

before I would say that God didn't hear me. He heard me when I prayed. If someone does die, God still heard me. And He sent the answer. They did not receive it.[3]

Frederick Price asserts that faith can lengthen one's life and lack of faith can shorten life: "I have watched people die, and my heart went out to them, but their faith was not developed, and it couldn't bring the healing to pass, and they died. It wasn't the will of God that they die, but their faith wasn't sufficiently developed."[4] Price further teaches that still-births or the death of young children is due to lack of faith exercised by the parents: "Children that are born dead had no control over their life, but their parents had that control. However, if the parents do not know the Word of God and to claim their rights in Christ, the child suffers the loss."[5] Capps implies that people have died prematurely because they failed to exercise their authority and speak words of life and health.[6] His daughter, Annette Capps, goes so far to say that healing ministers who successfully heal others, but become sick or die, have deficiently made use of their own faith for themselves.[7]

CRITICISM OF CONTEMPORARY FAITH TEACHING

McConnell characterizes Kenyon's assertion that the believer has no need to die sick as reckless abandon.[8] Further, he views the claim that believers should live to be seventy or eighty as rooted in New Thought metaphysics.[9] He criticizes Frederick Price's view that death of children is due to the parents' lack of faith: "Thus the responsibility for any premature death lies squarely with the believer."[10] MacArthur, who believes that the gift of healing is not for today, asserts that the heart conditions of Oral Roberts and Kenneth Hagin and the death of Kathryn Kuhlman invalidate the claims of others being healed through their ministries.[11] McConnell's most serious practical concern deals with attitudes toward the chronically sick and terminally ill, such as lack of sensitive, empathetic pastoral care and making a person feel guilty about lack of faith, like Job's comforters: "The time when a dying believer needs his faith the most is when he is told that he has it the least. . . . Perhaps the most inhuman fact revealed about the Faith movement is this: when its members die, they die alone.[12]

CLASSIC FAITH TEACHING

On Long Life. The idea that we can claim long life by faith goes back to at least the early 1800s. Tozer notes that "Finney used to teach that if you rest in the Lord and wait patiently for Him, you won't die until you're at least seventy-plus."[13] Considering that the death rate at that time was more frequent and at a much younger age, to make to the age of seventy was an accomplishment. It became a commonly accepted teaching in the Higher Life/Keswick movements, with their connecting of health and holiness. In these movements, Murray and Simpson exemplify the teaching that it was not necessary to die of sickness and that a person might live in health until age seventy or eighty.[14]

Similarly to and predating Kenyon, Simpson believed: "There is no need that we should die of disease. The system might just wear out and pass away as naturally as the apple ripens and falls in autumn, or the wheat matures and dies. It has simply fulfilled its natural period.... The promise of healing is not physical immortality, but *health until our life work is done.*"[15] Years before Simpson came to that conclusion, Spurgeon came to believe the same during the great cholera plague in London about 1855:

> One day, sick in heart, walking dejectedly down Great Dover Road on his way home from another funeral, he stopped and looked into an apothecary shop window. The shopkeeper, being a believer, had placed a placard in his window with a Scripture verse that read: "Because thou hast made the Lord, which is my refuge, even the Most High, thy habitation; there shall no evil befall thee neither shall any plague come nigh thy dwelling" (Psalm 91:9). Immediately, the Spirit of God impressed the truth on Charles' heart. He claimed the promise as his own. Dramatically he came out of his depression and went about his work completely confident God would care for him and keep him safe from the plague. The lines of an old hymn spoke to him: "Not a single shaft can hit, till the God of love sees fit." He remembered Cromwell's word, *"Man is immortal till his work is done."*[16]

Murray's wife likewise cited Cromwell's words in praying for her husband's health and strength in a time of weakness.[17] Contrary to some contemporary faith teaching that believes a person may die prematurely before the age of seventy because of lack of faith or failure to claim the promises of God or fight off the devil, Murray, Simpson, and Spurgeon all affirmed that a person who is walking in the will and obedience of God cannot die before their God-appointed time.

On Death Before Seventy or Death of an Illness. Many great men and women of faith have lived to advanced ages: Kenyon—80, Bosworth—81,

Müller—92, Murray—88, Simpson—76, Montgomery—87, Finney—83, Carter—79, Boardman—76, Hannah Whitall Smith—79, Taylor—73, Carmichael—84, Bounds—78, Wigglesworth—87, Meyer—82. In addition, John Wesley preached regularly up until three months before his death at 89. While this seems to support both classic and contemporary faith teaching, contemporary faith teaching is often absolutist, allowing no exceptions in God's will. Hagin, for instance, claimed that when prayer given in faith is not answered, it is not the fault of the person praying, but of the one being prayed for. It may be a lack of faith, sin, lack of desire, or one's own will.[18] This was not the classic faith teaching. On the contrary, while it is possible these factors may be involved, it must not be assumed so. It may be God's time for the person to go. While it is generally and universally God's will to heal, it must not be made an absolute.

Classic faith leaders believed God could make exceptions. Murray wrote, "The man of faith places himself under the direction of the Spirit, which will enable him to discern the will of God regarding him, if something should prevent his attaining the age of seventy. Every rule has its exceptions in the things of heaven as in the things of earth."[19] Simpson also recognized that in the sovereignty of God a person may die young: "Sometimes the Master is taking home His child and will He not, in such cases, lift the veil and show the trusting heart that its service is done? How often He does! . . . A dear young girl in Michigan who for some time claimed healing, awoke one day from sleep, her face covered with the reflection of heaven, and told her loved ones that the Master had led her to trust for life thus far, but now was taking her to Himself. It is well, and let no one dare to reproach such a heart with unfaithfulness."[20] Whereas some contemporary faith teachers would berate the child or parents for lack of faith, Simpson makes clear that her death at a young age was God's sovereign will, and admonished *let no one dare* accuse anyone of lack of faith. Nor did Simpson claim that his friend A.J. Gordon lacked faith or died prematurely out of the Lord's will when he died at 58.

Müller had exercised great faith and had seen both himself and many whom he prayed for become healed.[21] However, his own son died as a little boy. Bounds was a great man of prayer and faith who believed in healing, yet he buried his first wife and two children in a span of five years.[22] Both Phoebe Palmer and Hannah Whitall Smith, pioneering women of faith, lost children at young ages. Even Wigglesworth, whom contemporary faith teachers love to quote, recognized that God may sovereignly call people home to be with Him. When his own wife died in 1913, he rebuked death and she came back to life. But she told her husband that God wanted her and her work was finished, so he released her to the Lord at a young age. In contradiction to those who claim it cannot be God's will for a person to die young or die sick, his biographer records, "Wigglesworth willingly bowed to the will of God."[23] Additionally, Wigglesworth had the experience of praying for people and seeing them miraculously healed, yet at the same time suffered with kidney stones that were not healed.[24]

Bosworth, another favorite among contemporary faith teachers, also lost his son Vernon at the age of four. His first wife Stella, though having been healed several times, died of tuberculosis in the midst of his evangelistic ministry. Bosworth commented, "It seemed best to Him to call her, though still a young woman, home to Himself."[25] He did not blame their deaths on sin or lack of faith or failure, but rather went on to a greater ministry of healing. Hudson Taylor understood the sovereignty of God in healing for he lost a child, yet his wife Maria, near death, was restored miraculously. She died several years later, but still in the middle of her years.

In fact, many other great people of faith died young or of sickness as well: John Hyde, missionary to India who was known as "Praying Hyde" for his extraordinary life of prayer and faith, died at 29, saying he would rather burn out than rust out. Likewise, godly David Brainerd, missionary to North American Indians, died at 28. Spurgeon, who, as we have mentioned, had a great healing ministry, died at 57, from the long-term effects of gout and Bright's disease. Great Awakening revivalist Jonathan Edwards died at 54 from pneumonia, Pentecostal healing evangelist Charles Price at the age of 60, and the godly Tozer at 66.

Chambers, the man of faith who was totally abandoned to God, died at 43 from complications following an emergency appendectomy. While Chambers hovered near death, and seemed for a time to be recovering, his wife Biddy said, "Through all the days of the illness and its crises, the word which held me was, 'This sickness is not unto death, but for the glory of God,' and there were times when it seemed that the promise was to have a literal fulfillment. But again God had a fuller meaning."[26] Some would scoff and say she did not hear from the Lord. Others would say there was lack of faith. But she received assurance that there was "a fuller meaning." While agonizing over his death and asking, "Why?," "the last words she had heard Oswald speak came back to her powerfully in the twilight quiet, 'Greater works than these shall he do, because I go unto my Father.'"[27] Another dear friend who was disillusioned by his death, saw a vision of Oswald speaking words of comfort and encouragement to her. This was a further confirmation of God's sovereign purposes. Chambers' wife went on to compile his writings posthumously into what has become one of the greatest devotional classics, *My Utmost for His Highest*.

REFLECTIONS AND CONCLUSIONS

Scholars point out that Psalm 90:10 is stating an observation of life or a basic principle, not a hard and fast promise from God for long life. Even if it is recognized as a general principle of life as Finney, Murray and Simpson appear to have believed, they did not consider it an absolute. Contemporary faith leaders need to learn from these great leaders this balance. The contemporary faith and charismatic movements frequently lack a good practical theology of death that recognizes God's sovereignty.

In addition to the classic faith leaders cited above who died before seventy, or of an illness, or whose children or spouses died young, other contemporary examples can be cited. Evangelist Kathryn Kuhlman, well known for her faith healing ministry, died a year short of seventy of a heart condition contracted as a child through rheumatic fever. Contemporary charismatic leader Jamie Buckingham died at 59 of cancer after an earlier healing from cancer. Power healing advocate John Wimber died in his early 60s.

Can it really be said, as Annette Capps would claim, that these classic and contemporary leaders lacked faith to live to the age of seventy, when in reality their lives were such demonstrations of extraordinary faith? Of course not. Nor can it be claimed that they lacked faith or failed to exercise their authority because they died in sickness, not health. Likewise, if Frederick Price is to be believed, that death of a child is due to lack of faith on their parents' part, then Müller, Taylor, Palmer, Hannah Whitall Smith, Bounds, and Bosworth, were not great men and women of faith after all. On the contrary, I would affirm that these deaths were not an issue of faith, but of the sovereignty of God, as Simpson and Spurgeon have attested, "A man is immortal until his work is done."

As mentioned above, MacArthur declares the healing ministries of Kuhlman and Roberts as invalid because of their health problems. However, many people were healed through the prayers of great evangelical leaders like Müller, Spurgeon, Simpson, and Carmichael. Would MacArthur also claim that the healing ministries of all these are proven false because they themselves were not always healed? I would answer, "not at all," for it seems that some of God's choicest saints were not granted healing for purposes known only to God. Could it be that God's servants were afflicted by Satan in an attempt to hinder or discredit their ministries, yet they did not succumb (as Paul with his thorn in the flesh)? Could it be that God's purposes were fulfilled by His strength sustaining them in their weakness?

Ahijah was a prophet of God who had become blind through old age, yet operated in the supernatural gifts of prophecy and word of knowledge (1 Kings 14:4-5). Elisha performed many miracles, including raising the dead, but died of a sickness. Even more surprising, after his death, a dead man came back to life after his body touched Elisha's grave. So then, dispensationalists like McArthur cannot validly claim their supernatural ministries were proven hoaxes by their personal lack of healing.

On the other hand, it would be presumptuous to say that these men and women of faith were disobedient to God or lacked faith for healing. Contemporary faith leaders need to acknowledge what the classic faith leaders came to recognize—that while dying without sickness is an ideal to which *some* may attain, the effects of aging can occur in the most godly and strongest in faith. Simpson's close associate, Kenneth MacKenzie, humorously recalled the C&MA's earlier beliefs and the practical maturing of their understanding of health and the effects of aging:

> We were a hilarious company in those days of the flush of conquest, when with whole-souled enthusiasm, we were certified we should never have to adopt glasses, lose our teeth, behold falling or grey hair, nor suffer any impairment of physical faculties. . . . The high-flown exhilaration of those early years toned down in time, though there were radicals who would not compromise. At a convention at the Tabernacle, one woman remarked to me, "If I ever see glasses on A.B. Simpson's nose, I'll never again enter this place." One critic exultingly described a meeting for testimonies of healings, when a man arose and declared, "O yes, I know the Lord is your healer, but who is your dentist?"[28]

MacKenzie goes on to report that Simpson and the C&MA, in sharp contradistinction to Dowie, came to understand that in some cases the deeper purpose of God is indeed for the believer's strength to be perfected in weakness.[29] This will be discussed further in Chapter 22.

Contemporary faith leaders also need to concede, just as Simpson recognized, that in many cases, it is not a deficiency of faith, but rather that God has not imparted special faith for healing. A double portion of the Spirit rested upon Elisha, a great man of faith. Regarding his death, Simpson remarked, "His faith might easily have claimed exemption from his last illness, and possibly even from death itself, but like his great Master of whom he was the especial type, in all things he was made like unto his brethren, that he might teach us the faith that could glorify God, both in life and death. . . . All that was evil and of the enemy in connection with his illness was eliminated by the power of God, for we find his faith in the freest and fullest exercise, even on his dying couch. . . . We cannot doubt that a faith so mighty could easily have claimed his own recovery. But his work was done."[30]

Simpson recognized a dignity in dying of an illness that some contemporary advocates of faith fail to comprehend: "It is a beautiful picture of faith that even infirmity and approaching dissolution cannot subdue or even cloud, reminding us that the Christian's last hours may be his brightest and that the sublimest triumphs of his life should be in the face even of his foes. Have we not all seen such victories, the withering frame and worn out forces of nature . . . and the very frailty of the outward temple made it more transparent to the glory that was shining out from within, while the walls were crumbling into decay and the inward guest was fluttering for its flight to a brighter sphere?"[31] To Simpson then, dying of an illness may not be lack of faith, but may actually be the exercise of great faith.

Simpson's own experience fell short of his ideal of the ripe apple falling off a tree, but he triumphed even in sickness and death. He remained in vigorous health into his seventies, but the last two years of his life a stroke brought on some periods of depression and senility. Just hours before his death, Robert Jaffray and other C&MA leaders gathered around him to claim Scripture promises for victory over sickness and death. The aged sage remarked to them, "Boys, I can't go that far with you now."[32] He knew his time was drawing to an end. He knew that he had finished his course and his work was done. Simpson shows us that death, even after illness, can be for the Christian a triumph. This is a sound practical faith theology of death.

---

1. Kenyon, *Jesus the Healer*, 65.

2. See McConnell, 157; Kenneth E. Hagin, *Plead Your Case* (Tulsa, Okla.: Kenneth Hagin Ministries, 1979), 14.

3. Kenneth E. Hagin, *In the Name of Jesus* (Tulsa, Okla.: Kenneth Hagin Ministries, 1979), 141.

4. Frederick Price, *Faith, Foolishness or Presumption?*, 94.

5. Frederick K.C. Price, *Ever Increasing Faith Messenger*, Fall 1980, 3.

6. Capps, *How You Can Avoid Tragedy and Live a Better Life*, 94-96.

7. Annette Capps, *Reverse the Curse in Your Body and Emotions* (Broken Arrow, Okla.: Annette Capps Ministries, 1987), 91-92, cited in MacArthur, *Charismatic Chaos*, 240.

8. McConnell, 156-157.

9. Ibid., 157-158.

10. Ibid., 158.

11. MacArthur, *Charismatic Chaos*, 238-240.

12. McConnell, 166.

13. Tozer, *Success and the Christian*, 143.

14. Murray, *Divine Healing*, 41; Simpson, *How To Receive Divine Healing*, 10; Simpson, *CITB* (1992), 3:240.

15. Simpson, "Inquiries and Answers," *Word, Work and World*, Nov. 1886, 290-291. Italics mine.

16. Lewis Drummond, 221. Italics mine. Spurgeon also makes reference to this in *Faith's Checkbook*, 50.

17. Leona Choy, *Andrew and Emma Murray* (Winchester, Va.: Golden Morning Publishing, 2000), 63.

18. Kenneth E. Hagin, *What To Do When Faith Seems Weak & Victory Lost* (Tulsa, Okla.: Kenneth Hagin Ministries, 1979), 81-87.

19. Murray, *Divine Healing*, 41.

20. Simpson, "Inquiries and Answers," *Word, Work and World*, Nov. 1886, 294.

21. Müller, *Autobiography*, 66.

22. Dorsett, 39.

23. Hibbert, 26-27.

24. Ibid., 17.

25. Perkins, 72.

26. McCasland, 262.

27. Ibid.

28. Kenneth MacKenzie, "My Memories of A.B. Simpson VI," *AW*, Aug. 7, 1937, 500. Simpson did eventually wear glasses.

29. Ibid.

30. Simpson, *In the School of Faith*, 217-218.

31. Ibid., 218-219.

32. John A. MacMillan, "Grace's Consummation," *AW*, Dec. 8, 1945, 423.

CHAPTER 22

Faith, Suffering, Sickness, and Sanctification

The practical question arises to whether God can be glorified through suffering, especially through sickness and whether it is ever God's will for a person to be sick in order to achieve holiness. According to MacNutt, the early church fathers "moved gradually from a wholehearted belief in healing (St. Justin Martyr and St. Ireneaus in the second century) to a view that the body's suffering is preferable for the sake of the soul (St. Gregory the Great in the fifth century)."[1] Moreover, MacNutt attributes a major factor in the decline in the church's belief in healing to Platonic, Stoic, and Manichean thought which infected Christian spirituality and "tended to view our body as a prison that confines our spirit and hinders our spiritual growth."[2]

In the Middle Ages the belief developed that God causes sickness to purge out evil, even to the point of what some theologians called "purgative possession" by demons. This philosophy of negativism toward the body has been perpetuated through some forms of teaching on "bearing one's cross." MacNutt describes the typical attitude: "If you had a 'cross'-centered spirituality like this, wouldn't you feel guilty in asking to be healed from sickness? A healing would take away your opportunity to imitate Jesus and help redeem the world."[3] This kind of viewpoint hinders the practical exercise of faith. This section thus looks at the practical implications of classic and contemporary faith teaching regarding the relationship of faith, sickness, suffering, and sanctification.

CONTEMPORARY FAITH TEACHING

Some teaching today claims that Christians do not have to suffer and that those who do are either in sin, lacking in faith, or have failed to appropriate their inheritance in Christ. Gloria Copeland, wife of Kenneth Copeland, both well-known contemporary faith teachers, asserts, "Tradition says that God gets glory from sickness, because the world sees how marvelous the Christian bears the pain and agony. (*Tradition never adds up to the right answer*.) Anyone knows that the world has all the pain and agony it can stand. What the world wants is a way out of sickness—not a way into it. Suffering has no appeal to the world, but through tradition Satan has sold suffering to the church as being the will of God. . . . Realize that only Satan could be the source of such powerless, defeated beliefs sold to the family of the Almighty God."[4]

Hagin distinguishes between suffering from sickness and suffering from persecution. Christians may suffer persecution, but according to Hagin, they are not to suffer sickness. He believes according to 1 Peter 2:21 that Jesus "suffered so we won't have to."[5] Frederick Price also contends that God cannot be glorified through sickness.[6] Moreover, he teaches that God cannot desire to dwell within a sick body: "What makes you think the Holy Ghost wants to live inside a body where He can't see out from the windows and He can't hear with the ears? What makes you think the Holy Spirit wants to live inside of a physical body where the limbs and the organs and the cells do not function right?"[7] Contemporary faith leaders argue further that Paul's thorn in the flesh was not an illness and that all sickness is from Satan.[8]

CRITICISM OF CONTEMPORARY FAITH TEACHING

McConnell refutes contemporary faith teaching that Christians can be free from sickness in this life by noting that it is contrary to Paul's beliefs regarding redemption of the body.[9] Further, he criticizes the contemporary faith movement for an "over-realized eschatology" that believes healing can be complete in this age.[10] Moreover, critics point out that though some sickness does come from Satan, some also comes from God as correction or judgment.[11] Faith critics argue that Paul's thorn in the flesh was an illness.[12] Hanegraaff charges contemporary faith leaders with in sensitivity and cruelty when they tell the sick that they must be guilty of a lack of faith or some secret sin.[13]

CLASSIC FAITH TEACHING

Sources of Sickness and Suffering. Early church father Minucius Felix, writing about 210 A.D., asserts that to "feel and suffer the human mischiefs of the body is not punishment—it is warfare."[14] Again, Felix writes, "How beautiful is the spectacle to God when a Christian does battle with pain."[15] Thus whether the pain is sickness, deprivation, or persecution, it is regarded as warfare, doing battle with pain, which is viewed as harassment of demonic forces. Earlier he writes that demons "feign diseases, alarm the minds, wrench about the limbs."[16]

Classic faith leaders did not view sickness as caused by God except in cases of punishment, nor did they view all sickness as directly from Satan, but rather rooted in the Fall or a physical cause. To the question, "Is all sickness from the devil," Simpson answered that sickness can arise from several causes, among which include the chastening of God (in which case the devil is used as an instrument) or harassment from Satan when a believer is obedient and walking with God.[17]

Carmichael prayed for and believed for healing of chronic pain due to injuries from a fall, but never received more than occasional brief and temporary relief. She believed pain was from the Enemy, explaining, "Pain (like sin and cruelty) is the work of the enemy—'An enemy hath done this.' If it were not so, we should, I think, have no right to resist it. We do not resist our Lord; . . . All the wonderful easers of pain, which I believe are His gift, would be forbidden to us. Doctors and nurses would not be working with Him, but against Him."[18] For her, acceptance of the pain did not mean that God willed it or that she should give in to it. Rather, she maintained peace in perseverance, explaining, "So though through these months acceptance has been a word of liberty and victory and peace to me, it has never meant acquiescence in illness, as though ill-health were from Him who delights to deck His priests with health. But it did mean contentment with the unexplained."[19]

Carmichael viewed her work as being a soldier in the army of the Lord. Wounds and scars are a part of the territory as a soldier. To Carmichael, the trials of life, including sickness and pain, are God's way of "forging the blade" in the fire to become tempered instruments of God's warfare. Surviving on the spiritual battlefield of life requires enduring faith. Simpson also taught similarly, "Two things the Christian needs most are the power to believe and the power to suffer, and these two things can be taught to us by the enemy. . . . The Lord lets the devil acts as a drill sergeant in His army, teaching His children the use of His spiritual weapons."[20]

Penn-Lewis suggested a test to determine if the source of suffering is from God or Satan: "Suppose I say to you, 'Resist all suffering which comes from the devil.' You reply, 'How are we to know it is from the devil?' Test it by the declaration of your attitude. Say, 'If this suffering is given me from God, I take it; but if it is from the devil, I refuse it. Now let God settle which it is.' If it is from the enemy, it will pass away as you maintain the attitude of refusal. If God has some lesson in it to teach you, it will remain."[21] This is wise counsel.

Sickness and Sanctification. It is important to understand that these classic holiness and faith leaders did not accept the medieval belief that God puts a sickness on a person to sanctify him; rather that God desires healing and *uses* physical affliction to accomplish His sanctifying purposes in a person in order that he may be made truly and fully whole. The holiness movement, for the most part, did not believe that God causes sickness and suffering, but rather that God redeems it, using it for good. Scriptures often cited include:

> *Before I was afflicted, I went astray, but now I keep Thy word* (Ps. 119:67).

> *God does not afflict willingly* (Lam. 3:33).

> *God causes all things to work together for good* (Rom. 8:28).

Though God does not *cause* sickness and suffering to sanctify His people, classic leaders nonetheless viewed suffering as a means to growing in holiness or sanctification. Archbishop Leighton explained, "extraordinary afflictions are not always the punishment of extraordinary sins, but sometimes the trial of extraordinary graces. God hath many sharp-cutting instruments, and rough files for the polishing of His jewels; and those He especially loves, and means to make the most resplendent, He hath oftenest used His tools upon."[22] Spurgeon testified from his own experiences of suffering, including sickness, "I bear my willing witness that I owe more to the fire, and the hammer, and the file, than to anything else in my Lord's worship. I sometime question whether I have ever learned anything except through the rod. When my schoolroom is darkest, I see most."[23]

Though he viewed pain as warfare, early church father Minucius Felix, nonetheless also believed that illness can be used by God as a refining process: "For fortitude is strengthened by infirmities, and calamity is very often the discipline of virtue; in addition, strength both of mind and of body grows torpid without the exercise of labour. . . . But in adversity He looks into and searches out each one; He weighs the disposition of every individual in dangers, even to death at last; He investigates the will of man, certain that to Him nothing can perish. Therefore, as gold by the fires, so are we declared by critical moments."[24]

Similar to Felix, but contrary to some contemporary faith teaching, Simpson affirmed that God's voice can be discerned in illness: "God uses sickness. God uses trial. He lets the devil have a part in it, but it is by God's permission that all this has come."[25] Simpson was assured that it is ultimately God's will to heal. However, Simpson also perceived that people need first to be assured that they are in harmony with God's will and spiritually prepared for healing.[26] He warned of the danger of focusing on trying to claim healing without understanding God's purposes before healing can come: "Some dear ones have been so anxious to get well, and have spent so much time in trying to claim it, that they have lost their spiritual blessing. God sometimes has to teach such souls that there must be a willingness to be sick before they are so thoroughly yielded as to receive His fullest blessing."[27]

Similarly, Murray shed further light on the relationship between sickness and God's purposes for sanctification:

> One of the chief benefits, then, of divine healing will be to teach us that our body ought to be set free from the yoke of our own will to become the Lord's property. God does not grant healing to our prayers until He has attained the end for which He had permitted the sickness. He wills that this discipline bring us into a more intimate communion with Him. . . . This life of attention and action, of renouncement and of crucifixion, constitutes a holy life. The Lord brings it in the first place by sickness, and makes us understand that which we are lacking, and then also by the healing, which calls the soul to a life of continual attention to the voice of God.[28]

Stockmayer likewise counseled that holiness must precede and accompany healing: "God's children must not seek the healing of the body without taking at the same time by faith, all the new position which Christ's redemption gives us, . . . which amounts to this—Nothing more for self, but all for Christ. Before seeking freedom from sickness we must lay hold of the moral freedom which the Redemption of Christ has obtained for us, and by which we are cut off from any self-seeking: from the seeking of our own will, our own life, our own interests, or our own glory."[29] A.J. Gordon explained further the need for discernment: "For it is not alone that our poor diseased humanity needs a physician with divine skill to remove our deep-seated sicknesses, but especially one with divine insight to fathom and uncover them. The doctor's eyes are often more at fault than his hand. He cannot cure because he cannot comprehend the secret of our plague. How wonderful is the insight of the Great Physician. His penetrating glance goes to the root of disease when ours can only see the symptoms."[30]

Simpson also observed that mature Christians often have more problems with sickness than younger believers. He described how some believers receive healing in their earlier Christian experiences, "but when we meet them a little later in their life, we often find them struggling with sickness, unhealed and unable to understand the reason of their failure."[31]

This is not due to overt sin or lack of faith, but rather, "because God is leading them into a deeper spiritual experience. He is teaching them to understand His guidance, and some people cannot be guided any other way than by a touch of pain. . . . God is teaching them His finer touches."[32] In times like this God wants to work a "deeper healing." In such cases Simpson advises, "Our principal aim, therefore, should be to take our minds quite off our physical condition and the struggle for health, and to meet the Lord in His spiritual discipline. Then it will be very easy for Him to heal us, and our outward life will simply spring from inward conditions which must inevitably affect our whole physical being."[33] In a similar thought, Chambers declared, "We have no business being sickly, unless it is a preparatory stage for something better, or God is nursing us through some spiritual illness."[34]

As a practical example, Spurgeon, a godly man who had a great healing ministry, nonetheless was plagued by gout. He regarded this chronic painful condition as discipline from the Lord, remarking with a positive attitude, "I rejoice that I have such a God as that; and that if He would chasten me a thousand times worse than this, I would still love him; yea, though he slay me, yet will I trust Him."[35] When his wife Susannah was ill he wrote to his mother, "This hounding trouble has its bright side, and it abundantly sanctifies so that all is well."[36] But at the same time, Spurgeon did not believe that sickness was a punishment sent by God. Rather he believed that God could bestow blessing in the midst of sickness. Even when one of his critics was severely ill, he wrote to him, not in judgment, but in encouragement, praying, "May your sick chamber be the very gate of heaven to your soul, the presence of the Lord filling the house with glory."[37]

After the death of his son, Müller went through a period of illness, probably as a natural result of grief and depression. It continued about two months, until one night God gave him grace to discipline himself to pray when he just wanted to go to sleep. He testified of his experience: "No sooner had I begun to pray than His Spirit shone into my soul and gave me such a spirit of prayer as I had not enjoyed for many weeks. He graciously revived His work in my heart. I enjoyed that nearness to God and fervency in prayer for more than an hour. My soul had been panting for many weeks for this sweet experience. For the first time in this illness, I asked the Lord earnestly to restore me to health."[38] Müller understood that God had to do something in his heart and restore him to communion with God before he could even ask for healing. His prayer more than a month earlier had been, "May the Lord grant that I may be brought nearer to Him through this."[39] He recognized that spiritual or emotional healing often precedes physical healing; that we need to grow *through* illness before being delivered *from* illness.

Similarly, Pierson wrote of Müller's experience of sickness, "Sickness is often attended with strange self- disclosure."[40] He goes on to describe Müller's response to his severe illness: "As is often true in the history of God's saints, the sense of guilt, which seemed at first to have no root in conscience and scarce an existence, struck deeper into his being and grew stronger as he knew more of God and grew more like Him.... The more we live in God and unto God, the more do our eyes become enlightened to see the enormity and deformity of sin, so that we recognize the hatefulness of sin more distinctly.... As godliness increases, the sense of ungodliness becomes more acute."[41] Again Pierson commented of Müller, "He so delighted in the will of God as to be able from his heart to say that he would not have his disease removed until through it God had wrought the blessing it was meant to convey. And when his acquiescence in the will of God had become thus complete he instinctively felt that he would speedily be restored to health."[42]

Faith, Healing, and Sanctification. To classic faith teachers faith and sanctification went hand in hand. Palmer's principles of faith and confession were first expressed in the context of confessing one's sanctification and keeping it. Hannah Whitall Smith uses the terms "life of faith," "life of holiness," "life of full salvation," "land of promise," and "the interior life" interchangeably.[43] The life of faith ultimately entails victory over sin and temptation, not merely the receiving of blessings. In fact, Simpson believed that holiness is essential for walking by faith: "Faith requires for its heavenly vision the highlands of holiness and separation, the pure sky of a consecrated life."[44]

As a corollary to this principle, classic faith leaders understood that sanctification and healing also go hand in hand: "The link between Holiness and Healing is a very close and blessed one."[45] Murray lays down this axiom: "The more we give ourselves to experience personally sanctification by faith, the more we shall also experience healing by faith."[46] Likewise, Simpson avowed, "There is a spiritual law of choosing, believing, abiding, and holding steady in our walk with God, which is essential to the working of the Holy Ghost either in our sanctification or healing."[47]

Moreover, Murray stressed that healing is not an end in itself, but a means: "Most Christians see nothing more in divine healing than a temporal blessing for the body, while in the promise of our holy God, its end is to make us holy."[48] Somewhat similar to contemporary faith teaching that God gets glory from a believer's healing rather than from sickness, Simpson remarked that the "sanctifying influence of divine healing is greater than the sanctifying influence of sickness, and that the spiritual blessings which accompany healing have a greater value than the healing itself."[49] It should be noted, however, that in contrast to some contemporary faith teaching, Simpson did acknowledge that God can be glorified in sickness, though not as great as in healing. It is significant to note that contrary to the contemporary faith teaching cited above, but consistent with classic faith teaching, Oral Roberts asserted, "The sickness that glorifies God is the one He does not feel best to heal but that gives way to a greater miracle and to serve a larger purpose."[50]

REFLECTIONS AND CONCLUSIONS

I would conclude with classic leaders of faith that while healing is God's ultimate desire, God may use sickness and suffering to accomplish His purposes. God can be glorified in sickness, though greater glory comes through healing. What is most important is whether the sickness or healing contributes to Christ-likeness. We can learn from these classic faith holiness leaders that there is a connection between holiness and wholeness, that healing often results from growth in sanctification or that healing was delayed by lack of sanctification or obstacles to sanctification.[51]

C&MA leader Schenk wrote perceptively regarding the reason why divine healing is not widely practiced and experienced today: "Could the answer be found in the fact that man has become so self-sufficient today that there are few areas left in which he must trust the Lord? Why should men give up their secret and cherished sins to be healed of pneumonia when an injection of the doctor's needle will probably accomplish the same purpose with less sacrifice?"[52] Sanctification is God's ultimate purpose above and beyond healing, and what best accomplishes that purpose in each individual is the means that God will use.

I agree with Müller that "trials are the food of faith."[53] Whether through the trials of persecution, injustice, financial difficulties, traumatic experiences, or sickness, God wants to nurture faith and draw a person nearer to Christ. God does not willingly afflict His children, but He will allow pain, whether physical, emotional, mental, social, financial, or spiritual, if that is what will best accomplish His purposes. Paul Billheimer's more recent books *Don't Waste Your Sorrows* and *Adventure in Adversity* effectively articulate this classic faith view of sanctification and suffering to contemporary audiences.[54] An anonymous classic poem, "Watch God's Methods," quoted by Billheimer epitomizes this understanding of the connection between suffering and sanctification:

When God wants to drill a man
   And thrill a man
   And skill a man,
When God wants to mold a man
   To play the noblest part;
When He yearns with all His heart
   To create so great and bold a man
That all the world shall be amazed,
   Watch His methods, watch His ways!
How He ruthlessly perfects
   Whom He royally elects!
How He hammers him and hurts him,
   And with mighty blows converts him
Into trial shapes of clay which
   Only God understands;
While his tortured heart is crying
   And he lifts beseeching hands!
How He bends but never breaks
   When his good He undertakes;
How He uses whom He chooses
   And with every purpose fuses him;
By every act induces him
To try His splendour out—
   God knows what He's about![55]

                      —Author unknown

1. Francis MacNutt, *Healing* (Notre Dame, Ind.: Ave Maria Press, [1974] 1999), 51.

2. Ibid., 52.

3. Ibid., 63; see also Ken Blue, *Authority to Heal* (Downers Grove, Ill.: InterVarsity Press, 1987), 21-40.

4. Gloria Copeland, 8.

5. Hagin, *Must Christians Suffer?*, 3.

6. Frederick Price, *Is Healing for All?*, 87-112.

7. Frederick Price, cited in Hanegraaff, 260.

8. Frederick Price, *Is Healing for All?*, 6, 7, 21-36.

9. McConnell, 159.

10. Ibid., 160.

11. McConnell, 162-164; MacArthur, *Charismatic Chaos*, 266-267.

12. McConnell, 161-162.

13. Hanegraaff, 259-260.

14. Minucius Felix, *Octavius*, 36, *ANF*, 4:195.

15. Ibid., *Octavius*, 37; *ANF*, 4:196.

16. Ibid., *Octavius*, 27, *ANF*, 4:190.

17. Simpson, "Inquiries and Answers," *Word, Work and World*, Dec. 1886, 342. These are complex issues beyond the scope of detailed study here. Two works by Pentecostal scholars that deal exegetically and theologically with these issues extensively are: Michael L. Brown, *Israel's Divine Healer* (Grand Rapids: Zondervan, 1995), and John Christopher Thomas, *The Devil, Disease and Deliverance: Origins of Illness in New Testament Thought* (Sheffield, Eng.: Sheffield Academic Press, 1998). Brown views sickness as a result of God's wrath more commonplace in the Old Testament and the exception rather than the rule under New Covenant grace. He notes that "when disobedience is not a factor, sickness comes as a result of natural causes, the fallen state of man, demonic attack, or a large scheme in the plan of God" (p. 231). In the New Testament the veil has been lifted and the role and influence of the powers of darkness in sickness and suffering has been revealed (pp. 208-212). Thomas identifies three primarily causes of illness and/or infirmities in the New Testament: God, the devil and/or demons, and natural causes (p. 297). Differing from the usual viewpoint of his fellow Pentecostal colleagues, however, he concludes that "God is often attributed a role in the origins of sickness" in a multi-faceted manner "as a pedagogical device, an instrument of punishment, a source of sanctification, a means of spreading the gospel, or an instrument of salvation" (pp. 297-298).

18. Amy Carmichael, *Rose from Brier* (Ft. Washington, Penn.: Christian Literature Crusade, [1933] 1971), 27.

19. Ibid., 28.

20. Simpson, *A Larger Christian Life*, 89.

21. Penn-Lewis, *The Conquest of Canaan*, 41.

22. Archbishop Leighton, quoted in Cowman, *Streams in the Desert*, 113.

23. Spurgeon, cited in Cowman, *Streams in the Desert*, 114; see also Lewis Drummond, 558-559 for a similar statement.

24. Minucius Felix, *Octavius*, 36, *ANF*, 4:195-196.

25. A.B. Simpson, "God's Voice in Sickness," *Triumphs of Faith*, July 1902, 164.

26. Simpson, *The Old Faith and the New Gospels*, 60.

27. Simpson, *Days of Heaven on Earth*, June 18.

28. Murray, *Divine Healing*, 31, 76.

29. A.J. Gordon, *The Ministry of Healing*, 164-165.

30. Ibid., 243-244.

31. A.B. Simpson, "Two Stages of Divine Healing," *AW*, Jan. 28, 1953, 5.

32. Ibid.

33. Ibid.

34. Chambers, *Biblical Psychology*, 76.

35. Lewis Drummond, 464.

36. Ibid., 462.

37. Lewis Drummond, 559.

38. Müller, *Autobiography*, 68.

39. Ibid., 66.

40. Pierson, *George Müller of Bristol*, 55

41. Ibid., 55-56.

42. Ibid., 141.

43. See Smith, *The Christian's Secret*, 32, 58, 84, 85, 87, 90, 96-100.

44. Simpson, *A Larger Christian Life*, 13.

45. Andrew Murray, *Holy in Christ* (Toronto: Willard Tract Depot, 1888), 209.

46. Murray, *Divine Healing*, 13.

47. Simpson, cited in Cowman, *Streams in the Desert*, 31.

48. Murray, *Divine Healing*, 76.

49. A.B. Simpson, "The Sanctifying Influence of Divine Healing," *AW*, Sept. 17, 1952, 602.

50. Oral Roberts, cited in Ronald A.N. Kydd, *Healing Through the Centuries: Models for Understanding* (Peabody, Mass.: Hendrickson, 1998), 208.

51. I had a personal experience, practically illustrating this concept. I received a football injury that resulted in painful bursitis. Neither medication nor prayer brought healing. However, six months later I was healed after dealing with an issue of bitterness and unforgiveness toward another pastor. The injury had nothing to do with unforgiveness, but the pathway to healing did.

52. Schenk, cited in Ernest Gerald Wilson, *The Christian and Missionary Alliance: Developments and Modifications of Its Original Objectives*. Ph.D. dissertation, New York: New York University, 1984, 185.

53. Müller, cited in Cowman, *Streams in the Desert*, 117.

54. Paul Billheimer, *Don't Waste Your Sorrows* (Ft. Washington, Penn.: Christian Literature Crusade, 1977); Paul Billheimer, *Adventure in Adversity* (Wheaton, Ill.: Tyndale House Publishers, 1984).

55. Billheimer, *Don't Waste Your Sorrows*, 111, 112; Billheimer, *Adventure in Adversity*, 33, 34.

CHAPTER 23

Faith and Prosperity

Probably no other faith teaching engenders more controversy than teaching about prosperity. Teaching in the Church runs the whole gambit of believing that Jesus and His disciples were poor, to believing that they were rich. The medieval mendicants exalted voluntary poverty, while other leaders through the centuries have advocated that God desires Christians to be wealthy. One says believers are to deny themselves, others say God wants them to have their desires. For various Christian viewpoints on wealth throughout church history see Mullin, *The Wealth of Christians*, Sheils and Wood, *The Church and Wealth*, and Gonzalez, *Faith and Wealth: A History of Early Christian Ideas on the Origin, Significance, and Use of Money*.[1] This section investigates classic and contemporary faith teaching and practice regarding prosperity. Teaching on prosperity is based on several passages of Scripture, most notably:

> *Beloved, I pray that in all respects, you may prosper and be in good health, just as your soul prospers* (3 John 2).

> *Give and it will be given unto you; good measure, pressed down, shaken together, running over, they will pour into your lap. For whatever measure you deal out to others, it will be dealt to you in return* (Luke 6:38).

CONTEMPORARY FAITH TEACHING

It is very popular in the contemporary faith movement to quote 3 John 2, claiming that God wants believers to have material prosperity and divine healing. This is often referred to as the "prosperity gospel" or "health and wealth gospel." It is often associated with faith as a law and a force, believing that the positive confession sets in motion the laws of success and prosperity, as Copeland claims: "The success formulas in the Word of God produce results when used as directed."[2] I have mentioned earlier in Chapter 17 the role of positive confession expressed in popular slogans like "name it and claim it," "confess it and possess it," "you can have what you say."

Some contemporary faith teaching says that Jesus suffered so Christians do not have to suffer; Jesus became poor to make believers rich. Some interpret that into meaning that believers are "King's Kids" and should be living like royalty, not paupers, should always have the best and go first class.[3] Others claim that Jesus was really rich, not poor, and therefore wants believers to be rich.[4] Frederick Price asserts that he drives a Rolls Royce to follow in Jesus' footsteps.[5]

Contemporary faith teaching sometimes claims, that according to Mark 11:22-24, you can have whatever you desire. Some teach believers can claim a hundred-fold increase according to the law of sowing and reaping.[6] For instance, Gloria Copeland teaches, "You give $1 for the Gospel's sake and $100 belongs to you; give $10 and receive $1000; give $1000 and receive $100,000."[7] Others claim debt-cancellation and end-time transfer of the wealth of the wicked.

CRITICISM OF CONTEMPORARY FAITH TEACHING

Scholars such as Gordon Fee have pointed out that 3 John 2 really is a greeting, not a promise of Scripture, and so cannot be used to justify seeking prosperity.[8] Faith critics see in prosperity theology and praxis an attempt to manipulate God through formulas, with teachings such as "How to Write Your Own Ticket with God" and "God's Formula for Success and Prosperity."[9] MacArthur criticizes the view that believers have a divine right to prosperity because they are little gods.[10] McConnell faults the prosperity movement for its definition of prosperity as God wanting to give believers anything they desire and a consequent lack of teaching on self-denial, as well as degradation of the poor,[11] calling it "a gross example of the church's cultural accommodation to the worldly values of American materialism."[12]

MacArthur and Hanegraaff speak against Oral Robert's concept of "seed faith," likening it to making a down payment on a miracle or selling indulgences.[13] Hanegraaff speaks with contempt about teaching that Jesus was rich, replete with "designer clothes, big house, and a wealthy, well-financed advanced team," and rationalization that driving a Rolls Royce is following in Jesus' footsteps.[14] Especially noteworthy is that

Hagin in his later years became critical of some fellow contemporary faith teachers who teach extreme viewpoints regarding hundredfold return, debt-cancellation, end-time transfer of wealth, and other practices.[15]

CLASSIC FAITH TEACHING ON PROSPERITY

Puritan Roots. The idea that God wants to prosper believers is not confined to the contemporary faith movement, but is rooted in Puritanism and the Protestant work ethic, the belief that God rewards hard work and godly living. As mentioned in Chapter 1, seventeenth-century Puritan leader Thomas Brooks taught a form of prosperity doctrine based on the Puritan work ethic and Covenant theology, saying according to Deuteronomy 28:13 that believers will be the head and not the tail, and will have "much outward riches, prosperity, and glory."[16]

Baptist Roots. Some Baptist leaders promoted a form of prosperity teaching that was likely based on the Puritan ethic. One of these was renowned Philadelphia Baptist pastor Russell Conwell (born 1842) who founded Temple University and Conwell School of Theology (which eventually merged with Gordon Divinity School to form Gordon-Conwell Theological Seminary). He preached his famous prosperity message "Acres of Diamonds" 6,000 times throughout the United States. "Through this speech, he popularized the notion that hard work and godly living would and should result in wealth. In fact, he believed that becoming wealthy in order to use that wealth wisely was a Christian's responsibility."[17] Conwell's message sounds very much like the prosperity teaching today.

Classic Faith Use of 3 John 2. Even though this Scripture really is a greeting, not a promise of Scripture, as contemporary scholars such as Fee have pointed out, nonetheless, classic faith leaders did make use of this Scripture, considering it as a Spirit-led prayer.[18] Simpson and the early C&MA, for example, understood this Scripture as a prayer inspired by God, asserting, "We may expect to be 'in health' and prosper 'even as our soul prospereth.'"[19] However, they related this to primarily to health, not to financial prosperity. Simpson interpreted this Scripture to mean that health is interrelated with the spiritual and emotional state of the soul.[20] While Simpson included temporal blessing in his understanding of this invocation, he made no self-centered or materialistic application of this verse as do some prosperity teachers: "It implies that we cannot expect the Lord's blessing upon our bodies and our business, if we cherish in our hearts those spiritual conditions which bring divine chastening and produce misery and pain."[21]

Classic Faith View of Prosperity. Classic faith leaders were not, by and large, opposed to wealth. They did believe that God wants His people to prosper materially. Simpson, for instance, believed, "There is no harm whatever in having money, houses, lands, friends and dearest children if you do not value these things for themselves."[22] Charles Cullis, who influenced Simpson, avowed, "Living by faith in temporal as well as in spiritual things, had been regarded as one of 'the lost arts.'"[23] Hannah Whitall Smith likened the life of faith to the relationship of a child in the heavenly Father's house.[24] Giving the example of an adopted child she visited in a wealthy home, she explained, "If nothing would so grieve and wound the loving hearts around her as to see this little child beginning to be worried or anxious about herself in any way,—about whether her food and clothes would be provided, or how she was to get her education or her future support,—how much more must the great, loving heart of our God and Father be grieved and wounded at seeing His children taking so much anxious care and thought! . . . Who is the best cared for in every household? Is it not the little children?"[25]

Significant, however, is how the classic faith leaders defined prosperity and the attitude one should hold regarding prosperity. Simmons notes of these leaders:

> Although conspicuous consumption was officially condemned, the general flow of the Gilded Age [post-Civil War nineteenth century] was in the direction of a gospel of wealth. With this in mind, it is interesting to note that the representatives of the Higher Life movement were among the few who chose to swim against this tide. . . . In stark contrast to the main current of contemporary evangelicalism, Higher Life advocates actually spoke very little about *personal* prosperity. Instead, when they spoke of success it was usually within the context of ministry, including within that category anything from the salvation of individual souls to the establishment of a new orphanage, or the reception (through prayer) of just enough funds to meet the needs of their ministry for that specific day.[26]

Prosperity was not usually viewed as wealth or getting one's desires, but supply for all needs for oneself and accomplishing God's work. Cullis,

Hudson Taylor, Spurgeon, Carmichael, and Simpson practiced living by faith in similar manner as that of Müller, trusting God daily for financial and physical provision for their ministries. Hannah Whitall Smith likewise averred, "Better and sweeter than health, or friends, or money, or fame, or prosperity, is the adorable will of God."[27] This is not to say that God does not care about our material welfare, because God *is* interested in providing for our needs. Rather, the focus is not in getting, but trusting.

Some regarded their lives as enjoying the prosperity of God regardless of their circumstances. Simpson's view on prosperity is reflected in his quote of fourteenth century German mystic John Tauler, "Thou didst say, 'God prosper thee.' I have never been unprosperous, for I know how to live with God."[28] Hudson Taylor, who experienced severe privations as a missionary, nevertheless had a similar attitude looking back over his years of ministry, amazingly saying, "I never made a sacrifice."[29] His viewpoint on personal prosperity was, "Having now the twofold object in view . . . of accustoming myself to endure hardness, and of economizing in order to help those among whom I was laboring in the Gospel, I soon found that I could live upon very much less than I had previously thought possible. . . . My experience was that the less I spent on myself and the more I gave to others, the fuller of happiness and blessing did my soul become."[30] The attitude or motive for wanting to prosper is key, according to Müller:

> Suppose such a person had heard the promises about prayer, and should say, "Now I will try if these things are true, and I will ask God to give me a hundred thousand pounds sterling, and then I can give myself easy days; I can travel about and enjoy myself." Suppose he prays every day for this large sum of money, will he obtain it? Assuredly not! Why not? He does not ask for it that he may help the poor abundantly; that he may contribute to the work of God more liberally, but he asks that he may spend his life in idleness, and in enjoying the pleasures of the world.[31]

These people of faith had learned with the Apostle Paul: "I have learned to be content in whatever circumstances I am. I know how to get along with humble means, and I also know how to live in prosperity; in any and every circumstance I have learned the secret of being filled and going hungry, both of having abundance and suffering need. I can do all things through Him who strengthens me" (Phil. 4:11-13).

Classic Faith Practice on "King's Kid Christianity." What was the attitude and practice of the classic heroes of faith regarding "King's Kid Christianity?" Chambers chose neither first class, nor third class, but took the moderate place. On his voyage by ship to America his second class cabin was described as "not luxurious, but much more comfortable than the crowded compartments below."[32] Carmichael went farther, commenting regarding traveling first class: "I don't believe the Lord Jesus or His disciples would go in for it. It does not seem to me honoring to our Master, this missionary habit of going by the easier rather than the harder way, when He chose the harder. It is as if we put ourselves a little above Him."[33] When asked why she went third class, her reply was, "There is no fourth class."[34] She warned against "fashionable Christianity," which she regarded as worldliness.

But is it always wrong to go first class and desire the best? There was one occasion in which Carmichael did go against her own principle, and traveled first class on a ship in order to get sufficient sleep, cleanliness, privacy, and quiet when recovering from an illness. There were also times when she was willing to "go first class" in her buildings. She determined that it would be right to spend the Lord's money on more expensive materials if the money was given specifically for that purpose.[35] Spurgeon's biographer relates this story about Spurgeon boarding a train: "Spurgeon had been in conversation with a fellow minister. The reverend gentleman said to Charles, 'Well, I am going to the third class section of the train to save the Lord's money.' Spurgeon retorted, 'Well, I am going to the first class section of the train to save the Lord's servant.'"[36] Spurgeon recognized his legitimate need for better accommodations for his health and rest. So while normally these classic leaders would not choose to go first class, they sometimes thought it was appropriate for their well-being. They would spend money for the very best if it was for the good of the Lord's work or for others, not merely for their own convenience and comfort.

The Classic Faith Principle of Giving Up in Order to Gain. A common classic faith principle taught that abandonment of self is key to gaining the blessings of God. Murray, for example, asserted that without self-denial and letting go of the world faith cannot be exercised.[37] Likewise, Hannah Whitall Smith, Carrie Judd Montgomery, and Simpson all taught that abandonment precedes faith.[38] Smith and Montgomery claimed this was a "secret" to the Christian's happy or victorious life. Simpson advised that Jesus is "not a wealthy friend, advancing a large sum to aid us in our business, but coming into it Himself, and giving us His partnership, His counsel and His whole capital. And it is received by faith. . . . In one single act we renounce ourselves and all our sin and self-confidence, and take Him and His all-sufficiency for every future need."[39] Moreover, Simpson believed that the life of faith requires the continual exercise of a strong will, and "that faith itself is largely the exercise of a sanctified and intensified will, but in order to do this, it is necessary that our will be wholly renounced and God's will invariably accepted instead, and then we can put into it all the strength and force of our being, and will it even as God wills it, because He wills it."[40]

Contrary to some popular contemporary prosperity teaching, faith can only be properly exercised by renouncing self and putting on Christ day by day. To those who would claim that prosperity is the covenant right of the believer, Chambers would answer, "But if you are living the life of faith you will exercise your right to waive your rights, and let God choose for you."[41] It is noteworthy that Simpson, an early faith advocate of the rights and privileges of believers, nonetheless also emphasized, "The very test of consecration is our willingness . . . to surrender our rights."[42]

For classic faith leaders, the question involves setting one's affections on heaven rather than on earth. Simpson declared, "Faith [is] yielding up the world because it has a better inheritance."[43] Like Lot, Simpson perceived that people with an "earthly spirit" tend to "contend for the best of the land." But, in contrast, "the man of faith can let the present world go because he knows he has a better, but even as he lets it go God tells him that all things are his because he is Christ's."[44] Carmichael took that thought further, explaining,

> Those of us who are God's emissaries are to treat the world (not just its corruptions, but its legitimate joys, its privileges and blessings also), as a thing to be touched at a distance. . . . It is not that He forbids us this or that indulgence or comfort. . . . No, it is that we who love our Lord, and we whose affections are set on the things that are heaven for us today—we voluntarily and gladly lay aside things that charm the world, so that we may be charmed and ravished by the things of heaven. . . . to look upon the world, in all its delights and attractions, suspecting that traps are set there for us, reserving ourselves for a higher way. *The world is not for us.*[45]

Seeking after prosperity, in the minds of most of these classic faith leaders, is contrary to a heavenly-minded mindset. To the spiritually-minded, material considerations are secondary.

Classic Faith Cautions Regarding Prosperity. While classic faith leaders were not opposed to having wealth, they cautioned about the dangers that prosperity can bring. Blumhardt "detested the sort of prayer that presses God for one's own desires."[46] In contrast to the teaching that "you can have whatever you desire," Wigglesworth commented on Mark 11:22-24: "Desire toward God, and you will have desires from God and He will meet you on the line of those desires when you reach out in simple faith."[47] Carmichael also makes this important differentiation: "God has something much better for us than the thing we naturally desire. As we wait with all the desire of our mind fixed on Him, the thing we naturally long for becomes less pressing, the friction ceases, and we are set free to go on."[48] Thus, these classic faith leaders indicate that if a person is claiming prosperity for his own pleasure because he is a King's Kid, he is not in the will of God, but if he is praying that he may prosper for the sake of others, that prayer reflects God's will.

Whereas some associate financial abundance with God's blessing and approval, Bounds advised, "Material prosperity is not the infallible sign of spiritual prosperity."[49] Rather, prosperity may cause a person to grow farther away from God. Moody admonished, "We can stand affliction better than we can prosperity, for in prosperity we forget God."[50] Hudson Taylor likewise cautioned, "While the sun of prosperity shines upon me I may safely enjoy myself here without Him."[51] Simpson spoke of the "discipline of prosperity," that working of God in the believer's heart to be able to handle prosperity with a godly attitude:

> How few Christians really know how to abound. How frequently prosperity changes their temper and the habits and fruits of their lives! To receive God's blessing in temporal things, to have wealth suddenly thrust upon us, to be surrounded with the congenial friends, to be enriched with all the happiness that love, home the world's applause and unbounded prosperity can give, and yet to keep a humble heart, to be separated from the world in its spirit and in its pleasures, to keep our hearts in holy indifference from the love and need of earthly things, to stand for God as holy witnessed in the most public station, and to use our prosperity and wealth as a sacred trust for Him, counting

nothing our own, and still depending upon Him as simply as in the days of penury—this, indeed, is an experience rarely found, and only possible through the infinite grace of God.[52]

Commenting on Matthew 6:33 ("Seek first His kingdom and His righteousness, and all these things shall be added unto you"), Chambers advised, "We are not to seek success or prosperity."[53] Murray asserted that seeking after pleasure, honor, and riches actually stifles faith, and "only an unworldly spirit . . . can be strong in faith."[54] Simpson taught that the deeper and higher Christian life is not about receiving blessings, but about a change in priorities: "Once it was the blessing, now it is the Lord . . ."[55] All of these leaders agree that material blessings are secondary, as an old gospel song says, "My goal is God Himself, not joy, not peace, not even blessing . . ."[56] This is in stark contrast to so many people who seek God for what they can get from God, not for God Himself.

Interestingly, with his great wit and humor, Spurgeon adds a disclaimer to his own teaching on prosperity, which contemporary prosperity teachers would do good to heed: "Of course, I may not be sure of growing rich. I shall be fat, but not too fat. Too great riches might make me as unwieldy as corpulent persons usually are, and cause me the dyspepsia of worldliness, and perhaps bring on a fatty degeneration of the heart."[57] In a similar vein, Montgomery indicates that preoccupation with worldly things can even prevent healing: "If the things of the world are precious to us we will be occupied with them, and will not render unto the Lord according to all that He hath done for us. After a failure of this kind I have often seen it very difficult for people to receive healing again from the hand of the Lord."[58]

Classic Faith Principles of Prosperity. Keeping in mind the dynamic tension that, on one hand, classic faith leaders believed that God wants Christians to prosper, and, on the other hand, that motives must be pure, we will look at some of the classic practical faith principles for prospering.

1. Have a generous, giving attitude. Classic faith leaders usually did not legalistically demand a tithe, but viewed it as a beginning principle of liberality. Tithing was viewed as the minimum basis of generosity as early as Müller.[59] Montgomery cited Malachi 3:10, that the tithe must be sown in faith for the windows of blessing to be opened, claiming "I have many times found by experience that money which has been tithed, lasted much longer than that which had not been tithed."[60] Another connection between faith and financial prosperity can be seen in a 1915 article in Montgomery's *Triumphs of Faith* entitled "God's Rule for Financial Prosperity," emphasizing tithing.[61]

Oral Roberts' saying "The tithe is not a debt you owe, but a seed you sow," has its origin in this classic faith understanding of giving, based on Luke 6:38. Contrary to the claims of MacArthur and Hanegraaff, "seed faith" is not an invention of the contemporary prosperity movement. While motive, application, and practice of the principle may in some instances be questioned, the concept of planting a seed in faith for the purpose of receiving fruit is one which was taught by classic evangelical leaders. Murray, for instance, refers to exercising faith as a "seed-word."[62] Watchman Nee asserted that the way of God is not to save and get rich, but give and it shall be given.[63]

Oral Roberts has another popular saying derived from this Scripture, "Give to get to give." However, again he is not the originator of the concept, for Spurgeon asserted, almost exactly as Roberts, "Faith's way of gaining is giving. I must try this again and again; and I may expect that as much of prosperity as will be good for me will come to me as a gracious reward for a liberal course of action."[64] Roberts' phrase is so strikingly similar to Spurgeon's "give to gain" concept, one may wonder if he gleaned his idea from Spurgeon. Spurgeon appears to be one of the earliest faith leaders to make the connection between giving and financial prosperity: "I have noticed that the most generous Christians have always been the most happy and almost invariably the most prosperous. I have seen the liberal giver rise to wealth of which he never dreamed. . . . It takes faith to act toward our God with an open hand."[65] Yet we should not be surprised that he should make this connection, since he was influenced by the Puritans, who, as mentioned earlier, taught that Christians should prosper. Similarly, A.B. Simpson, while emphasizing the importance of pure motives, taught, "Thus we gain by giving. Thus we possess twice over by letting go."[66]

2. Stay out of debt. George Müller testified, "My wife and I never went into debt because we believed it to be unscriptural according to Rom. 13:8, 'Owe no man anything, but to love one another.' Therefore we have no bills with our tailor, butcher, or baker, but we pay for everything in cash. We would rather suffer need than to contract debts. Thus, we always know how much we have, and how much we can give away. Many trials come upon the children of God on account of not acting according to Rom. 13:8. . . . There is no promise that He will pay our debts."[67] Hudson Taylor, Spurgeon, Carmichael, Simpson, C.T. Studd, and a host of others influenced by Müller, have also practiced this principle. Bible seminar teacher Bill Gothard and his Institute in Basic Life Principles is a contemporary example of a ministry that has successfully practiced Müller's principles of staying out of debt and trusting God alone. Taylor avowed, "God's work done in God's way will not lack God's support. He is just as able to supply funds ahead of time as afterward and He much prefers doing so."[68]

3. Be satisfied with what you have. Hudson Taylor asserted, "The real secret of an unsatisfied life lies too often in an unsurrendered will."[69] Spurgeon wrote, "Happiness is not found when the barns are full and the vats are running over. Happiness is knowing that whatever you have, the Lord is your provider. You cannot have a better provider."[70] His attitude toward wealth was, "Prayer makes 'rich toward God,' and this is the best of riches."[71] Simpson believed the key to receiving blessing from God is: "When you become satisfied with God, everything else so loses its charm that He can give it to you without harm, and then you can take just as much as you choose, and use it for His glory. . . . Then every bank stock, and investment will be but a channel through which you can pour out His benevolence and share His gifts."[72] Contentment is thus a key to true prosperity.

Trust God, taking your needs to Him, not men. This concept Müller practiced and passed on to Taylor, Simpson, Spurgeon, Carmichael, and others, as with his principle on owing no debts. Carmichael explained, "We do not tell when we are in need unless definitely asked, and even then not always; for often the leading seems to be silent, except towards God."[73] Who is showing greater faith? Those who plead for funds, or those who do not broadcast their needs? The greatest demonstration of faith is to pray and trust God to provide without telling others.

5. Pray and believe for abundance. Many of the classic faith leaders believed in the concept of multi-fold increase. Commenting on the feeding of the 5,000, Carmichael testified, "And, as I believed, the promise was given to me then that there should be baskets over and above our daily supplies."[74] She understood that as we give of ourselves to others, by God's grace He will provide abundantly from the leftovers. Taylor trusted that God would provide even ten times over. Chambers testified that whenever he gave sacrificially, God doubled: "The Lord always gives double for all I give away."[75] They did not, however, like some contemporary faith teaching make a formula for obtaining a hundred-fold increase.

6. Make specific requests—believe for specific amounts. Müller would paraphrase James 4:1 to say, "You have not *exactly* what you need because you asked not for *exactly* what you needed." He believed that vague prayers get vague answers; specific prayer get specific answers. Müller prayed for precise amounts of money, and again and again would receive exactly what he needed. For instance, one time he asked the Lord for a thousand pounds of money, and received varying amounts from one shilling to a hundred pounds from several sources totaling exactly that amount. Also, he asked that the Lord would place on the hearts of people to donate time and articles of furniture and clothes for the children. As a result, he received every item he needed, plus food, volunteers to care for the children, and an offer of a house! Sometimes it took long periods of time, but he continued to pray repeatedly with precision. For one particular need, he prayed specifically for 134 days before receiving the answer. Carmichael recounts similar experiences.[76]

REFLECTIONS AND CONCLUSIONS

I conclude that, by and large, classic faith teaching and practice represents a balanced approach to prosperity that avoids the extreme polarities and maintains the dynamic tension of truth. The basic problem with the prosperity movement is not whether God desires to prosper believers, but rather how prosperity is defined. As we have seen, some in the contemporary faith movement define prosperity as having riches and living luxuriously as "King's Kids." How different in attitude and example were these classic pioneers of faith from some contemporary faith teachers who constantly appeal for money and teach a life of ease. I believe that we should look to these giants of faith as models through their characteristically simple, frugal, self-denying lives.

We must acknowledge and commend others, who have recanted or modified their view of the "health and wealth gospel," including Jimmy Swaggart, Jim Bakker and Benny Hinn. Also, it is noteworthy that Marte Tilton, the ex-wife of prosperity preacher Robert Tilton, now believes that prosperity is "having all your needs met and having enough to help other people. It is not a $1 million house or a Mercedes."[77] Hagin's recent book *The Midas Touch: A Balanced Approach to Biblical Prosperity*, goes a long way in correcting some of the errors of the prosperity movement and advocating balance. In it, Hagin clarifies misapplication of prosperity teachings, admits mistakes, retracting some of his earlier prosperity teaching, and also strongly critiques the teachings of some of his fellow prosperity advocates. In particular, he maintains that prosperity does not necessarily mean wealth, and stresses the importance of proper motives. Further, he repudiates or downplays the validity of such teachings as a literal hundred-fold return, end-time transfer of the wealth of the wicked, debt cancellation, tithing to an independent ministry rather than a church, giving to get, prosperity gimmicks, and other issues. While the book does not sufficiently deal with all pertinent issues, it is the soundest presentation of prosperity of any of the contemporary faith teachers, and receives my hearty recommendation.

As a practical application for believers today, I affirm with both the classic and contemporary faith leaders that God does want His people to prosper, to have everything we need in order to sufficiently accomplish all He desires. God does not want His people to be involuntarily impoverished. Yet the motives and goals for prosperity must be pure and Spirit-led. I would encourage those who are seeking prosperity to have the "holy indifference" toward wealth that the classic faith leaders advocated and modeled. They show us that we need to be content and moderate, not extravagant and self-indulgent. We must understand that in some situations God may want us to humble ourselves to the lowest, and in others it may be entirely appropriate for us to go first class. We should not assume that God always wants us to seek the best and finest in comfort and luxury, but neither should we assume that God always wants us to take the cheapest way. Seeking God's desire for the situation should be our desire. The classic faith leaders caution us that it is possible to focus so much on the material blessings that one can miss the greater blessings, which, ultimately, are not material.

---

1. Redmond Mullin, *The Wealth of Christians* (Maryknoll, N.Y.: Orbis Books, 1983); W. J. Sheils and Diana Wood, *The Church and Wealth* (Oxford: Basil Blackwell, 1987), and Justo L. Gonzalez, *Faith and Wealth: A History of Early Christian Ideas on the Origin, Significance, and Use of Money* (San Francisco: HarperSanFrancisco, 1990).

2. Copeland, *The Laws of Prosperity*, 20.

3. Frederick Price, *Faith, Foolishness or Presumption?*, 25-28, 34.

4. John Avanzini, cited in Hanegraaff, 35, 187, 397.

5. Frederick Price, cited in Hanegraaff, 187, 397.

6. John Avanzini, *30, 60, Hundredfold: Your Financial Harvest Released* (Tulsa, Okla.: Harrison House, 1989).

7. Gloria Copeland, *God's Will Is Prosperity* (Tulsa, Okla.: Harrison House, 1978), 54.

8. Fee, 4.

9. MacArthur, *Charismatic Chaos*, 325.

10. Ibid., 335.

11. McConnell, 175-183.

12. Ibid., 183.

13. MacArthur, *Charismatic Chaos*, 242, 348; Hanegraaff, 195-198.

14. Hanegraaff, 34, 35, 187.

15. Kenneth Hagin, *The Midas Touch*, 131-176.

16. Brooks, 131.

17. Editorial note, "About the Author," Russell Conwell, *Acres of Diamonds* (Uhrichville, Ohio: Barbour Publishing, 2003), 94.

18. For more on a history of interpretation of 3 John 2, see Heather L. Landrus, "Hearing 3 John 2 in the Voices of History." Paper presented at the 30th Annual Meeting of the Society for Pentecostal Studies, Oral Roberts University, Tulsa, Okla., Mar. 2001.

19. Simpson, *The Gospel of Healing*, 93; see also pp. 23-24, 44-45, 59; Simpson, *CITB* (1992), 6:387-388.

20. Simpson, *The Gospel of Healing*, 43-44.

21. Simpson, *CITB* (1992), 6:387.

22. Simpson, *Days of Heaven on Earth*, Oct. 6.

23. Charles Cullis, cited in Daniels, 55.

24. Smith, *The Christian's Secret*, 32.

25. Ibid., 32.

26. Simmons, *E.W. Kenyon*, 234.

27. Smith, *The Christian's Secret*, 36.

28. Simpson, *In the School of Faith*, 90.

29. Howard Taylor, *Hudson Taylor's Spiritual Secret*, 30.

30. Ibid., 26.

31. Steer, 87.

32. McCasland, 102.

33. Elliot, 98.

34. Ibid.

35. Ibid., 98, 208.

36. Lewis Drummond, 280.

37. Murray, *The Prayer Life*, 18.

38. Smith, *The Christian's Secret*, 38-40; Montgomery, *Secrets of Victory*, 15; Simpson, *Danger Lines in the Deeper Life*, 101.

39. Simpson, *In the School of Faith*, 35.

40. Simpson, *A Larger Christian Life*, 71.

41. Chambers, *My Utmost for His Highest*, May 25.

42. Simpson, *Days of Heaven on Earth*, Aug. 24.

43. Simpson, *In the School of Faith*, 52.

44. Ibid.

45. Amy Carmichael, *You Are My Hiding Place*, arranged by David Hazard (Minneapolis: Bethany House, 1991), 44.

46. Friedrich Zuendel, *The Awakening* (Farmington, Penn.: Plough Publishing House, 1999), 139.

47. Wigglesworth, *The Ever-Increasing Faith*, 11.

48. Carmichael, *Thou Givest . . . They Gather*, 110.

49. E.M. Bounds, *Book 2: The Essentials of Prayer*, from *The Complete Works of E.M. Bounds*, Book 2:114.

50. D.L. Moody, cited in *Heroes of the Faith* (Uhrichville, Ohio: Barbour Publishing Co., 1998), 18.

51. Hudson Taylor, *Union and Communion with Christ*, 42.

52. Simpson, *CITB*, (1992) 6:206.

53. Chambers, *Daily Thoughts for Disciples*, Nov. 7.

54. Murray, *The Holiest of All*, 459, 460.

55. A.B. Simpson, "Himself," *Hymns of the Christian Life*, 248.

56. Ibid., 265.

57. Spurgeon, *Faith's Checkbook*, 5.

58. Montgomery, *Secrets of Victory*, 100.

59. Steer, 104-105; see also Montgomery, *Secrets of Victory*, 36, 37.

60. Montgomery, *Secrets of Victory*, 37.

61. "God's Rule for Financial Prosperity," *Triumphs of Faith*, Nov. 1915, 242.

62. Murray, *With Christ in the School of Prayer*, 80. He further counseled, "Take the hidden feeble seed of the little faith you have, with the Word of promise on which you are resting; plant it in your heart. Give utterance to it in the contact with Jesus Christ and fervent prayer to Him." Andrew Murray, *The Secret of the Faith Life* (Ft. Washington, Penn.: Christian Literature Crusade, 1968), 69.

63. Angus Kinnear, *Against the Tide: The Story of Watchman Nee* (Wheaton, Ill.: Tyndale House, 1973), 87.

64. Spurgeon, *Faith's Checkbook*, 5.

65. Spurgeon, *Morning by Morning*, Oct. 26.

66. Simpson, *CITB* (1992), 1:392.

67. Müller, *Autobiography,* 43, 162.

68. Bill Gothard, *Men's Manual* (Oak Brook, Ill.: Institute in Basic Youth Conflicts, 1983), 2:84.

69. Hudson Taylor, *Union and Communion with Christ*, 20.

70. Spurgeon, *The Triumph of Faith in a Believer's Life*, 83.

71. Ibid., 89.

72. Simpson, *Days of Heaven on Earth*, Oct. 6.

73. Amy Carmichael, cited in Elliot, 189.

74. Elliot, 227.

75. McCasland, 147.

76. See Elliot, 289-290, for Carmichael's similar experiences.

77. Carol Chapman Stertzer, "She Found the Grace to Forgive," *Charisma*, Aug. 2000, 103.

PART 5

CONCLUSIONS

CHAPTER 24

Faith and Hermeneutics

Throughout this study I have alluded to various hermeneutical issues. Many, perhaps even most, of the controversies regarding contemporary faith theology and practice have involved the interpretation
of various passages of Scripture. Regarding the "health and wealth
gospel," Fee affirms: "The basic problems here are hermeneutical, i.e.,
they involve questions as to how one interprets Scripture. Even the lay
person, who may not know the word "hermeneutics' and who is not
especially trained in interpreting the Bible, senses that this is where
the real problem lies. The most distressing thing about their use of
Scripture . . . is the purely subjective and arbitrary way they interpret
the biblical text."[1]

HERMENEUTICS AND THE CONTEMPORARY
FAITH MOVEMENT

James W. Sire, in his book *Scripture Twisting*, addresses ways in which
cults misuse the Scriptures: inaccurate quotation, twisted translation,
ignoring the immediate context, collapsing contexts of two or more un-
related texts, speculation and overspecification, mistaking literal language for figurative language (and vice versa), selective citing, confused
definitions, ignoring alternative explanations, among others.[2] Many of
these misuses of Scripture in the contemporary faith movement have
been pointed out by their critics. However, this does not mean that the
contemporary faith leaders are cultic as some have claimed them to be,
but it does demonstrate that there is a serious problem with some contemporary faith exegesis.

Copeland appears at first glance to have a concern for proper interpretation of Scripture when he asserts "that we are putting the Word of

God first and foremost throughout this study, not what we *think* it says, but what it *actually* says!"[3] However, Fee responds:

> This is nobly said; but what does it mean? Implied is the hint that interpretations that differ from his are based on what people think, not on what the Bible says. But also implied is the truth that good interpretation should begin with the plain meaning of the text. The *plain meaning* of the text, however, is precisely what Copeland and the others do *not* give us, text after text. . . . But "plain meaning" has first of all to do with the author's original intent, it has to do with what would have been plain to those to whom the words were originally addressed. It has not to do with how someone from a suburbanized white American culture of the late 20th century reads his own cultural setting back into the text through the frequently distorted prism of the language of the early 17th century.[4]

To illustrate Fee's apprehension, a popular saying in the contemporary faith movement proclaims, "God said it; I believe it; and that settles it." That statement is true as far as it goes. But it leaves something out: what is it that God really said, and what does it mean? Often this is presumed, rather than thought through and studied exegetically. Lovett, formerly a professor at Oral Roberts University, also writes of his concern, explaining, "The problem with exponents of the Rhema [word of faith] interpretation is their biased selection of biblical passages, often without due regard to their context. The self-defined phrase 'confessing the Word of God' takes precedence over hermeneutical principles and rules for biblical interpretation. This approach not only does violence to the text but forces the NT linguistic data into artificial categories that the biblical authors themselves could not affirm."[5] Simmons concludes that the shaky hermeneutical foundation of the contemporary faith movement stems from its acknowledged founder: "In Kenyon's hands, even the texts that were a major focus of Keswickeans in general proved to be remarkably elastic. . . . Kenyon's tendency was to stretch a term or metaphor to a literal extreme that the original word or figure of speech did not intend."[6]

In addition to Kenyon's influence, Pentecostal circles generally had an aversion to formal education due to rejection of Pentecostal belief and practice by academics. As a result, some charismatic and word of faith leaders eschew theology and biblical exegesis as being traditional and not Spirit-led. James Zeigler, himself a former Rhema student and former director of the Holy Spirit Research Center at Oral Roberts University, pointed out that many of the Word of Faith teachers, not being schooled in the biblical languages, hermeneutics, and theology, rely heavily upon a literalistic rendering of the King James English version of the Bible.[7] They have mostly secondhand knowledge of Greek and Hebrew, based on helps such as *Strong's Concordance* or *Vine's Expository Dictionary, Dake's Annotated Reference Bible* and the *Amplified Bible* (which some scholars believe is deficient because it gives so many options, rather than defining a term within its context). One of my professors when I was a student at Oral Roberts University astutely remarked many years ago, "A little bit of knowledge [about Greek and Hebrew] can be a dangerous thing."

Derek Vreeland, a defender of the basic principles of contemporary faith theology, nonetheless acknowledges, "The writings of E.W. Kenyon lack theological sophistication and, in part, reveal a departure from the most sound of hermeneutical principles. However, the whole of his teachings falls within the bounds of historical orthodox Christianity, on the fringe perhaps, but still within orthodoxy."[8] Vreeland, even though a now and again supporter of contemporary faith leaders, also admits that Hagin uses a "loose pragmatic hermeneutic" and a "selective hermeneutic."[9] To illustrate this lack of theological and exegetical sophistication, a few examples of hermeneutical flaws in contemporary faith teaching include:

- Referring to Hebrews 1:6 where Jesus is called in KJV Bible "the first begotten," Copeland asserts, "He's no longer called the only begotten Son of God. He is called the first born from the dead, the first begotten of many brethren. . . . The next thing He does is include you and me in the begotten of God."[10] This appears to denigrate the deity of Christ and deify mankind. However, I do not believe Copeland is intentionally propagating heretical views here. Rather, he is showing his theological and exegetical ignorance by failing to distinguish between "first begotten" (*prototokos*—firstborn, prototype) and "only begotten" (*monogenes*—unique, one-of-kind).

- As mentioned earlier, Capps interprets Matthew 7:7 in light of his assumptions regarding other passages of Scripture, denying that it can mean to keep on asking and seeking. Ignorant of what the text really says and means in the original language, he comes to an erroneous conclusion. Barron points out correctly, "Capps's inflexibility demonstrates a major flaw in positive confession teaching: it attempts to make universal laws out of isolated texts."[11]

- Regarding Hebrews 11:1, I have several times heard contemporary faith teachers claim, "Now faith is. . .—that means faith is NOW." However, the problem with that interpretation is that the Greek word translated "now" (*de*) does not mean "now in time." Rather, it is a transitional word that can be translated, "therefore." It is valid to say that *sometimes* faith is now, but it cannot be claimed arbitrarily that faith is always now, nor can this verse legitimately be claimed as support for the teaching.

- As has been cited earlier, inferring from the wording in the KJV Bible, some contemporary faith leaders mistake the subject of Romans 4:17, believing that believers can "call those things which are not as though they are," when, in fact, God is the person being referred to in the context.

- MacGregor notes that Copeland "interprets Isaiah 40:12 in precisely the same manner as Mormon hermeneutics: 'The Bible says [God] measured out the heavens with a nine-inch span. Well . . . my span is eight and three-quarter inches long. So God's span is a quarter of an inch longer than mine. So you see . . . God . . . stands around 6'2", 6'3", weighs somewhere in the neighborhood of a couple hundred pounds, little better.'"[12] While MacGregor believes that Copeland is intentionally borrowing from Mormonism, I think it is more likely that Copeland, if he was being serious when he made the statement, was slavishly adhering to a literalistic wording of the KJV Bible, not comprehending Isaiah's hermeneutical use of anthropological metaphorical language to describe God in terms that ancient man could understand.

These are only a handful of the many erroneous interpretations pointed out by contemporary faith critics. Having pointed out these flaws, we must also recognize that Hagin before his death in 2003 acknowledged this problem in the contemporary faith movement and emphasized the need for interpreting Scripture in its context and not mistaking figurative for literal (though he needed to go farther with it).[13] It should also be noted that there are some contemporary faith leaders such as Bob Yandian and Rick Renner of Tulsa, Oklahoma, who have studied the original languages and seek to apply sound exegesis and exposition, bringing moderation to contemporary faith movement interpretation and praxis.[14]

HERMENEUTICS AND THE CLASSIC FAITH MOVEMENT

In contrast with most contemporary faith teachers, the major classic faith teachers and their predecessors, by and large, had received a scholarly theological education, as was customary at the time. Müller was a brilliant scholar, fluent in six languages, yet merged together scholarship and a vibrant faith. Wesley, Murray, Upham, Simpson, Chambers, and Torrey were all seminary-educated and studied the classical languages, such as Greek, Hebrew, and Latin. Simpson won academic awards for his scholarship. Jonathan Edwards was president of Princeton in its early days. Finney was trained in law. Torrey was highly educated as a graduate of Yale University and Yale Divinity School, and read the Bible in Greek, Hebrew, and German. Blanchard served as president of Wheaton College. Pierson wrote a book on hermeneutics.

Others who themselves were not scholars nonetheless availed themselves of academic materials and submitted and confirmed their teachings with academics. Palmer conferred with her husband who was a medical doctor and theologian. Moody became close friends with renowned professor Henry Drummond. Hannah Whitall Smith consulted pastors and theologians and pastors regarding her teachings, and wrote a booklet on interpreting the Bible. Amy Carmichael studied the Greek New Testament and scholarly reference material and commentaries. Tozer and MacMillan, though never completing high school, read voraciously the church fathers, mystics, reformers, and classical writers and theologians. MacMillan learned Greek and Hebrew through self-study, conversing with rabbis, consulting with professors, and attending college and seminary classes. Spurgeon obtained a working knowledge of Greek and Hebrew and read broadly a variety of classic writings.

Still, these classic faith leaders were not stodgy academics or ivory tower theologians who had little vital experience in a walk of faith. Rather, they walked close to God and practiced a life of daring faith, yet studied intensively, practically applied exegesis to life, and relied upon the Spirit to illuminate interpretation. Seminary-educated Murray counseled both the need for study and for revelation, saying, "As all the Word of God is given by the Spirit of God, each word must be interpreted to us by that same Spirit."[15] Simpson was concerned with grammatical-historical hermeneutics, but also perceived that God had provided much divine symbolism in Scripture: "It would be a great mistake to read the Bible only symbolically. But it is beautiful to see hidden truths beneath the history."[16] This is not to say that classic faith writers all had interpretations that would be accepted by scholarship today or that they would always agree with one another's interpretations in all matters.

REFLECTIONS AND CONCLUSIONS

Spirit-guided revelation and hermeneutics are not mutually exclusive entities that oppose each other. Again, this is not a case of "either-or" but "both-and," two polarities that are maintained in dynamic tension in the elliptical nature of truth. Scholarship and Spirit-led knowledge go hand-in-hand. Exegetical and hermeneutical study provides the banks needed to contain and maintain the flow of the river of God's Spirit. This is not to say that a person must be a scholar to be used by God or to hear from God. Moody, Wigglesworth, Tozer, MacMillan had not completed a high school education yet were greatly used by God and received genuine insights from God. Tozer stressed the need to be not just Bible taught, but Spirit taught.[17] Torrey, though a Yale graduate, did not denigrate lack of education. He too understood that a person may be well-educated but not Spirit-taught: "Prayer will do more than a theological education to make the Bible an open book. Only a man of prayer can understand the Bible."[18] Torrey balanced human education with divine education:

> The man who can be most fully taught of God is the one who will be most ready to listen to what God has taught others. . . . But we should not be dependent on them, even though we can learn much from them. We have a divine teacher: the Holy Spirit. We will never truly know the truth until we are taught by Him. No amount of mere human teaching, no matter who our teachers may be, will give us a correct understanding of the truth. Not even a diligent study of the Word, either in the English or in the original languages, will give us a real understanding of the truth. We must be taught by the Holy Spirit.
>
> The one who is thus taught, even if he does not know a word of Greek or Hebrew, will understand the truth of God better than someone who does know the original languages, but who is not taught by the Spirit. The Spirit will guide the one He teaches "into all truth"—not in a day, a week, or a year, but one step at a time.[19]

There is a need, therefore, on the one hand, for contemporary faith teachers to accept, learn and apply sound principles of hermeneutics, and, on the other hand, for those from a non-charismatic background to recognize that God does speak to people today and give special insight—whether it is called revelation or illumination or whatever. Those of us who are evangelical and/or charismatic scholars need to be open for the Holy Spirit to give new insights and fresh application to Scripture.

Contemporary faith people need to be willing to submit all supposed revelations to the tools of sound hermeneutics. (I once had a friend and colleague who was a Christian education director in a church where I was serving as assistant pastor. She often received insights into the Scriptures that could be described as revelations. However, since she had not studied the Bible in the original languages, she would come to me and say, "I believe God is saying to me that this passage means _____. Does this square with the Greek or the Hebrew?"). I would recommend this approach to contemporary faith leaders. Whenever they believe they have received a special revelation from God, it would be biblical and appropriate to submit it for confirmation to scholars of like mind who are open to the realm of the supernatural—for instance, professors at charismatic or Pentecostal colleges and seminaries—like Oral Roberts University, Regent University, Assemblies of God Theological Seminary, Church of God Theological Seminary, etc., or Pentecostal/charismatic scholars at other evangelical seminaries, such as Gordon Fee and Wayne Grudem.

Ultimately, Tozer's "two-wing" principle is needed in the issues of faith and hermeneutics to maintain a healthy tension of the contrapolarities. A.J. Gordon cited William Lincoln's insightful commentary on the need for balancing polarities of truth: "The only way for a believer, if he wants to go rightly, is to remember that truth is always two-sided. If there is any truth that the Holy Ghost has impressed upon your heart, if you do not want to push it to the extreme, ask what is the counter-truth, and lean a little of your weight upon that; otherwise, if you bear so very much on one side of the truth, there is a danger of pushing it into a heresy. Heresy means selected truth; it does not mean error: heresy and error are very different things. Heresy is truth; but truth pushed into undue importance to the disparagement of the truth on the other side."[20] I once heard Dr. Costa Deir, Dean of Elim Bible Institute, a Pentecostal school, proclaim this balance in a perceptive motto: "It is good to be highly educated; it is better to be educated from on High; it is best to be both."

ONLY BELIEVE

1. Fee, 3.

2. James W. Sire, *Scripture Twisting: 20 Ways the Cults Misread the Bible* (Downers Grove, Ill.: InterVarsity, 1980).

3. Kenneth Copeland, cited in Fee, 3.

4. Ibid., 3, 4.

5. L. Lovett, "Positive Confession Theology," *DPCM*, 720.

6. Simmons, *E.W. Kenyon*, 108.

7. Personal conversation with Zeigler, Tulsa, Okla., 1997. See also Vreeland, "Reconstructing Word of Faith Theology," 13.

8. Vreeland, 5.

9. Ibid., 12, 19. In fairness to Hagin, it should be noted that his most recent book, *The Midas Touch*, does show more concern for sound hermeneutics.

10. Kenneth Copeland, "The Prayer of Binding and Loosing," sound recording. Ft. Worth, Tex.: KCP Publications, 1987.

11. Barron, 102.

12. MacGregor, 89.

13. Hagin, *The Midas Touch*, 147, 150-153, 161.

14. I have heard Renner admit publicly, "We faith people have done some crazy things," and then proceed to teach a balanced approach to faith.

15. Murray, *The Spirit of Christ*, 162.

16. A.B. Simpson, *Divine Emblems* (Camp Hill, Penn.: Christian Publications, 1995), n.p.

17. A.W. Tozer, *The Root of the Righteous* (Camp Hill, Penn.: Christian Publications, [1955] 1986), 34-37.

18. R.A. Torrey, *How to Obtain Fullness of Power* (New Kensington, Penn.: Whitaker, [1982] 1984), 77-78.

19. Ibid., 51. Simmons (*E.W. Kenyon*, 93-94), however, misunderstands Torrey's statement as an anti-intellectual claim for not needing hermeneutics, perhaps not realizing that Torrey himself was a scholar and had studied biblical criticism at a German university.

20. A.J. Gordon, *The Ministry of Healing*, 261-262.

CHAPTER 25

━━━━◆·◆━━━━

Failures and Limitations of Faith

THE QUESTION OF FAILURE DUE TO SIN, UNBELIEF, OR WRONG CONFESSION

Hagin asserts, "We fail many times because we get ready to fail. We prepare for failure. We think it, believe it, and do it. But we as believers should never talk failure, doubt, or unbelief. We should talk faith. If you are defeated, you are defeated with your own lips."[1] That statement is true as far as it goes. Yes, people often do fail due to negativism or a self-fulfilling prophecy. Yet this statement cannot be absolute. A person may take a step in faith, and failure may still result. A person may pray, believe, and confess in faith, and healing still may not come. Kydd observes that Oral Roberts acknowledges this.[2] So Hagin, in this instance, contradicts Roberts and classic faith teaching, and thus errs when he says, "You *always* get and have in your life what you believe for and say."[3]

Hagin also claims, "You can have what you say."[4] Yes, that is true to an extent, but again it is not an absolute. You cannot have what you say if it is not God's sovereign will. You cannot have what you say if you have mixed motives. You cannot have what you say if you are being self-centered. Hagin's view is similar to conventional wisdom, which Fee argues is fallible:

> Conventional wisdom sees life always in terms of *quid pro quo*, one thing in return for another. For every evil, there is a direct, specific cause. . . . And for every good, especially every material blessing, there is also a direct specific cause. . . . But conventional wisdom is not biblical. Even though there are

special times when God does protect his own, it is clear from the whole of Scripture that *both* the rain *and* the hail fall on the just and the unjust alike. . . . The Fall has so permeated the created order that all people are affected by its consequences; and God has revealed Himself as abounding in mercy—even to the sinner.[5]

Thus, it is appropriate to acknowledge that *sometimes* sin or lack of faith or negative confession may indeed be involved in failure to receive a healing or answer to prayer. However, it needs also to be acknowledged that in many cases these factors are not responsible for the failure. As seen in this study, classic faith leaders recognized that apparent failures of faith may be due to many reasons.

ADDITIONAL REASONS FOR UNANSWERED PRAYER OR LACK OF HEALING

Delay for the purpose of growth and holiness. Contrary to some contemporary faith teaching, as I have noted in Chapter 22, lack of healing may be a part of the sanctification process. As Simpson remarked, even for the spiritual there may be "a deeper spiritual discipline."[6] Healing or answers to prayer may be delayed in order to bring about growth in the believer's life, even when there is no overt sin or unbelief. As mentioned earlier, Murray noted the connection that the more believers personally experience sanctification by faith, the more they also receive healing by faith.[7]

The sovereignty of God. While it is a general principle that God desires to heal and answer prayer, as pointed out earlier, classic faith leaders perceived that the sovereignty of God is a crucial factor in the answering of prayer. Faith healer Charles Price recognized that sometimes God knows better than we do in not answering our prayers: "More than once I have tried to exercise faith and have struggled to obtain an answer to my prayer only to find in the light of succeeding events that it were better by far to have that prayer unanswered. That is why God deals to every man the measure of faith that he needs to walk in harmony with the divine will. Beyond that point faith will not be imparted."[8] Kydd notes that Oral Roberts similarly oscillates between the poles of the certainty of healing and the sovereignty of God, maintaining the dynamic tension that keeps the two poles in balance.[9]

Faith has not been imparted by God. Trusting in one's own faith or another's faith or word, rather than receiving assurance or a touch from God can also be a reason for unanswered prayer. As mentioned in Chapter 10, classic faith leaders cautioned against acting on others' faith or word, or trying to prove faith. Referring to Matthew 9:20-21, Simpson counseled, "We cannot take the Lord's healing till we have this sense of spiritual touch."[10] Müller testified that it would be great presumption to get out of bed when severely ill if the Lord had not given him the faith to do it. A special gift or word of faith is needed. The key to praying in faith is seeking the Lord and knowing His express will in the situation. Such prayer is "prayer in the Spirit." Charles Price had a powerful healing ministry in which thousands were healed, but he also testified of times the Lord did not give him faith to heal.[11] S.D. Gordon answered the question, "How far may Christ's healing be expected?" by replying, "We may have all we can take, as His Spirit guides our taking."[12] Some contemporary faith teachers would claim the first part of Gordon's statement, "We may have all we can take," but they tend to leave off or de-emphasize the second part, which is the pivotal qualifier: "as His Spirit guides our taking."

Related to this, some people try to exercise more faith than they have or have been given. Carmichael also demonstrated this principle of faith: exercise the measure of faith God gives, then God will increase that measure of faith. She began by praying for one person to be converted, then a month later for two persons, then two weeks later for four persons, then several weeks later for eight persons. In each case, though others balked and doubted, God honored her faith and obedience, and granted the number of "souls" each time that He had impressed on her heart through "an irresistible divine pressure."[13] This is what Rosalind Rinker calls praying "faith-sized prayers."[14]

God has not promised what has been prayed. Some may expect more than God promises in this life. As noted earlier, Simpson avowed that God never promised that there would be no disease. He advised, "The Word places a limit to human life, and all that Scriptural faith can claim is sufficiency of health and strength for our life-work and within its fair limits."[15] While believers can claim inheritance in Christ, full inheritance or healing is not obtainable in this life.

A PROPER ATTITUDE TOWARD FAILURES OF FAITH

A person who is not healed or whose prayer is not answered should not be put down or made to feel guilty. Carter, who at one time held more extreme views, admonished, "No Christian should allow the Adversary to whip him because he is not healed, when he is conscious of a perfect acquiescence in the will of God."[16] Hannah Whitall Smith did not berate a person for lack of faith, but maintained that every believer has some faith, and can exercise that faith: "If you are a child of God at all, you must have at least as much faith as a grain of mustard seed, and therefore you dare not say again that you 'cannot trust because you have no faith.' Say rather, 'I can trust my Lord, and I will trust Him; and not all the powers of earth or hell shall be able to make me doubt my wonderful, glorious, faithful redeemer!'"[17]

Even if someone does lack in faith, that person should not feel guilty or be made to feel guilty. Seventeenth-century Puritan leader William Gurnall, in his classic writing *The Christian in Complete Armour*, assured the believer, "God accepts your weak faith."[18] Speaking out of the experience of his own life, Spurgeon, this great man of faith, acknowledged that sometimes he was weak in faith: "Faith is weakness clinging to strength and becoming strong in so doing."[19] Even in the midst of great bouts of depression and sickness, he found strength in the little faith he had. Influenced by Puritan thought, Spurgeon thus exhorts that even the weak in faith are not to be criticized, but encouraged that their small measure of faith can be effective:

> Faith exists in varying degrees according to the amount of knowledge or other causes. Sometimes faith is little more than a simple clinging to Christ in a sense of utter dependence. Thousands of God's people have no more faith than this. They know enough to cling to Jesus with all their heart and soul. Jesus Christ is to them a Savior strong and mighty, like an immovable, immutable rock. They cling to Him for dear life, and this clinging saves them. God gives to His people the propensity to cling. Though this is a very simple sort of faith, it is a very complete and effectual form of it. In fact, it is the heart of all faith, and that to which we are often driven when we are in deep trouble or when our mind is somewhat bemuddled by sickness or depression in spirit. We can cling when we can do nothing else, and that is the very soul of faith. Always cling to what you know. . . . Cling to Jesus, for that is faith.[20]

Moreover, Spurgeon did not berate people for their lack of faith, but rather encouraged them, "However feeble our faith may be, if it is real faith in Christ, we will reach heaven at last. . . . Your little faith has made you completely clean. You have as much right to the precious things of the covenant as the most advanced believers, for your right to covenant mercies lies not in your growth but in the covenant itself. . . . Am I poor in faith? Still in Jesus I am heir of all things."[21] This is healthy faith counsel for those who feel they may be inadequate in faith.

1. Kenneth E. Hagin, *You Can Have What You Say* (Tulsa, Okla.: Kenneth Hagin Ministries, 1979), 10.

2. Kydd, 204-211.

3. Hagin, *You Can Have What You Say*, 5. Italics mine.

4. Ibid., cover page.

5. Fee, 6-7.

6. Simpson, *The Gospel of Healing*, 64.

7. Murray, *Divine Healing,* 13.

8. Charles Price, *The Real Faith*, 90.

9. Kydd, 204-211.

10. Simpson, *CITB* (1992), 4:43.

11. Charles Price, *The Real Faith*, 91.

12. S.D. Gordon, *The Healing Christ*, 90.

13. Elliot, 91-93.

14. Rosalind Rinker, *How To Get the Most Out of Your Prayer Life* (Eugene, Ore.: Harvest House, 1981), 124-140.

15. Simpson, *The Gospel of Healing*, 64.

16. Carter, *Faith Healing Reviewed*, 91.

17. Smith, *The Christian's Secret*, 55.

18. Gurnall, Jan. 13.

19. Spurgeon, *The Triumph of Faith in a Believer's Life*, 87.

20. Ibid., 26.

21. Spurgeon, *Morning By Morning*, 80, 295.

CHAPTER 26

Claiming Inheritance or
Dying to Self: Theology of Glory
or Theology of the Cross?

Several years ago I read St. John of the Cross on mortification of self
and at the same time read Robert Schuller on self-esteem. I learned
from both, even though the writings of these two authors are poles apart.
Both teach elements of truth, but both represent opposite extremes. The
dynamic tension of the counter-polarities needs to be kept in balance. If
self-esteem is taught without the cross, the believer's thought and practice are skewed and become egocentric. If death to self is taught without
understanding the believer's exalted position in Christ, the believer's
thought and practice are again skewed and susceptible to self-centered
spiritual flagellation. The key to healthy Christian living and faith is to
hold these two truths in balance.[1] However, in relation to faith teaching,
claiming the believer's inheritance would seem to be at odds with dying to one's self. How can the two seemingly contradictory concepts be
reconciled?

In reality, healthy faith must maintain a healthy blend of both dying to self and claiming the rights and privileges of the believer. The
message of the crucified life is the one element often missing from contemporary faith teaching and practice, thus breaking down the dynamic
tension. Hagin does not negate the cross, but believes it has been over-
emphasized to the neglect of the abundant life in Christ: "The trouble
with us is that we have preached a 'cross' religion, and we need a 'throne'
religion. . . . The cross is actually a place of defeat, whereas the Resurrection is a place of triumph. When you preach the cross, you are preaching

death, and you leave people in death. We died all right, but we're raised with Christ."[2] The classic faith leaders of the Keswick and Higher Life movements would agree that we need a throne religion, but not to the neglect of the cross. Without the cross life the emphasis on obtaining the promised blessings of God is out of balance and susceptible to egocentricism and distortion.

Martin Luther distinguished a theology of glory (*theologia gloria*) from a theology of the cross (*theologia crucis*). The theology of glory "is concerned primarily with God and his glory, whereas the other sees God as hidden in his suffering."[3] According to Luther, man prefers the theology of glory or triumphalism because it exalts man: "He prefers works to suffering, glory to the cross, strength to weakness, wisdom to folly, and in general, good to evil."[4] In contrast, the emphasis of the New Testament exalts the humbling of Christ and denial of self: "Have this attitude in yourselves which was also in Christ Jesus, who, although He existed in the form of God, did not consider equality with God a thing to be grasped, but emptied Himself, taking the form of a bondservant, and being made in the likeness of men. And being found in appearance as a man, He humbled himself by becoming obedient to the point of death, even death on a cross" (Phil. 2:5-8).

Luther further declared, in contrast to some contemporary faith thought, that "God can only be found in suffering and the cross. . . . Therefore the friends of the cross say that the cross is good and works are evil, for through the cross works are dethroned and the old Adam, who is especially edified by works, is crucified. It is impossible for a person not to be puffed up by his good works unless he has first been deflated and destroyed by suffering and evil until he knows that he is worthless and that his works are not his but God's."[5] Other mystics likewise emphasized the life of the cross. Fenelon avowed, "We are nothing without the cross."[6] Thomas a Kempis likewise observed centuries ago, "The Lord has many lovers of His crown but few lovers of His cross."[7]

One of the men of the group of the "Friends of God," Nicholas of Basle, counseled John Tauler, "You must die, Dr. Tauler! Before you can do your greatest work for God, the world, and this city, you must die to yourself, your gifts, your popularity, and even your own goodness, and when you have learned the full meaning of the Cross you will have new power with God and man."[8] As mentioned in Chapter 1, Luther was influenced by Tauler and the *Theologia Germanica*. Because he became willing to die to himself, Tauler did indeed gain new power with God and man, having great impact on Luther and the Reformation.

Bounds follows these classic writers, saying, "All God's plans have the mark of the cross on them, and all His plans have death to self in them."[9] Tozer, speaking as a twentieth century prophet, declares that the same is true of this century, saying, "We do not want the cross. We are more interested in the crown."[10] This is true of much of evangelicalism, and especially of some in the contemporary faith movement who teach a triumphalistic theology of glory with its emphasis on having faith in one's own faith and claiming the rights, privileges, and authority of being a child of God or a "King's Kid." Classic faith teachers such as Simpson also emphasized the rights, privileges and authority of a believer, but with one crucial difference: they taught self-denial and the cross life—a theology of the cross. Simpson wrote, "How very much of the life of faith consists in simply denying ourselves."[11]

Charles Price noted the role of the cross in healing: "We have found that a broken spirit and a contrite heart and a feeling of unworthiness is generally an assurance of faith enough for healing, while on the other hand many people lose the blessing because they feel they are entitled to it."[12] Further, Price explained, "Faith must walk down the vales of self-abasement and humiliation in order that it might climb the mountain of divine revelation that is on the other side."[13] A.J. Gordon quoted faith healing pioneer Johann Christoph Blumhardt saying, "The way to have a strong faith is to think nothing of yourself."[14]

While I have disagreed with several of the assessments of Hunt and McConnell in this study, I would agree with their concern about the lack of emphasis in contemporary faith teaching (and much evangelical teaching as well) and practice on the crucified life. McConnell remarks that contemporary faith teaching and practice, especially regarding prosperity, "subverts the demands of the cross for self denial."[15] Though he paints the contemporary faith movement with too broad a stroke, nonetheless, there is an element of truth in his criticism. Hunt correctly and perceptively observes, "Were Andrew Murray alive today, he would vehemently disagree with the new self-centered gospel."[16] In contrast to much contemporary faith teaching, Murray taught, "Our lesson of today leads us to the very deepest roots of the life of faith. The deeper we are willing to enter into the death of self, the more shall we know of the mighty power of God, and the perfect blessedness of a perfect trust."[17] Murray believed in claiming the believer's covenant rights, but he also stressed that death to self must be at the roots of any covenant claims, writing further, "Selfishness is the death of faith. . . . Let us cease seeking faith in our own interest."[18]

Some contemporary faith teachers tend to imply that we can demand our rights from God. Biblical psychologists Larry Crabb and Dan Allender recognize that this problem is not confined to contemporary faith teaching: "The classic error of this culture: Demanding heaven now through some methodology or some person."[19] Classic faith teachers (and some contemporary faith teachers) agree we can demand of Satan, but, in contrast, we cannot demand from God. Wheaton College president Blanchard wrote a book on principles of faith and prayer entitled *Getting Things from God* that sounds similar to Hagin's *Write Your Own Ticket with God*. However, they are far apart in their theology. Blanchard wrote: "God takes no instructions from men. God does not permit men to give Him orders."[20] Likewise, in a similarly titled book, *Harnessing God*, Rader assures that believers cannot harness God, but as believers walk in faith and obedience, God puts Himself at their disposal so that they can harness the power of God.[21] Chambers asks the pivotal question: "Is the Son of God praying in me or am I dictating to Him?"[22] Chambers was not against claiming God's promises,[23] yet he exhorted, "But if you are living the life of faith you will exercise your right to waive your rights, and let God choose for you."[24] Yes, believers can claim their inheritance in Christ, but they will always be willing to exercise their right to waive their rights for God's sake. This is a healthy faith.

---

1. John Calvin discusses both mortification of the flesh *and* vivification of the Spirit in his *Institutes of the Christian Religion* ([Grand Rapids: Eerdmans, 1949], Vol. 1, Book 3, chap. 3:3), 651-654. He thus maintains more of a terminological balance than his contemporary, John of the Cross.

2. Hagin, *The Believer's Authority*, 16.

3. Gonzalez, *A History of Christian Thought*, 3:35. Luther vilified the theology of glory, referring to the Roman Catholic Church and scholastic theologians who taught a triumphalistic doctrine of glory.

4. Ibid.

5. Ibid.

6. Fenelon, 5.

7. Thomas a Kempis, cited in A.W. Tozer, *Men Who Met God* (Camp Hill, Penn.: Christian Publications, 1986), 115.

8. Meyer, *Five Musts of the Christian Life*, 41.

9. Dorsett, 213.

10. Tozer, *Men Who Met God*, 115.

11. Simpson, *Days of Heaven on Earth*, Oct. 19.

12. Charles Price, *And Signs Followed*, 129.

13. Charles Price, *The Meaning of Faith*, 43.

14. A.J. Gordon, *The Ministry of Healing*, 159.

15. McConnell, 180.

16. Hunt, *Beyond Seduction*, 163.

17. Andrew Murray, "Faith Counting on the Power of God," *Triumphs of Faith*, Nov. 1934, 243.

18. Murray, *The Holiest of All*, 467-468.

19. Larry Crabb and Dan B. Allender, *Hope When You're Hurting* (Grand Rapids: Zondervan, 1996), 132.

20. Blanchard, 134.

21. Paul Rader, *Harnessing God* (New York: George H. Doran Co., 1926), 16.

22. Chambers, *My Utmost for His Highest*, 221.

23. Ibid., 78, 322.

24. Ibid., 304.

CHAPTER 27

Summary of Healthy Practical Faith Principles for Today

This study has investigated nineteenth and twentieth century principles and practices of faith and their origins and development from
the Church Fathers, mystics, reformers, Pietists, Puritans, and the Wesleyan movement. It has been my thesis that we can glean healthy faith
principles and praxis from the teachings and practices of classic faith
leaders, principles and practices that are healthy because they are both
biblically sound and encourage strong development and exercise of
faith. I conclude that the following principles, adapted primarily from
classic faith leaders, constitute sound and strong faith praxis:

1. *Healthy faith believes in the reality of the supernatural both in the
Scriptures and in Christian life today.* Belief in the supernatural is
necessary for a strong and sound faith. Practice of the supernatural
should be encouraged, with the caution for need of discernment between what is of God, of the flesh, and of demonic origin.

2. *Healthy faith believes that Christians are in covenant relationship
with God and that there are rights and privileges as an inheritance
of that covenant.* Believers do not receive their full inheritance in
this life, but there are many more of the blessings of the covenant
that can be inherited in this life than are experienced by most Christians. Practically speaking, believers can and ought to claim their
inheritance, understanding that it must not be done with selfish motives.

3. As a corollary to the covenant inheritance of the Christian, *healthy faith understands that the believer can exercise spiritual authority on the basis of his position in Christ.* The believer has been given authority in the name of Jesus Christ over the dark powers and does not have to live a life of misery and defeat. That authority is delegated by Christ, not transferred. The believer can exercise that spiritual authority to overcome the influence and harassment of demonic powers through anger, fear, depression, sickness, physical endangerment, hindrances to evangelism, demonic oppression and control. Such authority can free people from bondage, open locked doors to evangelism and missions, and influence world events. Means of exercising such spiritual authority include persevering prayer, binding and loosing, speaking with commanding faith. Care must be taken not to abuse and misuse the believer's authority, recognizing that exercise of such authority must be in God's will and ultimately under God's control and sanction. Commanding in faith does not mean dictating to God.

4. *Healthy faith recognizes faith as a spiritual law and force that operates like natural laws, often as a cause-and-effect relationship in which acting and speaking in faith becomes a force that can set in motion other operations and effects, but also are not impersonal laws or forces, or mechanistic formulas that even non-believers can manipulate to get what one wants.* The laws of faith and force can only be exercised by believers in the will of God. God is not bound by these laws, for they find their source in His nature. God is always sovereign, transcending the laws He has placed in operation.

5. *Healthy faith is always primarily faith in God, not in one's self, one's own faith, or even in the Bible.* The object of faith is God, and the source of faith is always from God. Faith does not heal, but rather God. God is always the source of healing, faith is the agent or conduit of healing. Believers should have faith in the Bible as the Word of God, but this is secondary to faith in Christ. A believer can exercise the faith of God, that is the faith that is from God, that is His faithfulness, that is His own faith rooted in His omnipotence, that is a special mountain-moving faith. Such faith is not developed, but is imparted by God as a special higher level of faith. However, as a believer exercises the faith that he has, greater faith will be imparted to him.

6. *Healthy faith seeks the will of God and exercises faith based on an assurance from God.* When people do not know the will of God, they can pray, "If it be Your will," but it must not become an excuse for not knowing the will of God. When the will of God is known, praying "if it be Your will," is inappropriate and can hinder faith from being exercised. As a general principle, it is God's desire to heal, so that one can pray in faith for healing, unless God reveals otherwise. It must not be assumed that it is not God's will to heal, nor should it be assumed that in every case healing is God's will.

7. *Healthy faith recognizes that God does give a rhema, a leading of the Spirit, or fresh word from God, an assurance or special word of faith.* One cannot speak something into becoming a *rhema*, but one can confess the Word of God until God makes it a *rhema*, turning a written word of God into the living Word of God. In such a case, the word becomes alive, takes on new meaning and insight and becomes powerful and effective. Many steps of faith, such as abandoning medicine, should not be taken without receiving this special assurance from God. Caution should be taken in accepting all such impressions as a special word from the Lord.

8. *Healthy faith recognizes that revelation knowledge that comes from God through faith can be distinguished from sense knowledge that comes from the senses and the mind. God intends that revelation knowledge and sense knowledge be used hand-in-hand, not pitting one against the other.* Believers should use their senses, but ultimately depend on revelation of God's Word from the Holy Spirit. Satan can deceive the senses, so caution must be taken in accepting the signals of the senses. By the same token, revelation knowledge must be discerned, and believers must never become elitist, believing that they have superior knowledge than others.

9. *Healthy faith believes that healing is a provision of the atonement, thus, a person can rightly pray and believe for healing.* At the same time, it understands that *total* healing in this life is not a provision of the atonement, any more than complete sanctification can be obtained in this life. Healthy faith also always leaves room for the sovereignty of God.

10. *Healthy faith recognizes that the baptism or filling with the Holy Spirit that involves an empowering and intensive sanctifying is a valid spiritual experience, often occurring subsequent to conversion. Spiritual gifts or supernatural manifestations, such as speaking in tongues, may accompany such an experience, but since faith is the evidence, no physical manifestation is necessary as an evidence.* Those receiving this experience of the Spirit must be careful not to have an elitist attitude.

11. *Healthy faith recognizes the need for a positive mental attitude and an atmosphere of faith.* Attitudes of fear, doubt, or anxiety can have a negative effect upon one's faith, spiritual and emotional life, and health. One must be careful, however, not to adopt humanistic or New Age types of emphasis on PMA (positive mental attitude). A sanctified, Spirit-controlled imagination can be of great benefit, but humanistic and occultic types of imagineering and visualization must be avoided.

12. *Healthy faith maintains, along with PMA, that positive confession of the Word and truths of God is necessary, but this does not mean that believers can name and claim or confess and possess anything they want.* A person's words are not spiritual containers by which believers can speak things into existence. Just repeating words over and over again will not have spiritual effect unless they are coming from the heart and led by the Spirit of God. It is God that causes an effect through the believer's confession of faith, not the believer or his words themselves. Healthy faith does not become legalistically paranoid about speaking negatively, but is careful to maintain a consistently positive confession.

13. *Healthy faith recognizes that there is a time to pray once and a time to pray many times.* It perseveres through repeated prayer, but recognizes that when God gives assurance of the answer, there is no need to continue praying, but rather to start praising.

14. *Healthy faith may use a point of contact as an aid or stimulant to faith, but must not regard such contacts as fetishes, mediums, or magical actions.* No point of contact is effective unless it is accompanied by faith, and God is at work.

15. *Healthy faith accepts that God does communicate with believers through impressions and various types of revelation.* However, it also recognizes that impressions and supposed insights can also come from the flesh and even from Satan. Thus it is vital to exercise discernment and judge the impression through the Scriptures, circumstances, inner witness of the Spirit, sanctified reason, and the counsel of others.

16. *Healthy faith recognizes that God does sometimes heal supernaturally without medicine, but the believer does not abandon the use of medical means unless receiving a special assurance of faith from God to do so.* One should not feel guilty or be made to feel guilty for making use of doctors and medicine. Medical care and prayer can go hand-in-hand in God's plan to bring about healing.

17. *Healthy faith recognizes that as a general principle and ideal God gives a person seventy to eighty years of life, but it does not dogmatically assert that God promises at least seventy years.* God in His sovereign purposes may have designed a shorter life span for some. The classic teaching is that "a man is immortal until his work is done." No one should be berated for lack of faith or sin due to dying younger, or dying of an illness. There is a time to die, even of an illness, and a person can die with dignity, not fear, doubt, or guilt. Those who exercise a healing ministry, but who die younger or who are not healed should not be regarded as suspect, unless they are claiming something beyond healthy faith.

18. *Healthy faith recognizes that God desires believers to be healthy and does not cause sickness, except in rare cases of punishment.* However, it also recognizes that God often uses sickness to produce sanctification and spiritual maturity. God desires wholeness for the whole person, but especially for the spirit. Often growth in holiness precedes healing.

19. *Healthy faith recognizes that God does want His people to prosper, yet also acknowledges that prosperity does not necessarily mean wealth, but rather supply of all needs (not desires).* Seeking prosperity for one's self is an impure motive. God often desires that believers practice self-denial as a prelude to genuine prosperity. Believers

can prosper by giving generously beyond their tithe, practicing the principle of sowing and reaping.

20. *Healthy faith accurately handles the Scriptures as the Word of God, being careful to interpret them in proper context and balance with other Scriptures, and submitting all revelation knowledge to the Scriptures.* Sound hermeneutics and sound counsel from Spirit-led theologians can help to provide that balance for sound faith theology and practice.

21. *Healthy faith does not berate a person for apparent failures of unanswered prayer, but rather gives encouragement to faith.*

22. *Healthy faith recognizes that although believers have covenant rights, they willingly lay those rights at the foot of the cross, seeking God for His ultimate and best will.*

CHAPTER 28

Final Conclusions and Recommendations

THE NEED FOR BALANCE AND MODERATION

I would conclude that both contemporary faith teaching and its anti-faith critics are a "mixed bag," because both propagate elements of truth and both propagate elements of error. However, classic faith teaching and practice sometimes sides with contemporary faith teaching and practice, sometimes with contemporary faith critics, and sometimes with neither. I have affirmed that while there is error in the contemporary faith movement, yet much of what they teach is sound and based on classic faith teachings. I have pointed out both where contemporary teaching is in agreement with healthy classic faith teaching, and also where contemporary faith teaching has departed from healthy classic faith teaching. The positions of these classic faith leaders usually demonstrate a equilibrium that would be neither uncritically accepting of contemporary faith teaching, nor totally rejecting contemporary faith teaching.

The classic faith leaders, for the most part, show us the need for balance and moderation to achieve a healthy faith that is both strong and sound. As Spurgeon wrote, "The man believes one doctrine, perhaps, and that is so delightful that it swallows up every other. Then he gets hold of another, and he swings that way like a pendulum; no doctrine can be true but that one. Perhaps in a little time he swings back like a pendulum the other way. He is unsteady because, while his faith perceives the truth, it does not perceive the harmonies of truth. . . . He is half-blind, and cannot see far."[1]

Surprisingly, there are key similarities between contemporary faith leaders and their critics. Both have valid points, but take their positions to extremes. Both extremes have painted in broad brush strokes with absolutes, no middle ground, leaving room for no exceptions. Ironically, faith critics sometimes tend to do the same thing as contemporary faith leaders—using and quoting material of writers, ignoring context when it suits their purpose and ignoring other teaching when it does not fit into their system or argument. For instance, we have seen that contemporary faith teachers often cite classic faith leaders like Müller, Spurgeon, Simpson, Murray, MacMillan, McCrossan, Bosworth, etc. Faith critics fail to acknowledge classic faith influence on contemporary faith teaching. Just as some contemporary faith leaders have sometimes exercised selectivity in their choice of texts, and ignoring or rationalizing problem texts that do not fit their assumptions, so have some of contemporary faith critics. The problem, for instance, with Hunt is selective use of Tozer and Murray; with Hanegraaff is selective use of Kenyon, Hagin, and others. MacArthur and Hunt approvingly quote Tozer, but both criticize mysticism, which Tozer supports. Vreeland points out, "McConnell's inaccurate reading of Hagin's writings is an attempt to justify his own faulty historical analysis from Hagin's theology."[2] Such inaccuracies have had the practical consequences of stifling the genuine and healthy exercise of faith.

Both sides have often lacked discernment. Some contemporary faith critics have so focused on apparent bad theology among contemporary faith leaders that they have failed to discern the wheat from among the tares. They tend to regard all faith teaching as tares. Contemporary faith leaders have tended to do the opposite: failing to discern the tares in their own genuine wheat. While some books have engaged in a polemic against the contemporary faith movement, this study has sought practically to separate the wheat from the tares, to glean what is good and true from the contemporary faith movement and sweep away the chaff, to retain the nourishing meat of truth and spit out the bones. Both contemporary faith leaders and their faith critics need to read carefully these classic faith writers and retain their balance. Both need Tozer's two wings to make their truths fly, to maintain the dynamic tension of the polarities of truth.

Some of the scholarly charismatics who maintain a healthy faith balance, more in the classic faith tradition, include Wimber, Blue, and MacNutt.[3] It must be acknowledged that some contemporary faith teachers have modified their views or written clarifications of what they believe in order to stem radical beliefs and practices. Frederick Price, in his book *Faith, Foolishness, or Presumption*, addresses some extreme practices of faith, though he retains several questionable teachings as well. The book *Another Look at Faith* by Kenneth Hagin, Jr., more recently addressed some of the wrong conceptions, even contradicting his father's earlier statement that faith is a formula.[4] The more recent book by Kenneth E. Hagin (Sr.), *The Midas Touch*, restores much balance to contemporary faith teaching, especially in the area of prosperity, though he needs to address additional issues.

RECOMMENDATIONS TO CONTEMPORARY FAITH LEADERS AND FOLLOWERS

Do not disparage theology. Grenz and Olson, in their book *Who Needs Theology?*, note that fact that every believer is really a theologian—by definition, someone who thinks and teaches about God.[5] Thus every believer, not just a professional academic, is either a good theologian (thinking and teaching appropriately about God) or a bad theologian. Some of the movement's own critics are fellow charismatic and Pentecostal theologians who are on their side. Vreeland, who identifies himself as a part of the contemporary faith camp, nevertheless advocates "reconstructing" word of faith theology, retaining basic, sound principles, but abandoning or modifying some of its teachings.[6]

Do not disdain all "old" teaching as antiquated tradition. There is an old black Pentecostal preacher, known as "Mother Tucker," who for fifty years has been the Mother Teresa of Tulsa, Oklahoma, with her ministry to the poor and homeless.[7] She once spoke a word to a group of charismatic pastors that was really prophetic: "Everyone is looking for new revelation and God's new thing, but the Scripture says, 'Thus saith the Lord, Stand ye in the ways, and see, and ask for the old paths, where is the good way, and walk therein, and ye shall find rest for your souls.' (Jer. 6:16, KJV)." Some contemporary faith teachers have taken old principles of faith, modified them, and sometimes strayed from sound teaching and practice. In the name of innovation and new revelation, they have in some ways abandoned the old paths. They need to stand at the crossroads and ask for the ancient paths where the good way is, and walk in it, to heed the sound teachings and examples of the classic men and women of faith.

Be humble and teachable (as should their critics, and all Christians). Contemporary faith leaders especially need to be willing to sit down with charismatic and Pentecostal theologians of like mind, and have their teachings evaluated for soundness. Even if they believe they have revelation from the Lord, they need voluntarily to have it checked out and verified for theological, exegetical and hermeneutical soundness. Peter received revelation that Jesus was the Messiah, but shortly afterwards was deceived by Satan and rebuked by Jesus. No leaders, however great our anointing and walk with God, or how astute our education, are immune from error. If leaders in the charismatic and contemporary faith movements would be more self-critical, they would receive less criticism from non-charismatics.

Accordingly, *leaders need to be willing to admit and recant errors in theology and practice, while holding on to the nuggets of truth of faith,* publicly, both in written and oral form. Peter humbled himself and received rebuke from Paul, the junior apostle (Gal. 2:11-14). Some leaders have done this, but more needs to be done.

Teachers need to be careful what words they use, and what meanings they apply to those words. Ironically, though words play a crucial role in contemporary faith theology, practice, and effects, it is words—mistaken, imprecise, ill-defined, or misinterpreted words—that have gotten faith teaching into trouble. In the professional, business, and academic worlds, precise technical language is vital. For instance, having been a university professor and administrator, I have become aware that terms like "affiliated," "associated," "accredited," have particular technical and legal meanings and can be appropriately used only in certain contexts. In the theological world, terms have specific meanings as well. The church councils that formulated the great Christian creeds such as the Nicene and Athanasian Creeds, and the Chalcedonian Definition were concerned with precise words and meanings. In fact, battles were even fought over single words.

It is thus vital for ministers of the Gospel to be knowledgeable about the nuances of meaning both in the text (the task of hermeneutics) and especially careful in our choice of words in conveying those meanings (communication). James 3:1 exhorts that teachers come under stricter judgment. All of us who are teachers—of any stripe—must not be sloppy and carefree in our language, assuming the anointing of the Spirit on our thoughts and words. Even though Hunt, Hanegraaff, and McConnell are wrong about some of their assumptions and conclusions, have made judgments without full knowledge or understanding, and have sometimes unfairly and inaccurately charged contemporary faith teaching with cultism and heresy, they have done a service to the contemporary faith movement by challenging its leaders to think and clearly define what they mean and the practical consequences of how they teach it.

Contemporary faith leaders and followers (as well as their critics) need to avoid taking positions to an extreme or being legalistic, dogmatic, or absolutist. As a caution, for instance, Chambers, who believed in faith, divine healing, and revelation knowledge, somewhat similar to contemporary faith positions, nevertheless admonished, "The fanatical element in the saint is the element that is devoted to a principle instead of to consistent conduct before God. For instance, I may become a devotee to the doctrine of Divine healing which means I must never be sick, and if I am sick then I say I must have gone wrong. The battle all through is against the absurdity of being consistent to an ideal instead of to God."[8] Such thinking breaks down the dynamic tension of the polarities of truth.

Be willing to evaluate and change questionable aspects of contemporary faith theology. Vreeland, from within the contemporary faith movement, gives sound counsel for reconstructing contemporary faith theology:

> If the vitality of the word of faith movement is to remain, second and third generation word of faith leaders must enter the process of restructuring word of faith theology. Pastors and ministers who have been influenced by the word of faith perspective cannot sit by and allow poor hermeneutics and unreflective theology to undermine a movement with such potential. Reflective theology must begin in the pastor's study. Solid theology must be preached for [sic] the pulpit. Pentecostal history has taught the lesson that charismatic movements begin in the fury of spiritual intensity that produce a raw and somewhat primitive theology. Only conscientious biblical reflection illuminated by the Holy Spirit can develop a "systematic" word of faith theology. . . . It requires humility to admit areas of excess and biblical weakness. . . . The anti-intellectual feelings that have plagued the development of Pentecostal theology must be shaken off in the building of word of faith theology.[9]

RECOMMENDATIONS TO CONTEMPORARY FAITH CRITICS

Be careful not to overreact. Yes, there have been some poor theology and some harmful practices, but not all contemporary faith teaching has been wrong. Thus we must be careful not to "throw out the baby with the bathwater" and watch out for the danger of knee jerk reaction. Hanegraaff, McConnell, and Hunt have, by their mistaken assumptions, shown us that just because a teacher uses certain terminology that may *sound* questionable, heretical, or cultic, it does not follow that they really are. They have claimed as cultic those, for example, who teach faith as a law or a force. But we have shown that orthodox evangelicals have been using such terms for well more than a century, without such language being considered as cultic or heretical.

Bowman, once an associate of Hanegraaff at Christian Research Institute (CRI) and himself a faith critic, albeit a more moderate and irenic one, makes a noteworthy point in this vein. He mentioned that he had read a statement to a fellow-researcher at CRI, who then responded that the statement was heresy. It was, in actuality, a statement made by Walter Martin, Hanegraaff's deceased predecessor at CRI that was almost identical to a word of faith teaching condemned by Hanegraaff as heretical.[10] Would Hanegraaff condemn his own mentor as a heretic? The research in this book has turned up many such quotes from Spurgeon, Chambers, Simpson, Murray, Bounds, Tozer, etc., that sound virtually identical to statements made by contemporary faith teachers that have been condemned by their critics. Ironically, although Bowman has attempted to be fair and even-handed with the contemporary faith teachers, some of what even Bowman labels "unbiblical" comes from these earlier classic evangelical writers who have been considered generally sound in theology.

This places such faith critics in a presumptuous and embarrassing position of declaring heretical and cultic respected leaders known for their staunch orthodoxy. Certainly, if they are guilty of heresy, it needs to be exposed. However, the evidence has shown that while there may be misinterpretation and misapplication of such concepts, most of the concepts themselves are not necessarily heretical. Before making assumptions and jumping to conclusions, such critics need to do their own hermeneutics of the teaching: what do these writers mean when they use these terms? How have they been used by earlier evangelicals? How have other evangelicals interpreted these concepts and Scriptures? What other sources can these terms have come from besides cultic and heretical sources?

Recognize that though contemporary faith teaching still has weaknesses, some teachers have modified their teachings. Even some contemporary faith critics such as Farah, have acknowledged that they have moderated their teachings and practices.[11] In a judicious statement, Ken Blue, after critiquing some of the weaknesses of the contemporary faith movement, nonetheless acknowledges, "And in defense specifically of 'faith formula' teachers, let me say that while I believe that they exaggerate what is fully available to us now, they are still closer to the truth than those who deny the availability of healing now."[12]

Be careful not to lump all faith teachings and teachers together as one. Hanegraaff has done this—piecing together questionable teachings from various sources—and thus created a monstrous and distorted caricature of contemporary faith teaching. Contemporary faith teaching is far from monolithic. Vreeland correctly observes, "The theological systems of the various word of faith ministries, churches and faith teachers lack precise similarity. The faith theology of Hagin differs somewhat from the theology of Copeland, etc."[13] We have seen such differences in this study. Critics need to recognize and affirm the good in faith theology and practice and those in the movement who maintain a balance—such as the Hagins' recent books and moderate leaders like Bob Yandian and Rick Renner, who maintain faith theology and practice, but who make more effort to use sound exegesis and hermeneutics of Scripture.

It should also be recognized that the followers of contemporary faith teachers have often gone far beyond what the teachers themselves would advocate. Joe McIntyre, a Kenyon scholar, notes about Kenneth Hagin:

> As I have observed Hagin's ministry and writing over the years, he has addressed many issues in more depth as he observed his "sons" take things beyond what he thought was healthy. For example, in his tapes on intercession he taught on travail or groaning in the spirit. When some of his followers took this idea to a ridiculous extreme he brought some balancing teaching in his next prayer school. *The Midas Touch* is obviously motivated by the same concerns. When some seemed to be thinking he was saying we should never suffer if we have faith, he came out with his book on suffering which clarified what he thought we should suffer and what we should resist. When Kenneth Copeland was teaching (in the way his black and white temperament often does) on the necessity of fasting, Hagin came out with "A Common Sense Guide to Fasting" which sought to bring balance to what (I think) Hagin perceived as an overemphasis on fasting by Copeland. . . . Hagin seems to have spent a lot of time addressing excesses in his own camp. In his series on confession

he talks about the crazy things people have done in the name of positive confession. . . . Much of the correction in his material seems to be based on his ongoing discovery that people don't have much common sense. He mistakenly assumed that they did and is amazed at how wrong he was![14]

Admit that contemporary faith leaders do teach some valid principles of faith in accord with classic teachings. Though they have sometimes taken the concepts beyond the usual biblical balance of classic faith teachers, such principles should not be abandoned, just because they are easily identified with extreme faith and New Thought teachings. Acknowledging areas of agreement between classic faith teaching does not mean blanket acceptance of all contemporary faith teachings. Bowman acknowledges that some of what contemporary faith leaders teach is indeed true, concluding that the movement is "neither soundly orthodox nor thoroughly heretical."[15] He has demonstrated inconsistent logic and bad fruit in some contemporary faith teaching, yet also the danger of too quickly labeling a statement as heretical.

ABOVE ALL—LOVE

Paul Billheimer, one who stands in the tradition of classic faith teaching, yet has been conciliatory to those in the contemporary faith camp (though not without strong disagreements), stresses that the bridge over the gulf between these two camps is *agape* love, a love that forgives, forbears, and does not keep a record of wrongs.[16] Yes, there are valid and serious concerns about contemporary faith teaching and practice. But such concerns must be expressed in a tone of *agape* love, not by accusing teachers of being cultic and heretical. Passantino stresses that those who are "theologically ignorant, ill-advised, untrained, or sloppy" should not be judged as heretics, but rather, "Our response to ignorance and irresponsibility . . . should be with gentle exhortation, lovingly explaining the truth to a brother in sin."[17]

Yes, some contemporary faith critics have at times illegitimately portrayed contemporary faith leaders as heretical and cultic, and sometimes misrepresented contemporary faith teaching. But a godly response does not call such criticism "doctrinal doo-doo" or express a desire that they be cursed or dead, as some contemporary faith leaders have done.[18] Both sides need to drop the unloving, condemning diatribe and rhetoric. Instead, both need to seek openly opportunities for dialogue without rancor. Then both sides can learn how to have a truly healthy faith that

FINAL CONCLUSIONS AND RECOMMENDATIONS

is both strong and sound—an ideal toward which we all strive. I encourage readers to rediscover and apply classic faith teaching for a strong and sound faith.

---

1. Spurgeon, *1000 Devotional Thoughts*, 148.

2. Vreeland, 14.

3. This is not to say that I would embrace everything they teach.

4. As mentioned earlier, compare Hagin, Jr., *Another Look at Faith*, where he declares, "Faith is not a formula," with Hagin, Sr., (*New Thresholds of Faith*, p. 25) where he writes, "Here is a formula for faith" (see also pp. 23, 96).

5. Stanley J. Grenz and Roger E. Olson, *Who Needs Theology?: An Invitation to the Study of God* (Downers Grove, Ill.: IVP, 1996), 12-14.

6. Vreeland, "Reconstructing Word of Faith Theology."

7. In May 2001 Mother Tucker received an honorary doctorate from Oral Roberts University, Tulsa, Oklahoma, for her selfless and outstanding ministry.

8. Oswald Chambers, *Not Knowing Whither: The Steps of Abraham's Faith* (London, Edinburgh: Oswald Chambers Publications Association; Marshall, Morgan, and Scott, 1934), 143, 144.

9. Vreeland, 20.

10. Bowman, *The Word-Faith Controversy*, 53. For more such examples and further discussion of this problem of too quickly condemning a teaching as heresy, see James R. Spencer, *Heresy Hunters: Character Assassination in the Church* (Lafayette, La.: Huntington House Publishers, 1993).

11. Personal conversations with Farah.

12. Blue, 50.

13. Vreeland, 12.

14. E-mail correspondence with Joe McIntyre, June 7, 2004. Cited by permission from Joe McIntyre.

15. Bowman, *The Word-Faith Controversy*, 10.

16. Paul Billheimer, *Love Covers: A Viable Platform for Christian Unity* (Ft. Washington, Penn.: Christian Literature Crusade, 1981), 40, 106-126.

17. Bob and Gretchen Passantino, *Witch Hunt* (Nashville: Thomas Nelson, 1990), 147.

18. See MacArthur, *Charismatic Chaos*, 360, 361; Hanegraaff, 39, 112, 114, 219.

BIBLIOGRAPHY

Aldridge, Alfred Owen. *Jonathan Edwards*. New York: Washington Square Press, 1964.

Alexander, Joseph Addison. *The Gospel According to Mark*. Grand Rapids: Baker, [1858] 1980.

Anderson, May Mabette. "The Prayer of Faith," *The Christian and Missionary Alliance Weekly*, Feb. 17, 1906, 98.

———. "The Prayer of Faith: Part II," *The Christian and Missionary Alliance Weekly*, Feb. 24, 1906, 24:106-107.

Anderson, Neil T. *Living Free in Christ*. Ventura, Calif.: Regal Books, 1993.

———. *Victory over the Darkness*. Ventura, Calif.: Regal Books, 1990.

Andrews, Leslie A. "Alliance Practice and Cultural Diversity in Relation to Women in Ministry," Report of the Committee to Study the Role of Women in Ministry, General Council, May 1995, 109.

Avanzini, John. *30, 60, Hundredfold: Your Financial Harvest Released*. Tulsa, Okla.: Harrison House, 1989.

Bailey, Keith. *The Children's Bread*. Harrisburg, Penn.: Christian Publications, 1977.

———. Audiotape of message, delivered January 1996.

Ballard, Paul. "Practical Theology as an Academic Discipline," *Theology* XCVIII 1995 (782):112-122.

Barnes, Alfred. *Barnes Notes on the New Testament*. Robert Frew, ed. Grand Rapids: Baker, [1851, 1884] 1985. Vol. 1.

Barron, Bruce. *The Health and Wealth Gospel*. Downers Grove, Ill.: IVP, 1987.

"The Believer and Positive Confession," an official statement as approved by the General Presbytery of the Assemblies of God on August 19, 1980. *Pentecostal Evangel*, November 16, 1980, 8ff.

Bernard of Clairvaux. *The Works of Bernard of Clairvaux: Treatises II*. Washington, D.C.: Cistercian Publications, 1974.

Billheimer, Paul E. *Adventure in Adversity*. Wheaton, Ill.: Tyndale, 1984.

———. *Destined for the Throne*. Fort Washington, Penn.: Christian Literature Crusade, 1975.

———. *Don't Waste Your Sorrows*. Fort Washington, Penn.: Christian Literature Crusade, 1977.

———. *Love Covers: A Viable Platform for Christian Unity*. Fort Washington, Penn.: Christian Literature Crusade, 1981.

Blanchard, Charles A. *Getting Things from God: A Study of the Prayer Life*. Chicago, Ill.: The Bible Institute Colportage Assn., 1915.

Blue, Ken. *Authority to Heal*. Downers Grove, Ill.: IVP, 1987.

Bloesch, Donald G. *Jesus Christ: Savior and Lord*. Downers Grove, Ill.: IVP, 1997.

Boardman, William E. *The Higher Christian Life*. Boston: H. Hoyt; Chicago: William Tomlinson, [1858]; New York: Garland, 1984.

Boardman, Mrs. William. "Simple Truths about Faith," *Triumphs of Faith*, November 1890, 242.

Bosworth, F.F. *Christ the Healer*. Grand Rapids: Fleming H. Revell, 1973.

Bounds, E.M. *The Complete Works of E. M. Bounds*. Grand Rapids: Baker, 1990.

———. *Power Through Prayer*. Grand Rapids: Baker, 1978.

———. *Prayer and Praying Men*. Grand Rapids: Baker, 1977.

———. *The Preacher and Prayer*. Grand Rapids: Zondervan, 1950.

———. *Purpose in Prayer*. Chicago: Moody Press, n.d.

———. *Winning the Invisible War*. Springdale, Penn.: Whitaker, 1984.

Bowman, Jr., Robert M. *The Word-Faith Controversy*. Grand Rapids: Baker, 2001.

———. "'Ye Are Gods?' Orthodox and Heretical Views on the Deification of Man," *Christian Research Journal* (Winter-Spring 1987), 18ff. San Juan Capistrano, Calif.: Christian Research Institute, 1993).

Bromiley, Geoffrey W. *Historical Theology: An Introduction*. Grand Rapids: Eerdmans, 1978.

Brooks, Thomas. *Precious Remedies Against Satan's Devices*. London: Banner of Truth Trust, [1652, 1866] 1968.

Brother Lawrence. *The Practice of the Presence of God*. Grand Rapids: Baker, 1975.

Brown, Colin, ed. *The New International Dictionary of New Testament Theology*. Grand Rapids: Zondervan, [1971] 1978. Vol. 3.

Brown, Michael L. *Israel's Divine Healer*. Grand Rapids: Zondervan, 1995.

Browning, Don S. "Practical Theology and Political Theology," *Theology Today*, 1985/86, 42:15-33.

Bushnell, Horace. *Nature and the Supernatural*. New York: Charles Scribner's Sons, 1885.

Calvin, John. *A Compendium of the Institutes of the Christian Religion by John Calvin*. Hugh T. Kerr, ed. Philadelphia: Westminster Press, [1939] 1964.

———. *The Institutes of the Christian Religion*. Vol. 1. Grand Rapids: Eerdmans, 1949.

Capps, Annette. *Reverse the Curse in Your Body and Emotions*. Broken Arrow, Okla.: Annette Capps Ministries, 1987.

Capps, Charles. *Authority in Three Worlds*. Tulsa, Okla.: Harrison House, 1982.

———. *God's Creative Power Will Work for You*. Tulsa, Okla.: Harrison House, 1976.

————. *How You Can Avoid Tragedy and Live a Better Life*. Tulsa, Okla.: Harrison House, 1980.

————. *Releasing the Ability of God*. Tulsa, Okla.: Harrison House, 1978.

————. *The Tongue, a Creative Force*. Tulsa, Okla.: Harrison House, 1976.

Carmichael, Amy. *Mountain Breezes: The Collected Poems of Amy Carmichael*. Fort Washington, Penn.: Christian Literature Crusade, 1999.

————. *Rose from Brier*. Fort Washington, Penn.: Christian Literature Crusade, [1933] 1971.

————. *Thou Givest . . . They Gather*. Fort Washington, Penn.: Christian Literature Crusade, 1958.

————. *You Are My Hiding Place*. Arranged by David Hazard. Minneapolis: Bethany House, 1991.

Carter, Russell Kelso. *The Atonement for Sin and Sickness*. Boston, New York: Willard Tract Repository, 1884.

————. *Faith Healing Reviewed After Twenty Years*. Boston, Chicago: The Christian Witness Co., 1897.

————. "Standing on the Promises," *Hymns of the Christian Life*. Harrisburg, Penn.: Christian Publications, 1978, 329.

Chadwick, Samuel. *The Path of Prayer*. London: Hodder & Stoughton, 1931.

Chambers, Oswald. *Biblical Psychology*. Grand Rapids: Discovery House, [1962] 1995.

————. *Daily Thoughts for Disciples*. Grand Rapids: Discovery House, [1976] 1994.

————. *My Utmost for His Highest*. New York: Dodd, Mead, and Co., [1935] 1963.

————. *Not Knowing Whither: The Steps of Abraham's Faith*. London, Edinburgh: Oswald Chambers Publications Association; Marshall, Morgan, and Scott, 1934.

————. *Oswald Chambers: His Life and Work*. London: Simpkin Marshall, 1941.

————. *The Place of Help*. Grand Rapids: Discovery House Publishers, [1935] 1989.

————. *The Psychology of Redemption*. London: Marshall, Morgan and Scott, [1930] 1963.

————. *Still Higher for His Highest*. Grand Rapids: Zondervan, 1970.

Chappell, P.G. "Healing Movements," in Stanley M. Burgess and Gary B. McGee (ed.), *Dictionary of Pentecostal and Charismatic Movements*, 353-374. Grand Rapids: Zondervan, 1988.

The Christian and Missionary Alliance Weekly. March 9, 1909, 397.

Chrysostom. *Homilies on First Corinthians*, Homily 29." *Nicene and Post-Nicene Fathers*, First Series. Philip Schaff, ed. Grand Rapids: Eerdmans, 1979. Vol. 12.

————. *Homilies on Timothy*: Homily 6, Homily 10. *Nicene and Post-Nicene Fathers*, First Series. Philip Schaff, ed. Grand Rapids: Eerdmans, 1979. Vol. 13.

Clarke, Adam. *Clarke's Commentary on the New Testament*. New York: Abingdon Press, [1830]. Vol. 1.

Clement of Alexandria. "First Principles of Faith," cited in *You Give Me New Life*, ed. David Hazard, Minneapolis: Bethany House, 1995, 36-38.

————. *The Strommata, or Miscellanies*, Book 2, Chapters 2, 4. *The Ante-Nicene Fathers*. Alexander Roberts and James Donaldson, eds. Grand Rapids: Eerdmans, 1979, 2: 348–350.

The Cloud of Unknowing, The Book of Privy Counseling. William Johnson, ed. Garden City, N.Y.: Image Books, 1973.

Collins, Kenneth J. "Abiding in the Kingdom of God: The Disciplines of the Liberated Life," *The Asbury Herald*, (Spring 1997) 108:2:3.

Conwell, Russell. *Acres of Diamonds*. Uhrichville, Ohio: Barbour Publishing Co., 2003.

————. *Life of Charles Haddon Spurgeon: The World's Great Preacher*. Philadelphia: Edgewood Publishing, 1892.

Cook, F.C., ed. *The Bible Commentary: Matthew to Luke*. Grand Rapids: Baker, [1871] 1981. Vol. 7.

Copeland, Gloria. *God's Will for Your Healing*. Fort Worth, Tex.: Kenneth Copeland Ministries, 1972.

————. *God's Will Is Prosperity*. Tulsa, Okla.: Harrison House, 1978.

Copeland, Kenneth. *The Force of Faith*. Fort Worth, Tex.: KCP Publications, 1983.

————. *Forces of the Recreated Human Spirit*. Fort Worth, Tex.: Kenneth Copeland Ministries, 1982.

————. *Freedom from Fear*. Fort Worth, Tex.: KCP Publications, 1983.

————. *The Laws of Prosperity*. Fort Worth, Tex.: Kenneth Copeland Publications, 1974.

————. *Our Covenant with God*. Fort Worth, Tex.: Kenneth Copeland Publications, 1976.

————. "The Prayer of Binding and Loosing," sound recording. Fort Worth, Tex.: KCP Publications, 1987.

Coray, E.A. "A Power of Attorney from God," *Alliance Weekly*, Oct. 26, 1929, 689.

Cowman, Mrs. Charles. *Springs in the Valley*. Minneapolis: World Wide Publications, [1939] 1968.

————. *Streams in the Desert*. Grand Rapids: Zondervan, [1925] 1972. Vol. 1.

Crabb, Larry, and Dan B. Allender. *Hope When You're Hurting*. Grand Rapids: Zondervan, 1996.

Cyril of Jerusalem, *Catechetical Lectures*, Lecture 5. *Nicene and Post-Nicene Fathers*, 2nd Series. Philip Schaff, ed. Grand Rapids: Eerdmans, 1979. Vol. 7.

BIBLIOGRAPHY

Daniels, W.H., ed. *Dr. Cullis and His Work*. New York: Garland Publishers, [1885] 1985.

Dayton, Donald W. *Theological Roots of Pentecostalism*. Peabody, Mass.: Hendrickson Publishers, 1987.

DeArteaga, William. *Quenching the Spirit*. Lake Mary, Fla.: Creation House, 1996.

Dillenberger, John. *Martin Luther: Selections from His Writings*. New York: Doubleday, 1961.

Donnally, Ed. "He's Still Not Afraid to Confront," *Charisma*, August 2000, 66-69.

Dorsett, Lyle Wesley. *E.M. Bounds: Man of Prayer*. Grand Rapids: Zondervan, 1991.

————. "The Pietist Tradition in Evangelical Spirituality: A Bibliographic Essay," *The Christian Educator's Handbook on Spiritual Formation*. Kenneth L. Gangel and James C. Willhoit, eds. Grand Rapids: Baker, 1994.

Douglas, William M. *Andrew Murray and His Message*. Grand Rapids: Baker, 1984.

Drickamer, J.M. "Communication of Attributes, Communicatio Idiomatum," *Evangelical Dictionary of Theology*, 2nd Edition, ed. Walter A. Elwell, Grand Rapids: Baker Academic, 2001, 277.

Drummond, Henry. *The Changed Life*. Westwood, N.J.: Fleming H. Revell, n.d.

————. *Natural Law and the Spiritual World*. New York: H.M. Caldwell Co., n.d.

Drummond, Lewis. *Spurgeon: Prince of Preachers*. Grand Rapids: Kregel Publications, 1992.

Edman, V. Raymond. *They Found the Secret*. Grand Rapids: Zondervan, 1960.

Edwards, Jonathan. "The Distinguishing Marks of the Work of the Spirit of God," *Jonathan Edwards on Revival*. Edinburgh: The Banner of Truth Trust, 1984.

Edwards, Troy J. "The God-Kind of Faith—A Biblical, Historical, and Theological Defense," n.d., available on the Internet at www.100megspop2.com/victoryword, accessed July 25, 2001.

Eller, Vernard, ed. *Thy Kingdom Come: A Blumhardt Reader*. Grand Rapids: Eerdmans, 1980.

Ellicott, Charles John, ed. *Ellicott's Commentary on the Whole Bible*. Grand Rapids: Zondervan, 1959. Vol. 6.

Elliot, Elizabeth. *A Chance To Die: The Life and Legacy of Amy Carmichael*. Old Tappan, N.J.: Fleming H. Revell, 1987.

Erb, Peter C., ed. *Pietists: Selected Writings*. New York: Paulist Press, 1983.

Fant, Jr., Clyde E., and William M. Pinson, Jr., eds. F.B. Meyers, "The Fulness of the Spirit," cited in *Twenty Centuries of Great Preaching*, Waco, Tex.: Word, 1971. Vol. 6:380.

Farah, Jr., Charles. "A Critical Analysis: The 'Roots and Fruits' of Faith Formula Theology." Paper presented at the Annual Meeting of the Society for Pentecostal Studies. Tulsa, Okla.: Oral Roberts University, 1980.

———. *From the Pinnacle of the Temple: Faith or Presumption*. Plainfield, N.J.: Logos, n.d.

Fee, Gordon. *The Disease of the Health and Wealth Gospel*. Cosa Mesa, Calif.: Word for Today, 1979.

Fenelon, Francois. *Let Go*. Springdale, Penn.: Whitaker, 1973.

Finney Charles G. *Revivals of Religion*. Virginia Beach, Va.: CBN University Press, 1978.

Foster, K. Neill, with Paul L. King. *Binding and Loosing: Exercising Authority Over the Dark Powers*. Camp Hill, Penn.: Christian Publications, 1998.

Foster, K. Neill. *Sorting Out the Supernatural*. Camp Hill, Penn.: Christian Publications, 2001.

Foster, Richard J. *Celebration of Discipline*. San Francisco: HarperSanFrancisco, [1978] 1988.

———. *Prayer: Finding the Heart's True Home*. San Francisco: HarperSanFrancisco, 1992.

———. *Streams of Living Water: Celebrating the Great Traditions of the Christian Faith*. San Francisco: HarperSanFrancisco, 1998.

Foster, Richard J., and Emilie Griffin, eds. *Spiritual Classics*. San Francisco: HarperSanFrancisco, 2000.

Foster, Richard J., and James Bryan Smith, eds. *Devotional Classics*. San Francisco: HarperSanFrancisco, 1993.

Friesen, Gary, with Robin Maxson. *Decision Making and the Will of God*. Portland, Ore.: Multnomah, 1980.

Gilbertson, Richard. *The Baptism of the Holy Spirit*. Camp Hill, Penn.: Christian Publications, 1993.

Gill, John. *Gill's Commentary*. Grand Rapids: Baker, [1852] 1980. Vol. 5.

"God's Rule for Financial Prosperity," *Triumphs of Faith*, November 1915, 242.

Goforth, Jonathan. *By My Spirit*. Grand Rapids: Zondervan, 1942.

Goforth, Rosalind. Cited in *World Shapers: A Treasury of Quotes from Great Missionaries*. Wheaton, Ill.: Harold Shaw Publishers, 1991.

Gohr, G.W. "Price, Frederick K.C.," *Dictionary of Pentecostal and Charismatic Movements*, 1988, 727.

Gonzalez, Justo L. *Faith and Wealth: A History of Early Christian Ideas on the Origin, Significance, and Use of Money*. San Francisco, Calif.: HarperSanFrancisco, 1990.

———. *A History of Christian Thought*. Nashville, Tenn.: Abingdon Press, 1971. Vol. 2 and 3.

Gordon, A. J. *How Christ Came to Church: A Spiritual Autobiography* with A. T. Pierson, "The Life Story, and the Dream as Interpreting the Man." Philadelphia: American Baptist Publishing Co., 1895.

BIBLIOGRAPHY

——. *The Ministry of Healing*. Harrisburg, Penn.: Christian Publications, n.d.

Gordon, S.D. *The Healing Christ*. New York, N.Y.: Fleming H. Revell. Ann Arbor, MI: Vine Books, 1924] 1985.

——. *Quiet Talks on Prayer*. Chicago, Ill.: Fleming H. Revell, 1911.

Gothard, Bill. *Men's Manual*. Oak Brook, Ill.: Institute in Basic Youth Conflicts, 1983. Vol. 2.

Gräb, Wilhelm, and Richard R. Osmer. "Editorial," *International Journal of Practical Theology*, 1997. Vol. 1:1-5.

Graf, Jonathan L. comp. and ed. *The Three Great Classics on Divine Healing*. Camp Hill, Penn.: Christian Publications, 1992.

Grenz, Stanley J., and Roger E. Olson. *Who Needs Theology?: An Invitation to the Study of God*. Downers Grove, Ill.: InterVarsity, 1996.

Grou, Jean-Nicolas. Cited in *The Alliance Weekly*, July 2, 1952, 424.

Grubb, Norman P. *C.T. Studd: Cricketer and Pioneer*. Fort Washington, Penn.: Christian Literature Crusade, 1933.

——. *Rees Howell Intercessor*. Fort Washington, Penn.: Christian Literature Crusade, [1952] 1984.

Grou, Jean-Nicolas. *How To Pray*. Nashville, Tenn.: The Upper Room, 1973.

——. "On Being Truly Spiritual," *The Alliance Weekly*, September 10, 1952, 592.

Gurnall, William. *The Christian in Complete Armour*. James S. Bell, Jr., ed. Chicago, Ill.: Moody Press, [1655] 1994. .

Guyon, Madame. *Experiencing God through Prayer*. Springdale, Penn.: Whitaker House, 1984.

Hagin, Kenneth E. *The Art of Intercession*. Tulsa, Okla.: Kenneth Hagin Ministries, 1980.

——. *The Art of Prayer*. Tulsa, Okla.: Kenneth Hagin Ministries, 1991.

——. *The Believer's Authority*. Tulsa, Okla.: Kenneth Hagin Ministries, 1984.

——. *Exceedingly Growing Faith*. Tulsa, Okla.: Faith Library, 1983.

——. *God's Medicine*. Tulsa, Okla.: Kenneth Hagin Ministries, 1977.

——. "Healing: The Father's Provision," *Word of Faith*, August 1977, 9.

——. *Having Faith in Your Faith*. Tulsa, Okla.: Faith Library Publications, 1980.

——. *How to Turn Your Faith Loose*. Tulsa, Okla.: Kenneth Hagin Ministries, n.d.

——. *How to Write Your Own Ticket with God*. Tulsa, Okla.: Kenneth Hagin Ministries, 1979.

——. *In the Name of Jesus*. Tulsa, Okla.: Kenneth Hagin Ministries, 1979.

——. *The Midas Touch: A Balanced Approach to Biblical Prosperity*. Tulsa, Okla.: Faith Library Publications, 2000.

———. *Mountain Moving Faith*. Tulsa, Okla.: Kenneth Hagin Ministries, 1993.

———. *Must Christians Suffer?* Tulsa, Okla.: Kenneth Hagin Ministries, 1982.

———. *New Thresholds of Faith*. Tulsa, Okla.: Kenneth Hagin Ministries, 1985.

———. *Plead Your Case*. Tulsa: Kenneth Hagin Ministries, 1979.

———. *The Real Faith*. Tulsa, Okla.: Kenneth Hagin Ministries, n.d.

———. *Right and Wrong Thinking*. Tulsa, Okla.: Faith Library Publications, 1977.

———. *Seven Things You Should Know About Divine Healing*. Tulsa, Okla.: Kenneth Hagin Ministries, 1979.

———. *What To Do When Faith Seems Weak & Victory Lost*. Tulsa, Okla.: Kenneth Hagin Ministries, 1979.

———. *You Can Have What You Say*. Tulsa, Okla.: Kenneth Hagin Ministries, 1979.

Hagin, Kenneth, Jr. *Another Look at Faith*. Tulsa, Okla.: Kenneth Hagin Ministries, 1996.

———. *Healing: A Forever Settled Subject*. Tulsa, Okla.: Kenneth Hagin Ministries, 1981.

———. *Word of Faith*. November 1984, 3.

Hanegraaff, Hank. *Christianity in Crisis*. Eugene, Ore.: Harvest House Publishers, 1993.

Hardesty, Nancy A. *Faith Cure: Divine Healing in the Holiness and Pentecostal Movements*. Peabody, Mass.: Hendrickson, 2003.

Harper, J. Steven. "Renewal—The Wesley Way," *The Asbury Herald*. Spring 1996, 10.

Harrell, David Edwin, Jr. *All Things Are Possible: The Healing and Charismatic Revivals in Modern America*. Bloomington, Ind.: Indiana University Press, 1975.

Harris, E. Lynn. *The Mystic Spirituality of A.W. Tozer, A Twentieth-Century American Protestant*. San Francisco: Mellen Research University Press, 1992.

Hartzfeld, David F., and Charles Nienkirchen, eds. *The Birth of a Vision*. Camp Hill, Penn.: Christian Publications, 1986.

Hayford, Jack. *The Beauty of Spiritual Language*. Dallas: Word, 1992.

Henry, Marie. *Hannah Whitall Smith*. Minneapolis: Bethany House, 1984.

Henry, Matthew. *A Commentary on the Whole Bible*. Old Tappan, N.J.: Fleming H. Revell, 1935.

Henry, Matthew, and Thomas Scott. *A Commentary on the Whole Bible*. Nashville: Thomas Nelson, [1710, 1792] 1979. Vol. 3.

Henry, Matthew. *A Commentary on the Whole Bible*. Old Tappan, N.J.: Fleming H. Revell, 1935. Vol. 4.

BIBLIOGRAPHY

Heroes of the Faith. Uhrichville, Ohio: Barbour Publishing Co., 1998.

Heschel, Abraham Joshua. *God in Search of Man: A Philosophy of Judaism*. New York: The Noonday Press / Farrar, Straus and Giroux, 1955.

Hibbert, Albert. *Smith Wigglesworth — The Secret of His Power*. Tulsa, Okla.: Harrison House, 1993.

Hicks, Roy. *Avoiding Ditches: Keeping on the Highway of Balance*. Tulsa, Okla.: Harrison House, 1995.

———. *Praying Beyond God's Ability*. Tulsa, Okla.: Harrison House, 1977.

Hunt, Dave. *The Berean Call*, September 1995, 2.

———. *Beyond Seduction*. Eugene, Ore.: Harvest House, 1987.

Hunt, Dave, and T. McMahon. *Seduction of Christianity*. Eugene, Ore.: Harvest House, 1985.

Hurtado, Larry W. "Normal, but Not a Norm: Initial Evidence and the New Testament," *Initial Evidence*. Gary B. McGee, ed. Peabody, Mass.: Hendrickson, 1991, 189-201.

Hus, Jan. "Faith Formed in Love," *Christian History*. Issue 68, n.d. (Vol. 19:4), 33.

Hyatt, Eddie. "The Nineteenth Century Roots of the Modern Faith Movement," unpublished paper. Tulsa, Okla.: Oral Roberts University. April 25, 1991.

Hymns of the Christian Life. Harrisburg, Penn.: Christian Publications, 1978.

Jones, Brynmor Pierce. *The Trials and Triumphs of Mrs. Jessie Penn-Lewis*. New Brunswick, N.J.: Bridge-Logos Publishers, 1997.

Jones, E. Stanley. *Abundant Living*. New York, Nashville: Abingdon-Cokesbury Press, 1942.

Kärkäinen, Veli-Matti. *Christology: A Global Introduction*. Grand Rapids: Baker, 2003.

Kelley, C.F. *Meister Eckhart on Divine Knowledge*. New Haven, Conn., and London: Yale University Press, 1977.

Kenyon, E.W. *The Blood Covenant*. Seattle: Kenyon's Gospel Publishing Co., 1969.

———. *The Hidden Man: An Unveiling of the Subconscious Mind*. Seattle: Kenyon's Gospel Publishing Co., 1970.

———. *Jesus the Healer*. Seattle: Kenyon's Gospel Publishing Co., [1940] 1943.

———. *In His Presence*. Seattle: Kenyon's Gospel Publishing Co., 1969.

———. *The Two Kinds of Faith*. Seattle: Kenyon's Gospel Publishing Co., 1942.

———. *The Two Kinds of Knowledge*. Seattle: Kenyon's Gospel Publishing Co., 1942.

———. *Two Kinds of Righteousness*. Seattle: Kenyon's Gospel Publishing Co., 1965.

———. *The Wonderful Name of Jesus*. Seattle: Kenyon's Gospel Publishing Co., [1927] 1963.

Kinnear, Angus. *Against the Tide: The Story of Watchman Nee*. Wheaton, Ill.: Tyndale, 1973.

King, Paul L. "A. B. Simpson and the Modern Faith Movement." *Alliance Academic Review*. Ed., Elio Cuccaro, Camp Hill, Penn.: Christian Publications, 1996, 1-22.

————. *A Case Study of a Believer with Authority: The Impact of the Life and Ministry of John A. MacMillan*. Doctor of Ministry dissertation. Tulsa, Okla.: Oral Roberts University, 2000.

————. *A Believer with Authority: The Life and Message of John A. MacMillan*. Camp Hill, Penn.: Christian Publications, 2001.

————. *Genuine Gold: The Cautiously Charismatic Story of the Early Christian and Missionary Alliance*. Tulsa, Okla.: Word & Spirit Press, 2006.

————. "The Historical C&MA View of Fallible Prophecy." Unpublished paper, 2001.

————. "Holy Laughter and Other Phenomena in Evangelical and Holiness Revival Movements." *Alliance Academic Review*. Elio Cuccaro, ed., Camp Hill, Penn.: Christian Publications, 1998, 107-122.

————. *Moving Mountains: Lessons in Bold Faith from Great Evangelical Leaders*. Grand Rapids: Chosen Books, 2004.

————. *A Practical-Theological Investigation of Nineteenth and Twentieth-Century "Faith Theologies."* Doctor of Theology thesis. Pretoria, South Africa: University of South Africa, November 2001.

————. "The Restoration of the Doctrine of Binding and Loosing," *Alliance Academic Review*. Elio Cuccaro, ed. Camp Hill, Penn.: Christian Publications, 1997, 57-80.

————. "Why Not Tongues without Controversy?—A.B. Simpson's Model and Appeal for Pentecostal Ecumenicity." Paper presented at the 35th Annual Meeting of the Society for Pentecostal Studies, Fuller Theological Seminary, Pasadena, California, March 23-25, 2006.

Kittel, Gerhard, ed. *Theological Dictionary of the New Testament*. Grand Rapids: Eerdmans, 1964. Vol. 2, 4.

Knapp, Martin Wells. *Impressions*. Cincinnati: Revivalist Publishing House, 1892.

Knight III, Henry H. "God's Faithfulness and God's Freedom: A Comparison of Contemporary Theologies of Healing," *Journal of Pentecostal Theology*, 1993. Vol. 2:65-89.

Koch, Kurt E. *Between Christ and Satan*. Western Germany: Evangelization Publishers, n.d.

————. *Demonology Past and Present*. Grand Rapids: Kregel Publications, 1973.

———. *Occult Bondage and Deliverance*. Western Germany: Evangelization Publishers, 1970.

Kreeft, Peter, and Tacelli, Ronald K. *Handbook of Christian Apologetics*. Downers Grove, Ill.: InterVarsity, 1994.

Kydd, Ronald A.N. *Healing Through the Centuries: Models for Understanding*. Peabody, Mass.: Hendrickson, 1998.

La Combe, Pere. "Spiritual Maxims," Francois Fenelon and Madame Guyon, *Spiritual Progress*, http://ccel.org/f/fenelon/progress/spirit06.htm, accessed 2000.

Ladd, George Eldon. *A Theology of the New Testament*. Grand Rapids: Eerdmans, 1974.

Lake, John G. *Spiritual Hunger and Other Sermons*. Ed., Gordon Lindsay. Dallas: Christ for the Nations, 1993.

Landrus, Heather L. "Hearing 3 John 2 in the Voices of History." Paper presented at the 30th Annual Meeting of the Society for Pentecostal Studies, Oral Roberts University, Tulsa, Oklahoma, March 2001.

Latourette, Kenneth Scott. *A History of Christianity*. New York: Harper and Row, [1953] 1975. 2 vol.

Law, William. *The Way of Divine Knowledge*. Albany, Ore.: AGES Software, 1997.

Lawson, James Gilchrist. *Deeper Experiences of Famous Christians*. Anderson, Ind.: Warner Press, [1911] 1970.

Lederle, Henry I. *Systematic Theology (Honors B.Th.): Guide 2 for STH403-T (History of Theology)*. Pretoria, South Africa: University of South Africa, 1979.

———. *Systematic Theology: Honors B.Th. STH403: Guide 2*. Pretoria, South Africa: University of South Africa, 1980.

———. *Treasures Old and New: Interpretations of "Spirit-Baptism" in the Charismatic Renewal Movement*, 1-36. Peabody, Mass.: Hendrickson Publishers, 1988.

———. "Initial Evidence and the Charismatic Movement: An Ecumenical Appraisal," *Initial Evidence*. Gary B. McGee, ed. Peabody, Mass.: Hendrickson, 1991, 131-141.

Lewis, Alan E. *Between the Cross and the Resurrection: A Theology of Holy Saturday*. Grand Rapids: Eerdmans, 2001.

Lie, Geir. "E.W. Kenyon: Cult Founder or Evangelical Minister? An Historical Analysis of Kenyon's Theology with Particular Emphasis on Roots and Influences." Masters thesis, Norwegian Lutheran School of Theology, 1994.

Lindner, William. *Andrew Murray*. Minneapolis: Bethany House, 1996.

Lloyd-Jones, D. Martyn. *The Christian Warfare*. Grand Rapids: Zondervan, 1976.

————. *God's Ultimate Purpose: An Exposition of Ephesians 1:1-23*. Edinburgh: Banner of Truth, 1978.

————. *Revival*. Wheaton, Ill.: Crossway Books, 1987.

Lockyer, Herbert. "Three Abiding Forces," *The Alliance Weekly*, September 2, 1953, 10.

Lovett, L. "Positive Confession Theology," in Stanley M. Burgess and Gary B. McGee (ed.), *Dictionary of Pentecostal and Charismatic Movements*, Grand Rapids: Zondervan, 1988, 718-720.

Luther, Martin. "Sermon for the 3rd Sunday of Epiphany, Matthew 8:1-13," *The Sermons of Martin Luther*. Grand Rapids: Baker, 2000, Vol. 2.

MacArthur, John F. *Charismatic Chaos*. Grand Rapids: Zondervan, 1992.

————. *Our Sufficiency in Christ*. Dallas: Word, 1991.

MacArthur, William T. *Ethan O. Allen*. Philadelphia: The Parlor Evangelist, n.d.

————. "Fabrics Filled with Power," *The Alliance Weekly*, September 14, 1912, 390.

MacGregor, Kirk R. "The Word-Faith Movement: A Theological Conflation of the Nation of Islam and Mormonism?" *Journal of the American Academy of Religion*, Vol. 75, No. 1, (March 2007).

MacKenzie, Kenneth. "Healing or Helping?," *Triumphs of Faith*, January 11, 1903.

————. "My Memories of A. B. Simpson VI," *The Alliance Weekly*, August 7, 1937, 500.

MacMillan, John A. "Authority," *The Alliance Weekly*, June 19, 1937, 386.

————. *The Authority of the Believer*, Harrisburg, Penn.: Christian Publications, 1980.

————. "All Authority," *The Alliance Weekly*, March 2, 1940, 130.

————. "Broadening Sympathies," *The Alliance Weekly*, December 10, 1938, 787.

————. "Commanding God," *The Alliance Weekly*, October 7, 1939, 626.

————. "Contacting God," *The Alliance Weekly*, November 9, 1940, 706.

————. "Divine Protection," *The Alliance Weekly*, December 6, 1947, 770.

————. *Encounter with Darkness*. Harrisburg, Penn.: Christian Publications, 1980.

————. "The Family Altar," *The Alliance Weekly*, May 5, 1945, 30.

————. "Fasting as an Aid to Prayer, *The Alliance Weekly*, March 4, 1950, 130.

————. *The Full Gospel Adult Sunday School Quarterly*, October 28, 1934, 12.

————. *The Full Gospel Adult Sunday School Quarterly*, December 23, 1934, 36.

————. *The Full Gospel Adult Sunday School Quarterly*, May 3, 1936, 17.

BIBLIOGRAPHY

———. *The Full Gospel Adult Sunday School Quarterly*, October 15, 1939, 10.

———. *The Full Gospel Adult Sunday School Quarterly*, November 26, 1939, 28.

———. *The Full Gospel Adult Sunday School Quarterly*, November 22, 1942, 25.

———. "Go Forward!" *The Alliance Weekly*, May 11, 1946, 290.

———. "The Goodness of God," *The Alliance Weekly*, November 20, 1948, 743.

———. "Grace's Consummation," *The Alliance Weekly*, December 8, 1945, 423.

———. "Mount of Transfiguration," July 21, 1934, 450.

———. "The Oppression of the Enemy," *The Alliance Weekly*, June 21, 1947, 386.

———. "Our Alliance Message," *The Alliance Weekly*, December 27, 1941, 826.

———. "Our Mohammedan Problem in the Philippines," *The Alliance Weekly*, June 22, 1929, 396, 401, 404.

———. "Our Most Stubborn Foe," *The Alliance Weekly*, June 27, 1942, 402.

———. "Praying Geographically," *The Alliance Weekly*, September 14, 1946, 578-579.

———. "Raging Chariots," *The Alliance Weekly*, May 15, 1937, 307.

———. "Self-Deception," *The Alliance Weekly*, July 24, 1937, 467.

———. "The Weakness of Power," *The Alliance Weekly*, April 2, 1938, 211.

MacNutt, Francis. *Healing*. Notre Dame, Ind.: Ave Maria Press, [1974] 1999.

McCasland, David. *Oswald Chambers: Abandoned to God*. Grand Rapids: Discovery House Publishers, 1993.

McConkey, James H. *The Three-fold Secret of the Holy Spirit*. Chicago: Moody Press, 1897.

McConnell, D.R. *A Different Gospel*. Peabody, Mass.: Hendrickson Publishers. 1988.

McCoy, Charles Sherwood. *The Covenant Theology of Johannes Cocceius*. Ph.D. Thesis, Yale University, 1956.

McCrossan, T.J. *Bodily Healing in the Atonement*. Reedited by Roy Hicks and Kenneth E. Hagin. Tulsa, Okla.: Kenneth Hagin Ministries, [1930] 1982.

———. *Christ's Paralyzed Church X-Rayed*. Youngstown, Ohio: Rev. C.E. Humbard, 1937.

———. *Speaking with Other Tongues: Sign or Gift—Which?* Harrisburg, Penn.: Christian Publications, 1927.

McGee, Gary B., ed. *Initial Evidence*. Peabody, Mass.: Hendrickson, 1991.

McGrath, Allister E. *The Christian Theology Reader*. Cambridge, Mass.: Blackwell Publishers, 1995.

McIntyre, Joe. *E. W. Kenyon and His Message of Faith: The True Story*. Lake Mary, Fla.: Creation House, 1997.

Maddox, Randy L. "The Recovery of Theology as a Practical Discipline," *Theological Studies* 51 (1990), 650-672.

Marsh, F.E. *The Spiritual Life, or Helps and Hindrances*. Des Moines, IA: Boone Publishing Co., 1958.

Meyer, F.B. *Abraham or the Obedience of Faith*. Fort Washington, Penn.: Christian Literature Crusade, 1983.

———. *Changed by the Master's Touch*. Springdale, Penn.: Whitaker House, 1985.

———. *Five Musts of the Christian Life*. Chicago: Moody Press, 1927.

———. "The Fulness of the Spirit," cited in *Twenty Centuries of Great Preaching*, 6:380. Clyde E. Fant, Jr., William M. Pinson, Jr., eds. Waco, Tex.: Word Publishers, 1971.

———. *The Secret of Guidance*. Chicago, Ill.: Moody Press, n.d.

"Minutes of General Council 1995 and Annual Report 1994," The Christian and Missionary Alliance, 1995, 142.

Montgomery, Carrie Judd. "Faith Rest Cottage," *Triumphs of Faith*, April 1888, 96.

———. *The Prayer of Faith*. Chicago: Fleming H. Revell, 1880.

———. *The Secrets of Victory*. Oakland, Calif.: Triumphs of Faith, 1921.

———. *Under His Wings*. Oakland, Calif.: Triumphs of Faith, 1936.

Moody, D.L. "How To Get Faith," *Triumphs of Faith*. May 1887, 117.

Morgan, G. Campbell. *The Gospel According to Matthew*. Old Tappan, N.J.: Fleming H. Revell, 1929.

———. *The Teaching of Christ*. New York: Fleming H. Revell, 1913.

Müller, George. *The Autobiography of George Müller*. Springdale, Penn.: Whitaker House, 1984.

Mullin, Redmond. *The Wealth of Christians*. Maryknoll, N.Y.: Orbis Books, 1983.

Murray, Andrew. *Abiding in Christ*. Springdale, Penn.: Whitaker House, 1979.

———. *The Blood of the Cross*. Springdale, Penn.: Whitaker House, 1981.

———. *Divine Healing*. London: Victory Press, 1934.

———. "Faith Counting on the Power of God," *Triumphs of Faith*, November 1934, 243.

———. *God's Best Secrets*. Grand Rapids: Zondervan, 1971.

———. *The Holiest of All*. New Kensington, Penn.: Whitaker House, 1996.

———. *Holy in Christ*. Toronto: Willard Tract Depot, 1888.

———. *The Inner Life*. Springdale, Penn.: Whitaker House, 1984.

———. *Key to the Missionary Problem*. Contemporized by Leona Choy. Fort Washington, Penn.: Christian Literature Crusade, 1979.

BIBLIOGRAPHY

———. *The Prayer Life*. Basingstoke, Hants, U.K.: Marshall, Morgan and Scott, 1968.

———. *The Secret of the Faith Life*. Fort Washington, Penn.: Christian Literature Crusade, 1968.

———. *The Spirit of Christ*. Springdale, Penn.: Whitaker House, 1984.

———. *The Two Covenants*. Fort Washington, Penn.: Christian Literature Crusade, 1974.

———. *With Christ in the School of Prayer*. New York: Anson D.F. Randolph and Co., [1886].

———. *With Christ in the School of Prayer*. Springdale, Penn.: Whitaker House, 1981. (revised)

Nee, Watchman. *God's Plan and the Overcomers*. New York, N.Y.: Christian Fellowship Publishers, Inc., 1977.

———. *Latent Power of the Soul*. New York: Christian Fellowship Publishers, Inc., 1972.

———. *A Living Sacrifice*. New York: Christian Fellowship Publishers, Inc., 1972.

———. *The Spiritual Man*. New York: Christian Fellowship Publishers, Inc., 1968.

———. *Spiritual Reality or Obsession*. New York: Christian Fellowship Publishers, 1970.

Nevius, John L. *Demon Possession and Allied Themes*. Chicago: Fleming H. Revell, n.d.

New American Standard Bible. Carol Stream, Ill.: Creation House, [1960, 1962, 1963, 1968] 1971.

New International Version. Grand Rapids: Zondervan, [1973, 1978] 1984.

Nienkirchen, Charles W. *A.B. Simpson and the Pentecostal Movement*. Peabody, Mass.: Hendrickson Publishers, 1992.

Niklaus, Robert L., John S. Sawin, and Samuel J. Stoesz. *All for Jesus*. Camp Hill, Penn.: Christian Publications, 1986.

Nuzum, C. *The Life of Faith*. Springfield, Mo.: Gospel Publishing House, [1928] 1956.

Oesterreich, T.K. *Possession: Demoniacal and Other*. New Hyde Park, N.Y.: University Books, 1966.

Palmer, Phoebe. *Faith and Its Effects*. New York: Palmer and Hughes, [1848] 1867.

Pardington G.P. *Twenty-five Wonderful Years*. New York: Christian Alliance Publishing Co., 1912; New York: Garland, 1984.

Parham, Charles. *The Everlasting Gospel*. Baxter Springs, Kan.: n.p., 1911.

Parker, Larry. *We Let Our Son Die*. Irvine, Calif.: Harvest House, 1980.

Passantino, Bob and Gretchen. *Witch Hunt*. Nashville: Thomas Nelson, 1990.

Peale, Norman Vincent. *The Power of Positive Thinking*. Englewood Cliffs, N.J.: Prentice-Hall, Inc., 1952.

Peck, George B. *Throne-Life, or The Highest Christian Life*. Boston: Watchword Publishing, 1888.

Pember, George H. *Earth's Earliest Ages and Their Connection with Modern Spiritualism and Theosophy*. Toronto, Ontario: A. Sims, Publisher, n.d.

———. *The Great Prophecies of the Centuries Concerning Israel and the Gentiles*. London: Hodder and Stoughton, 1909.

Penn-Lewis, Jessie. *The Conquest of Canaan*. Fort Washington, Penn.: Christian Literature Crusade, 1989.

———. "How To Pray for Missionaries," *The Alliance Weekly*, June 12, 1937, 373-375; June 26, 1937, 406-407.

———. *Life in the Spirit*. Dorset, Eng.: Overcomer Literature Trust, 1910.

———. *Prayer and Evangelism*. Dorset, Eng.: Overcomer Literature Trust, [1921].

———. *Releasing Your Spirit*. New Kensington, Penn.: Whitaker House, 1997.

———. *Soul and Spirit*. Dorset, Eng.: Overcomer Literature Trust; Fort Washington, Penn.: Christian Literature Crusade, n.d.

———. *The Warfare with Satan*. Dorset, Eng.: Overcomer Literature Trust, 1963.

Penn-Lewis, Jessie, with Evan Roberts. *War on the Saints* — Unabridged Edition (Ninth Edition). New York: Thomas E. Lowe, Ltd., 1973.

———. *War on the Saints*. Abridged edition. Fort Washington, Penn.: Christian Literature Crusade, 1977.

Perriman, Andrew ed. *Faith, Health and Prosperity*. Carlisle, Cumbria, U.K.; Waynesboro, GA: Paternoster Press, 2003.

Perkins, Eunice. *Fred Francis Bosworth, The Joybringer: His Life Story*. River Forest, Ill.: F.F. Bosworth, 1927.

Petrie, Arthur. "Ruth the Redeemed," *The Alliance Weekly*, Nov. 21, 1942, 743.

Pierson, Arthur T. *The Acts of the Holy Spirit*. Harrisburg, Penn.: Christian Publications, 1980.

———. *Forward Movements of the Last Half Century*. New York: Funk and Wagnalls, 1900.

———. *George Müller of Bristol*. New York: Fleming H. Revell, 1899.

———. *Lessons in the School of Prayer*. Dixon, Mo.: Rare Christian Books, n.d.

Bibliography

———. "The Life Story, and the Dream as Interpreting the Man." in A.J. Gordon, *How Christ Came to Church: A Spiritual Autobiography.* Philadelphia, Penn.: American Baptist Publishing Co., 1895), 95-149.

———. *The New Acts of the Apostles.* New York: Baker and Taylor, 1894.

Price, Charles S. *And Signs Followed.* Plainfield, N.J.: Logos, [1972].

———. *The Creative Word.* Pasadena, Calif.: Charles S. Price Publishing Co., 1941.

———. *Golden Grain,* August 1932, 10.

———. *The Real Faith.* Pasadena, Calif.: Charles S. Price Publishing Co., [1940] 1968.

———. *See God!* Pasadena, Calif.: Charles S. Price Publishing Co., 1943.

———. *Spiritual and Physical Health.* Pasadena, Calif.: Charles S. Price Publishing Co., 1946.

———. *The Meaning of Faith and the Sick Are Healed: Resolving the Mysteries of Faith.* Shippensburg, Penn.: Destiny Image Publishers, 2002.

———. *The Story of My Life.* Pasadena, Calif.: Charles S. Price Publishing Co., 1935.

———. *Two Worlds.* Pasadena, Calif.: Charles S. Price Publishing Co., 1946.

Price, Frederick K.C. *Ever Increasing Faith Messenger,* Fall 1980, 3.

———. *Ever Increasing Faith* program on TBN. November 16, 1990.

———. *Faith, Foolishness or Presumption?* Tulsa, Okla.: Harrison House, 1979.

———. *Is Healing for All?* Tulsa, Okla.: Harrison House, 1976.

Rader, Paul. *Harnessing God.* New York: George H. Doran Co., 1926.

———. "Old Time Power," *Hymns of the Christian Life.* Harrisburg, Penn.: Christian Publications, 1978, 145.

Raser, Harold E. *Phoebe Palmer: Her Life and Thought.* Lewiston, N.Y.: E. Mellon Press, 1987.

Rawlinson, A.E.J. *Westminster Commentaries: St. Mark.* London: Methuen & Co., Ltd., 1925.

Rawlinson, George. *The Pulpit Commentary: Isaiah,* eds. H.D.M. Spence and Joseph S. Exell. Chicago: Wilcox and Follett, n.d.

Reynolds, Lindsay. *Footprints.* Beaverlodge, Alberta, Canada: Buena Book Services, 1981.

———. *Rebirth.* Beaverlodge, Alberta, Canada: Evangelistic Enterprises, 1992.

Rice, John R. *Prayer: Asking and Receiving.* Murfreesboro, Tenn.: Sword of the Lord Publishers, 1942.

Rinker, Rosalind. *How to Get the Most Out of Your Prayer Life.* Eugene, Ore.: Harvest House, 1981.

———. *Prayer: Conversing with God.* Grand Rapids: Zondervan, 1959.

Riss, R.M. "Copeland, Kenneth," in *Dictionary of Pentecostal and Charismatic Movements*, 343-374. Grand Rapids: Zondervan, 1988.

Robeck, Jr., Cecil M. "William J. Seymour and 'the Bible Evidence,'" *Initial Evidence*. Gary B. McGee, ed. Peabody, Mass.: Hendrickson, 1991, 72-95.

Roberts, Alexander, and James Donaldson, eds. *Ante-Nicene Fathers*. Grand Rapids: Eerdmans, 1979. Vol. 2.

Robertson, A. T. *A Grammar of the Greek New Testament in Light of Historical Research*. Second Edition. New York: George H. Doran Co., 1915.

Sattler, Gary R. *God's Glory, Neighbor's Good: A Brief Introduction to the Life and Writings of August Herman Francke*. Chicago: Covenant Press, 1982.

Scougal, Henry. *The Life of God in the Soul of Man*. Minneapolis: Bethany Fellowship, 1946.

Schaff, Philip, ed. *The Nicene and Post-Nicene Fathers*. Grand Rapids: Eerdmans, 1979. Series 1, Vol. 6. Vol. 13; Series 2, Vol. 9, 12, 13.

Schuller, Robert H. *Self Esteem: The New Reformation*. Waco, Tex.: Word, 1982.

———. *You Can Become the Person You Want to Be*. Old Tappan, N.J.: Fleming H. Revell, 1973.

Seymour, William. *The Doctrines and Disciplines of the Azusa St. Apostolic Faith Mission*. Los Angeles: Apostolic Faith Mission, 1915.

Sheils, W.J., and Diana Wood. *The Church and Wealth*. Oxford: Basil Blackwell, 1987.

Shelton, James B. *Mighty in Word and Deed: The Role of the Holy Spirit in Luke-Acts*. Peabody, Mass.: Hendrickson, 1991.

Simmons, Dale H. "Mimicking MacMillan." Unpublished paper, Graduate School of Theology. Tulsa, Okla.: Oral Roberts University, 1984.

———. *E.W. Kenyon and the Postbellum Pursuit of Peace, Power, and Plenty*. Lanham, MD and London: Scarecrow Press, 1997.

———. "Say You Have It and You Have It: The Expanding Role of Positive Confession from Phoebe Palmer to Peter Popoff." Paper presented at the joint meeting of the Society for Pentecostal Studies and Wesleyan Theological Society at Church of God Theological Seminary, Cleveland, Tennessee, Mar. 14, 1998.

Simpson, A.B. "According to Your Faith," *Christian and Missionary Alliance Weekly*, September 8, 1906, 146-148.

———. *The Alliance Weekly*, February 10, 1917, 290.

———. *Annual Report, The Christian and Missionary Alliance*. May 1908.

———. "The Authority of Faith," *The Alliance Weekly*, April 23, 1938, 263.

———. *Christ for the Body*. Nyack, N.Y.: The Christian and Missionary Alliance, n.d.

———. *Christ in the Bible*. Camp Hill, Penn.: Christian Publications, 1992. Vol. 1, 3, 4 and 5.

———. *Christ in the Bible: Luke*. Harrisburg, Penn.: Christian Publications, n.d., Vol. XIVB.

———. *Christ in the Bible: Matthew*. Harrisburg, Penn.: Christian Publications, n.d., Vol. XIII.

———. *Christ in the Bible: Gospel of John and the Acts of the Apostles*. New York: Christian Alliance Publishing Co., 1891, Vol. X.

———. *Christian and Missionary Alliance Weekly*. Mar. 27, 1891, 195.

———. "The Connection Between Spiritual and Physical Life," *The Alliance Weekly*, Aug. 2, 1919, 292.

———. *Danger Lines in the Deeper Life*. Camp Hill, Penn.: Christian Publications, 1991.

———. *Days of Heaven on Earth*. Camp Hill, Penn.: Christian Publications, 1984.

———. *Divine Emblems*. Camp Hill, Penn.: Christian Publications, 1995.

"Editorial," *The Christian Alliance and Missionary Weekly*, November 1890, 274.

———. *The Four-fold Gospel*. Harrisburg, Penn.: Christian Publications, n.d.

———. *Friday Meeting Talks: Series # 3*. Nyack, N.Y.: Christian Alliance Publishing Co., 1900.

———. *The Gentle Love of the Holy Spirit*. Camp Hill, Penn.: Christian Publications, 1983.

———. "God's Voice in Sickness," *Triumphs of Faith*, July 1902, 164.

———. *The Gospel of Healing*. Harrisburg, Penn.: Christian Publications, 1915.

———. *The Highest Christian Life*. Harrisburg, Penn.: Christian Publications, 1966.

———. *The Holy Spirit*. Harrisburg, Penn.: Christian Publications, 1896. Vol. 2.

———. *How to Receive Divine Healing*. Harrisburg, Penn.: Christian Publications, n.d.

———. "The Imperative Mood and the Present Tense of Faith," *The Alliance Weekly*, September 23, 1953, 6.

———. *In the School of Faith*. New York: Christian Alliance Publishing Co., [1894].

———. *The Land of Promise*. Harrisburg, Penn.: Christian Publications, 1969.

———. *A Larger Christian Life*. Harrisburg, Penn.: Christian Publications, n.d., accessed via website: http://online.cbccts.sk.ca/alliancestudies/simpson/larglife.html

———. *The Life of Prayer*. Camp Hill, Penn.: Christian Publications, 1989.

———. *Life More Abundantly*. New York: Christian Alliance Publishing Co., 1912; Harrisburg, Penn.: Christian Publications, 1965.

———. *The Lord for the Body*. New York: Christian Alliance Publishing Co., n.d., accessed via website: http://online.cbccts.sk.ca/alliancestudies/simpson/LORDBODY.HTM

————. *The Lord for the Body*, revised edition. Camp Hill, Penn.: Christian Publications, 1996.

————. *The Old Faith and the New Gospels*. Harrisburg, Penn.: Christian Publications, 1966.

————. *Present Truths or the Supernatural*. Harrisburg, Penn.: Christian Publications, 1967.

————. "The Sanctifying Influence of Divine Healing," *The Alliance Weekly*, September 17, 1952, 602.

————. *Seeing the Invisible*. Camp Hill, Penn.: Christian Publications, 1994.

————. "Spiritual Talismans," *The Alliance Weekly*, June 14, 1919, 178.

————. *Triumphs of Faith*, November 1921, 253.

————. *Triumphs of Faith*, November 1922, 252.

————. "Two Stages of Divine Healing," *The Alliance Weekly*, January 28, 1953, 5.

Sire, James W. *Scripture Twisting: 20 Ways the Cults Misread the Bible*. Downers Grove, Ill.: IVP, 1980.

Smail, Thomas, Andrew Walker, and Nigel Wright. "'Revelation Knowledge' and Knowledge of Revelation: The Faith Movement and the Question of Heresy," *Journal of Pentecostal Theology*, 1994, 5:57-77.

Smith, David L. *A Handbook of Contemporary Theology*. Wheaton, Ill.: Bridgepoint/Victor Books, 1992.

Smith, Hannah Whitall. *The Christian's Secret of a Happy Life*. Old Tappan, N.J.: Fleming H. Revell Co., 1942.

————. *The God of All Comfort*. New Kensington, Penn.: Whitaker House, 1984.

————. *Living Confidently in God's Love*. Springdale, Penn.: Whitaker House, 1984.

————. *The Unselfishness of God*. Princeton, N.J.: Littlebrook Publishing Co., 1987.

————. *The Unselfishness of God and How I Discovered It*. New York: Garland Publishers, [1903] 1985.

Smith, S. M. "Perichoresis," *Evangelical Dictionary of Theology*, 2nd Edition, ed. Walter A. Elwell. Grand Rapids: Baker Academic, 2001, 906-907.

Snyder, James L. *In Pursuit of God: The Life of A.W. Tozer*. Camp Hill, Penn.: Christian Publications, 1991.

Spence, H.D.M. and Joseph S. Exell, eds. *The Pulpit Commentary*. Chicago: Wilcox & Follett Co., n.d. Vol. 36.

Spencer, James R. *Heresy Hunters: Character Assassination in the Church*. Lafayette, La.: Huntington House Publishers, 1993.

Spurgeon, Charles. *Faith's Checkbook*. Chicago: Moody Press, n.d.

BIBLIOGRAPHY

———. *The Metropolitan Tabernacle Pulpit*. Pasadena, Tex.: Pilgrim Publications, 1979. Vol. 7, 11, 17, 19, 24, 36.

———. *Morning by Morning*. Old Tappan, N.J.: Fleming H. Revell, 1984.

———. *The New Park Street Pulpit*. Grand Rapids: Zondervan, 1964. Vol. 6.

———. *Power in the Blood*. New Kensington, Penn.: Whitaker House, 1996.

———. *The Power of Prayer in a Believer's Life*. Robert Hall, comp. and ed. Lynnwood, Wash.: Emerald Books, 1993.

———. *Spiritual Warfare in a Believer's Life*. Lynnwood, Wash.: Emerald Books, 1993.

———. *1000 Devotional Thoughts*. Grand Rapids: Baker, 1976.

———. *The Treasury of the Bible: Matthew to Luke 15*. London: Marshall, Morgan and Scott, 1952. Vol. 1.

———. *The Triumph of Faith in a Believer's Life*. Lynnwood, Wash.: Emerald Books, 1994.

———. *What the Holy Spirit Does in a Believer's Life*. Lynnwood, Wash.: Emerald Books, 1993.

Steer, Roger. *Spiritual Secrets of George Müller*. Wheaton, Ill.: Harold Shaw Publishers, 1985.

Stertzer, Carol Chapman. "She Found the Grace to Forgive," *Charisma*, August 2000, 103.

Stockmayer, Otto. "Faith Opposed to Sight," *Triumphs of Faith*, June 1891, 124.

Strachey, Ray. *Religious Fanaticism: Extracts from the Papers of Hannah Whitall Smith*. London: Faber & Gwyer, Ltd., 1928.

Strang, S. "Tilton, Robert," in *Dictionary of Pentecostal and Charismatic Movements*. Grand Rapids: Zondervan, 1988, 845.

Susanto, Johanes Lilik. "A Practical Theological Evaluation of the Divine Healing Ministries of Smith Wigglesworth and John G. Lake: A Continuationist Reformed Perspective," Doctor of Theology Thesis, University of South Africa, Pretoria, South Africa, June 2007, accessed at: http://etd.unisa.ac.za/ETD-db/theses/available/etd-06262008-113048/unrestricted/thesis.pdf

Swaggart, Jimmy. *The Balanced Faith Life*. Baton Rouge, La.: Jimmy Swaggart Evangelistic Assn., 1981.

Synan, H. Vinson. "Capps, Charles Emmitt," in *Dictionary of Pentecostal and Charismatic Movements*. Grand Rapids: Zondervan, 1988, 107.

———. *The Holiness-Pentecostal Tradition: Charismatic Movements in the Twentieth Century*. Grand Rapids: Eerdmans, [1971] 1997.

Taylor, Dr. and Mrs. Howard. *Hudson Taylor in the Early Years*. London: The China Inland Mission, [1911] 1930.

———. *Hudson Taylor's Spiritual Secret*. Chicago: Moody Press, 1932.

Taylor, Mrs. Howard. *Pastor Hsi (of North China): One of China's Christians.* London: Morgan and Scott, 1907.

Taylor, J. Hudson. Cited in *World Shapers: A Treasury of Quotes from Great Missionaries.* Wheaton, Ill.: Harold Shaw Publishers, 1991.

Taylor, J. Hudson. "Reckon on God's Faithfulness," *Triumphs of Faith,* July 1902, 159.

———. *Union and Communion with Christ.* Minneapolis: Bethany House, n.d.

Taylor, Jack R. *The Key to Triumphant Living.* Nashville: Broadman Press, 1971.

Taylor, Jeremy. *The Rule and Exercises of Holy Living.* London: J. M. Dent and Co.: Aldine House, 1900.

Ten Boom, Corrie. *Defeated Enemies.* Fort Washington, Penn.: Christian Literature Crusade, [1963] 1970.

Thayer, Joseph H. *Thayer's Greek-English Lexicon of the New Testament.* Grand Rapids: Baker, 1977.

Theologia Germanica, ed. Thomas S. Kepler. Cleveland, Ohio, New York: World Publishing Co., 1952.

Thomas a Kempis. *Of the Imitation of Christ.* Grand Rapids: Baker, 1973.

Thomas, John Christopher. *The Devil, Disease and Deliverance: Origins of Illness in New Testament Thought.* Sheffield, Eng.: Sheffield Academic Press, 1998.

Thompson, Phyllis. *Hudson Taylor: God's Venturer.* Chicago: Moody Press, n.d.

Tibbetts, Pearle. "A Serious Call to a Devout and Holy Life," *An Introduction to Five Spiritual Classics.* New York, N.Y.: Board of Missions of the Methodist Church, 1955, 107.

Torrey, R.A. *Divine Healing.* Grand Rapids: Baker, 1924.

———. *The Power of Prayer and the Prayer of Power.* Grand Rapids: Zondervan, 1924.

———. *How to Obtain Fullness of Power.* New Kensington, Penn.: Whitaker Books, [1982] 1984.

Tozer, A.W. *Born After Midnight.* Harrisburg, Penn.: Christian Publications, 1959.

———. *The Christian Book of Mystical Verse.* Camp Hill, Penn.: Christian Publications, 1963.

———. *The Divine Conquest.* Old Tappan, N.J.: Fleming H. Revell, 1950.

———. *Faith Beyond Reason.* Camp Hill, Penn.: Christian Publications, 1989.

———. *Jesus, The Author of Our Faith.* Camp Hill, Penn.: Christian Publications, 1988.

———. *Jesus Is Victor.* Camp Hill, Penn.: Christian Publications, 1989.

———. *Let My People Go! The Life of Robert A. Jaffray.* Camp Hill, Penn.: Christian Publications, 1990.

Bibliography

————. *Man: The Dwelling Place of God*. Camp Hill, Penn.: Christian Publications, 1966.

————. *Men Who Met God*. Camp Hill, Penn.: Christian Publications, 1986.

————. *The Next Chapter After the Last*. Camp Hill, Penn.: Christian Publications, 1987.

————. *Of God and Men*. Harrisburg, Penn.: Christian Publications, 1960.

————. *The Pursuit of God*. Camp Hill, Penn.: Christian Publications, [1948, 1982] 1993.

————. *The Pursuit of God: A 31-Day Experience*. Compiled by Edythe Draper. Camp Hill, Penn.: Christian Publications, 1995.

————. *The Root of the Righteous*. Camp Hill, Penn.: Christian Publications, [1955] 1986.

————. *The Size of the Soul*. Camp Hill, Penn.: Christian Publications, 1992.

————. *Success and the Christian*. Camp Hill, Penn.: Christian Publications, 1994.

————. *That Incredible Christian*. Harrisburg, Penn.: Christian Publications, 1964.

————. *Whatever Happened to Worship?* Camp Hill, Penn.: Christian Publications, 1985.

————. *Who Put Jesus on the Cross?* Camp Hill, Penn.: Christian Publications, [1975] 1996.

Tuttle, Jr., Robert G. *John Wesley: His Life and Theology*. Grand Rapids: Zondervan, 1978.

Underhill, Evelyn. *The Mystics of the Church*. Cambridge: James Clarke and Co., Ltd., [1925] 1975.

Upham, Thomas. *The Life of Faith*. Boston, Mass.: Waite, Pierce; New York, N.Y.: Garland, [1845] 1984.

————. *Life, Religious Opinions and Experience of Madame Guyon*. Fort Washington: Christian Literature Crusade, Allenson and Co., Ltd., 1905.

Vine, W.E. *Vine's Expository Dictionary of New Testament Words*. McLean, Va.: MacDonald Publishing Co., n.d.

Vreeland, Derek E. "Reconstructing Word of Faith Theology: A Defense, Analysis and Refinement of the Theology of the Word of Faith Movement." Paper presented at the 30th Annual Meeting of the Society for Pentecostal Studies, Oral Roberts University, Tulsa, Oklahoma, Mar. 2001.

Warner, W.E. "Moise, Mary Gill," in Stanley M. Burgess and Gary B. McGee, eds. *Dictionary of Pentecostal and Charismatic Movements*. Grand Rapids: Zondervan, 1988, 626.

Watson, George D. *Bridehood Saints*. Cincinnati: God's Revivalist, n.d.

————. *Holiness Manual*. Boston: McDonald, Gill, & Co., Publishers, 1882.

————. *Steps to the Throne*. Cincinnati: Bible School Book Room, n.d.

————. *White Robes and Spiritual Feasts*. Cincinnati: God's Revivalist Press, n.d.

Watts, John D. W. *Word Biblical Commentary*, ed. David A. Hubbard and Glenn W. Barker. Waco, Tex.: Word, 1987. Vol. 25.

Wigglesworth, Smith. *The Ever-Increasing Faith*. Springfield, Mo.: Gospel Publishing House, 1924.

————. "Faith," *Triumphs of Faith*. November 1922, 249.

————. *Faith That Prevails*. Springfield, Mo.: Gospel Publishing House, 1938.

William of St. Thierry. *The Mirror of Faith*. Kalamazoo, Mich.: Cistercian Publications, 1979.

Williams, J. Rodman. "Opinion," *Logos Journal*. May-June 1977, 35.

Wimber, John and Kevin Springer. *Power Healing*. San Francisco: HarperSanFrancisco, 1987.

Wilson, Ernest Gerald. *The Christian and Missionary Alliance: Developments and Modifications of Its Original Objectives*. Ph.D. dissertation, New York, N.Y.: New York University, 1984.

Woodworth-Etter, Maria. *Acts of the Holy Ghost: The Life, Work and Experience of Mrs. M. B. Woodworth Etter*. Dallas: John F. Worley Printing Co., [1915].

————. *Marvels and Miracles*. Indianapolis: M.B.W. Etter, 1922.

Young, Brad. *Jesus the Jewish Theologian*. Peabody, Mass.: Hendrickson, 1995.

NAME INDEX

Alexander, Joseph Addison 186, 190n81, 191n99, 227

Allen, Ethan O. 47

Allender, Dan B. 353

Anderson, May Mabette 283, 285

Anderson, Neil T. 2, 259, 267n48

Anselm 27, 232

Aquinas, Thomas 26

Aristotle 25, 218

Athanasius 95

Augustine 26, 30, 32, 254, 258

Avanzini, John 332n4,6

Bailey, Keith 56, 76, 227, 288

Bakker, Jim 67, 331

Barnes, Alfred 138n81, 190n81

Barron, Bruce 15, 253, 254, 257, 339

Baxter, Mrs. Michael (Elizabeth) 44, 46, 49, 53, 246

Baxter, Richard 74

Bengel, Johann Albrecht 34, 35, 78

Benson, Joseph 74

Bentham, Jeremy 48

Bernard of Clairvaux 28, 29, 32, 57

Billheimer, Paul E. 55, 63, 67, 96, 121, 122, 317, 368

Blanchard, Charles A. 56, 178, 270, 271

Bloesch, Donald 180

Blue, Ken 318n3, 362, 367

Blumhardt, Johannes 24, 36, 43, 45, 47, 126, 173, 176, 177, 246, 270, 271, 327, 352

Boardman, William E. 24, 34, 44, 46, 48, 49, 52, 53, 63, 158-60, 164, 174, 198, 255, 292, 303

Boardman, Mrs. William 174

Bohler, Peter 37, 254

Böhme, Jacob 28, 217

Bonar, Andrew 31

Bonar, Horatius 119

Bosworth, F.F. 16, 53, 56, 61-63, 66, 108, 113, 158, 160, 180, 195, 236, 237-39, 246, 297, 302, 304, 305, 362

Bounds, E.M. 2, 17, 23-25, 36, 43,

56, 64, 76, 80, 81, 127, 131, 148, 155-57, 159, 160, 177, 183, 199, 218, 219, 271, 294, 303, 305, 327, 352, 366

Bowman, Jr., Robert M. 15, 64, 65, 68n11, 172, 173, 179, 182, 186, 192n105, 290, 293, 366, 368

Brainerd, David 304

Branham, William 68, 270

Brooks, Thomas 35, 90, 92, 322

Brother Lawrence 29

Brown, Michael L. 318n17

Buckingham, Jamie 238, 305

Bushnell, Horace 24, 43, 74, 144

Calvin, John 32, 228, 229, 248, 353n1

Capps, Annette 301, 305

Capps, Charles 66, 98, 112, 113, 117, 153, 244, 253, 264, 269, 270, 273, 278, 285, 301, 339

Carmichael, Amy 2, 24, 29, 34, 36, 44, 45, 58n7, 64, 74, 77, 155, 156, 158, 160, 208, 211n29, 38, 260, 303, 305, 311, 324-27, 329-31, 334n76, 341, 347, 375

Carter, Russell Kelso 24, 54, 63, 109, 149, 178, 198, 228-30, 246, 247, 294, 295, 299n46, 303, 347

Catherine of Sienna 28, 29

Chadwick, Samuel 157

Chambers, Oswald 2, 24, 26, 28, 34, 36, 42, 55, 64, 89, 96, 106, 110, 148, 156, 160, 162, 164, 174, 177, 179-81, 183, 185, 186, 198, 199, 207, 210, 218-21, 227-29, 233, 236, 248, 258, 304, 305, 314, 325, 326, 328, 330, 341, 353, 365, 366

Chappell, P.G. 18, 53, 54, 290, 293

Cho, David Yonggi 147

Christensen, Larry 238

Christlieb, Theodore 43, 77, 78

Chrysostom 127, 137n161, 153, 156, 165n15, 182

Clarke, Adam 37, 42, 183, 190n81

Clement of Alexandria 25, 26, 27, 30, 38n8, 159, 182, 187, 216-18, 223n26

Cocceius, Johannes 32, 34

Robeck, Jr., Cecil M. 240n26

Rogers, Hester Ann 37, 42, 105, 255

Sattler, Gary R. 36, 41n85

Scougal, Henry 29, 34, 156, 157-159

Schuller, Robert H. 13, 57, 170, 244, 259, 350

Scofield, C.I. 53

Seymour, William J. 63, 81, 236, 237, 240n26

Shelton, James B. 240n26

Simmons, Dale H. 7, 64, 65, 95, 101n68, 150n33, 215, 266n21, 296, 323, 338, 344n19

Simpson, A.B. 2, 16, 17, 23-25, 30, 31, 33, 34, 36, 42-44, 46, 47, 49, 50-57, 58n7, 61-64, 66, 72-75, 77-79, 87-94, 96-99, 105, 106, 108, 109, 111, 119, 121-23, 126, 127, 130, 133, 134, 146, 148, 155-164, 174, 176-78, 181-83, 185, 191n99, 195-99, 202n25, 207, 216, 219, 227, 229, 230, 233-235, 237, 238, 239n4,245-47, 254, 257, 258, 260-63, 265, 271-73, 279, 280, 282-84, 289-97, 302, 303, 305-7, 308n28, 311, 313-16, 322-30, 341, 346, 347, 352, 362, 366, 380, 382, 385, 388-90

Sire, James W. 337

Smith, Hannah Whitall 2, 24, 33, 42, 45, 48, 49, 52, 55, 64, 80, 89, 97, 104, 107, 144, 145, 148, 155, 156, 160, 161, 173, 177, 196, 205, 219, 234, 237, 238, 247, 255, 257, 258, 261-63, 280, 281, 284, 303, 305, 315, 323-25, 341, 348

Smith, Wilbur M. 190n81

Spener, Philip Jacob 34, 35

Spurgeon, Charles 2, 17, 24, 33, 44-45, 50-53, 55, 61, 64, 66, 73, 75, 76, 83n7, 87, 89, 90-92, 94, 96, 98, 99, 107, 119, 124, 126, 127, 130, 132, 134, 144, 146-48, 154-63, 165n15, 173, 174, 176, 177, 179, 180, 183, 185-87, 195, 206, 215, 216, 219, 222, 227, 229, 238, 245, 247, 256, 257, 270-73, 302, 304, 305, 308n16, 312, 314, 324, 325, 328-30, 341, 348, 361, 362, 366

Steele, Daniel 37, 110

Stockmayer, Otto 24, 46, 49, 52, 53,

55, 174, 227, 235, 313

Stott, John 234

Studd, C.T. 45, 292, 329

Swaggart, Jimmy 15, 19n4, 67, 331

Synan, H. Vinson 20n13; 58n2, n23; 59n29; 68n21; 234

Tacelli, Ronald 38n9

Tauler, John 28, 30, 324, 351

Taylor, Dr. and Mrs. Howard 178

Taylor, Jack R. 166n31

Taylor, J. Hudson 2, 24, 33, 44, 45, 50, 55, 62, 64, 72, 74, 75, 104, 106, 108, 111, 112, 174, 178, 180, 186, 207, 233, 246, 292, 294, 303-5, 324, 327, 329, 330

Ten Boom, Corrie 218; 224n35, n36

Teresa of Avila 28, 248

Thayer, Joseph H. 151n44, 209, 211n32

Theophilis 205

Theron, Jacques 7

Thomas a Kempis 28, 30, 57, 351, 353n7

Thomas, John Christopher 318n17

Tilton, Robert 67, 118, 131, 331

Timothy, H.B. 25, 38n9

Torrey, R.A. 17, 24, 49, 51, 55, 56, 63, 64, 76, 91, 157 ,174, 175, 183, 190n81, 198, 206, 227-30, 233, 236, 261, 271, 272, 289, 341, 342, 344n19

Tozer, A.W. 2, 13, 16, 17, 28-30, 34, 36, 39n32, 43, 53, 64, 97, 98, 102n85, 104, 108, 112, 155, 156, 160, 162, 164, 165, 176, 178, 185, 207, 216, 218, 219, 221, 222, 243, 248, 249, 251n43, 262, 263, 273, 301, 304, 341-43, 352, 362, 366

Trudel, Dorothea 24, 31, 36, 46, 47, 52, 89, 118, 246

Treat, Casey 97

Tucker, Mother 363

Turnbull, Walter 237

Underhill, Evelyn 31

Upham, Thomas 24, 43, 52, 53, 104, 106, 144, 145, 147, 154, 160, 163, 245, 284, 341

Vine, W.E. 211n2, 212n33, 204, 209, 339

Vreeland, Derek E. 7; 40n63; 68n8; 339; 344n7, n8; 362; 363; 365; 367

SUBJECT INDEX

SCRIPTURE INDEX

21 282
21:4 283
21:10-14 283
26:19 176

Romans
3:3 180
3:27 143, 146
4:17 253, 262, 340
5:17 89
8:1 178
8:5-6 243
8:16-17 86
8:27 194
8:28 312
10:8 203, 204, 206, 209
10:8-9 252
10:8-10 265
10:9-10 255, 258
10:10 194
10:17 27, 104, 203, 209, 252
13:8 329
15:32 194

1 Corinthians
2:4-5 178
2:10-14 213
3:21 88, 97
12:9 180, 182, 184
14 80
14:27-29 81

2 Corinthians
3:2 96
5:7 13, 232
5:21 88
10:4-5 178, 244
12:4 209

Galatians
2:11 364
2:15-21 181
2:20 172, 174, 180, 181, 182,
    183, 185, 186
3:3 174
3:13 87, 92, 98
4:7 86
6:7-8 253

Ephesians
1-2 119
1-3 122
1:20-23 116
1:21-23 90
2:6 73, 116, 119
3:10-11 125
6:12 152
6:17 203, 204, 209

Philippians
2:5-8 351
4:8 243
4:11-13 324

Colossians
2:12 153, 154

Titus
2:1-2 13

Hebrews
1:6 339
3:1 252
4:14 252
10:23 252
11 52
11:1 232, 340
11:6 13, 200
11:11 180
12:2 106, 174
13:8 73

James
1:6-7 109, 182
1:7 108
4:1 331
4:15 194
5 171, 227, 268
5:14-15 46
5:15 32, 76, 183
5:16 153

1 Peter
2:9-10 31
2:21 310
2:24 225, 226

2 Peter
1:4 87, 89

1 John
4:1-3 282
5:4 219
5:14 194
5:14-15 269

3 John
2 320-23, 333n18

Revelation
1:6 31
17:17 209
21:4 226